About Island Press

Island Press is the only nonprofit organization in the United States whose principal purpose is the publication of books on environmental issues and natural resource management. We provide solutions-oriented information to professionals, public officials, business and community leaders, and concerned citizens who are shaping responses to environmental problems.

Since 1984, Island Press has been the leading provider of timely and practical books that take a multidisciplinary approach to critical environmental concerns. Our growing list of titles reflects our commitment to bringing the best of an expanding body of literature to the environmental community throughout North America and the world.

Support for Island Press is provided by the Agua Fund, The Geraldine R. Dodge Foundation, Doris Duke Charitable Foundation, The Ford Foundation, The William and Flora Hewlett Foundation, The Joyce Foundation, Kendeda Sustainability Fund of the Tides Foundation, The Forrest & Frances Lattner Foundation, The Henry Luce Foundation, The John D. and Catherine T. MacArthur Foundation, The Marisla Foundation, The Andrew W. Mellon Foundation, Gordon and Betty Moore Foundation, The Curtis and Edith Munson Foundation, Oak Foundation, The Overbrook Foundation, The David and Lucile Packard Foundation, Wallace Global Fund, The Winslow Foundation, and other generous donors.

The opinions expressed in this book are those of the author(s) and do not necessarily reflect the views of these foundations.

A Field Guide to Conservation Finance

Story Clark

ISLANDPRESS

Washington • Covelo • London

To my husband, Bill, and our two daughters,
Avery and Felicia,
for their patience, love, and support.

Library of Congress Cataloging-in-Publication data.

Clark, Story.
   A field guide to conservation finance / Story Clark.
      p.   cm.
   Includes bibliographical references and index.
   ISBN-13: 978-1-59726-059-6 (cloth : alk. paper)
   ISBN-10: 1-59726-059-2 (cloth : alk. paper)
   ISBN-13: 978-1-59726-060-2 (pbk. : alk. paper)
   ISBN-10: 1-59726-060-6 (pbk. : alk. paper)
   1. Nature conservation—United States—Finance. I. Title.
   QH76.C53 2006
   333.72068′1—dc22   2006021693

British Cataloguing-in-Publication data available.

Printed on recycled, acid-free paper ∞

Design by Paul Hotvedt
Manufactured in the United States of America
10 9 8 7 6 5 4 3 2

Contents

Acknowledgments

Putting pen to paper is a huge learning experience. During the process, I imposed on busy conservationists, taking hours of their time asking them for advice, and then more advice. I depended on LTAnet and RallyNet, the Land Trust Alliance's research Web sites. I learned so much. For their knowledge and for the generous way that conservationists donated their time to this project, I would like to thank the following people.

Liz Iliff assisted me every step of the way. Without her help researching, interviewing, following up, organizing, tying up of loose ends and general good sense, this book could never have been written.

Two experts in the conservation field, Bill Hutton and Peter Stein, gave many, many hours reading drafts and offering invaluable suggestions.

My good friend and fellow conservationist Roger Altman kindly set the stage with his foreword.

The editors at Island Press, particularly my primary editor, Jeff Hardwick, as well as Heather Boyer and others, guided and encouraged me.

Many experts read and commented on specific chapters, giving hours of their time. For their excellent thoughts and additions, I offer special thanks to Timothy B. Barnard, Elizabeth Bell, John Bernstein, Patrick Coady, Andrew C. Dana, Jean Driscoll, Jay Espy, Donna Fletcher, Brad Gentry, Bland Hoke, Peter Howell, Lloyd Irland, Jim Kitendaugh, Lawrence R. Kueter, Tim Lindstrom, Leslie Mattson-Emerson, Linda Mead, Stefan Nagel, Henry C. Phibbs, James P. Richter, Catherine S. Scott, Bill Sellers, Paul Sihler, Stephen J. Small, Julie Turrini, Tammara Van Ryn, Brooke Williams, and Terry Tempest Williams.

Other experienced conservationists gave me multiple interviews, answered questions requiring extensive research, suggested new contacts, and more. Thank you to Lise Aangeenbrug, Mark C. Ackelson, Robert F. Aldrich, Jill Arango, Stephen M. Bartram, Brad Chalfant, Rebecca Chapman, Vicki Church, Richard D. Cochran, George M. Covington, Michael Dennis, Gene Duvernoy, Denis Hayes, Renee Kivikko, Gil Livingston, Michael Mantell, Betsy Martens, Ezra Milchman, Anne Murphy, Mary Anne Piacentini, Mark Robinson, Chuck

Roe, Will Shafroth, Brian Steen, Ciona Ulbrich, Phillip Wallin, Leah Whidden, and Donna Windham.

Many other generous people participated in informative interviews that provided the valuable information forming the core of this book. Others commented on specific sections, arranged interviews, contributed art, and followed up on many other details, which immeasurably contributed to the book. For all of this good work, I would particularly like to thank the following people: John Adams, Tim Ahern, Nancy Ailes, Jason Anderson, Judy Anderson, Marty Anderson, Laurie Andrews, Hugh Archer, Christine Arvidson, Tom Bailey, Tracy Bakalar, Barry Banks, Barbara E. Barker, Tina Batt, Julie Beach, Ralph Benson, Robert Berner, Connie Best, Ian Billick, Peggy J. Birk, Bowen Blair, Dale Bonar, Rex R. Boner, Renee J. Bouplon, Rob Bowers, Marian D. Brailsford, Whitney L. Brice, Frances Brody, Jamie Brotherton, Chip Brown, Consuella Brown, James Brown, Randy Brown, Norman Brunswig, Teresa Buckwalter, Bruce Bunting, Dan Burke, Emily Burnett, Laura Callanan, Jane Calvin, Neil Carlson, Michael Catania, Timothy J. Caufield, Michael Chamberlain, Glen Chown, Edward Sortwell Clement Jr., Martha Cochran, George Cofer, Dennis Collins, Tony Colyer-Pendas, Susan Connolly, Carol Connors, Ernest Cook, Terrie Cooper, Terry Corwin, Glo Cunningham, Fred Danforth, Adam Davis, Tom Dean, Lois R. DeBacker, Kristin DeBoer, Allen Decker, Chris DeForest, Mike DeHart, Nicholas H. Dilks, Peter Dittmar, Gage Dobbins, Daniel F. Donahue, Tom Duffus, Sharon Dunn, Tom Dureka, Barbara Dye, Fred Ellis, Mark W. Elsbree, Bill Eyring, Kent Faerber, Tom Faragher, Michael Feeney, Barbara Finfrock, Wendy Fisher, Anne Fleming, Kathleen Fluegel, Kathleen Fosha, Fred Freyer, Suzanne Fusaro, Paul Gallay, Annette Gibavic, Carol Glover, Martin Goebel, Mariah Goode, Jane C. and John T. Griffith, Darla Guenzler, Brent Haglund, Dawn Haight, John v. H. Halsey, Dale Hamilton, Chris Hanson, Joan Harn, Ron Harrison, James Hathaway, Peter Hausmann, Will Haynie, Peter Helm, Richard Hendry, Camilla M. Herlevich, Ray Herndon, Mac Herrling, Ethan Hicks, Jennifer Hill, Karen Hobbs, Jean Hocker, John Hoffnagle, Kim Honor, Ann P. Hooke, Rebecca Howard, Tom Howe, Jerry C. Huang, Rich Hubbard, Paul Hurt, Robert Hutchinson, Mary Pope Hutson, Christine P. Iffrig, Jon M. Jensen, Andrew Johnson, Gary P. Johnson, Laura Kamala, George Kelly, Mike Kelly, Jamie Kendall, Chris Killingsworth, Pam Kimball-Smith, Sue Kinde, Gordon King, Julie Klein, Michelle Knapik, Rich Knox, Peg Kohring, Kate Kuhlman, Jon Kusler, Tom Lagerstrom, Kris Larson, Bill Leahy, Jim Leape, Jim Light, Brenda Lind, William Long, Jennifer Lorenz, David

MacDonald, Betty Manganiello, Kristen Manguso, Mike Martin, Wade Martin, Alex Mas, Allen May, Laurel Mayer, Carol Harris Mayes, Catherine M. McFarland, Kevin McGorty, Tim McGowan, Peggy McNutt, Kevin Mendik, Shannon Meyer, Robert Miller, E. Gay Mills, Rich Mogensen, Joe Moll, Jim Moses, Sopac McCarthy Mulholland, Molly Murfee, Fay R. Nance, Dan Nees, Dru Anne Neil, Jean C. Nelson, Ann Nichols, Patrick Noonan, Conn Nugent, Anna Nygaard, Richard Ober, Vincent Ollivier, Mari Omland, Stephen Outlaw, Van Parker, Mary Patno, Nancy Perlson, Daniel E. Pike, Karin Marchetti Ponte, Pat Porto, Hal Poster, Alana Preston, Brian R. Price, Glenn Prickett, Jim Promo, Andrea Erickson Quiroz, Jerry Rankin, Richard Reagan, Asha Rehnberg, Aaron Revere, Joanne Riccitelli, Mary Ellen Richardson, Curt Riffle, Mary Anne Rodgers, John Roe, Melissa Rowitz, Bruce Runnels, Audrey Rust, Moriah Salter, Michael W. Sands, David Santomenna, Chris Sawyer, Jonathan Schechter, Dan Schlager, William H. Schlesinger, Susanne Scholz, Debra Schwartz, Ann Taylor Schwing, Peter Seligmann, David Shactman, Carl Silverstein, Marc Smiley, Marsha Smith, Ted Smith, Vicki Sola, James Gustave Speth, Robert Stark, Judith Stockdale, Jamie Sweeting, David J. Swift, David Tately, Charlie Thomsen, Bill Turner, Robin Underwood, Jeanne B. Van Alen, Richard R. Veit, Carolyn Vogel, Terry Vogt, Robert Vosskuhler, Jon Wagar, Jason A. Walser, Justin Ward, Stephanie Ward, Wesley T. Ward, Emily Warrington, Laurie Wayburn, Abigail Weinberg, John Weiser, Dan Wells, Rand Wentworth, Michael Whitfield, Terry Whittaker, Karen Wilkinson, Bob Williams, Nick Williams, Lisa Wilson, Marla Wilson, Mary Alice Wilson, Carol A. Witzeman, John Woodbury, Kellie Wright, Leigh Youngblood, Mark W. Zenick, and Lynn Zimmerman.

In memorium, I thank Tom Rossetter, former chair of the Jackson Hole Land Trust board of directors, who always teased me by saying I would have made a successful developer.

Foreword

The importance of conservation has never been more clear. In recent years, the cataclysmic threat of climate change has permeated the consciousness of most Americans. Many of the most important and iconic species of mammals and fish are disappearing around the world at frightening rates. Moreover, the Earth's population is projected to double by 2050, which will put even more acute pressure on the planet.

These threats have turned many Americans into motivated conservationists. Some of these devoted people work on a global scale, but most concentrate on their own communities or their favorite places. They dedicate themselves to preserving open lands and the ecosystems and wildlife within them.

To protect these places, local conservation organizations are springing up everywhere. They range from land trusts to park conservancies to historical associations. Some of these are professionally run and well financed, but they are the exception. Most are young organizations, which are feeling their way and trying to cobble together some funding. They need guidance on choosing their precise missions, organizing, and staffing themselves correctly and, in particular, on techniques of financing and executing land conservation transactions.

Fortunately, Story Clark has written this extraordinary guidebook for them. It is the bible on organizing and financing local conservation. Every single task involved—from forming a board of directors to choosing a code of ethics to raising and borrowing money and, of course, to executing transactions—is covered in this uniquely readable "how to" format.

Any organization whose goal is land protection should read this book. Many of them should go further and adopt it, lock, stock, and barrel, as their handbook for operations. It will enable numerous such organizations to professionalize themselves and to accomplish conservation transactions more quickly and efficiently.

The book is that good because Story Clark has seen it all and experienced it all. She is one of America's most experienced and successful conservationists. Story was a leader at one of the best land trusts in the country in Jackson

Hole, Wyoming, has consulted extensively for some of the largest U.S. foundations involved in conservation, and is one of the longest-serving board members of the profoundly effective organization Conservation International. I have known and worked with Story for nearly twenty years, and no one is better qualified to have written this pathbreaking and practical guide to making conservation happen. There is nothing comparable.

Roger C. Altman

Chairman, co-CEO, and cofounder of Evercore Partners

Introduction: A Field Guide

The land conservation movement is rooted in a love of the land. This deep attachment gives it passion. Its qualities of self-reliance and creativity make it nimble. Its strong connection to community and people gives it the power to succeed.

Conservation finance is the best place where people, land, and money meet. It is populated with individuals who are passionate about land and are contributing special skills and great new ideas to its protection. Most are people of conservation organizations responding with ingenuity to the pressure to stretch limited funds for greater outcomes. However, new diversity is entering the conservation finance scene. Some of these new participants work behind cash registers at local retail enterprises. Others are realtors and developers. Some are commercial and investment bankers who may look a little out of place in their gray suits with *Wall Street Journals* tucked under their arms.

Like many of us, they started out leading two lives: the one a life of loving land, going back to making childhood visits to the grandparents' farm or the New Jersey shore or taking annual hunting and fishing trips; the other, a life of work. Somewhere along the way, they discovered that their work could save land, and they blended the two. They honed their skills on behalf of conservation, and the sparks of creativity and innovation started to fly.

Mostly, these are the people of finance who wandered into the world of conservation. They had friends who were involved, and they ended up on land trust boards. They went on to contribute meaningfully and to enrich their own lives. They were hooked.

I understand how natural this blend of financier and ardent conservationist can be because I grew up in New York City with an investment banker father who loved the land: Central Park, the beaches of the Atlantic Coast, and Wyoming. A walk through the meadows and around the sparkling water of the reservoirs of Central Park reveals the diversity of people who are drawn to open land. I came to expect secret passions for land from most everyone, even urban capitalists. That view is continually reenforced. After college, my colleagues and I made hundreds of cold calls throughout the country in search of support for new national parks in distant Alaska. Enthusiasm was everywhere. The same proved true in twenty-five years of fundraising in Wyoming. Those "red state" conservatives connect with the land daily and deeply and quietly love it. They will do just about anything, short of calling themselves environmentalists, to keep those special places—whether wild or covered with cattle—open. I have come to expect the strength of that connection.

Hope for conservation lies in the world of finance, where people understand the art and the science of raising, borrowing, investing, and managing funds. The people in finance use a different lexicon. They talk about such things as equity investments and credit. They are in a successful parallel universe to ours—the for-profit world. They understand the for-profit market that invests abundantly in land, but not for conservation purposes. Our system, fueled almost entirely by philanthropy, simply cannot keep pace.

If we want sustainable conservation outcomes, we must engage this other universe and integrate it into ours. Without what they know, we will never get ahead of the bulldozers. This other universe has been managing money for hundreds of years. It is where attractive deals are constructed, where money is raised from lenders and investors, where multiple moving parts are managed, and a return on investment is generated. Conservation deals need this same expertise. Our unique challenge is ensuring that conservation is an essential part of the return.

How do we put these people and the money they control to work for conservation? We start by understanding their language and culture. This is not as hard as we might think. We know the value of understanding the many cultures of landowners. We already know that a working knowledge of, say, the cattle business helps us to work with ranchers. The same is true with bankers.

Once we speak the language, we can meet on their terms and in their comfort zones. This should not be hard either. We do our best work sipping coffee in farmhouse kitchens. So now step out just a little farther. Venture into those gaping bank lobbies, Wall Street high-rises, chamber of commerce meetings, and real estate association luncheons. Don't wait for them to find us.

Then make that connection to land. I was always in awe of how Mardie Murie, noted conservationist and advocate for protecting Alaskan lands, could connect her audiences to the vast wildernesses of faraway Alaska. She personalized wilderness and celebrated its human element. People responded.

Stepping into a banker's office, the last thing we are likely to think about is our mutual appreciation of land. We are more likely to bring up the weather or launch right into our pitch. But what if our banker grew up on a ranch? Or had a vegetable garden as a child and longs for one in the city? Or has a little weekend place in the woods of Connecticut? Now that is a foundation to build on.

Two generations from now in this urbanizing world, we might not have the luxury of this connection. For now though, the human attachment to land goes far beyond hiking or fishing. It follows us into boardrooms and corporate headquarters.

I have met bankers, lawyers, accountants, and financiers from around the country who jumped at the chance to blend their careers with their deep passion for land. Conservation finance gives them that chance. It is a portal through which that parallel universe of finance can support the natural one.

A Guide to Private Money for Conservation

Conservation finance involves raising and managing money to pay for conservation. As in for-profit markets, the money we need is capital for equity (ownership) and debt (loans) from the private sector.

Money is the common currency of our culture. We cannot conserve land without paying for it at some point and in some way. The money is all around us. Our challenge is to access it.

Traditionally, we have used private, philanthropic capital and public, governmental funds in the form of tax incentives, bond measures, and other agency appropriations and loans. We have had great projects and the generous individuals and institutions needed to pay for many of them. Traditional fundraising from private institutional and individual donors fundamentally enabled us to move quickly and to find money to protect critical land before the trees are cut, the soil is turned, and the asphalt rolled. Even projects funded by the increasingly popular public bond measures usually used privately fundraised dollars to cover the requisite private matches, down payments, loans, stewardship endowments, and administrative costs. Most other publicly funded acquisitions have similar private fundraising requirements.

From traditional fundraising, creative conservationists have moved into leveraging their fundraised dollars in numerous ways. They attract partners to share the financial burden. They match it with money from less traditional sources, such as business. They understand the value of responsibly borrowing money for greater flexibility. As they take on bigger and more complicated projects, they recognize that these fundraising and financing skills become invaluable, making it possible to align multiple moving parts and synchronize capital to close the deal. These conservationists are figuring out how to attract more and different private money to conservation and how to use the money we have more effectively. Some of these trailblazers contributed to James Levitt's book *From Walden to Wall Street.*[1] The Nature Conservancy has been particularly innovative in this way, as described in Bill Ginn's book *Investing in Nature.*[2] However, conservation still lacks what Pat Coady, an investment banker and writer on this subject, calls "a system of finance."[3] This is an integrated market that invests in conservation finance.

Such a market is not easy to create. It has impediments that are less troublesome to the for-profit world. First and foremost is the core problem that conservation land does not easily produce a large financial return, nor does it produce a stream of income to carry debt while still conserving its natural resources. In addition, organizations working with charitable dollars must, to a great degree, be more averse to risk. Sustainably scaled conservation can also require prohibitively large sums of money. Our own still-fragmented system for capitalization, to the extent that we have one, is not widely understood. Major gaps in experience and information exist between conservation organizations that know how to do deals and everyone else. Smaller land trusts are trying creative financing but need support, financial and otherwise. Staffs are eager to get into finance but have boards that are risk averse.

The more creative among us have shown that by engaging for-profit professionals and markets, financing conservation can become more effective and efficient. The conservationists I interviewed for this book, whether new to land conservation or more seasoned, understand this. They leap over cultural borders into that parallel universe to entice the for-profit world into conservation; these leaders have listened and learned from these communities. They are members of the Rotary Clubs and serve on the boards of the community foundations and banks. They recognize that a community must value something before it will pay for it, because, as historian Bill Cronon tells us, "the protection of nature is a cultural project, not just a biological one. Whether we protect deep wilderness or an inner city community garden, from a human cultural point of view we are protecting a human *symbol* of nature."[4]

Successful, local conservation finance is based on understanding these cultural landscapes: city, suburban, working or wilderness, business, religious, youthful or old. Because every person relates to the land differently, the challenge is not finding the money but finding out how to make the connections with the people who control it. Thus, conservation finance makes for odd bedfellows: real estate brokers and conservation program directors, bankers and biologists, ranchers and foundation lenders. But when our common language speaks, it speaks loudly, and conservation interests are served.

A Guide to This Book

This volume is a tool kit of the most basic techniques of conservation finance, or finding and managing funds (in this case, nongovernmental funds) for the conservation of land and water. The book describes the tools to try first, though none of them are simple. It integrates the fundamental components of conservation finance, including honing fundraising skills and systems, which is guaranteed to raise more money. It also offers a sampling of other approaches, including voluntary surcharges, transfer fee programs, and partnerships.

This book gets a conservationist started with the simple but still revenue-rich programs. It does not explore the newest and most sophisticated means of conserving land through new tax incentive programs or REITs (real estate investment trusts) or timber or ecological service payments. I plan to follow this edition with a second volume that will dive more deeply into the tool kit and describe more complex tools.

My hope is that this book will do two things. First, it should help fill knowledge gaps about the conservation finance techniques that many conservationists, but not enough, already use. Second, it should create a new vehicle for communication by bringing financing to life through stories from the people who are using it. Stories of success should give comfort to the unconvinced that conservation finance offers opportunity and greater leverage.

This book covers financing in the general sense (i.e., raising and managing money from different sources to pay for a project) and in the narrow sense (i.e., assuming debt to do the same). A land trust may be in the middle of a transaction as a buyer (or a seller), or it may facilitate the transaction by finding someone else to buy the land and conserve it. A landowner may be looking for a way to sell certain rights to the land to pay estate taxes or generate income while keeping ownership.

To understand how to make those tools useful and be cautious about their pitfalls, it helps to hear firsthand the experiences of others using them. This book is filled with lessons from people working on new strategies—often for the first time—who know how scary it is to take out that first loan but who also know the sweet joy of success. However, hearing from the experts all the time can be intimidating. When I looked for people using these private financing techniques, I went to the small and medium-sized land trusts on the theory that if the little guys can do it, then everyone can.

Some of these tools are best suited to fund operations (e.g., annual giving) or stewardship (e.g., transfer fees) or acquisitions (e.g., capital campaign). But for most land trusts, a mix of sources will create stability and opportunity. I hope and fully expect that public funding will remain a critical component of that mix as well.

Financing takes a land trust beyond the reactive, emergency-driven approach to conservation (easy to say!) to become strategic and proactive. This book will lead you down that road. It describes techniques that support a stable, functioning land conservation operation that enables a land trust to step responsibly into the more proactive realm of acquisition. I offer tips and tools on how to get organizationally, financially, and programmatically ready (part 1, chapters 1 to 3).

Financing, whether borrowing money or raising it, can also involve serious legal and ethical questions. Though no more important than they have always been, legal and ethical considerations will likely play a more prominent role in the future. I review those considerations here (part 1, chapter 4).

I assume that most land trusts or landowners do not have on hand all the money they need, so we will consider how to raise the money (part 2); look at the benefits, pitfalls, and techniques of borrowing money (part 3); and then explore ways to reduce the overall cost of acquisition so the financial burden is less (part 4). Finally, I consider backup strategies in case everything does not go as planned, discuss how to package different techniques and offer a look to future opportunities to improve on the system we have now (Conclusion).

Throughout the book, you will encounter innumerable references to the Land Trust Alliance (LTA) and its *Land Trust Standards and Practices*. The Land

Trust Alliance is the national convener, strategist, and representative of more than 1,500 land trusts across the United States.[5] *Land Trust Standards and Practices* is a set of guidelines, with accompanying templates for policies, forms, and checklists, recommended by LTA. These guidelines should be central to the operations for any land trust. They also form the basis of land trust accreditation.[6] LTA provides indispensable tools to start a land trust and to strengthen it so that it is in a position to use finance effectively.

The novice conservationist may feel a little overwhelmed. However, know that conservation finance is rewarding right from the start and is in no way reserved for organizations with a lot of money. I talked to many small land trusts that had successfully completed their first capital campaign, set up surcharge programs, and used external revolving loan funds.

This is the book I wish I had when I entered the conservation business. It combines many personal stories of the successes and pitfalls of managing money for conservation with the hard facts of the business. I have not shied away from laying out my own errors along the way; they are as instructive as the stories of success.

My hope is that the collective value of this information will become another point along the immense learning curve of conservation finance. As we expand our knowledge and dialogue, and involve more good minds in conservation, we will eventually put the power of the universe of finance squarely to work for conservation.

Part 1

Positioning Your Organization

Chapter 1
Organizational Readiness

Ready or Not: The Hardeman Meadows

It was a "must buy" ranch. Three quarters of a mile of highway corridor defining the edge of one town and the gateway to another, and half a mile deep, dotted with grazing cattle. The pasture and elegant barn preserved the area's rural character. The ranch offered a tranquil foreground to the dramatic backdrop of the mountains. A beloved, local agricultural family owned it, but they were forced to sell due to family reasons. The father was a popular local auctioneer. The children were star ropers and basketball players. They were kind community people pushed to make a tough decision.

The family had approached the local land trust a year earlier. At the time, this young land trust was accepting donated easements and was not in a position to purchase expensive land. Because of the perceived risk, the land trust responded with a modest offer to purchase the ranch. In this conservative community, the land trust had been working quietly with landowners at their kitchen tables, soliciting conservation easement gifts. It was not interested in controversy or high-profile issues, fearing that they would jeopardize these essential relationships. While the land trust very much wanted to protect the ranch, it could not imagine risking money it didn't have.

The family turned to a developer who planned to blanket the pastures with townhouses. Once the negotiations were public, the community reacted; everyone was in an uproar. Newspaper headlines tracked the developer's every move and the public's angry responses. Eyes turned toward the land trust to find a solution.

The land trust could hide no more. Saving or losing the ranch was quickly becoming its defining moment. Although the community was activated to help

Figure 1.1

The Hardeman Ranch epitomizes the agricultural heritage of Jackson Hole, Wyoming. Once threatened by development, the southern part of the ranch be-came the Jackson Hole Land Trust's first major conservation purchase. (Jackson Hole News & Guide)

the land trust succeed, it was an untested volunteer force—affluent but un-tapped to do more than support the land trust's $70,000 annual budget. The land trust's two-and-a-half-person staff was eager to take on the project, but its board of ranchers and donors was understandably hesitant. A crucial fac-tor, though, was the land trust's board chair, who had run a major corporation.

In the eleventh hour, the land trust bit the bullet and risked its entire sav-ings ($100,000) to buy a nonrefundable option. Then it set out to raise almost $2 million dollars in three months to buy the property. Before it signed the op-tion, the land trust considered where it would find the money. It talked to a few donors. But in all honesty, it had little idea how it was going to pay for the land and had no commitments from donors for funds. The whole project was dan-gerous. It placed the fledgling land trust's existence at risk and threatened to dash the hopes of many in this new land conservation movement.

Over the next three months, the land trust threw its first big community fundraiser outdoors in a park in Wilson, Wyoming. It snowed the night before and into the morning. The county committed $500,000 to the project, only to withdraw its commitment when sued for authorizing the expenditure. Never having worked with a bank before, the land trust hastily arranged for a loan to cover the county's share. After the three months, with the county lawsuit still pending, the land trust had not raised all the money needed. It exercised its option anyway and squeezed out the last $100,000 in the final days. Less than six hours before closing, it completed a complex resale agreement with a con-servation buyer for part of the ranch and a ten-year lease with another local nonprofit for the barn.

So why so much struggle and all the surprises? The land trust was not ready. When a land trust faces its first big acquisition, it can let the situation get desperate and risk everything—stressing its board and panicking its donors—or it can get ready in advance. Pushed by seemingly uncontrollable circumstances, many land trusts take the panic route. The impending threat of development has catalyzed the creation of many land trusts. Those that survive grow from the experience. But it is an unnecessarily difficult and perilous way to grow. Some readers may choose to skip this first section of the book because they are too busy saving land to get ready. But they will be back if they survive that first big deal, because no one wants to do it that way again.

How do I know? Because the "Campaign to Save the Hardeman Meadows," described above, was my first exposure to big money and time-pressured purchases by my small land trust. I wanted to do this deal more than anyone, but I had no idea what I was getting into. When the heat was on, a group of us had cornered our board chair, and against his better judgment, he agreed to recommend the project to our board. That decision cost him and others four months of sleepless nights, for only one reason: we were not ready. We had cultivated landowner contacts, but we hadn't cultivated other key community members, donors, and leaders who would have stood ready to help us in important ways.

Hard work by many, the business acumen of our chair, and lots of luck got us through. We made the contacts, but in a big rush. The project defined us and made us a stronger, more active land trust. It built up our donor base, and it makes me proud every time I pass by the beautiful Hardeman Ranch. But we could have gone under. There are easier and safer ways to mature.

I have done it both ways—the unprepared way and the prepared way—and I highly recommend the latter. Even when you are fully prepared, deals can be scary and unpredictable, so there is no reason to be unprepared as well. It is really not so difficult to begin getting ready now for that crucial moment when that most important place is threatened and the land trust must step in.

What does it mean to be prepared? It means being organizationally and financially ready and having the right project. I have made plenty of mistakes in all these categories. For the Hardeman Meadows project, our land trust didn't have an optimal board for purchasing land; we didn't have a large established donor base or prospects ready to write checks. We had not done a thorough feasibility study and didn't have a clear idea of our sources of funding or a plan for the land. These are organizational and financial issues. Fortunately, the ranch gave us a good place to start because it was an important conservation project and so many people wanted to save it.

Since then, again through trial and error, I have learned many strategies that will help any land trust move into the land or conservation easement purchase business. What follows in this section is not an exhaustive list of the dos and don'ts but a brief primer on organizational, financial, and project-related strategies that should make acquisitions easier.

Organizational Readiness

Some of the basic principles of getting ready to buy conservation interests (land or conservation easements) are the same as those relevant to preparing a fundraising campaign.[1] You cannot jump into a fundraising campaign without preparatory work. Land or easement purchase is no different. Just as any company will reorganize with structural and even personnel changes if it moves into a new business, a land trust must do the same. An organizational assessment is a good way to sort out internal needs, prioritize them, and develop timelines for change.[2] An assessment does not have to be an elaborate process. It can be gratifying to assess a land trust's strengths—there are always many. But for this new line of work, some degree of organizational change is usually needed. It should begin at the top with the board of directors and move through every aspect of the organization.

Board of Directors

The board of directors is the most crucial element of a successful organization. It should be the policy- and direction-setting body of any conservation organization. It has the fiduciary responsibility for the organization—a serious role. Most important, the board offers leadership. A land trust can have all the best plans and best staff, but without board leadership, nothing will change. When a land trust is small, the board should also supply valuable manpower. The board of directors is the perfect place for a land trust to get the skills, experience, and wisdom it needs but for which it can't afford to pay. A founding board should be passionate and generous with time and money. As the organization evolves, especially if it becomes staffed, the board must develop a bigger view with larger goals. It can then take on substantial fundraising roles and oversee management. But leadership always remains a key element to success.[3]

Figure 1.2
Board Chairman Alan
Hirschfield at the closing for
the Hardeman meadows.
(Courtesy of Jackson Hole
Land Trust)

Building and maintaining a strong board is not a matter of luck. It takes careful consideration of what skills and expertise the organization needs and who will make its mission a high priority and be compatible for working intensely together. Small organizations rarely take a critical look at their boards. Often, they are so appreciative of anyone willing to serve that they don't think about the overall composition. An effective board will attract other talented people more easily. People like to be part of an effective, well-functioning operation. An ideal board is composed of people who are committed to the organization and offer a variety of skills. The traditional three W's for nonprofit board composition—wealth, wisdom, and work—still hold true. Don't forget that leadership ability, often overlooked as an essential board skill, is part of that wisdom.

Nonprofit board size varies. I serve on the board of one large, sophisticated conservation organization with thirty-four members and on another board with eight members. All boards must have an effective decision-making structure. For a large board, an active executive committee is essential. A small board may put less emphasis on an executive committee. A big board takes more management but brings more skills in-house. Without good management, members of a large board can lose interest. A small board can be more nimble.

As part of an organizational assessment, a board and staff (if there is staff) should ask what skill sets are currently on the board and what skills are needed for the new course charted for the organization. Professionals with skills that may benefit a land trust include bankers, landscape architects, surveyors, engineers, title company personnel, and real estate lawyers (who do not represent the land trust while serving on the board), appraisers, and investors.

What about real estate agents or brokers and developers? There are pros and cons to adding them to a land trust board. The obvious benefits are their working knowledge of land transactions and pricing, their negotiating skills, and their purchase and sale expertise. On the negative side is the potential for conflict of interest, or at least the appearance of a conflict of interest. Real estate agents and developers who work with the same type of real estate as the land trust in the same service area may, or may be perceived to, gain a professional advantage from connections with buyers and sellers involved with the land trust. The image of developers—and, to a lesser degree, realtors—working in conflict with conservation can also taint a land trust's image.

In a cutthroat real estate environment, the choice of one realtor or developer over another can hurt a land trust's reputation among the rest of the real estate community. On the other hand, the wealth of information that comes with the right person can be worth the trouble. If, after weighing the pros and cons, a board decides to invite a realtor or developer to join, then extra care is needed to avoid these ethical and public relations issues. (In the Hardeman Meadows project, the fact that a successful realtor was on our board, and in the spotlight for being there, while also serving on the county commission led to the lawsuit against the county and the subsequent withdrawal of the county's $500,000 share from the project.)

Not all of the necessary land acquisition experts will fit on the board or are right for it. The board should have a comfortable balance of landowners, donors, citizens, scientists, and land-related professionals. Nonetheless, people with all of the skills essential to acquisition should be encouraged to join the land trust team, whether on the board or in some other capacity.

In addition to their own expertise, board members' connections are invaluable. For instance, if a land trust is considering borrowing money (and many acquisition strategies require it), then board members should ask, "Have I taken my local banker to lunch to talk to him [or her] about the land trust?" When we needed a bank loan for the purchase of the Hardeman Meadows, I had no real contacts with bankers. Fortunately, our board chair had frequent dealings with the local bank. (For more information on bank loans, see chapter 11.)

Paid Staff

Having a paid staff for a land trust helps immensely. Because running a land trust can be exhausting, a volunteer-run organization tends to be more reactive. It simply has less time to plan a proactive course. A land trust with staff has more time to develop and carry out a long-term conservation plan. It can focus on its highest-priority projects and use its resources for highest return. A volunteer land trust faces so many tasks just to stay afloat that it must focus on immediate threats.[4] In its early years, a land trust usually has plenty of important reactive conservation work. Eventually, though, it must take the time, whether staffed or unstaffed, to set that work in the context of a land trust's vision for the future.

Generally, the more staff, the more proactive a land trust can be. For example, having in-house real estate knowledge opens deal-making doors. If the land trust is small, it must rely on its board and others closely associated with the organization who have time and real estate skills to invest. Chris DeForest, of the Inland Northwest Land Trust, which operates in Washington State and northern Idaho, explains the situation when his land trust suddenly had to negotiate a purchase option and raise the $50,000 to pay for it: "If we hadn't had Asha on staff we would have been in real trouble. She had worked in real estate and knew how to negotiate and write up the agreements. It was my rapport with the landowner and her expertise that got us through that first acquisition." Of course real estate skills can be learned. As Chris says: "Now that we know how to write up an option, we could do it again much more easily." But it is best not to learn at the negotiating table with critical land on the line. If a board member has good experience in this area, be sure to team up staff with that person so that these skills can begin to be transferred for the next transaction.

Staff and volunteer roles and responsibilities should be clear before heading into a big project, because life can get pretty chaotic during any project. Everyone wants to be part of the excitement of protecting a critical piece of land—and everyone can be. But staff, board, and volunteers should understand their responsibilities. One person must be the project leader and direct the negotiations. Other individuals should take charge of fundraising, communications, and managing documents. Remembering that negotiations are handled in confidence, there are still ways to involve members of the land trust community so that no one feels left out. For most projects, opportunities to participate exist with stewardship assessments, fundraising events, strategy sessions, and administration. Someone has to be assigned to coordinate those assignments, too.

Unpaid Staff or Volunteers

Approximately half of all independent land trusts in the country have no paid staff. Even staffed land trusts have unpaid boards, easement monitors, fundraisers, and many other valuable volunteers. Volunteers are the foundation of land conservation in America. Without volunteer leadership, the great parks, nature preserves, and trail systems would not exist. It is not surprising then that most land trusts begin as a volunteer group energized by a threat to a precious parcel of land, and they often stay volunteer. The passion of a young land trust and its volunteers is contagious. That first victory is exhilarating and attracts more people who want to help.

Land conservation is that way—it compels friends and neighbors to get involved and to take up the work needed to succeed. This level of motivation is particularly impressive because the work of land trusts can be pretty technical. Still, they manage very well. The volunteer land trust board on which I served for many years partnered with another land trust for its more technical functions and hired a good lawyer to draw up the documents. This allowed the board, committees, and volunteers to initiate contact with landowners, to negotiate conservation transactions, to design and implement a stewardship program, and to raise funds.

An all-volunteer land trust should not shy away from setting an ambitious strategic vision, negotiating tough deals, or borrowing money for financing deals. But to make such achievements possible, volunteers must give huge amounts of time. Ultimately, these dedicated people need reinforcements. Having been a volunteer myself, I know how much time must be given and that a limited number of members often carry the lion's share. A lucky land trust has a band of volunteers who have chosen this cause to be their life's work. An ongoing recruitment effort that helps generate a steady supply of new leaders and supporting volunteers will make this model sustainable.

Once a land trust has a few staff members, volunteers' roles change. Whereas volunteers do everything in a volunteer organization, in a staffed organization, as board members they set policy and share with staff the planning and do much less of the implementation of the program. Sometimes volunteers will back away with the hiring of staff, either because they are so relieved not to have to do all the work anymore or because they feel a little pushed out by staff. It may be harder to reengage the volunteers as staff members assume the core tasks of working with landowners and writing easements. At this critical juncture, it is important to keep volunteers close. Their savvy and their connections with the community are often what have built the organization. It is their institutional history that prevents mistakes from being repeated. This knowledge cannot be substituted easily, if ever. Volunteers participating in an organization build broader ownership. Also, they are twice as likely to be donors than are nonvolunteers.[5]

Box 1.1   Tips for Working with Volunteers

- Use volunteers' ideas as much as possible.
- Pay attention to each volunteer project.
- Hold regular meetings to monitor progress.
- Be prepared to spend lots of staff time offering suggestions for more people who can help, for sources of supplies, and for encouragement.
- Remind volunteers of upcoming meetings. (It may be necessary to have one volunteer call to remind the others.)
- Thank them!

Just weeks after I had started running a new environmental organization in Wyoming, I passed a couple on the road. The woman said that they had just retired to Jackson Hole and that she had a little experience raising money for hospitals back in Connecticut. Might I be able to use her help? Little did I know at the time that an energetic and experienced fundraiser had entered my life. Finding donors for conservation in Jackson Hole became Addie Donnan's full-time volunteer job. She was at work early in the morning and left late in the afternoon. She wrote letters and thank-you notes, and she took me to lunch with people she had just met. She and her husband, Ted, held fundraising parties at their home. Addie initiated a lucrative silent art auction that continues today. We now had two desks and chairs. Addie set the example. Soon we had others reviewing government documents, providing legal support, and writing position papers. I learned how much knowledge and work unpaid staff can provide—a lesson I never forget.

Box 1.2   Tips for Events

- Check all community calendar sites for possible scheduling conflicts before choosing an event date.
- Events are stressful so make sure the person in charge can handle the stress very well. If necessary, use someone on staff with experience in and a passion for events and grassroots organizing.
- Don't be afraid to ask anyone for help with ideas, time, supplies, or money.
- If you want a varied crowd, plan a variety of activities/programs.
- If you want people to stay, invite their children. If they have fun, the parents will stay longer.
- Identify experienced, capable volunteers to run specific parts of the event. Make sure they and others know who is in charge of each part. Be sure they are reliable. If you have any doubts, team people up and check in on their progress frequently.
- More people are needed to help than are usually estimated. So don't plan for a more complex event than you have volunteers and staff available to handle.
- Use volunteers' ideas as much as possible. Open up the event planning meetings to suggestions.
- Match volunteers carefully with projects. Make sure they have the time to handle and are happy with what you give them to do.
- Keep the spirits of event planners up. Strong leadership and lots of enthusiasm are contagious and make event planning more fun.
- Be organized and keep track of everything: new ideas, phone numbers of volunteers, schedules and deadlines, supplies and their sources, and whom to thank. Keep a master notebook for reference, and use it often. It will also be useful for planning the next event.
- Make contingency plans for rain. Rent a bigger tent than would be needed for good weather.
- Publicity is important. Use every means available (paid service announcements, paid radio, TV and newspapers, posters, community calendars, e-mail, your Web site, box-holder mailings), and promote the event well in advance.
- Make a final schedule for everything that should happen at the event, and give a copy to all volunteers.
- Get someone to take good photographs for the write-up and for future marketing.
- Publicly thank everyone associated with the event.

Take pains to explicitly redefine the roles of board, staff, and volunteers. It may seem like overkill to actually write out job descriptions, but it is amazing how many questions about roles emerge in the writing. This also helps place volunteers and paid staff on more equal footing—both should be seriously engaged with clear expectations. Here are some valuable roles in which volunteers can stay involved:

- Board members
- Advisory board members
- Volunteer consultants when their expertise matches a land trust need, be it, for example, design assistance for an invitation, real estate expertise for a transaction, or banking experience for a bank loan
- Members of committees (strategic planning, stewardship, fundraising)
- Interns (or offering internships to family members and friends of volunteers)
- Easement monitors as part of the stewardship program
- Fundraisers and sources of donor prospects
- Links to landowners
- Office assistants (for example, mailing newsletters and answering phones)
- Event organizers, planners, and workers
- Well-informed community ambassadors for the land trust.

There is nothing like a big new project to attract a whole new group of volunteers. Momentum and enthusiasm are more easily sustained through big group projects, such as a stewardship or restoration project, or through participation in a strategic planning process or new fundraising drive. It may seem more difficult for a staffed organization to involve volunteers in other ways, but your organization will be healthier and have greater community support if you do. Try to become the person on staff who is always thinking of projects that volunteers can do. Then ask them to learn about the organization, and participate at every appropriate opportunity (see online appendix at www .conservationguide.com).

A fundraising event is the classic means of getting valuable assistance from volunteers because it requires so many tasks with a range of time commitments and skills. Like many privately funded land acquisition projects, the Hardeman Meadows campaign centered on a big community event with fundraising activities ranging from a pet show to a hobby horse race to a "cattle maze" labyrinth to an auction. Volunteers stepped forward with new booth ideas weekly, and daily preparations kept people streaming in and out of the land trust's small offices. Simply planning the event created an atmosphere of excitement. Prospective large donors would step into the office chaos and feel the urgency, the joy, and a contagious sense of the project's value. They wanted to be part of it. Volunteers can create that buzz in a community as well.

By eleven a.m. on the day of the Hardeman Meadows event, despite the snow (which melted by late morning), seventy-five volunteers were hurrying to finish building booths and carting in supplies. Most had arrived much earlier to dig the snow out of their booths. As the event prepared to open, just watching the sea of activity and hearing the sound of staple guns and hammers making ready was exhilarating.

Each booth had its memorable moment: the master of ceremonies of the pet show with a very large snake wrapped around his shoulders, the shouts of encouragement from parents as their small children competed on just-crafted (at the hobby-horse booth) stick hobby horses decorated for the rodeo, older children disappearing into the "cattle maze" cleverly designed by a local contractor. One thousand people—almost a tenth of the county's population—attended.

For a big community event sponsored by a small land trust, nonboard volunteers must take on a great deal of responsibility. This builds tremendous ownership in the organization and its mission, but it has its risks because the capability and reliability of those volunteers may not have been tested. This is why volunteers should work in teams and should report to the larger group frequently. For specific projects, such as writing, it is wise to informally interview the volunteer first to determine writing experience. You might even ask for a writing sample. Be up front about why; neither of you wants a big investment of time to result in a product that does not meet the organization's needs. Writing styles are personal, and significant editing can cause disappointment.

Even without a specific land project around which to organize, finding a good reason to hold a limited number of events is a wonderful way to build support and involve new people in the organization as workers and attendees. Organizations can use the excuse of an event to encourage their board members and friends to pull out their holiday card mailing lists for invitees, which ultimately builds donor prospect files. A good speaker or the occasion of honoring past supporters is enough of an excuse for an appealing event. Volunteers should be asked to help. Afterward, the land trust will find itself in a new

Figure 1.3
The Jackson Hole Land Trust hosted a western-style
carnival to fundraise for its Hardeman Meadows project.
(Jackson Hole News & Guide)

and elevated place with its donors, its volunteers, and the community at
large.

The article "The Care and Feeding of Volunteers," by Michael McKee, sum-
marizes well some of the ways to attract and keep good volunteers.[6] It is well
worth the effort and sometimes substantial time investment it takes to make
sure volunteers are part of what the land trust does for many reasons—not just
because of the good work they can do. A land trust is a business, and community members (including volunteers and donors) are land trust customers, just
as landowners are. Whatever volunteers do to help, their experience should
be enjoyable and they should be thanked privately *and* publicly.

Community Support

Community support is essential. The community, whether a small town or
larger region, is full of people and institutions that can help build momentum for conservation and spread the word about what the land trust does and
why. Necessary for the long-term survival of conservation work, community
support fuels all aspects of a land trust and its projects, especially when money
must be raised. For the Hardeman Meadows project, people stepped forward
from every corner. Without any prompting, the local cycling club donated the

Figure 1.4
The Little Traverse Conservancy encourages community support through fun outdoor activities. (Courtesy of Little Traversee Conservancy)

proceeds of its Mother's Day race, the ski patrol came forward with $4,500, the local sporting goods store donated 10 percent of its profits for a period of time, musicians played fundraising concerts, and newspapers published editorials supporting the project. Obviously, the more visible the land trust's projects are, the easier it is to build support. But that community support, once established, will carry over to less visible projects.

If your land trust is unsure about whether it has community support because it has maintained a low profile, you should find out. How to test the water depends on the characteristics of the town or region. In a small community, systematically asking newspaper editors, political officials, businesspeople, and donors will gauge support, often uncovering misinformation and criticisms that the land trust can then address. Inviting a critic out for coffee, or better yet to the land trust offices, and carefully listening to the person's concerns is the best way to bring skeptics around and learn about the perception problems that the land trust must overcome. When I discovered that a member of the town council thought our program was restricting public access, I invited him out to lunch. We talked about fishing, a mutual interest. I told him about the number of miles of spawning streams we were protecting and the public park projects we were planning. He suggested a couple of new park opportunities. We have been friends ever since.

You can't get to know a community by sitting in an office all day. Participate in community organizations, such as the Rotary Club or the Chamber of

Commerce. Join a tennis group or a book club or the Parent-Teacher Association. The community needs to find out that the land trust is a collection of real people who have a spectrum of interests and are not single-minded land conservationists.

Knowing the community *and* having already familiarized it with your land trust will be especially valuable when the crunch of an acquisition is on. It helps to have key politicians, newspaper reporters, and editors already knowledgeable about the land trust and just an easy phone call away. The list of people who can help a land trust is nearly endless. So make friends everywhere, then, for example, the banker will know you when a project needs financing and the title company staff will be familiar with conservation easements.

Having ways to build support more systematically can expand the network exponentially. For example, creating a good database of landowners by neighborhood saves last-minute researching in county records. Sophisticated record keeping can track relationship data to identify who knows whom and to introduce the land trust to people who make decisions regarding the project and who might support it.

The goal is to know what community relations work lies ahead, who is on the team, and who needs cultivation before they read about the project in the newspaper. If our land trust had been working with the broader community, we might have anticipated the frustrations that led to the lawsuit and the county's retraction of the $500,000 from the Hardeman Meadows project. As it turned out, the plaintiffs wanted to be heard. If our ears had been to the ground, we probably could have addressed their issues before they were elevated to the courts. Eventually, the lawsuit was settled and the county money paid. But the delay nearly killed the deal.

Project Criteria

Even the smallest and newest land trust must have project criteria. Standards for accepting projects will keep a land trust focused on projects that are consistent with its mission so that it can use its limited resources most effectively. The project criteria should flow out of the mission and out of any more-specific conservation plans, if the organization has them. Project criteria give credence to an organizational decision to undertake a project, and they help distinguish its choices from those of other organizations. Ultimately, project criteria help a land trust create a cohesive and meaningful conservation legacy, whether it involves wildlife or agriculture or a mix of conservation resources.

Since a land trust's project criteria will guide its projects, the criteria must be consistent with the trust's charitable purposes, follow all applicable laws and regulations, and address organizational and conservation sustainability. They should be developed by the organization as a whole, and all projects should meet the criteria without exception.

Project criteria can start as a few lines outlining acquisition guidelines and addressing such issues as minimum parcel size and resource characteristics. As a land trust matures, the criteria can become more specific. The powerful tool of geographic information systems (GIS) facilitates a more organized approach. Using GIS, a land trust can integrate other plans and information into its own. It can, for example, overlay trail corridors and county parks and recreation plans to drive an open space program, soils and land use to drive an agricultural program, or wildlife corridor and habitat mapping to drive a wildlife program. For starters though, simple written criteria are sufficient. *Land Trust Standards and Practices* Standard 8, "Evaluating and Selecting Conservation Projects," and its online appendices (available at www.conservationguide.com) offer excellent guidance on project criteria.

Strategic Planning

Strategic planning is the process of identifying realistic objectives and creating a road map for accomplishing and evaluating them within a specific time period, usually a number of years. At some point, not necessarily in its very first year, a land trust should take the time to develop a strategic plan, even when money and time are scarce and development is advancing on many fronts. Such a plan ensures that a land trust's work adds up to something meaningful for the trust's staff and volunteers, its constituents, and its conservation mission.

Strategic planning starts by building consensus around the big picture: the land trust's overriding reason for existence. It works from the general to the specific, creating consensus and clarity regarding the mission, goals, strategies, and programs and then pricing out the cost of the plan and its programs.

Because its driving goals are conservation focused, a land trust must know enough about the conservation and community values it strives toward in order to identify the necessary ingredients for success. Often, such long-term plans aim to keep intact ecological resources (such as watersheds, migration routes, and critical habitat), blocks of agricultural land, continuous scenic road

Box 1.3   Steps in Strategic Planning

1. Develop the process (board chair, executive director, consultant responsibility).
   • Hire a consultant.
   • Appoint a planning committee, or assign the planning task to an existing committee.
   • Establish a timeline for planning.
   • Set the date for a full board retreat.
   • Determine the scope (subject matter) of the plan.
2. Inform the key players (board chair).
3. Do a preplanning assessment, and present a written report to the board (consultant).
   • Assess the external environment. What is the current political climate? What is the status of federal, state, and local policy? What are the economic and technological trends? What is the status of the competition?
   • Assess the internal environment. What is the status of the organization's programs, finances, governance, and administration?
4. Conduct a full-day board retreat (consultant, chair, executive director).
   • Discuss the organizational assessment.
   • Identify the critical issues facing the organization and the strategic directions the organization will take in response to those issues.
   • Develop or refine the mission statement.
   • Identify the broad organizational goals to guide the organization for the next three to five years.
5. Develop objectives for each goal—that is, quantifiable accomplishments that establish progress toward the goal (staff, consultant, planning committee).
6. Develop implementation plans for each objective (staff, chair, committee chairs, consultant).
7. Develop a staffing plan (executive director).
8. Develop three- to five-year financial projections (executive director, consultant, treasurer).
9. Create a first draft of the plan for review by the planning committee (executive director).
10. Plan a review by relevant board committees (staff, committee chairs).
11. Produce a second draft of the plan (executive director).
12. Present the plan to the board for approval (chair).

Courtesy of Marc Smiley, "The Three-part Planning Process," LTA Rally, Madison, Wisconsin, October 2005, available at http: //www.ltanet.org/ attached-files/0/54/5476/Rally_2005_E14_1.pdf (accessed August 30, 2006).

corridors, or a series of community gardens. Here again, GIS technology can aid strategic planning at any scale.

A strategic plan need not be a huge undertaking. But it should have a programmatic and financial component, a timeline and measurable outcomes, and result from an inclusive organizational process. Leading with words, and supported by a financial picture of what change will mean, the plan will demonstrate internally, to the community, and to funders, that the land trust has realistic plans and the rigor to achieve them. When completed, each member of the organization should be invested in the organization's future and better understand their roles and relevance to the mission.

Iterations of the strategic plan keep the organization incrementally moving toward more ambitious outcomes. As a land trust increases its expertise using such tools as financing, it can become more proactive with its strategic planning—its agenda will no longer be set by which landowner wants to donate and when. Of course, getting to this point takes time, usually several years. Conserving agricultural, recreational, scenic, and ecological values is more easily accomplished when a land trust systematically chooses its course.

The process can engage community members and a plan summary can help them grasp the relevance of a land trust's mission. Once the community does, other benefits ensue. The planning and priority-setting project of the small Cacapon and Lost Rivers Land Trust in West Virginia is a case in point. With a grant from the National Fish and Wildlife Foundation, executive director Nancy Ailes assembled experts from all around the country to help define the ecological importance of the Cacapon River, a large tributary to the Potomac River, which flows through Washington, D.C., and into the Chesapeake Bay. Before priority setting, the land trust had eight hundred acres in donated conservation easements; after priority setting, two years later it had five thousand acres. Through outreach during the planning process, the community (and its landowners) found that they were part of an area of ecological importance. With this knowledge, they were more willing to support the land trust financially and through easement gifts. Nancy has some good advice: "Define the significance of your area, its priorities and how you intend to protect them. Otherwise, money won't flow your way."

Decision Making

How a nonprofit organization makes decisions demonstrates its stability and transparency and, in the end, its effectiveness during those fast-paced campaigns for land or easement acquisition. Clear roles as to who makes what decisions and when are crucial. What are the lines of authority? What decision-making responsibilities does the board retain? What decisions are delegated to paid or unpaid staff? Is there accountability? *Land Trust Standards and Practices* Standard 3, "Board Accountability," addresses some of these questions.

While negotiating a purchase, for example, who in the organization can make decisions about price and terms? It is useful to have a board committee work with whoever is representing the land trust to directly convey parameters set by the board as a whole. Then, if decisions need to be made between board meetings (which they always do), the parameters to work within are already known. This said, there is negotiating value in having to go back to the board on big decisions, so the committee's latitude should have practical application but not be limitless.

Good Record Keeping

Get it right. Don't track more information than you can handle absolutely correctly. Recognize, though, that record keeping is more than keeping accurate, organized files. It also involves questions about who has access to those files, and privacy and confidentiality considerations that come into play as soon as you buy your first filing cabinet.

A land trust must keep many different kinds of records, including but not limited to donor, land/easement, stewardship, financial, personnel, and board records. Be thoughtful and educated about how to manage each. Good guidelines and templates of policies are available. *Land Trust Standards and Practices* Standards 2D, "Compliance with Laws: Records Policy"; 5B, "Fundraising: Accountability to Donors"; 6B, "Financial and Asset Management: Financial Records"; 9G, "Ensuring Sound Transactions: Recordkeeping"; and supporting appendices offer guidance here. Other aspects of land trust work also require good record keeping, including evaluation and selection of conservation projects (addressed in Standard 8), tax benefits (addressed in Standard 10), ensuring sound transactions (addressed in Standard 9), conservation easement stewardship (addressed in Standard 11), and fee land stewardship (addressed in Standard 12). The Land Trust Alliance's web-based member database, LTAnet, offers extensive other sources of information on record keeping.[7]

In addition to the obvious legal and financial reasons for good record keeping, there is the matter of sanity. This is perpetual stuff. Making sure those memos cover enough information so that, for example, a new stewardship director can pick up where the old one left off keeps the next generation of practitioners from having to scrabble around for missing facts.

When raising money, attention to detail and good organization is particularly important because donors care that you get it right. It is more important to know the spelling of a donor's name than whether she likes horseback riding. We had a wealthy donor whose summer mail was routinely sent to her winter address. She became very annoyed because she thought we had not invited her to two of our big summer events—an avoidable mistake.

A good donor database makes a big difference, but more important is what is asked of it. Basic information includes the following:

- Name, mailing addresses (including seasonal), phone numbers, and e-mail addresses
- Relationship to the land trust: easement/fee donor, financial supporter, in-kind donor, volunteer, professional advisor, board member (dates of service)
- History of involvement with the land trust: gift history (including ask amounts), estate donor, and other participation
- Dates of contact with person and by whom (staff/board), including when thanked.

Useful information to add as the capacity to track more information increases:

- Expertise/profession (e.g., attorney, accountant)
- Land trust events attended
- Location of residence (useful in relation to past and future land trust projects)
- Interests (e.g., fishing, biking, bird-watching)
- Future potential involvement: conservation buyer prospect, estate donor, large donor.

Write memos, even if they are only two lines long, on all contact with individual donors, foundations, bankers, and anyone who can help you in any way. The memo should be dated and should explain the purpose of the meeting, contain insights into the contact's interests, record questions asked, and detail follow-up action to take (see appendix 1.2). Large donors, prospects, and other important contacts should have individual files. A chronological file for all internal memos and donor correspondence ensures that every piece of donor information has a backup place where it can be found.

Appreciation

All "investors" in a land trust program, from board to staff to donors to volunteers to businesses to landowners, deserve to and must be thanked for whatever they have done for the organization. Thanking is the opportunity to put the "fun" into fundraising. Good humor, good times, and appreciation are the secret ingredients that bring supporters back again and again to help, to attend events, and to give. The mission of land conservation is the driving force behind support for a land trust, but the important intangibles make the experience enjoyable and the memories worth living again.

Think of all the ways that supporters can be recognized for their generosity:

- Personally, immediately after their work is completed
- At regular land trust events
- In the land trust's newspaper or newsletter
- On the land trust's Web site
- At a small appreciation event
- By staff and board individually
- With a small gift (nothing too fancy, because donors don't want to think that their donation is just paying for gifts)[8]

Figure 1.5
To show appreciation to supporters, the Jackson Hole Land Trust presents awards at its annual picnic. (Courtesy of Jackson Hole Land Trust)

- With a personal note signed by the executive director or board chair or by the whole board or staff
- With a special opportunity (e.g., fishing on a private fishing stream or riding on a conserved ranch; attending a dinner in the person's honor)
- A naming opportunity for a park or park bench or on a list on a public sign (see chapter 6).

The need to thank supporters can be forgotten in the chaos of daily land trust life. But it must not be. If your supporters are private people, they may want to be acknowledged only privately, so be sensitive to these nuances by asking them first. But most people are very pleased to be acknowledged publicly.

Conclusion

Many land acquisitions have been done on the fly, but why risk it? Why not start getting ready for the big project as soon as the land trust forms? As you may have guessed by now, I think *Land Trust Standards and Practices* and its appendices offer excellent information in all of these areas and should be the standard guidelines for operating a land trust. They are also central to land trust accreditation, which is explained in detail on the Land Trust Alliance's Web site.[9]

Getting prepared gets everyone involved because it means expanding the network. We all have to eat lunch. Ask the board, staff, and volunteers to use a lunch or two not only to meet with landowners but also to talk up the land trust with important community members and listen to what they have to say. It is easy to stay in the comfort zone at the office, but don't. Get out and meet the people that the land trust needs to know. Then, when the big project comes along, the land trust will be better prepared to negotiate it, close on it, *and* pay for it. You may stumble along the way, but as you do the advance work you can take comfort in knowing that you are getting much more prepared than we were when we bought the Hardeman Meadows.

Chapter 2
Financial Readiness

The key to purchasing land or conservation easements is to be financially stable. There is nothing worse than worrying about meeting payroll while trying to close on a land transaction. A land trust on financially sound footing is also more likely to have developed a variety of potential sources of funding for an acquisition. Armed with these, the land trust can prepare a financial road map or plan that outlines the strategy and budget for the project, possible sources of revenue, and how much each revenue source might generate. If, instead, pressures are forcing the organization to focus on other money matters, this plan cannot be prepared or adequately implemented.

A Stable Organization

A land trust must have a board-approved annual budget to direct expenditures, recorded and monitored by balance sheets and income statements. Land trusts usually have three primary categories of expenditure: operating, protection, and stewardship. The operating program includes administration of fundraising, staffing, reporting, record keeping, board of directors, and office expenses. The protection program covers specific protection project expenses. The stewardship program includes the plans and costs associated with stewardship monitoring and restoration, amendment, and any other plans associated with property and easement management. Land trusts also have endowments, quasi or board designated endowments, dedicated funds and reserves.[1] These are like savings accounts for various purposes. A land trust's first account of this kind is usually a reserve to help manage cash flow. The second is a stewardship fund that eventually should have sufficient value to be able to pay for ongoing stewardship for all easements and fee acquisitions from its interest revenue. A legal defense fund can be part of the stewardship fund or can be separate. Another very useful fund as a land trust moves to purchase acquisitions is a protection fund.

These categories of expenditure and accounts vary depending on the land trust. For example, many land trusts pay for basic protection and stewardship work out of their operating fund—in an effort to let the protection and stewardship funds grow—and use these dedicated funds only for major costs, such as options and purchases (protection) and lawsuits (stewardship). Regardless, land trusts should plan for anticipated expenditures in each program area annually. Within each program, there are many line items of expenditure and activity. Most land trusts pay for these expenditures primarily from unrestricted charitable gifts from individuals. Others depend heavily on foundation support. Some have very unusual revenue sources. The Land Trust of Santa Cruz, for example, paid most of its bills for years with timber revenue from its sustainable tree farm and with rental income on office space and cabins.

One big advantage of individual giving is that it is more likely to be unrestricted, and thus the land trust can spend it where the need is. Some foundations also make unrestricted "general support" grants, but more often they make grants for specific projects, or "restricted" grants. For this reason, most land trusts look for flexible financial support mostly from individuals. Ideally, these individuals become regular donors to the land trust through its annual giving program.

Before creating a new funding need for a conservation purchase, a land trust should be certain that its sources of annual revenue are reliable by reviewing the revenue numbers and the individual donors behind them. Is annual giving revenue consistent? Are there donors who give every year, and does the land trust support and cultivate them? Is the outreach program doing more than replacing attrition? Is attrition low? What is the capacity of annual donors to give more? Not only is a strong annual giving campaign the basis for financial stability, it is also the launching pad for a capital campaign to buy, protect, and steward land and conservation easements.

Annual donors should be knowledgeable about the organization's activities and, if possible, personally acquainted with its board and staff. Find ways to inform donors throughout the year with newsletters, a Web site, and personal correspondence. Bringing donors and prospects closer to the land trust's activities leads to greater interest, involvement, and financial participation. If it is possible to entice supporters with an invitation for a field visit or a workday or to help monitor a property, their commitment will grow because they will have invested time as well as money. If, for instance, a donor spends a day

Figure 2.1
The Jackson Hole
Land Trust offers field
trips on preserved
properties—such as
the Walton Ranch,
shown here—to the
public, donors, and
donor prospects.
(Courtesy of Jackson
Hole Land Trust)

walking a restoration project with the land trust manager and design engineer, then that person might attend a fundraising event for the same project. A larger annual gift is likely at the end of the year. When personal investment grows, so does the interest in protecting that investment.

Some land trusts conduct field trips to visit protected properties. This is a particularly attractive opportunity for supporters if the properties are under easement and not regularly accessible to the public. Other land trusts create trail systems that encourage citizens to see and enjoy the landscape. Some sponsor workdays, fishing trips, hikes, mountain bike trips, and overnight camping trips; others bring in speakers, take on educational projects such as inviting schools to use protected land, and hold events featuring stories by old-time landowners or discussions by biologists and ecologists. Remember that donors are volunteers and vice versa. Treat them as part of the family, because they are.

Although the details of soliciting gifts from individuals, foundations, and corporations are discussed in more detail later in this book, public or governmental funding is not. For many land trusts, public funding will cover the actual purchase price of a conservation acquisition. Accessing public funding is an art unto itself involving alignment with agency priorities, access to decision makers, and significant community education and mobilization. Many land trusts have developed close relationships with agencies that take advantage of the nimble nature of land trusts to implement public acquisition programs.

Regardless of the role that public funding plays in a land trust's program, there will always be a need for private funding, ranging from general costs associated with running a land trust to options or down payments, closing costs, and matching dollars required by some public programs; stewardship costs; and, in many cases, the acquisition cost itself.[2]

A Word about Fundraising

Fundraising comes in many shapes and sizes. It is central to any land trust, even one with its funding already in place. All active land trusts soon arrive at a point where even reliable sources of money are not enough. A land trust supported by foundations laments that it does not have a base of major donor support. A land trust with lots of major donors is concerned about being elitist, and one with only small donors is frustrated that it can't undertake more ambitious projects. A broad base of support is always best, no matter how hard it is to develop. A land trust should be funded to some degree by a combination of small annual donors or members, major donors, board members, special events, foundations, investments, planned giving donors, and public funding where such programs exist. Long-term financial plans developed with clear criteria and implemented meticulously can help an organization get out ahead financially rather than always running to catch up. As a land trust becomes more proactive, fundraising becomes less of a challenge and more of an opportunity.[3]

Fiscal Controls

If no one in the organization has the ability or the desire to track the finances, then make that first part-time hire a bookkeeper. Knowing what money is coming into the organization and from whom, as well as what money is going out and to where, is essential for an organization of any type. Both the board and staff should be responsible for fiscal matters. At the board level, a member good with details and numbers should get the job of treasurer and be expected to report to the board at least quarterly with written financial information (which can be prepared by the bookkeeper or staff member). In a staffed organization, a senior staff member or chief financial officer should be watching the books even more closely. The responsible staff person and the board treasurer should meet regularly (monthly or quarterly depending on the scale and activity level of the organization) to review all of the organization's financials.

The financial reports should be prepared by a bookkeeper whose reports are in turn reviewed by a qualified financial advisor, preferably by a Certified Public Accountant (CPA), in an annual audit.[4]

If a land trust is blessed with savings accounts, how the land trust invests these accounts depends on its investment policy (developed by the board's investment committee and approved by the full board; see online appendix at www.conservationguide.com), and on what they will be used for and when. Ideally, a land trust's operating fund and reserve should be very liquid, its protection fund should be somewhat liquid based on a partly predictable acquisition schedule, and its stewardship fund(s) should be invested for the long term. An active protection fund is most challenging to invest because predicting transaction closings is never easy. Land protection and financial staff (paid or volunteer) should meet regularly to review the status of all impending projects in order to plan for when the protection fund portfolio must be liquid.

Land trust accounting can be tricky because a small organization may be working with large amounts of money for a short period of time during an acquisition. A good accountant with nonprofit experience can help design a financial structure that builds in standard fiscal controls and Generally Accepted Accounting Procedures.[5] Donors and the Internal Revenue Service expect these procedures to be in place and followed.

Opening Doors and Creating Options

Consider the Hardeman Meadows example described in chapter 1. What should the land trust have done to create financial options well in advance of having to purchase the ranch? It should have been building relationships with friends, banks, county officials, and the business community so that these parties could have known enough and cared enough about the land trust to help at the right moment. Instead, the land trust had to do all that relationship building at the same time that it was raising money and while the option clock was ticking.

How could it have gotten ahead of the game? It was struggling just to raise its annual budget, spending its days talking to landowners about giving easements, not selling them. It was not lacking in ambition to get into the acquisition business, but it had enough on its plate.

The secret to taking a step toward purchasing conservation interests for the overtaxed young land trust is subtle. Success lies in the support of a broader community. It rests on more than just the support of donors and target landowners, or money and land; it rests on the ongoing and truly enjoyable task of getting to know the community and the community getting to know the land trust.

Once a land trust has the network, then it can brainstorm likely sources of support and funding for those special properties that may become available. For instance, take a productive wetlands that the land trust hopes someday to purchase and is rumored to soon be for sale. Where are the most realistic sources of revenue to pay for it? State and federal fish and wildlife departments? The National Fish and Wildlife Foundation? NAWCA (North American Wetlands Conservation Act) funding? Neighbors? Bird clubs? A partnership of several organizations? Will matching funds be needed?

The Inland Northwest Land Trust was caught off guard when Reardan's Audubon Lake, located outside of Reardan, Washington, came on the market in July 2003. This 278-acre property with an 80-acre pond and surrounding wetlands and shrub-steppe uplands was rich in bird life and a popular viewing area for bird-watchers from the adjacent highway, and for the lucky few who had permission to visit the property. The land trust had to negotiate its first complicated option immediately and raise a payment of $51,000 from its membership base of four hundred people. Fortunately, it had a well-developed relationship with the Spokane Audubon Society, which appealed to its own broader membership for money. Numerous other Audubon chapters, as well as the state office of the Audubon Society, also supported the project. Two national organizations—Trust for Public Land (TPL) and The Nature Conservancy (TNC)—encouraged the state to appropriate funds to buy the property. As one staff member says: "Part of readiness is having a network of organizations and people who are older and wiser to help." The Washington Department of Fish and Wildlife approved the acquisition in March 2006, though only after the Inland Northwest Land Trust had purchased the property with a loan from the Bullitt Foundation.

The Inland Northwest Land Trust's purchase is an example of a project requiring both public and private funding. The option was paid for with gifts from individual donors, and the purchase had to close before the state money was available. The land trust needed and received private interim funding to bridge the timing gap. In these circumstances, a land trust should know the nearest conservation revolving loan fund (see chapter 12) or whether a friendly foundation loans money through a program-related investment program (chapter 15) and should be on great terms with local bankers (chapter 11).

Figure 2.2
Reardan's Audubon Lake, now permanently protected thanks to Inland Northwest Land Trust's many dedicated volunteers and conservation partners, is home to a rich variety of birds, such as this marsh wren. (Photo by Robert M. Griffith)

A Financial Plan[6]

Whether at the single-project or larger landscape level, a financial plan is vital to financial success in land acquisition. A financial plan is both a thinking process and a final document. The rigor of preparing a plan, even the simplest one for a single project, clarifies ideas around the project, ensures creative strategizing early in the process, and creates a vehicle for the whole organization to support the project. Land trusts that send detailed memos and budgets for each project to the board for approval are already doing most of the work of financial planning.

A financial plan should map out every step for a transaction, from the initial feasibility study to the celebration party, before getting involved in the project. The plan should anticipate as many of these steps as possible. Part of developing the plan is considering appropriate types of funding and financing and the sources for them.

The planning stage is the perfect time to do "out-of-the-box" brainstorming on all possible conservation outcomes and all possible ways of achieving them. A land trust might find that the obvious outcome is only one of several worth pursuing. This is also the time to prioritize the strategies and create a backup plan.

As a land trust grows more sophisticated, it can use its financial plan to develop larger landscape-scale initiatives and to broaden its financing options at that scale. In one ambitious plan, twelve land trusts working in an iconic western landscape identified the costs of protection for the key sites within a

28-million-acre system, the cost of protecting them, and where the money might realistically come from. The resulting document identified ten sources of funding to conserve the most critical one million privately owned acres in the ecosystem and estimated the potential revenue from each source based on past performance and consultation with local experts. It laid out a ten-year plan for generating that revenue, including the cost of the fundraising and a two-year initial start-up phase. This kind of blueprint is valuable in articulating and guiding conservation activity throughout a region.

On a much smaller scale is a single-project financial plan that identifies the components of a single transaction. Such a plan includes the following:

- A description of the project and its importance (including supporting information)
- Desired rights to be acquired: conservation easement ownership, fee title ownership, or other rights (e.g., lease)
- A desired interim ownership and long-term ownership outcome (land trust, government, or private ownership)
- A desired use outcome and justification (park, private ownership, wildlife sanctuary)
- An optimal vehicle for protection (single purchase, phased purchase, exchange, bargain purchase)
- Desired sources of short-term and long-term revenue (local, state, federal programs, foundations, individuals, corporations)
- Backup sources of revenue
- An analysis of the risk
- A detailed budget
- Implementation steps and approval points.

Determining the desired outcome for the project is the first step in developing the financial model. Establishing the best outcome will lead to identifying the most likely sources of funding. If, for example, the property is best suited for a town park, then the town government is a good first place to go for money. The ultimate disposition of the property affects the terms of the purchase and the land trust's ability to succeed at raising the money. Looking at the suite of options can start the creative thinking that it takes to find funding. Some questions to consider follow:

- Could the land be resold to a government agency?
  - Is the parcel on a government priority list for acquisition? Is an acquisition proposal before that agency and is the congressional delegation (or state legislators or county commissioners) aware and supportive of the acquisition? Is there a signed letter of intent to purchase?
  - If a government purchase is in the works, are interim property stewardship needs in the budget in case there is a delay with appropriations?
- Could the land be sold to a conservation-minded buyer directly?
  - How likely is finding an individual buyer within the transactional time frame? What do the experts (realtors) advise about finding a conservation buyer?
  - Is the land trust prepared to take the risk of selling the land unrestricted to a buyer, or is it planning to sell restricted and make up the difference in price through fundraising?[7]
  - Is financing (e.g., borrowing interim capital) likely and in the budget?
- Could the land be resold to an institution?
  - Will the uses be compatible with the land trust's goals and its representations about future use?
  - Is there a signed contract with the institution?
- Should it be retained as a park or preserve or for other uses?
  - Have stewardship and management costs been fully budgeted into the cost of the property?
  - Have government permitting issues been addressed?
- Should the land be restored and then sold?
  - Have restoration costs been realistically budgeted?
  - If wetlands restoration is involved, does the land trust know enough about this business? Have the appropriate specialists assessed the restoration needs? Has the Army Corps of Engineers assessed the opportunity for mitigation funding?

For the Hardeman Meadows purchase, we had an idea that we would sell the ranch to a conservation-minded buyer subject to a conservation easement allowing one new homesite and would fundraise for the difference between the purchase price and the restricted resale price. We hoped to receive part of the value of the conservation easement from a windfall state payment to the county of $500,000. But we had not fully scoped out the conservation buyer

Figure 2.3
Rancher and favorite auctioneer Earl Hardeman presided over the auction fundraiser for the Hardeman Meadows. (Jackson Hole News & Guide)

market or undertaken a formal feasibility study. In the end, we used a variety of sources of revenue to pay for the 137-acre ranch. We divided the property into two parcels, separating the barns from the new homesite—something that realtors advised us to do when we couldn't sell the parcel as one. We also could not find a buyer in our short, ninety-day time frame. Instead, a land trust donor stepped forward and bought the bulk of the property, taking the risk of resale for us. The barns, which we had assumed would be the draw for any conservation buyer, were leased separately to an educational institution. We took out a loan to cover the easement value when the county withdrew its commitment to pay for it. Then we sold our only other liquid asset, a lot in a development, to pay off the loan when the lawsuit dragged on. Eventually, we received the $500,000 from the county—one year after closing—when the lawsuit was settled.

A financial plan not only clarifies the land trust's own ideas about strategy and provides a document for board discussion and approval, it can also be customized into a financial marketing document to present to prospective donors, partners, investors, and lenders. The packaging of a project into a financial plan draws heavily from the private financial world. Developing a financial plan is an important step toward broader thinking about identifying, marketing to, and using the robust funding sources that help for-profit private finance to thrive.

In for-profit finance, multiple institutions serve financing needs. The opportunity to engage several institutions in conservation finance (e.g., banks, foundations, investor groups, and intermediaries) is just now emerging and could ultimately support land trusts with multiple sources of capital and backup financing. But we aren't there yet.

Protection Fund

Many land trusts have set aside funds specifically to pay for conservation purchases or simply to begin working on a project before they have raised the money to purchase it. These segregated protection funds are typically used for the early costs of due diligence and for securing the property. Expenses include option payments, appraisals, legal fees, hazardous material (HAZMAT) environmental reviews, and whatever other expenses are not donated. These costs can amount to tens or even hundreds of thousands of dollars. Some land trusts have built up very large war chests that they also use for acquisition. They try to recapitalize the fund following an acquisition so that the fund "revolves" (see chapter 14). Having even a small amount of money in a protection fund can be extremely useful for cash flow when starting work on an acquisition. Otherwise, these initial costs, which may be substantial, can strain the operating budget. The land trust should create policy for the protection fund to determine where contributions come from, how the fund is used, and who can authorize expenditures.

Conclusion

Now that your organization is prepared and its finances are in order, it is time to look for the right project. Of course it never happens this way. The right project doesn't just cool its heels waiting for you. Still, choosing between two or more pressing, and seemingly right, projects is difficult and the choice can greatly affect your land trust's future.

Chapter 3
The Deal

"You never really know how deep the water is until you jump off the cliff."
Chris DeForest, executive director, Inland Northwest Land Trust

That critically important piece of land is now for sale. The large parcel is the lynchpin in your conservation plan. It is along a river with important migratory bird habitat, visible from a highway approach, and backs up to a state park. It meets all of your project criteria, including the public benefit test. The seller is sympathetic but has to sell. It is close to a trendy resort. For a developer, these 120 acres would be perfect for retail and a large residential subdivision.

The more appealing the project is, the easier it can be to finance, especially privately. If it has a combination of special attributes, it can attract a more diverse following and a greater variety of funding sources. The above hypothetical parcel would appeal to commuters along the highway, bird-watchers, business interests that want to keep the approach corridors to the trendy resort attractive, users of the state park, and river users (e.g., fishers and float trip operators).

Your parcel may not have all those attributes though. It may be only an acre and a half, located behind a grocery store and too wet to easily see or visit. This was the case for a hidden jewel donated to the Jackson Hole Land Trust that required $54,000 for restoration and access to create an outdoor laboratory for a nearby public school and an elevated walkway to a nearby park. We named it the Wilson Wetlands Trail. These less visible projects can be as important as the more prominent ones. Paying for any project, especially the hidden ones, is easier if the land trust positions the project carefully.

How a land trust presents a project is almost as important to its success as the project itself. For example, a time-sensitive deadline can add a strong element of urgency. Strategic marketing begins well before the initial documents are signed. If organizational systems are in place and the land trust has developed a thoughtful financial plan, then positioning is founded on the *feasibility analysis,* the *structure of the offer,* and the *financial support.*

Feasibility analysis starts with early investigation of the project: acquisition challenges, costs, likely financial support, and due diligence (or determination of the legal and real estate issues). This information informs the land trust's financial plan. Structure of the offer reflects likely acceptable terms to the seller. Financial support means finding the money to pay for the project and structuring the payment to meet both seller and buyer requirements.

Marketing the project will build support among the land trust's constituencies, additional project constituencies, and the community as a whole for fundraising, political, and other purposes. Detailed information and documentation for these and other pieces of the puzzle are found in the *Land Trust Standards and Practices* and supporting appendices online.[1]

As soon as a land trust takes on an acquisition project, it has a relationship with the landowner whether it intends to or not. Well before the first thoughtfully orchestrated meeting with the landowner, a relationship exists. Despite the necessary confidentiality of preparations for negotiation and the negotiations themselves (emphasized to all involved), the land trust has to assume that word of its interest may reach the seller. Particularly in a small community, there are too many connections and overlapping interests to ensure that board discussions, feasibility interviews with donors, research in the courthouse records, and mapping will stay completely confidential. Despite your best intentions, the landowner may hear about the land trust's interest in the worst

Figure 3.1
The Wilson Wetlands Trail became an ideal outdoor laboratory for the nearby Wilson Elementary School. (Courtesy of Jackson Hole Land Trust)

way, from the wrong person, and your intentions may be entirely misunderstood. The sooner the landowner hears of your interest *from you*, the better.

Feasibility Analysis

Testing the fundraising "water" with a fundraising feasibility study has many benefits. Not only does it give a land trust a good sense of how much money it might raise, but it creates interest, and even ownership, in the project early on among the project's likely funders. Some land trusts undertake informal feasibility studies by contacting a handful of major donors. Others take a more formal approach by hiring a consultant to conduct confidential interviews using a list of standardized questions. The more formal approach is safer, especially if the project is expensive, the land trust is new to project (capital campaign) fundraising, or the fundraising campaign will involve multiple projects.

Whatever the approach, the fact that a land trust asks donors for their opinions signals to them that they are valued. Prospective donors to the project are now on the inside track even before the land trust has decided to take it on and well before it has taken it public. Even if a donor interview discloses that the donor is reluctant to support the project, the conversation with the land trust representative brings the donor closer to the organization and provides the land trust with valuable feedback. However, if enough people react negatively, the land trust ought to rethink the financial plan and even the merits of the project. If it chooses to proceed, these naysayers should be cultivated rather than ignored.

A feasibility study can identify many issues in addition to the likely sources of the bigger donations. It can test how arguments in favor of the project resonate and can help the land trust develop new and stronger ones. It can also identify issues that the land trust may not have considered.

I have heard some land trusts complain that consultant feasibility studies have misled them. Here we are talking about garbage in and garbage out. If a land trust doesn't have a good list of potential donors to interview, then the study may conclude that an adequate base of support for the project is lacking. The study may not have considered that the land trust will partner with another organization that has a great donor list. It may have been too early in the process for the feasibility consultants for the Foothills Land Conservancy in Tennessee, for example, to know of or have access to the donor network of the campaign's prominent, popular, and active campaign chairs, Senator Lamar

Alexandra and Governor Phil Bredesen. Land trusts such as the Inland North-west Land Trust or the Foothills Land Conservancy might have been short on donors initially and therefore to interview, but both had the elements in place to generate new donor support—and they did.

Marketing and Relations

I address marketing and public relations strategies here, after feasibility, be-cause these activities should start long before the commitment to purchase is made and extend past the closing. Marketing and public relations starts with the board's first discussions of the project. The board acts essentially as a focus group. Its questions, reservations, and excitement about the project indicate the strengths and weakness of initial arguments for the project. Then, during the feasibility phase, discussions with donors offer another early opportunity to give donors the facts before they hear them from someone else and a chance to get more feedback to shape the message. If project funding depends on pri-vate fundraising or community support for public funding, early marketing is particularly important because a land trust will need all the time it can get to build that support.

Community opinion can also influence the seller. If a seller thinks protec-tion will be popular, that is one more incentive to sell to the land trust instead of another buyer. Community members will have opinions on the ultimate use and ownership of the project, the appropriateness of the location, how the land trust is acquiring it, the way the seller is treated by the land trust—on just about every aspect of the transaction. Knowing community sentiment ahead of time can prevent surprises at later stages of negotiation and can help focus mar-keting efforts on promoting the project's strengths and addressing anticipated community concerns. Also, the ability to fundraise locally will greatly depend on community opinion.

Unanticipated community and political concerns do emerge. However, if the land trust uses its project criteria to select the project, if the project is pro-moted well, and if its planned uses are consistent with the land trust's mission, community criticisms can usually be overcome. Following are some issues that the community may raise:

- Property tax revenue loss
- Self-dealing (that the transaction will particularly benefit a land trust board or staff member or large donor)

- Uncertainty about future uses
- Distrust of land trust leadership because some leaders may be new to the community or, in a resort area, only seasonal residents
- Lack of understanding and thus fear of conservation easements
- Conflict with the town's growth plans or other community or private interests or plans
- Permanent choices about land being made without public input.[2]

It is useful to ask, "Who might benefit from the project?" Benefiting community interests and groups should be highlighted in promotional material. Not everyone will be aware of a project's benefits to *them*, especially before the deal is completed. As an example, the Jackson Hole Land Trust suggested that a neighboring elementary school use the Wilson Wetlands Trail for science projects. The creative fifth grade teachers integrated water quality testing into their curriculum. A donor donated rubber boots for the whole class, and soon the children were using the stream regularly. They took on the responsibility of cleaning up the trash every year. At the end of the first year, the class planted a tree along the stream to commemorate their graduation from elementary school.

Land trust staff, board members, volunteers, and *users and potential users* are the primary marketers of any land trust project. Build interest and excitement first among this core group. Enthusiasm is contagious, so spread it around. To efficiently spread the word, develop the "elevator speech," which describes the project in the time it takes for an average elevator ride. The elevator speech should be scripted and used by everyone who is promoting the project. Here are some other media tips:

- Preempt the press by writing a land trust press release. Highlight the human-interest reasons for buying the property, as the group of people who are interested in wildlife is usually much smaller than the group associated with and affected by the project. Also include a quote from a senior land trust representative (like the board chair) and, if possible, a prominent community member.
- Find a press champion. A third person promoting the project is even better than the land trust promoting it. Quote this person in the press release.
- If the press is not supporting the project, back up and do more homework.

Figure 3.2
The Jackson Hole Land Trust, other participating nonprofits, and public agencies held a ribbon-cutting ceremony to celebrate the opening of the Wilson Centennial Trail and to thank volunteers. (Tim Young)

Ask supporters to write letters to the editor. Find a mutual friend, and take the newspaper editor out to lunch.

- Remember to use all forms of media, from newspapers to radio to mailings to the Internet (blogs, Web sites, links) to the e-mail lists of project supporters.

When it's all done, promote the project's success in the media as well as at an event. Here volunteers, donors, advisors, and the whole community can celebrate *and be thanked*. The public relations value of the celebration broadens the land trust's positive exposure through the press and therefore in the community.

Risk Assessment

A careful inventory of the risks associated with a project takes a land trust past the emotional enthusiasm for it and into the practical challenges of its protection. An assessment of risk may lead a land trust to back away, but in most cases it leads to greater attention to key issues and fewer surprises down the road. A typical issue emerging from risk assessment is what to do about the presence of hazardous materials on the site. In one project, we identified an environmental issue during this stage but believed we could solve it by getting an extended due diligence period in the purchase contract. I spent the entire period under the contract working with a consultant on whether the ground near a fencepost treatment vat was contaminated by treated logs dragged from the vat to be dried. At the end of the period, we still didn't know.

But all parties were forewarned, and we were able to escrow $1 million for cleanup, only part of which was needed.

Other kinds of risks also need to be assessed, including political opposition, stewardship issues (such as serious invasive species infestations or major restoration requirements), potential impacts from adjacent land uses, or constraints on time and funding. A few land trusts use risk assessment checklists to evaluate these (see the online appendix at www.conservationguide.com for an example). Others use their acquisition and criteria checklists or think about risks rigorously but less formally.

Failure to anticipate risks has serious costs. Difficult as it is, attempt to identify as many as you can and to weigh the risks dispassionately. Do not take on a project that has more risks than your land trust can reasonably handle.

Due Diligence

Due diligence addresses all of the investigations into the real estate and legal questions that might affect the purchase and ownership of a parcel of land. The purpose of careful due diligence is to learn exactly what is being purchased (warts and all) and to avoid surprises after the land trust makes a purchase—chances are those surprises will not be the fun kind. They can be costly, jeopardize a transaction, or endanger the organization.

On one project, a survey error during county permitting for a lot split required us to amend the permit, which delayed the sale of the conservation easement by several months. The appendices accompanying the *Land Trust Standards and Practices* include comprehensive checklists for site inspections and other aspects of due diligence.

Site Inspection

One visit to the property, at the very minimum, is necessary because understanding land cannot be reduced to a review of relevant documents and maps. For large projects or those with complicated elements, many visits will be necessary. Having the landowner come along, if possible, is especially helpful because an owner, especially a long-time owner, usually knows the land well. Spend an afternoon with the owner discussing the land. You will learn a lot, *and* it is a great way to start building a personal relationship for negotiating the purchase down the road.

I like to hire a surveyor to mark the property lines before I visit the property, so I can see where they really are, not just the locations of the fences or

Figure 3.3
Representatives of the Jackson Hole Land Trust review restoration plans for the Hardeman Meadows. (Courtesy of Jackson Hole Land Trust)

hedges, which can be far off the legal boundaries. I always look for evidence that suggests problems such as environmental concerns or other hazards, buildings requiring maintenance or potentially creating a liability, easements of sight that won't show up on the title report, or access easements or other right-of-ways.

Unraveling the mysteries of land takes getting to know it. It requires time and experience to understand what to look for. Budget the time, use the checklists, take notes, bring along people who understand land, and be very observant yourself.

PROPERTY TITLE REPORT

A property title report is a report on the property that documents in detail most of the burdens on the title. A title company usually prepares this report—also known as a preliminary title report, title commitment, or title abstract—in anticipation of a sale and as a first look at the aspects of the title that company is willing to insure. The subsequent title insurance policy lasts for the duration of the new owner's (e.g., the land trust's) ownership paid for with one payment made at closing. A good title report prepared by a reputable company represents a systematic investigation of the title using courthouse land, tax, and legal records. In some jurisdictions, lawyers do their own title abstracting and render a legal opinion regarding the soundness of title. Parts of Massachusetts use this approach. In some remote places, title insurance is simply not available. A land trust should consult with an experienced local real estate attorney to find out local conventions dealing with title abstracting and title insurance matters.

An important and revealing document, the title report should be commissioned as early as possible, especially if the initial due diligence raises any legal or title questions, or ownership is complicated. For simple transactions, the title report can be requested in preparation for closing. But transactions with likely issues can benefit tremendously from an earlier review when the land trust is deciding whether to proceed with the deal.

A title report can be hard to understand at first, but the title company staff or preparing lawyer can walk the land trust representative through it. Then that representative and the land trust's attorney should read it carefully again. Most important is the list of the conditions that the insurance *will* cover and the ones that it *will not* (the exceptions). There is a standard group of exceptions the title will not insure against.[3] The extent to which individual exceptions can be addressed and then removed from the list so the insurance can be more comprehensive varies from state to state. In certain states, all exceptions can be removed with other supporting documentation. In others, exceptions regarding certain aspects of the title, such as mineral ownership, cannot be removed. If the land trust is concerned with mineral ownership, for example, it will have to research that separately. Any exceptions, or *defects,* other than the standard ones will signal immediately that there are title issues. The goal is to resolve those so that the final list of exceptions includes only the standard exceptions.

The title company representative or the land trust's attorney can help distinguish the defects that require special attention, such as mortgages, liens, notice of *lis pendens* (i.e., pending lawsuits), clouds on title, ownership claims, and certain right-of-way easements that may impact the conservation or re-sale value of the property. These issues must be resolved or at least addressed before closing, or the insurance policy, which carries with it the same exceptions from coverage as the title report, will not protect the land trust from potentially serious claims that could threaten the land trust's ownership in the property or compromise its future protection.

This is not to say that all title issues will appear in the preliminary title report. The following defects may not appear:

- Problems that arise after the date of the report
- Unrecorded claims against the property
- Mineral rights and associated issues, unless a mineral report is also commissioned

- Timber or water rights
- Hazardous materials liability and associated permitting questions that might not appear in county records, such as federal hazardous materials issues
- Claims that might suddenly appear because the property is being sold and money will change hands.

Unanticipated claims can raise their ugly heads at the worst times. Just days before we were to close on what had already been a very difficult purchase for the Jackson Hole Land Trust, a new party came forward with a quitclaim deed claiming an ownership interest in the property. The deed did not show up on the title report because it had never been recorded. This project had already been riddled with title issues. The seller's first attorney had left town with the money for the property's prior commercial venture and was in jail in Florida. Extricating the property from those legal proceedings and lining up the sale to the land trust had been a major achievement for the seller's current attorney. For him, this new development was the final straw. He threw up his hands, pulled out his personal checkbook, and wrote a check for $500 to the interfering party. It was enough to get him to sign over his quitclaim to the seller and go away.

Exacting research on property ownership, a careful review of the title report, a visit to the zoning office, and thorough site visits can avoid many problems, though not all surprises.

Structure of the Offer

The offer is the document that translates what you have heard from the seller about his or her needs and your own requirements into writing. When presented, it should not be a surprise to anyone because all parties should have discussed its terms and even seen them in writing. This doesn't mean that the structure isn't creative at addressing issues. It just shouldn't, in most cases, be full of surprises. The exception is when there is no time or opportunity to talk to the seller. In that case, keep it simple. For a less sympathetic seller, frontload it with cash. After all, it is often for a less than full-value cash need that the seller is selling. If you can satisfy his or her immediate need, you have a better chance at making a deal.

Price

Cash is only one form of compensation that a land trust can offer a seller. The land trust must always think of its proposal to the seller as a combination of elements that can best meet the requirements of a landowner as well as its own. Those include tax benefits and other benefits (see chapter 16). The cash component should be discounted from market value if at all possible, not simply because it is only one of many benefits the land trust can offer but because the land trust rarely has the money to routinely pay full market value.

A discounted or "good" price is a relative term. In a popular area like a resort community, prices will be much higher than in a less popular area. A good price in these different areas will be very different numbers. Don't be fooled though. There is a reason why a particular property sells at a really low price relative to the real estate values in that area. Is it because the buyer negotiated well with the seller or because the seller is sympathetic to conservation, or is there a defect on the title? If you don't know the reason—and your land trust has a fiduciary responsibility to know so that it is not paying over market value—don't wait until after the closing to find out. Do a little more due diligence. It might be a buried fuel tank with removal costs that will eliminate that great savings of a "low" price.

Before starting any negotiations, the land trust must have an idea of what the property is worth and the land trust's price range. If the land trust is operating regularly in the real estate market, it will be able to estimate the land's value. Land trusts often track comparable sales as a matter of course. Appraisers and real estate brokers also track sales data. In some places where sales information is public, the land trust must sort out which past sales are most comparable for assessing the value of the property in question. In other places where sales are not public, you must collect sales information from helpful appraisers, real estate brokers, and landowners, or out of appraisals that the land trust commissions. Keeping a running spreadsheet with the size, type, price, and date of sale of parcels of interest to the organization allows valuation information to become institutionalized.

In almost all situations, an appraisal or opinion of value is still necessary.[4] If the land trust pays for the appraisal, the document becomes the organization's proprietary information. A land trust working as a team with the seller to achieve the best outcome for all parties tends to share valuation information. But there are other times when the land trust should keep the appraisal confidential.

Appraisals are more an art than a science. They are historical reviews for property sales. In a steeply falling market they tend to be high, and in a steeply rising market they tend to be low. Also, even good appraisers are not infallible, so it is a good idea to have one's own opinion (based on comparables tracked by the land trust), to know enough about appraisals to be able to intelligently scrutinize one, and to raise any questions with the appraiser. Thus a land trust, as a charitable organization, cannot pay over appraised value except in special circumstances. A formal appraisal will set limitations on how much money a land trust can pay without additional documentation.[5]

Appraisers can play several roles in the negotiating process. They can advise on real estate values before giving a formal appraisal. They can estimate how a change in a condition of the sale, such as a change in the restrictions of a conservation easement (if purchased or retained), can affect value. The appraiser can help identify ways to structure a deal so that the price is lower (or higher) by explaining the factors that affect the price.[6]

Too frequently, the land trust's conservation criteria are met but the price is too high. There is no need to walk away in this situation. Instead, consider the following options for overcoming the price barrier (also see chapter 16 for more strategies for lowering the price):

- Negotiate with the seller to lower the price, being clear about your land trust's financial limitations.
- Determine whether there is another benefit that the land trust can offer, such as a desirable parcel in trade or the benefits of a tax deduction from a discounted sale.
- Ask whether the seller is willing to phase the transaction, selling part now and part later.
- Partner with another organization, either another land trust or a private or public partner, if part of the land is suited for a residential, institutional, public, or commercial use.
- Look for ways to save, including on purchase terms, loan rates, commissions and fees, or professional services.
- Figure out whether ways to conserve the property other than by immediate or even eventual purchase exist. For example, the land trust might be able to do one of the following:
  - Lease it or find another conservation-minded entity to lease it.
  - Lease it with an option to buy.
  - Purchase (or be given) a right of first refusal.
  - Purchase (or be given) a right of first offer or look, by which the seller offers the land to the land trust first. If the land trust cannot meet the price, the seller can offer it elsewhere.

Negotiations

How does a land trust get its price when it is very eager to buy and the seller is not that interested in selling, especially to a land trust or under any condition?

The first rule is to *listen to the seller.* As a successful real estate broker friend told me, "Don't say anything more than you absolutely have to. If you can, don't open your mouth. Don't inject yourself into the conversation. Listen, listen, listen." Sometimes it takes a long time for the seller to get around to saying what is really on his or her mind. Along the way, other important information emerges.

The goal is to gain an understanding of the seller so that buyer and seller can build a relationship of open communication. "A lot of success comes down to establishing trust with the landowner and having mutual respect," explains Ted Sortwell Clement, executive director of Aquidneck Land Trust in Rhode Island. In a successful $3 million acquisition of a conservation easement for the Escobar's Highland Farm, Ted says, "The landowner and I had talked for years about his love of the property, which had been in his family since the 1930s. The success of deals hinges on taking time, as we did on many occasions, laying out the financial scenarios of selling vs. keeping the property."

The issues for the seller may or may not have to do with money. While listening, first and foremost think about what the seller really wants from the deal in a broad context (see chapter 16 for more on the following options).

- Is it a tax deduction? Then offer a bargain sale.
- Is it income-producing property? Suggest a 1031 exchange.
- Is it a place to live? Carve the house out of the deal, or offer a life estate.
- Is there a difficult relative involved? Who might be the right person to approach that relative, and what does the relative need?

A land trust also should remember its priority: conservation. With that in mind, it is easier not to sweat the little stuff. Losing a deal over a small fraction of the purchase price or a small element of the terms is simply not worth it. In the heat of negotiations, it is easy to lose perspective. My same broker friend describes all the refrigerators he bought to make deals close. By this he means that a buyer or seller can get hung up on something small like the kitchen having the wrong kind of refrigerator. My friend was always happy to buy a new refrigerator to get a deal done. The same goes for a land negotiation. Small differences in anything, even price, can be absorbed if they get the deal done.

Always look for common ground and then build on it. Start with easy issues, and work up to the tough stuff. Common ground usually begins with a love of land. If the seller has owned the land for any length of time, then he or she usually has an attachment to it. Land trusts by their mission share that love. Start by admiring the land.

The next place to look for common ground is with personal relationships. Negotiators are people first.[7] If a board member knows the seller, has kids at the same school, or belongs to the same club, bring that person along. Then look for other areas of common interest:

- Land preservation
- Respect for the land's care
- Personal connections (with members of the board, staff, or volunteers)
- Confidentiality
- Community goodwill.

A land trust can often be flexible in how it structures its transactions, and because it is a nonprofit charitable organization, it can offer structures that allow the seller to utilize valuable charitable tax benefits. Meeting the seller's personal or financial needs may involve a variety of elements, only one of which is cash. As an example, a land trust can offer the opportunity to be memorialized through the naming of a park or simply the perpetuation of the status quo for the land. For landowners who have lived in the area for many years, a land trust can bring an interested audience for stories about the history of the area or simply a sympathetic ear.

A land trust can be perceived negatively because of suspicions about its unusual nonprofit motives, the age of its staff (generally younger than the sellers), or concerns that it is representing the wrong elements of the community (newcomers, wealthy people). Landowners may appear to be interested when they are sometimes just being polite. Poke around a bit with questions that might help unearth perceptions. Then listen carefully to the responses.

Legal ownership and family dynamics play a complicating and often unpredictable role in negotiations. If multiple landowners are involved, keep them all in the loop if at all possible and if the lead negotiator doesn't object. If—in the common case of a husband negotiating for his wife and her family—the land trust is not negotiating with the primary owner, then involve the wife and the others as much as the husband will permit without undermining the primary negotiator (the husband). The wife may choose to stay in the background, but when she is asked to sign away her family's property, she is bound to have questions. At the very least, know who all the owners are and be ready for their questions and their new issues, even when everything appears to be settled with the primary negotiator.

If a bank or corporate owner is involved, the dynamics of the negotiations will be different than if the owners are individuals who have a personal investment in the land. Even on the family level, one member of a couple may seem very sympathetic to the land trust but may not be calling the shots. You can get sucked into thinking that the sympathetic member will prevail. Sometimes that person does, and that is always wonderful. Give this member as much support as you can without alienating other parties.

Family dynamics, in play even from nonowners, can take their toll in negotiations. Kids may be pressuring their parents for money, or parents may be making decisions that the kids want to make for themselves. Siblings may not trust one another. Land trust negotiators will inevitably learn more about these relationships than they ever want to know. Some of that knowledge may at least prove helpful in designing mutually acceptable outcomes. Keeping quiet during interfamily conversations, using discretion, and honoring confidentiality are the best guides.

Not everyone is a good negotiator—someone who listens, stays focused, doesn't sweat the unimportant aspects of the deal, meets the needs of the seller, reaches agreement on a price within the range that the land trust has determined it can afford, and gets the deal done. This last point is very important: a negotiator is a deal maker and that means not just negotiating, but *closing the deal* if humanly possible. A good negotiator has confidence backed up with experience. Less adept is someone who gets nervous and talks too much. Some negotiating skills, such as understanding the nuts and bolts of real estate contracts, can and should be learned before stepping into a room with a seller. But the ability to hear the needs, concerns, and wants behind the words and find that common ground often comes naturally. Choose the best negotiator you can find, and don't be hurt if it isn't you. Then send two people to meetings with the seller, so that there are two sets of eyes and ears, because negotiating is only part of what must happen in the room with the seller. Collecting information is also essential to constructing a successful final deal.

Though it is a point of much debate, I believe that good realtors, real estate agents, or brokers earn their keep. In cases where the land is listed with real estate agents, if the agents are doing their job, they can play a critical role in the negotiations and with due diligence. It is entirely in their best interest to see that the transaction is successfully completed—that is how they make their commission. That said, realtors could be more motivated to sell to a developer than to a land trust if subsequent commissions on lot sales for a subdivision follow. Assess the orientation of their motivation. If it is pointed in your direction and they are working for the success of your deal, they can answer questions about the land, handle all the paperwork, and be creative about finding common ground. Many states now allow intermediary or transactional brokers, who are not compelled to exclusively represent the seller or the buyer. This reduces the potential for an adversarial dynamic between the buyer-realtor and the seller-realtor.

If the land is listed and the land trust is the buyer, it still must decide whether to hire its own realtor or use the listing realtor. If two realtors are involved, they must split the commission, reducing the reward for each. The listing realtor is more highly motivated if receiving the entire commission. This is an important consideration if the land trust is experienced enough in the real estate market to not need its own representation. On the other hand, the land trust may want its own advisor who is not directly connected to the seller to offer advice and to buffer the land trust from the seller. This can be a good thing if the seller does not work well with the land trust, or it can be a bad thing if, like most realtors, the realtor is unfamiliar with the workings of land trusts and unknowingly misrepresents its purposes. It helps to have some contact directly with the seller for this reason.

The listing realtor is also obligated to inform buyers of the property's "defects." Good realtors do, but some realtors do not. Knowing some, if not all, of these defects can reduce the need for due diligence, though it will not absolutely eliminate it.

Because land trusts are not the usual sort of buyer or seller in the real estate market, introducing your land trust to the real estate community through targeted outreach before getting into the middle of a specific deal gives everyone some background and personal connection.

If the property is not listed and the land trust is confident about negotiations, it can hire a real estate lawyer instead of a realtor. A real estate lawyer must review all legal documents on the land trust's behalf anyway. Realtors tend to use sales agreement templates that then must be customized by the land trust's lawyer to meet a land trust's often unusual requirements.

Real estate lawyers, however, do not need to play a direct role in the negotiations. Hiring a lawyer in negotiations instead of a realtor can be a less expensive strategy for very expensive land, because realtors usually charge a 5- to 7-percent commission on the gross sale price. However, attorneys who participate in the actual negotiations can strongly influence them. Their often-conservative nature (after all, their job is to protect their client, not the deal) can add an element of formality to negotiations, dampen a land trust's entrepreneurial spirit and, if given too much authority, inadvertently frustrate a deal. On the other hand, a knowledgeable lawyer can reassure the landowner's own advisors (and therefore the landowner), who may be less familiar with conservation organizations and conservation tax benefits. But realtor or no realtor, someone has to manage the sales documents. The land trust and its attorney will have to do that work if a realtor isn't involved.

Time is a critical factor in negotiating. It can work for or against the land trust. Obviously, if a landowner is determined to sell or a developer is pressuring to buy, the land trust has very little time to negotiate. It should do its very best to honor all deadlines. Under other circumstances, sometimes slowing everything down can give the seller (and the land trust) a chance to think about and improve the deal structure in meaningful ways. There are times when politely walking away from a deal can produce results. It takes great self-control to put a halt to unworkable negotiations. Leaving the table in the most politic manner for a period of time does not mean that negotiations cannot be picked back up in the future, even a few years later. Leaving the table angrily, however, can ruin the future chance for negotiating. I left the table furious and in tears once. It took years for the land trust to patch that relationship back together. Possibly because of my actions or maybe for other reasons, the land trust had to pay a high price when a deal was finally struck.

Another time, we finally walked away from another important parcel, respectfully and openly, because neither party could see a way to common ground. Two years later, the landowners approached us indirectly when facing a claim for back taxes. The purchase price ended up being 80 percent of our offer two years earlier (in a rising real estate market) because we had not alienated them then, and now *they* were in a hurry.

Patience helps, too. Time gives the landowner a chance to think and talk to relatives or advisors. Patience also gives the land trust time to think. A new good idea from either party can change the direction of negotiations overnight—one reason that negotiating is fun and exciting. But whatever happens, never act on impulse. Develop a strategy for each move with your support team and co-negotiators.

Here are a few more suggestions that have helped me in negotiations over the years:

- There may be *big cultural differences* between the land trust and the seller that can lead to misunderstandings. Periodically checking in with the seller on where the seller thinks negotiations stand should clarify the situation. Stating where you think things stand also helps to keep communication open.
- Some landowners *don't relate well to the written word.* Just because they have seen the document, doesn't mean they understand it. If you think this might be the case, suggest that you walk through the document together. You can summarize each section as a starting place for discussion.
- *Sellers take their land very personally.* If there is something you don't like about the land, keep it to yourself.
- On a similar note, landowners always *think their land is worth more* than buyers do. Try not to argue about the *value.* Instead, argue, if you must, about the *price.*
- *Long gaps in communicating with the seller are dangerous.* The seller could be talking to other buyers, or there may be some misunderstanding eating at the seller and creating hard feelings. Whatever the reason, you lose momentum and often much more. If you are negotiating, keep it active.
- *Finding a solution together* builds the most ownership in the process. Try to hold collective brainstorming sessions to work through barriers in the negotiations.
- Just because you are far apart on price doesn't mean that the seller doesn't want to sell to you. *Your positions may be different, not your interests.*[8]
- Just as in asking for a big gift from a donor, *don't be scared off by the seller's reaction to your first offer,* and don't immediately try to soften it with a better offer. Let your offer sit out there. It will set the parameters and let the seller know what you can actually pay comfortably.
- There are *many parts to a purchase that must be negotiated*—including price, down payment, terms (cash payment, installment), option conditions, contingencies, timing, closing date—so keep up the momentum even after settling on the big issues.

- *Don't negotiate against yourself.* If you must make a concession, the seller should too. Just because you represent a nonprofit doesn't mean you aren't subject to the same rules of negotiating that the seller is. But again, don't sweat the small stuff if you are only that far away from a final deal.
- *A wily negotiator will ask for concessions right at the end of the negotiations* when you consider them to be over. Be careful here. If the seller is committed at that point too, there is no reason to give more just because that is how people like to play it.
- *Make sure that the seller can save face* if the land trust seems to come out ahead in some way.
- *Confidentiality is assumed in negotiations.* The problem is that a land trust has a board and often a staff who need to know what is going on. Stress and restress the importance of confidentiality, and discuss only what others need to know, not all the personal details you end up hearing unless they are essential to constructing the best outcome.

Commitment to Purchase

Just as in the rest of life, it is hard (and scary) to make a commitment. To raise money to pay for a conservation purchase, the urgency of a deadline and a guaranteed purchase must exist. The option deadline on the Hardeman Meadows project ratcheted up that campaign in an instant. A fast-approaching deadline will keep a project high on everyone's list, including the donors'. Such a deadline is exhausting but very useful.

Any less firm commitment on the part of the seller can come back to haunt you. Again, I learned this the hard way. On one project, I had a purchase commitment sealed with a handshake. But the landowner apparently had a change of heart in the months that it took to round up conservation-minded buyers. I suspect that the family was not psychologically ready to sell. In another, too much time passed between when the selling family said that they wanted to sell and when we worked out a financing plan. In the meantime, circumstances changed and the deal fell through.

Moving from negotiations to a commitment to sell can be challenging. Here, too, the character of the negotiating team can make all the difference. If the land trust negotiator is new to the community, consider adding a well-established member of the board for the final discussions; this will add legitimacy to the agreement in the seller's mind. If the board member is a community member of means, the seller may know this and be better assured that the land trust will find the money to close on the purchase.

Sometimes experience and confidence can carry the day. On two different occasions, I asked a well-known conservation attorney, Bill Hutton, to join our negotiating team when we were down to the final issues. In the first case, the negotiations were for the Hardeman Meadows. The staff (including me) was new to negotiating land deals, and the tax issues were novel for the family. Bill brought a gentlemanly, quiet confidence to the table that even won over the family's very skeptical attorney. On another occasion, the communication was taking place over the phone (never a good idea) and the negotiations weren't going well. Once again, I asked Bill to help with the final two calls, and we got the deal done.

Getting the commitment to purchase involves writing down the terms and having both parties sign them. Here is when one sometimes finds out whether there really is a meeting of the minds. To ensure that all the new language doesn't sink the deal, write down the agreements as they are being made along the way, not as a means of negotiating but as a way to document, communicate, and confirm what has already been agreed.

The commitment is essential. This is what good realtors do so well. I have found that persistence plays a big role in success here. However, persistence can morph into nagging. Carefully timed but relentless persistence is the key.

The Financial Structure

How to pay for conservation acquisitions is discussed in much greater detail elsewhere in this book, where we will explore how to raise the money, how to borrow it, and how to reduce costs. I will review here the most common elements of the deal structure.

Options and Purchase Agreements

How can a land trust commit to a purchase without the money in hand? This is where the purchase instrument and its terms come in. Several legal instruments can give a buyer time to raise money. They include options, lease options, rights of first refusal, and certain structures of sales contracts. Low-cost options are the best because they buy time during which the buyer can decide whether to make the purchase but the seller cannot sell to another party.

Contingencies in sales contracts allow time too but are more risky because the buyer must make the purchase if the conditions are met. For these, a good real estate lawyer can write up the offer with ways to get out of the deal if absolutely necessary.

During the option period, the land trust raises the money to make the purchase and then exercises its option if it has the money in hand or is confident that it will have the money before closing. The option period may be used to arrange financing if raising money will take longer than the land trust has to close on the purchase (see part 3 of this book). However, not every landowner is willing to sign an option, especially if the landowner is highly motivated to sell or unsympathetic to the land trust's goals, or if the market is very strong and other sale opportunities loom. The seller may not want to relinquish the right to sell elsewhere while waiting to see whether the land trust can come up with the money.

Options have benefits to sellers, though. First, a motivated seller likes an option because, if the option consideration is high enough, it is likely that the option holder will buy. Second, an option payment can be a significant amount of money that is not subject to taxes until the option is exercised or the land trust fails to exercise it. An option payment cannot be characterized as income or capital gains until the buyer purchases or does not purchase. If the land trust exercises the option, then the option payment applies toward the purchase price and is generally treated as capital gains subject to capital gains tax. If the land trust does not exercise the option, then the option payment is treated as ordinary income and is taxed as such. Thus the seller has use of the option money without paying taxes on it for the entire option period.

If the option payment is large, there can be significant value in deferring the tax for the seller. However, in order to be construed as an option and not a down payment, the payment cannot be so large that a full commitment to purchase has effectively been made. There must be a reasonable chance that the land trust would still walk away from the deal. This is a judgment call, one best discussed with the land trust's attorney. I have used large option payments when it was very likely that we could raise the purchase price, as in the case of pre-acquisitions when takeout public funding is primarily a matter of timing.

Sales contracts can be written with contingencies that can give a land trust time and ways out if it is unable to raise the purchase price. Once the contractual conditions are met, the land trust has to buy. Some legitimate conditions that may necessitate more time include the following:

- Securing financing (the best condition)
- Addressing title issues
- Determining zoning compliance
- Assessing the extent and cost of hazardous materials remediation.

Whether through an option or a conditioned sales contract, the land trust should try to get as much time as possible, especially if the transaction is complicated or expensive. For transactions that involve fairly predictable outcomes, a committed and hardworking organization with real estate manpower (staff or volunteer) can get just about anything done in six months. If, however, the land trust is dependent on a public takeout source that might be delayed at many points in the political and bureaucratic process, six months is never enough time. Options may be extended for more money. At some point, though, the land trust must decide if it is going to do the deal or not. If it is certain that it can raise the money but can't do it in time for the closing, it should borrow (see part 3).

Consider a couple more tips:

- With seller approval, record options in the public land records so that others are aware of the encumbrance on the property and won't violate it.
- Write into the contract (option or otherwise) a thirty- or sixty-day period after exercising the agreement to close, which buys more time to get those final dollars raised or contingency plans in place.

A land trust must take an option agreement very seriously. An option should be used only when it is likely that the land trust will exercise it and complete the purchase. This caution is for two reasons: First, a land trust makes a financial and time investment in an option. Second, if a buyer gets a reputation for not exercising options, sellers will hear about it and be less likely to agree to them in the future.

Closing

The closing is the event when the documents that transfer the real estate are signed and the money is exchanged. The office of the title company that issues the title insurance or a lawyer's office is a typical place for a closing. The convention in many jurisdictions is to conduct "virtual" closings electronically. Real estate transactions are also closed through the mail or sequentially with

Figure 3.4
The Wilson Centennial Trail provides
public access through protected land in
the community. (© David J. Swift)

the various parties stopping by a central location to sign documents. The parties open an escrow account a few weeks before the closing date with instructions to distribute the funds when the parties meet the conditions of the escrow instructions, such as signing documents and depositing appropriate funds. A land trust can also host an actual closing at its offices, where all parties meet followed by a small celebration.

Closings take a certain amount of preparation. Before the closing, read and have someone else carefully read every document and check each exhibit. The actual prenegotiated costs must be allocated correctly among the parties. Real estate taxes, for example, are usually the responsibility of the seller to the date of closing and of the buyer after that date. The seller will advance his or her pro rata payment to the buyer by discounting the sale price accordingly. The purchase contract also details costs that are split according to its terms. A title company, for a fee, will prepare the closing statement, which is very useful.

Signature lines throughout the documents should be noted in advance to make sure everything gets signed. Even a simple transaction can have several places for notarized signatures. If a bank or a government agency is involved, there will be additional documents requiring signatures. Get all of the documents ready in advance, and clearly identify all signature lines, who gets which copies, the number of copies needed of each, who is going to record the deed, and who is responsible for the checks.

There are two schools of thought about how to conduct closings. One school keeps a closing as simple as possible, with the minimum number of people attending so it can be executed quickly. The other school argues that land trusts should make closings a bigger deal. I am of the second school because a closing marks the culmination of months of effort on the part of all the parties. The negotiations are finally finished. The signing of the documents is a momentous event. It can also be a time to strengthen the land trust's relationship with the sellers (or buyers). A glass of champagne and a toast can help smooth over any rough moments in the negotiations and launch the relationship positively. An enthusiastic seller becomes one more ambassador for land conservation.

The danger of having numerous people at a closing is that amid the commotion a document may not be signed or may get misplaced or covered with champagne. So get the business of the closing out of the way first. Then remove all the documents from the room before the champagne starts flowing.

Conclusion

Conserving land is a land trust's business, and buying land or other conservation interests is one very good way to do it. If the land trust has a good

Figure 3.5
Jackson Hole Land Trust board chairman preseenting a check to the sellers at the Hatchet Ranch closing. (Courtesy of Jackson Hole Land Trust)

project and adequate sources of money, then it should be able to close most deals. The process may be challenging organizationally because so many decisions must be made in a short time. It may be difficult personally because negotiations are full of surprises and require adapting quickly to changing circumstances. But one's skill level and tolerance for acquisition and risk grows with each difficult decision and each new deal successfully completed. The results are very satisfying, even exhilarating, and they strengthen the organization.

Chapter 4
Legal and Ethical Considerations

OK, it is time to come clean. On more than one occasion, I have been completely carried away with a deal. I have gone down to the wire trying to meet that deadline of all deadlines: December 31.[1] With pressure from the landowner, the landowner's lawyer, and my own board members, I have considered taking shortcuts. I became more concerned about getting the deal done than about any other issue. I admit now that, consciously or not, I planned to barge through whatever barriers stood in the way to close the deal.

Once in this potentially dangerous mind-set, with everyone anxiously awaiting the outcome, I would kid myself into thinking that a little more word-smithing or maybe a small concession (or a big one) could pull it all together. In the wild hope that a few more hours could resolve tough issues, I would call to see how late the county clerk would keep her offices open so I could record the deeds. But more often, there were more complicated ethical issues at play.

In these final hours or at any time when dealing with a special property, a conservation negotiation can deteriorate quickly. My colleagues and I would stare at one another in disbelief when lawyers would send back the documents highlighting only some of their changes. We would have to compare our original to theirs line by line to find them all. On more than one occasion, parties made themselves entirely unavailable until the last hours of the last day of the year. In one case, we found a lawyer hiding at his house with his phone disconnected, apparently hoping that we would not find him to respond to changes in the last version of documents he submitted.

Many a clever seller representative pushed us right to the end in the hopes that we would make major last-minute concessions just to get the deal done. I thank my lucky stars that I was able to make that eleventh-hour call to a trusted land trust associate for advice. In one case, we walked away from a deal with a former United States cabinet member over whether or not there should be square footage limitations on the buildings. In these cases and others, I learned a valuable lesson: put checks and balances in place so that, in those vulnerable moments, the passion for the deal doesn't completely rule the day.

Pressures can be intense when a tax deduction is in play, but they are even more so when cash is involved. Money ups the ante *and* money ups public scrutiny. When conservation land is purchased, especially with private, charitable gifts, donors demand assurances that the money was spent well, newspapers take a new interest in land trust activities, and a previously disinterested community finds something to say.

Most of us in the land conservation movement understand or can learn what *legal* behavior entails: we must follow the law. The laws of land conservation are complicated, involving the tax code as well as laws governing nonprofit and charitable organizations' activities, conduct, and reporting. Still, a land trust is expected to know how to follow them (see box 4.1). Fortunately, there are regulations written by the federal, state, and local agencies and further explained and reenforced through excellent commentaries, books, conferences, and seminars of the Land Trust Alliance and others.

But what is *ethical* behavior in a world where the rules for land conservation keep changing and where each transaction is unique? Ethics are built on a foundation of moral values of what is good and bad or what is right and wrong.[2]

As Stephen Small, an attorney and a frequent writer and speaker on conservation ethics, says, "Ethics is the art of what should be done, as opposed to what can be done."[3] Ethics go beyond the law and embrace the spirit of the law. Ethics reach for a higher standard and in the nonprofit world are defined with such words as *public trust, integrity, fairness, openness,* and *responsibility.* The public gives the special benefit of tax-exempt status to nonprofit, charitable organizations; with this status, it bestows its trust that charitable dollars will be spent well and ethically in pursuit of a stated mission. Land trusts are fortunate to hold the public trust, and they must earn it and re-earn it every day.

In addition to the overriding need for land trusts to do what is right—in other words, to act legally and ethically themselves—the Internal Revenue Service has made it clear that it expects more. It asks land trusts to help prevent abuses by any of the parties in a land conservation transaction, including donors. "Taxpayers who want to game the system and the charities that assist them will be called to account," states Steven Miller, commissioner for tax-exempt and government entities, Internal Revenue Service, referring to a public statement made by his boss, Mark Everson, the commissioner of internal revenue.[4]

Box 4.1   Some of the Important Legal Requirements for Land Trusts

- Obtaining nonprofit corporate status
- Obtaining and maintaining federal tax-exemption and public charity status
- Avoiding substantial unrelated business income
- Avoiding inurement and private benefit
- Avoiding participation in political campaigns and complying with limitations on lobbying
- Reporting changes in organizational form, purposes, or activities to the IRS
- Meeting fundraising requirements
- Meeting the public support test
- Meeting federal and state filing requirements
- Paying appropriate state and local taxes
- Maintaining corporate records and complying with corporate procedures
- Complying with evolving nonprofit best practices, guidelines, and laws, including nonprofits and Sarbans-Oxley Act related voluntary reforms
- Maintaining good standing relating to governance, fiscal controls, accountability transparency, and fundraising fundamentals

This information was summarized from an excellent handout available through LTAnet forum "Legal and Ethical Aspects of Managing a Nonprofit Organization," workshop at the Land Trust Alliance National Conference: Rally 2005, October 17, 2005, Madison, Wisconsin. Http://www.LTANET.org/objects/view.acs?object_ID=17496. Courtesy of Stefan Nagel, of Stephen J. Small, Esq. P.C., and Konrad Liegel, partner, Preston, Gates & Ellis.

A series of 2003 *Washington Post* articles on The Nature Conservancy sounded the first alarm.[5] These articles highlighted issues that caught the attention of the public, of Congress, and of much of the land conservation community for the first time, despite the fact that Steve Small, the Land Trust Alliance and others had been talking about them for years. The multipart, front-page articles accused The Nature Conservancy of, among other things, undertaking land transactions with large companies and individuals close to the organization without inviting competitive offers, facilitating charitable deductions in real estate transactions where the charitable intent might be in doubt, and undertaking real estate transactions that lost sight of ecological goals. Although these accusations were, in many people's minds, questionable, the fact that they appeared in a major newspaper brought them to the public's attention.

In the conservation business, there are so many decisions and judgment calls to make. The deeper one gets into a project, the more detailed the decisions become and the easier it is to lose perspective. Knowing exactly how to act both legally and ethically gets less and less clear. Since ethical behavior must be the sum of all of those choices, it is hard to view them collectively in the midst of a deal. Yet the days of complacency with regard to our own actions and the actions of those with whom we work are over. The decisions and choices of all parties involved are not always clear, but the consequences of improper actions are.

The Land Trust Alliance's *Exchange* magazine has published extensively on the issue of conservation ethics. Most of what has been written, though, pertains to ethical issues when a landowner receives a tax deduction for a gift. In this chapter, I change the context a bit, addressing ethics when money is involved, as in the purchase of conservation interests. The presence of money further complicates these issues.

Take, for example, a situation where a land trust board member's enthusiasm for conservation has captured the attention of his farmer neighbor. This fourth-generation farmer owns wildlife-rich riparian land and is willing to sell an easement at a bargain price to the land trust on which the board member serves. The board member knows that the land trust has money to buy conservation easements. He and the farmer discuss the terms of an easement. He is pleased with the willingness of the farmer to discount the easement price. Now the board member brings the deal to the land trust. Does this sound like an exciting project? Does it sound familiar and fraught with potential ethical issues? Yes and yes.

So what is ethical behavior in this example? We will explore this question throughout this chapter.

Checks and Balances

The first step in helping an organization maintain a high ethical standard is to put in place a set of checks and balances. Then, when the heat is on, good ethical decisions will continue to be made despite growing pressure to get the deal done at any cost.

There are many reasons to adopt and follow the Land Trust Alliance's (LTA's) revised *Land Trust Standards and Practices.*[6] One of the more compelling reasons is to create a framework within which consistent legal and ethical practices can operate. *Standards and Practices* offer an ethical rudder by which to steer through land trust work. Using the example of a board member advocating the purchase of a neighboring farmer's easement, here are some of the suggested practices that will help as guides through otherwise murky waters:

1. *Practice 3D, Preventing Minority Rule.* A land trust should have a policy to "prevent a minority of board members from acting for the organization without proper delegation of authority." In our example, this practice would prevent a board member from determining whether and how a transaction would occur without the majority of the board in support.

2. *Practice 4A, Dealing with Conflicts of Interest.* A land trust should have a written conflict of interest policy "to ensure that any conflicts of interest or appearance thereof are avoided or appropriately managed through disclosure, recusal or other means." In our example, the board member has a direct interest in what happens on the adjacent farmer's property. If the land trust acquires an easement on this property, the board member's adjacent property will likely be aesthetically and financially enhanced. The board member's personal and financial interests may influence or appear to influence the land trust's decision to purchase the easement.

3. *Practice 4C, Transactions with Insiders.* "For purchases and sales of property to insiders, the land trust obtains a qualified independent appraisal prepared in compliance with the Uniform Standards of Professional Appraisal Practice by a state-licensed or state-certified appraiser who has verifiable conservation easement or conservation real estate experience. When selling property to insiders, the land trust widely markets the property in a manner sufficient to ensure that the property is sold at or above fair market value and to avoid the reality or perception that the sale inappropriately benefited an insider." In our example, the board member is defined as an insider.[7] Though not the seller of the conservation easement, he is closely associated with the seller personally and through the physical location of his property. The appearance of insider dealing strongly suggests that careful procedures should be followed.

4. *Practice 7E, Board/Staff Lines of Authority.* "If the land trust has staff, the lines of authority, communication and responsibility between board and staff are clearly understood and documented." If a board member brings a project to the staff, the staff has the authority and responsibility to eval-

uate it on its merits, answering to the executive director rather than to the board member, despite the advance work by the board member. If the land trust has no staff, the decision-making process must still be clear. Usually, the board would delegate responsibility to the appropriate board committee, which would answer to the board as a whole.

5. *Practice 8B, Project Selection and Criteria.* "The land trust has a defined process for selecting land and easement projects, including written selection criteria that are consistent with its mission." Project evaluation criteria create a measure for land trust engagement. Despite our example board member's enthusiasm, the project must meet standardized criteria.

6. *Practice 9J, Purchasing Land.* "If the land trust buys land, easements or other real property, it obtains a qualified independent appraisal to justify the purchase price. However, the land trust may choose to obtain a letter of opinion (see definitions) from a qualified real estate professional in the limited circumstances when a property has a very low economic value or a full appraisal is not feasible before a public auction. If negotiating for a purchase below the appraised value, the land trust ensures that its communications with the landowner are honest and forthright." As in the case of all real estate purchases, the land trust in our example must obtain an appraisal of the farmer's easement. Since the farmer intends to sell the easement at a discounted price, the land trust must be sure that the farmer is fully aware of the gift he is making. This should be communicated to him by an appropriately designated party who is less self-interested than the neighboring board member.

Our board member–farmer example improves ethically if the land trust adopts *Land Trust Standards and Practices.* Adoption of *Land Trust Standards and Practices* does not happen by simply a single vote by the board of directors. No matter what the resources of a land trust are, adoption takes careful consideration and time. A thorough process would involve the board, the staff (if any), and review and approval by the land trust's attorney.

The Land Trust for Tennessee (LTTN), a fairly small land trust with eight staff members, invited people with expertise in relevant fields to participate in its process of adopting the *Land Trust Standards and Practices* and developing its own associated policies. LTTN's Web site describes their adoption process.[8] A smaller land trust would not require such an extensive approach and could use the sample policies provided by LTA for smaller organizations. But LTTN's work provides a good model worthy of review.

First, LTTN assessed its current compliance with *Land Trust Standards and Practices*. Knowing which areas would require more work allowed LTTN to plan its adoption process. Then it compiled a notebook of existing policies and applicable sample LTA documents. Next, it set priorities and delegated the work of developing policies in these priority areas, meeting regularly to assess progress. The staff consulted with board and committee members, other land trusts, and attorneys on suggestions in the drafting process. Ad hoc subcommittees focused on specific areas, such as land protection. From the subcommittees, the draft policies went to the full committees. The recommended documents were posted for several weeks on LTTN's Web site for review by the board. Then the board voted to adopt the LTTN Standards and Practices and its own associated policies. The whole process took about a year.

LTTN's staff is very willing to help other land trusts develop an adoption process. Rebecca Howard, LTTN's staff attorney, who oversaw the process, says that people enjoyed working on it once they got into it. She feels that having those standards and practices in place strengthened the organization in many ways, including helping it to run more efficiently.

Beyond adopting the *Land Trust Standards and Practices* and the policies and procedures, other measures can help. Here are a few:

* *Get educated.* How can you play by the rules if you don't really know them? Ask everyone on staff and on the board to read section 170(h) of the Internal Revenue Code, *The Conservation Easement Handbook*, and Steve Small's very readable *The Federal Tax Law of Conservation Easements*, which gives valuable commentary on the law and regulations.[9]
* *Understand the meaning and consequences of private benefit and inurement.*[10]
* *Adopt a multitiered board approval process* so that the board gets a chance to consider a project before the organization becomes thoroughly invested in it.
* *Empower the board executive committee* or the protection committee to review projects in detail and be fully informed about them before recommending approval to the full board. This can be accomplished by structuring the board decision-making process so that a subgroup of the board meets to review each project in depth in advance of full board approval.

- *Establish a board ethics committee* to advise on difficult ethical issues.
- *Annually evaluate performance* relative to *Land Trust Standards and Practices* to keep these helpful guidelines fresh in everyone's minds. One staff or board member can take on the job of reviewing how the land trust is faring and can lead the discussion.
- Have board and staff *review and sign conflict-of-interest disclosure statements annually.* Many organizations do.
- *Take a look at your mission.* Land trusts work for it daily but sometimes forget how it can be a guide in situations involving ethics. Focusing on the mission can put the issue into a long-term view, setting it in the context of its other priorities and the stewardship responsibilities.
- Early in discussions with a seller, *disclose as many of the standards and procedures that a land trust must follow as possible.* Issues of private benefit and inurement and signing the Form 8283 in the case of a donation or bargain sale are examples of the conduct required by *Land Trust Standards and Practices.* Then the seller will better understand early in the transaction the choices a land trust must make.
- When things get really complicated, *explain the situation to an associate, advisor, or board chair* to help you see the way.

The Tests

In a moment of crisis, taking a look at the big picture really helps. That is why conservation movement leaders often talk about the "tests." These are broad-

(a) Does it smell fishy?

(b) Could you explain it to your grandmother with a straight face?

(c) Would your project be defensible under questioning by the media?

(d) How would your project fly at the local coffee shop?

(e) Are you staying focused on your mission?

Figure 4.2
Can your deal pass these tests?

brush, layperson assessments of whether a deal is ethical, safe in other ways for the organization, and generally a good idea. In his plenary speech on ethics at the National Land Conservation Conference: Rally 2003, Darby Bradley, outgoing president of the Vermont Land Trust, started a good list of "tests":

1. *The smell test.* Does it smell fishy?
2. *The grandmother test.* Could you explain it to your grandmother with a straight face?
3. *The Mike Wallace test.* Could your explanation of what happened hold up to questioning on *60 Minutes*?[11]

To these tests, Michael Whitfield, executive director of the Teton Regional Land Trust (TRLT) in eastern Idaho, has added the "coffee shop" test: Could you explain the land trust's actions to the farmers, ranchers and local opinion leaders who meet for breakfast at the local coffee shop? Says Michael: "Our standing as open, ethical and fair-minded community members is our key asset. If we are accurately viewed as having mistreated a well-intentioned landowner, we are, appropriately, toast."[12]

To all of these I would add a fifth test based on a reminder by Jean Hocker, former LTA president, to also remember the land trust's mission and make sure that all of the land trust's actions follow from and are consistent with that mission. The test would be the "mission" test, or perhaps the "eyeglass" test: Are you staying focused on your mission?[13]

One final assessment: Do you find yourself justifying the project solely based on the public benefit? In other words, does the end justify the means?

Knowing the Law

One set of state and federal laws governs the conduct of tax-exempt organizations, and another set governs conservation transactions. For tax-exempt organizations, a good reference is *Law of Tax-exempt Organizations,* by Bruce Hopkins. For land conservation transactions, there is *The Federal Law of Conservation Easements,* by Stephen Small, among many other good publications.[14] For any land trust, numerous federal and state statutory and regulatory operating requirements exist—as well as severe penalties for not adhering to them. But two minefields—inurement and private benefit—are particularly worth noting here because they affect most, if not all, purchase transactions.

Inurement occurs when an organization knowingly or unknowingly provides financial benefit to a person who is related to the organization—for example, in the case of a board member, employee, or possibly a donor or even their family members, often called "insiders."

One activity that can result in inurement is excessively compensating a board member or staff person for services. *Land Trust Standards and Practices* Standard 4B recommends that the board president or treasurer never be compensated for services.

Other actions risk creating financial benefits for insiders, such as protecting land that enhances the value of neighboring real estate owned by a board member. If these benefits are incidental *and* there is good conservation justification for land trust action, then remedies may be attainable. Inurement is tricky though, and the statutory prohibition is absolute. IRS penalties include fines to improperly benefited insiders and even to the board, whether the member voted for the transaction or not. In egregious cases, the loss of tax-exempt status is likely.

The second minefield, private benefit, results from excessive payments or advantage to unrelated parties, as in the case of payment of greater than fair market value, absent adequate justification, to a seller for land. Similarly, private benefit arises when a land trust sells land, absent valid justification, for less than fair market value. In either case, a land trust is giving special privileges to certain individuals beyond what is generally granted to the public.

The IRS recognizes that business reasons do exist to convey private benefit, such as paying in excess of an appraisal for property. A delicate case could arise in our board member/neighboring farmer example. If the board member's property significantly appreciates in value as a result of the land trust buying a conservation easement on the neighboring parcel, inurement will be an issue. The land trust must decide whether the easement purchase is justified under its mission and established priorities to take on the potential inurement issues. If there is any question that the benefit to the board member is more than "incidental," the land trust might ask the board member to appraise the enhancement in value of his property and to make a contribution to the land trust without tax benefit to compensate for the enhancement.

Another law that affects nonprofit organizational accountability is the American Competitiveness and Corporate Accountability Act of 2002, known as the Sarbanes-Oxley Act. The United States Congress passed this law in response to corporate scandals, such as at Enron, to rebuild public trust in the corporate sector by addressing governance, accounting, and accountability issues. While the law applies primarily to publicly traded corporations, two of its provisions apply to both for-profit and nonprofit corporations. All of the provisions of the act, however, are relevant to nonprofit organizations and their governance procedures, and many states have or may enact statutes applicable to nonprofits patterned after Sarbanes-Oxley, as in the case of California's Nonprofit Integrity Act.

The Sarbanes-Oxley Act has served as a wake-up call and set in motion a valuable self-evaluation by nonprofits that inevitably is revealing some weaknesses. The particularly relevant procedures set forth in this law have been incorporated into the Land Trust Alliance's 2004 *Land Trust Standards and Practices* and will likely be addressed in greater detail in the LT Accreditation Commission Standards and Practices Curriculum.[15] A 2003 report on the Sarbanes-Oxley Act concluded that "for all of us in the [nonprofit] sector, the Sarbanes-Oxley Act has caused a renewed realization that nonprofit organizations rely on—and must protect—the indispensable and unequivocal confidence and trust of our constituencies."[16]

Stefan Nagel, of counsel with the law office of Stephen J. Small, and Konrad Liegel, partner with the law firm of Preston Gates & Ellis LLP, recommend in their article in the fall 2005 issue of LTA's *Exchange* that "all land trusts consider how to incorporate the spirit and concepts of Sarbanes-Oxley into how they conduct their nonprofit activities, such as:

- Avoidance of conflicts of interest
- Use of independent audits
- Disclosure of transparent financial statements
- Guidance by a corporate code of ethics."[17]

It almost goes without saying that a land trust must always work within the context of its charitable purposes. Whether the project is donated or purchased, a land trust must not act in any way that betrays its charitable purposes. These purposes are well defined in the Internal Revenue Code.

Five Ethical Issues Particularly Relevant for Purchased Conservation

For purchased or partially purchased or bargain-sale transactions, five broad and often interrelated ethical issues are particularly bothersome and threaten to cause problems: (1) conflict of interest and the appearance of conflict of interest, (2) undue board or donor influence on decision making, (3) valuation, (4) fundraising, and (5) the potential for conflicting duties. Other ethical issues that can arise in the course of a transaction should not be downplayed, but in my experience these five can cause the greatest problems. With the help of experienced conservation practitioners, I will discuss these ethical issues and offer specific guidance.

Conflict of Interest and the Appearance of Conflict of Interest

Conflicts of interest arise when a person is in a position to influence the decisions of an organization or otherwise has access to information that is not readily available to the general public.[18] These individuals are defined as "insiders" or disqualified persons under Internal Revenue Code section 4958. When this knowledge or access overlaps with a person's private interests, financial or otherwise, the best interests of the organization may be compromised. Thus conflict-of-interest situations usually apply to board and staff members and to major donors or active volunteers who are privy to information resulting from their closeness to the organization. The IRS has sample guidelines for conflict-of-interest policy for community boards of health care organizations. These provisions, which offer good guidance as to the IRS's concerns with regard to conflict of interest, should be incorporated into the policies of every land trust.[19]

Conflicts of interest and even the appearance of conflict of interest can greatly damage a land trust's reputation and its ability to maintain the public's trust, seriously limiting the effectiveness of the organization. Negative effects can linger for years despite efforts by the land trust to overcome them.

Often the appearance of a conflict can be as damaging to an organization as the conflict itself. For this reason, Stefan Nagel recommends that the appearance of conflict be treated as seriously as a real conflict and that the organization use the same procedures for both to protect its operations.

The *Washington Post* series on The Nature Conservancy's transactions with insiders raised a red flag particularly concerning conflict of interest and the appearance thereof.[20] Though no illegal action by The Nature Conservancy has been found, the accusation and appearance of conflict seriously damaged the reputation of the organization. While insiders are often the most sympathetic, trustworthy, and generous people with whom a land trust can conduct business, their closeness raises serious and legitimate conflict-of-interest issues. The *Land Trust Standards and Practices* Standard 4C, "Transactions with Insiders," explains what steps should be taken in these situations. Even with good procedures a land trust opens itself up to accusations of favoritism and worse.

Disclosure is key. Like other legal and ethical issues, conflict of interest is resolvable if the parties at risk disclose their interests up front. Then the board can evaluate the situation and determine whether the circumstances warrant action to protect the organization. In our board member/neighboring farmer example, if the board member immediately makes known that he is promoting conservation of his neighbor's land, then the board can recuse the board member from discussions of and votes on the project and from further negotiations on the easement. It might also decide to retain a third party—a biologist, for example—to evaluate whether the neighbor's land meets the land trust's conservation criteria, rather than relying on the opinions of internal staff or other board members (in a volunteer land trust). If the land trust decides to make the purchase, it might contract for two appraisals of the easement, or one appraisal and a reviewing appraisal, to determine the value of the conservation easement.

Protecting against the appearance of a conflict of interest will be more challenging. If the property is sufficiently important to the land trust to go through with the purchase, it can take steps to address these concerns. If, for example, the farmer's riparian land is clearly within the land trust's existing area of interest, the land trust might do well to publish a map of its plan showing how this purchase fits in. Despite these measures, the board might still determine that the neighboring board member should step down from the board to ensure that he is not present for any discussions or decisions regarding the project. However, stepping down wouldn't solve the problem if the board member initially participated in the project while still a board member.

One of the practical and negative effects of grappling with conflict of interest issues is that organizations may choose not to undertake important projects that have the potential to harm their reputations. Because the land conservation movement is relatively new at resolving these issues, we have much to learn about how to avoid conflicts without compromising a conservation plan. It is clear that land trusts must be cautious, but how cautious? Some recommendations follow for addressing many of these variations on conflict of interest.

- Create a policy. Whether part of a comprehensive code of ethics or freestanding, it should identify situations when conflicts or the appearance of conflicts arise, such as when an employee or board member owns land near or adjacent to targeted conservation projects or has a relationship with another organization that performs services for the land trust.
- Keep clear board meeting minutes that document procedures followed.
- Require that board members and staff disclose any real or apparent conflict. Some land trusts require board and staff to sign a disclosure form annually. Orientation for new board members should seek disclosure of any conflicts.
- Explain the importance of the strictest confidence and prohibit any improper disclosure of information except that needed in conducting organizational responsibilities.
- Require that board and staff recuse themselves from board or committee discussions or votes on any project involving their conflict, unless they are requested by the board to provide information on the conflict.

Box 4.2   The Land Trust for Tennessee Statement of Ethics

LTTN is dedicated to preserving the unique character of Tennessee's natural and historic landscapes and sites for future generations. LTTN's goals are established and its actions are taken with a long term vision for conservation. As a private, non-profit organization, LTTN has an obligation to provide a public benefit and therefore strive to avoid any conflict of interest or provide any private benefit to any of its Board members, staff or other insiders.

LTTN pledges to conduct its land protection and organizational activities under the highest professional standards and in accordance with the Land Trust Alliance's *Standards and Practices*. LTTN acknowledges the trust placed upon it by its donors, landowner partners and the public by being fiscally responsible, by always considering its long term responsibility to the lands it protects and by building a sustainable, capable land trust organization. In addition, LTTN pledges to foster open and productive relationships with landowners, its fellow land trusts and the general public.

LTTN strives to undertake only those actions which enhance the reputation and credibility of the land trust community. When appropriate, LTTN works co-operatively with other land trusts, government agencies, private individuals and conservation organizations to accomplish high quality, lasting conservation of important natural and historic landscapes.

- If requested by the board, the person involved in the conflict should resign from the board or take a temporary leave of absence until the board has resolved the related matter.[21]

Beyond a policy, Tim Barnard, an attorney who represents the Willistown Conservation Trust, encourages land trusts to adopt a set of standards of conduct. This is a set of specific responses developed internally to consistently address sensitive questions the public might ask of the organization. According to Tim: "There is a tendency of a group to say, 'This is all normal and expected! We unavoidably deal with people whom we know and trust.' But that is not good enough for the public." For example, the public may ask how the land trust chooses its consultants, lawyers, bankers, and real estate brokers and on what basis it makes referrals. Or, why is its banker a board member's brother-in-law? The land trust should make these choices responsibly, and in specific (but not all) cases the decisions should be open to public scrutiny. Standards of conduct offer the organization protection by creating consistent, careful responses that answer these questions or explain why they are not answered. In this way, a land trust further demonstrates organizational transparency and attention to ethical considerations.

As a member of a volunteer land trust, you might ask, "How can we avoid conflicts when our board members do all the project work?" In a small land trust, board members must be actively involved in making the deals, and often those deals involve land close to where they live. For a land trust working in a small geographic area, this is particularly a problem. Land conservation can and must continue. It just takes more care and more deliberate attention to the dangers of conflict of interest. As with a larger organization or one with a bigger service area, if a board member has conflicts, these should be defined and disclosed and the board member should not participate in any related discussions or votes.

Undue Board or Donor Influence on Decision Making

Board members, as well as other members of a community, can exert pressure on a land trust—for financial gain or otherwise—by making large contributions or lobbying board members or staff. Though not necessarily a conflict-of-interest issue, this creates ethical problems for the land trust nonetheless. While it is to the credit of all land trusts that so many people get wrapped up in the excitement of conserving land and find the thought of destroying a special area unbearable, that enthusiasm can create pressure to jump the gun and approve a project while overlooking normal cautions. A successful land trust develops a big network, even in a small community, and pretty soon everyone wants to protect land in his or her own part of town. The land trust becomes the obvious vehicle for salvation.

But not all conservation is equally important. This is particularly true when conservation land is purchased with scarce resources. In the board member/neighboring farmer example, the project actually sounds pretty good and seems to be a legitimate expenditure of land trust resources, but sometimes the suitability is less clear.

In this situation, a real conflicting interest may not even be in play. The person or group might simply love the parcel of land. But the pressure is still there, and it can still create ethical issues and at least the appearance of a conflict of interest. It can raise other questions, including the following: Who has decision-making responsibility? Is staff working for a certain board member who called because she got a call from an agitated neighbor, or is staff working for the executive director and the land trust's mission as a whole? What are your obligations to the community, to your donors, to the land, or to your mission? All this pressure can be subtly, but persistently applied.

So why shouldn't the land trust simply protect that parcel of land? Perhaps it should. If, however, the parcel doesn't meet land trust criteria, the organization must focus its limited time and money elsewhere. The land trust should take the time to explain this reasoning to the interested parties. It can suggest other ways for the neighbors to protect the land by finding a conservation buyer or making the purchase collectively.

Valuation

Says Steven T. Miller of the Internal Revenue Service: "I hear all the time from charities that I should not hold them accountable for the misconduct of their donors. I believe that is nonsense. If you perceive there is something out of whack with a transaction—walk away."[22]

These are strong words. The Tax Reform Act of 1984 was the first step toward bringing charitable organizations into the dialogue with the IRS on the valuation of charitable gifts. The act requires a donee organization to acknowledge receipt of any noncash charitable gift valued over $5,000 and to submit Form 8282 if the donee organization sold certain contributed property within two years. The IRS has recently made several other noteworthy changes in the acknowledgement on what is now Form 8283.[23]

So what does all this have to do with the *purchase* of conservation interests? A lot. First, many purchases have a charitable element. Sellers working with land trusts as buyers can and often do claim a partial gift when selling property at below fair market value. This gift is subject to the same valuation scrutiny as a full donation. Second, the IRS's growing interest in the value of donated conservation signals an overall change in the role they are asking charitable organizations to play. Abuses of the system are, they say, more and more a land trust's responsibility. Third, for conservation purchases, if the price paid by the land trust is too high then it risks private benefit. This is a very serious violation that must be avoided at all costs.

Valuation and the appraisals that estimate it play a critical role in purchased conservation transactions. They can make or break a deal; they can create unrealistic expectations or dash hopes. Despite the fact that appraisals have an element of art as well as science, they offer the factual basis for negotiating a purchase. They can create the path through the emotions and tensions of trying to agree on the price. For a full value purchase, an appraisal assures the land trust that it is not overpaying—or creating inurement or private benefit. Thus, with the heightened interest of the IRS in valuation, there are ramifications for purchased as well as donated conservation easements and fee land.

In addition to the IRS, other public agencies are scrutinizing the appraisal process for their acquisitions. The Department of the Interior and the U.S. Forest Service, as examples, have reorganized the way they review appraisals from contract appraisers and now expect strict adherence to agency appraisal rules. Land trusts working on pre-acquisition projects are often surprised by the extent to which agency review of contract appraisals results in downward adjustments in value. They assume that once the appraiser has produced a value, the agency will accept it. The outcome of this new scrutiny of every aspect of the appraisal by agency appraisal review teams is often less compensation to landowners and land trusts.

Form 8283

When a partial (bargain sale) or full donation is involved, the dilemma for land trusts is what to do if the valuation claimed by the donor seems out of line. Form 8283 (revised in 2005), which the donor must submit to the IRS with his or her tax return, requires that the donee organization acknowledge the gift. Opinions within the conservation community differ on whether or not to sign Form 8283 when, in the extreme case, the appraisal value appears very far off the mark or is otherwise indefensible. Though the form's instructions are pretty clear about when to sign, they beg the ethical questions being raised by the IRS commissioner and other IRS agents.

Though there is the spectrum of opinions on when not to sign, to simplify, one school recommends always signing the form, unless the gift is inaccurately described—for example, if the legal description is wrong or if the donor did not make the gift at all. The other school argues that ethical considerations and direction from the IRS commissioner seem to raise the stakes and compel land trusts to consider the accuracy of an appraisal before signing Form 8283. If the appraisal is clearly deficient or fraudulent, a land trust should not sign Form 8283.

Specifically, some trust advisors take the IRS's written instructions for Form 8283 at face value. Form 8283 specifically states that "this acknowledgement does not represent agreement with the claimed fair market value."[24] The instructions require only that the donee organization complete part 4 of the form, which asks the organization to acknowledge that it is a qualified organization, that the description of the property donated is accurate, and unrelated other questions.

The conservation gift acceptance policy of certain land trusts represent this view. Though the form creates no obligation for the landowner to share the appraisal with the land trust, or even to disclose the value of the gift, some land trusts request a copy of the appraisal. They alert the landowner to its reasons for requesting it, and if they find clearly demonstrable deficiencies, then as a matter of courtesy and good practice (but not legal obligation) they delay signing the form and alert the landowner and appraiser to the deficiencies. A land trust's concern is that a landowner might rightly hold the land trust responsible for refusing to sign Form 8283 if objections over valuation are the basis of the refusal. Attorneys and land trusts sharing this view believe that a land trust cannot substitute its layperson's estimation of comparable values for the appraiser's professional judgment. Nonetheless, they think that a land trust has an *ethical* responsibility to review the reported value of gifts it accepts if the donor shares the value and to alert the donor of demonstrable irregularities. It is not inconceivable that a land trust might step outside its policy if it decided that the appraised value was indefensible, and was able to support that conclusion with say, a second appraisal. An unwritten extension of a policy might be: to sign unless advised by counsel that the risks of signing were greater than the risks of not signing.

Larry Kueter, attorney with Isaacson, Rosenbaum P.C. in Colorado, who was recently appointed chair of the Land Trust Accreditation Commission, an independent program of the Land Trust Alliance, has written extensively on the ethical issues raised by Form 8283. Larry recommends that land trusts review all appraisals before signing the form and, in extreme cases, he recommends that they not sign. He suggests a three-tiered approach to evaluating whether or not to sign.

1. The acceptable appraisal warranting the signing of Form 8283 is generally in line with the expected value of the donated portion of the transaction and is not missing any elements required by the IRS.
2. The acceptable appraisal, with caveats, is aggressive in its value or is missing a key element (or both). In these circumstances, the land trust should sign the Form 8283, but it should thoughtfully share with the donor in writing its concerns regarding the appraisal. The written comments should be cautionary, or should direct landowners or their appraisers to an issue

for them to resolve, and should include the caveat that the donor must rely on his or her advisors, not on the land trust, regarding these matters.

3. The unacceptable appraisal is one that is indefensible as to its conclusion of value, or the land trust believes that either no gift has been made or that the gift described in the appraisal is not the gift received. Any of these problems will result in an appraisal that is, or borders on being, fraudulent, and the land trust should not sign Form 8283.[25] Exactly what constitutes an "indefensible" appraisal is left to the judgment of a land trust and its counsel.

In any of these cases, a land trust must have some knowledge of appraisals so it can identify problems. The policies differ, however, on what to do if a land trust finds deficiencies in the appraisal. Land trust policies also differ on whether to request a copy of the appraisal and whether to receive it before accepting the conservation easement or signing Form 8283. Obviously, judgments of valuation are difficult if the landowner does not provide the land trust with an appraisal, which the landowner is under no legal obligation to do.

Both interpretations put a land trust in a difficult position. If it signs the form knowing that there are serious deficiencies in the appraisal, it may be acting legally (following the form's instructions) but possibly not ethically. If it doesn't sign the form, it is supplanting the role of the appraiser and ignoring the form's instructions but is following the verbal directive from the IRS commissioner and alerting the IRS to potential issues with valuation.

Following the letter of the instructions and form, certain attorneys suggest not requesting or reviewing the appraisal. However, begging the ethical question makes some land trusts very uncomfortable. They would rather be on what they consider the right side of the ethical question and the wrong side of the law. A "don't ask, don't tell" strategy may not be right for the conservation movement as a whole either, leaving it open to guilt by association and worse.

It should be noted that *Land Trust Standards and Practices* does not offer a clear directive on whether or not to sign Form 8283. It recommends that a land trust see the declared value of the gift and sign only if that information is filled in on the form. It states: "If the land trust has significant reservations about the value of the gift, particularly as it may impact the credibility of the land trust, it may seek additional substantiation of value or may disclose its reservations to the donor."[26]

To attempt to avoid these issues, land trusts should encourage their donors to retain state-certified, respected appraisers who are knowledgeable in this area of valuation and to follow Uniform Standards of Professional Appraisal

Practice. However, in many parts of the country, such appraisers are hard to come by.

In the real world of working in the field, a land trust's hesitancy in taking a seemingly aggressive role in evaluating the appraisal is rooted in an interest in maintaining a good relationship with a landowner. Let's say, as in the case of our board member/neighboring farmer example, that the farmer has sold a conservation easement to the land trust at a very generous bargain sale price, but the appraisal vastly inflates the value of the gift portion of the transaction. We have a very generous landowner, but after the transaction is completed, the land trust, after reviewing the appraisal, has concerns about the gift's value. Now, after the landowner has made such a generous gift, should the land trust question the size of it, which might be interpreted as questioning his generosity? Ethically, the answer is probably yes. But this is not a comfortable situation for the land trust or the landowner.

In an effort to avoid these situations, it might be prudent to prepare the seller/donor beforehand, as some land trusts do, by asking the landowner for a copy of the appraisal, explaining the reason for this request, and offering to discuss this policy with landowners or their advisors. In our example, it is possible that the farmer is unaware of the error made by the appraiser—many landowners are unfamiliar with the details of appraisals.

Land trust boards have debated long and hard whether to write a letter to the donor expressing their concerns about appraisals. To satisfy its own ethical concerns, the land trust should try to review the appraisal or preliminary draft before the easement is signed or at least before the landowner's tax return is filed so that there is time to discuss any issues with the landowner. In the extreme case, if, after reviewing the appraisal, the land trust concludes that the appraised value is so high as to be clearly fraudulent, it is faced with a choice. Should it take the legal approach and sign Form 8283 anyway? Or should it do what some say is more ethical and not sign?

Until we have greater clarity from the IRS on these issues, each of the approaches outlined above seem defensible. It is important, however, that land trusts think through these issues and develop a well-reasoned policy that they share with easement donors at the outset of discussions.

VALUATION OF CONSERVATION DEVELOPMENTS

Recent articles have put the spotlight on so-called conservation developments, which are land developments, usually residential, that conserve or represent to protect parts of the property with high conservation value. There are numerous very legitimate conservation developments that conserve significant conservation land with minimum development. But others use the tax code to offer investors and lot owners tax deductions for little or no true conservation gift. The arrangement works something like this: The house lots on a development are clustered on part of the property, and the remaining land is left as green space. The developer gets an appraisal demonstrating that the zoning would allow much greater density development; by "giving away" that density, the developer or the investors receive a tax deduction. In some cases, this is an appropriate and valuable gift, but in other cases—where although the zoning might allow greater density, the market indicates that the highest-value use of the property is lower density—no gift of monetary value is made.[27]

In addition, for an easement donor to receive a tax deduction, the land being conserved must meet the conservation purpose provisions of the Treasury Department regulations and the criteria of a legitimate conservation organization or public agency and have the easement accepted by that entity. These conditions are not always met. Land trusts are usually involved in these projects as recipients of donated easements. In such cases, they should be sure the conservation interest given meets the land trust's project criteria, and do not get sucked into the developer's hype over a large easement that gives away market value without much conservation value. How to respond to any overstatement of value in the appraisal depends on how your land trust comes down on the sign–not sign debate discussed earlier.

VALUATION OF CONSERVATION BUYER TRANSACTIONS

In a conservation buyer transaction, a purchaser of priority conservation land donates a conservation easement or enables a land trust through a cash donation to retain or receive a conservation easement on land protecting its conservation resources and values. In recent years, conservation buyer transactions have been subject to intense scrutiny regarding valuation of easement gifts as well as the appropriateness of various conservation buyer transaction structures, raising questions about how the tax law should be interpreted in this context.

In July 2004, the IRS issued Notice 2004-41, "Regarding Improper Deductions for Conservation Easement Donations." This notice represents the IRS's concern that, in certain conservation buyer transactions, taxpayers "may be improperly claiming charitable contribution deductions under Section 170 of the Internal Revenue code."[28] The notice effectively shut down many land trust conservation buyer programs where the land trust did anything more than just match conservation-minded buyers with conservation property. There is speculation that the Treasury Department may issue new rules that could prohibit seemingly ethical conservation buyer transactions, but nothing has emerged from the IRS yet.

To further understand the notice and its implications, land trust boards and staff should familiarize themselves with the notice itself; read two articles in *LTA Exchange*, "IRS Notice Could Be Good News," by Stephen J. Small (Fall 2004), and "The IRS and Conservation Buyer Transactions: Throwing the Baby Out with the Bath Water?," by Tim Lindstrom (Winter 2005); and keep abreast of the Land Trust Alliance's efforts to seek resolution of these questions. Conservation buyer transactions will be discussed in more detail in the second volume of this book.

Paying over Fair Market Value

Beyond Form 8283, land trusts face other valuation issues. One of the biggest is when the land trust must pay more than the appraised value to acquire a conservation interest.

There are circumstances where paying modestly above fair market value may be acceptable. But that decision should be supported by very good justification, such as compelling conservation values that would be lost through land trust inaction, or because the purchase is the last parcel in an important area or a "completion" parcel where the seller knows that he or she can hold out for more, or if there is direct competition from a developer who is using speculative numbers.

Another reason for seemingly overpaying is a low appraisal. Since appraisals are historical views of the real estate market, they look at past sales. In a quickly appreciating market, the appraisal may not reflect all of the appreciation in the marketplace and may come in low. If a land trust finds itself paying above appraised value, then to avoid private benefit issues, it is good practice to document the reasons why you paid more for each specific transaction. Here again, arranging for a second appraisal or review appraisal or simply requesting a range of value from one appraiser gives the land trust a better foundation for negotiations and increases the chances of paying near an appraised value.

Paying under Fair Market Value

The flip side of paying over market value is paying below market value. This requires a real judgment call on the part of the land trust. If the landowner is fully aware of the discount that he or she is offering the land trust, is that enough reason for the land trust to accept it? No. There are times when a landowner may be making a decision that could jeopardize his or her own well-being. *Standards and Practices* 9L speaks to part of this question: "If negotiating for a purchase below the appraised value, the land trust ensures that its communications with the landowner are honest and forthright." In certain situations, however, a land trust should do more than communicate honestly. To the extent possible, it should not enter into an agreement with a landowner that is likely, in the land trust's view, to cause future economic problems for the landowner. If the land trust is perceived to have taken advantage of a landowner, its position as a fair player in the community could be jeopardized—at significant cost to the organization. (See conflicting duties section.)

Fundraising

Raising money for a land project or for general operations seems like a simple ethical matter, but it too can get complicated because a land trust may have two conflicting purposes—first, spending donated money effectively to meet its goals, and second, keeping donors happy so they will continue to donate. There are many ways that a land trust's actions can be at cross-purposes with its donors' interests. The secret to minimizing these is good communication.

Sometimes it is difficult or impossible to know what the future open space use of a conserved property will be because of unfinished negotiations with the takeout agency or changes in community priorities. If any uncertainty exists, the land trust should inform the donors up front whenever possible. Small changes are less problematic, but bigger ones will matter to donors.

One land trust executive director told me how her fundraising campaign hit a bump in the road when the land trust, working with the community, decided to build a bike path through a newly purchased property. Some donors with adjacent land opposed that use and withdrew their pledges. I had a less dire situation in which our fundraising materials explained that the land would be used for playing fields. When we finally worked out the plan with the county, the playing fields moved to a nearby parcel. We then chose to lease the land to a rancher for grazing. Fortunately, it was early enough in the process that we could go back to the handful of donors to explain the change and get their approval to use their contributions in this fashion. Here are a few possible situations and related suggestions on how to handle communicating with donors on the expenditure of donated funds:

- *Use of funds if the fundraising campaign is unsuccessful.* Let's say that a land trust has an option to purchase land and is raising money to exercise that option. What happens to the donations if the land trust doesn't raise enough money and has to let the option expire? Giving back the money is problematic, especially in a new tax year, when the donor has already claimed a deduction for the gift. The best approach is to work through in advance how to handle the situation. Some land trusts give their donors a choice. The money can go into a fund for future acquisitions, or the gift can be made as a pledge to be called if sufficient money is committed.
- *Use of excess funds from a fundraising campaign.* This is the last thing a fundraiser wants to discuss in a fundraising appeal. However, accurate representation of how all the funds will be used can prevent misunderstandings with donors. If the use of the money is in line with the intended use—say, for acquisition or stewardship or for the protection fund—then there is no problem. In any other situation, donors must be informed.
- *Donation for a specific purpose.* The purpose must clearly fall within the mission and intended purpose of the land trust. Don't be bribed into doing a project. On the other hand, if the project is within your mission and is a priority, welcome the gift!
- *Requests by donors for special action or treatment.* While organizations can provide special field trips and events to a class of donors that make major gifts, individual donor requests for special treatment that has quantifiable value—such as a request to do a detailed review of an appraisal for personal property—is not appropriate.

Conflicting Duties

This is an easy label for all land trust ethical issues. Larry Keuter defines these duties as follows. The first duty is to good conservation—after all, that is the land trust's mission. A well-thought-out and appropriately implemented strategic plan and a well-funded stewardship program are elements of fulfilling this duty.

The second duty is to protect the land trust and its assets, and not to expose those assets to liability. Fulfilling this duty is one reason land trusts are properly advised not to give legal or tax advice to donors of conservation easements. If the advice is wrong, the land trust could be liable.[29]

A third duty is to a land trust's donors to spend their money effectively to further the organization's mission. A fourth duty is to landowners to help them achieve their conservation goals. A fifth duty is to be a responsible and responsive member of the community (for example, by not entering into perpetual conservation contracts that might block publicly approved growth plans). A sixth duty is to the greater land trust community to participate in credible transactions and not set bad precedents. The continued success of the land trust movement depends on retaining the public's confidence in the public programs and tax incentives that are essential to meeting the conservation mission.

Now the IRS appears to have added a seventh duty: to ensure that the land trust is not party to any transaction in which other participants are not following the law and good practices.

Conflicting duty issues come into play with land trusts that accept conservation interests without having the funds to adequately steward or defend them against violations. On the one hand, the land trust has the duty to conserve important conservation land, to give landowners conservation options, and to serve community interests. On the other hand, the land trust has a responsibility to protect its assets and to follow through on the stewardship commitments it makes. But what if critical land is threatened today and the land trust simply hasn't been around long enough to raise a large stewardship or legal defense fund? Should the land trust walk away from this important project for those reasons? Leaders of larger well-funded land trusts might say yes. Leaders of new, small land trusts might say no. It is a tough dilemma since the industry as a whole does not have adequate stewardship funds and even the best land trusts have legitimately taken years to raise sufficient funds to meet their estimated stewardship obligations for existing projects.

For many years, the land trust community has been exploring business models to support conservation easement defense. Currently, at least one such model is being piloted. We must be hopeful that a collective easement defense program emerges, given the high potential costs of future lawsuits. One way that a land trust can help itself is to integrate the estimated monitoring and administrative stewardship costs (or a contribution toward a fund whose interest will cover those costs) into the overall cost of the project. Then work separately to raise a legal fund for collective legal defense, which will also raise awareness of the need to defend these conservation interests.

I know how hard raising stewardship money can be. We know more about these costs now than we did originally, when conservation was collected like baseball cards and it was an acreage game. Our obligations are different now, and stewardship must stand on equal footing with acquisition even if it makes an already difficult job much tougher (see Part 11, Chapter 5, Raising Money). A land trust will not be well served if it collects land that it cannot adequately steward.

Conflicts in duty show up all over the place. One not so uncommon example occurs when landowners are poorly advised. What if a land trust witnesses a landowner's lawyer offering uninformed information—for example, by saying that it is not necessary to consider mineral ownership in a transaction that could have serious tax ramifications for the landowner? Should a land trust give contradictory advice despite warnings not to give tax advice? Larry Keuter again recommends a good rule of thumb: if a landowner is headed over a cliff, it is the land trust's responsibility to stop him. Otherwise, the land trust and its personnel will be the first ones criticized.

Keuter also advises that in thinking about these situations, try reversing roles: what would you want someone else to do for you in a field in which you are not familiar (say, in the area of medicine)?

In another common situation, some landowners have no representation at all because they are not well-off or because they are culturally suspicious of consultants and want to rely on the land trust or its advisors. This is not a good idea because of the very real conflict of interest, especially if something goes wrong. The problem arises with cattlemen's land trusts because ranchers as a rule are suspicious of outside professionals. When accepting a donated easement, the right approach may be to raise a fund for landowners to use to pay for a conservation planner, an appraisal, or a lawyer. In the case of purchased conservation, what should the land trust do? The same.

Michael Whitfield, of the Teton Regional Land Trust (TRLT), has seen several situations where these duties to conservation, donors, and the landowner seemed to conflict. Six years ago, TRLT worked with a ranching family with four young children and very limited financial resources. Their ranch was their only asset. They lived in marginal housing and barely made ends meet. The family owned over 1,000 acres of riverfront land, which was identified as very high priority through TRLT's conservation planning because of nesting bald eagles, abundant water birds, wintering elk, and trumpeter swans. TRLT had also protected some of the adjoining land.

The family loved the natural resources and open space of their ranch and was willing to give away much of its value in a generous bargain sale, despite their weak financial situation. A developer had also started conversations with them for a particularly sensitive stretch of riverfront land. The family had no personal advisors and lacked the resources to hire legal and financial help.

After deliberating, the TRLT board offered to pay the family's legal costs so they could hire a lawyer, which they did. It was tempting to accept the family's offer of a large bargain sale, because TRLT did not have nearly the resources to pay the full value of a conservation easement to protect the ranch. But TRLT didn't think the offer would give the family the financial cushion that it obviously needed. "It didn't feel right, didn't look fair," Michael said. In a creative move, TRLT bought a no-development conservation easement on as much of the ranch as it could afford and, on another portion, purchased a ten-year arrangement with the owners with allowance for some building areas and a provision to buy permanent protection in the future.

TRLT decided that ethical considerations required them to counsel the family to be less generous than they might have been. This is the coffee shop test. Would the old-timers chatting in the coffee shop agree that TRLT had dealt with this family in a fair manner, or would the land trust be viewed as having taken advantage of their good intentions? Would the deal feel right in the long term?

As the end of the ten-year period approaches, TRLT is in a stronger financial position and, despite the fact that real estate has substantially appreciated, it is more likely to be able to purchase a permanent easement on the rest of the ranch. TRLT continues to have a good relationship with the family, which makes stewardship more sustainable. The family is in a better position financially to meet their own stewardship obligations. TRLT's reputation at the coffee shop has since led to many bargain sale easements with old-time ranchers who view the land trust as fair in its dealings with landowners.

Michael writes that of the people with whom he works, "many are older landowners who have worked the land their entire lives, have never had much in the way of financial resources, and who now find themselves very land rich if still cash thin. We need to tread very carefully in not only being completely forthright in presenting our assessment and appraisal of their land values, but also in some cases insisting that, as appropriate to the project, we 1) insist that the landowner retain some modicum of development rights to retain some future value, or 2) find resources to partially or fully compensate the landowner for development value, or 3) in the extreme case where we don't have the requisite resources, refuse a gift."[30]

While some might disagree with this approach, in eastern Idaho, where most landowners are very skeptical of government or nonprofit use and of conservation in any form, TRLT has successfully designed a very strong program that suits the culture of the region.

Conclusion

The responsibilities of land trusts in transactions are changing, and with these changes come new debates over ethical expectations. At one time, a land trust could stand by while an appraiser produced an aggressive report, but now some land trust advisors believe that the land trust should weigh in. As the Treasury Department continues to scrutinize the practices of nonprofits, including land trusts, the debate won't likely stop here. The IRS currently has under way several hundred audits of conservation easement donations. Based on what it learns through these audits, it intends to revise its forms and instructions accordingly. This will prompt new debates about what is legal and what is ethical and the difficulties in certain situations of accomplishing both. "We are at the crucible of an evolving practice," says LTA president Rand Wentworth. "Land trusts are being asked to actively discourage people who push the ethical envelope. Part of ethics is being a good partner with open communication to landowners. We are obligated as a movement to act more proactively in this regard."

So how is a land trust to protect itself in this changing environment? The best advice is to assemble a strong team of advisors, be vigilant about keeping up with new government directives and the law, and have an internal process that is as resistant to abuse as possible. Then, absent further direction, make sure that all your transactions have clear public purpose and do what seems right.

Beyond that, the process of developing policies and codes of conduct alone can start good organizational thinking about these important issues. There is nothing as valuable as that conversation about what is right for a particular part of the country and a particular community. One size does not fit all. The pressures and concerns of a regional land trust, for example, can be very different from those of a land trust with a small geographic area with innumerable opportunities for conflict of interest.

In the new world of rising standards of conduct in increasingly complicated transactions and with greater public scrutiny of nonprofit governance, taking a crack at a set of documents that govern land trust ethical behavior is a very good idea. We forget that, often, new land trust board members may never have served on a board before and know little if anything about their roles and proper conduct. The same is true for new staff members, who commonly are right out of school or coming from jobs where confidentiality was less important. A simple board and staff orientation notebook that includes these policies can be a first step toward bringing everyone onto the same playing field.

Land Trust Standards and Practices spells out what these policies should address with sample documents in its appendices. Certain land trusts, including the Land Trust for Tennessee, are willing to help too.

There is no doubt that ethical issues are tough. You can be a very good person who understands the difference between right and wrong and still be stumped by these questions. Strong policies are not enough. Land trusts must also have defensible practices. Compliance with legal guidelines is clearly needed, but so is the need to be ethical, which takes land trust responsibilities to another level.

Ethical conduct, however, requires many judgment calls. Unfortunately, no clear answer exists that applies to every situation. Reassuringly, these issues are indeed solvable, but resolution takes time and work and discussion with trusted people, such as your lawyer, board chair, and associates. So take the necessary time, and do not make these decisions too quickly.

"It is no longer *ethical*, in my view, to say that the job of a land trust is to conserve land, and that meeting all the other needs of the community is somebody else's job. We must consider the larger big picture and the context within which we do our work." Darby Bradley told us this at the National Land Conservation Conference: Rally 2003 plenary on ethics. This is what the IRS commissioner earlier in this chapter was saying as well. As we become a bigger player in land use, our obligations to a bigger community grow. Darby continued: "We are no longer minor actors on the fringes of the land use stage. The land trust community has been incredibly successful, and with that success has come new responsibilities."

Part 2
Raising Money

Chapter 5
Raising Money

Author Terry Tempest Williams told me the story of her young Utah land trust's efforts to raise $180,000 to buy a pristine stretch of desert in the canyon country. This sixty acres of state land, directly across from the Colorado River, had just been sold to the highest bidder. Development was imminent. At this worst possible moment, Terry had to leave to make a long-scheduled trip to speak at the Peninsula Open Space Trust (POST) annual meeting in Northern California. Terry, along with the whole community, was distraught at the prospect of losing the land, and she hated to leave her compatriots at this particularly stressful moment. Audrey Rust, president of POST, picked her up at the airport. Terry got in the car, emotionally charged, explained their situation to Audrey, and asked for her advice. Raising $180,000 for this tiny desert community seemed virtually impossible. But Audrey said, "Money is energy. You can do this." Audrey told Terry story after story of how POST had raised millions of dollars to protect land in the San Francisco Bay Area.

Terry composed herself for the meeting, focused her attention on the audience, and made her speech about why open space matters. She explained what the town of Castle Valley was facing and how the "Castle Rock Collaboration" would protect wilderness areas. She spoke from her heart. She talked about how land trusts are like water seeping into the smallest of cracks to create openings. She explained how Audrey Rust and POST's work gives others courage to do the same bold work. When it was over, Audrey handed Terry a check for $180,000 from an anonymous donor.

The Castle Rock Collaboration purchased the land and stopped the development slated to begin that very next Monday. Suddenly, this small grassroots effort had credibility. They went on to raise $2 million and protect fragile desert with the help of other concerned partners.

This is a story about the power of land and the desire to protect it. It is also about the power of a speaker like Terry, who lifts up the heart; a land trust president like Audrey Rust, who is a great and generous fundraiser; and a donor like this anonymous one, who understands the power of giving and receiving. Land gives back so much, even to a donor a thousand miles away.

Raising money for conservation is powerful and passionate. If you love land enough to work to save it, you can learn to use its magic to inspire others to give. Then you can raise money the traditional way, or motivate hotel owners to institute a surcharge, or convince developers to establish a transfer fee, or invent new revenue-generating techniques (all discussed in this part of the book).

It is never easy in the beginning. Speaking well is part of the program and that takes practice. Fortunately, the subjects—people and land—make the task easier.

The first talk I ever gave was about the Alaska National Interest Lands Conservation Act. It was an exciting subject, and I knew the information backward and forward. But I was very nervous, and the high school gym was too dark and crowded. The next time I gave the speech, I was still very nervous but it worked better. After a few more times, I was able to crack a joke, which relaxed the crowd and me. In 1980, after thousands of people had made speeches, written letters, and filled hearing rooms, the bill passed, and over 100 million acres of federal lands in Alaska were protected, doubling the size of the country's national park and refuge system, tripling the amount of land designated as wilderness, and creating ten new national parks.

A speech is important no matter how you are raising money. So practice it by yourself first, then in front of friends who will give you honest feedback. Remember not to rush through it. Work on cadence, emphasis, and humor. Then let it carry you away, and it will carry away the audience too. I always laugh or cry when I hear Terry Tempest Williams speak. I do the same when I speak. Land is an emotional matter, so let it rip.

Direct, frequent substantive communication helps, including emails and face-to-face meetings with pictures and maps. Did I mention emails? The Peconic Land Trust has even posted signs on properties alerting neighbors to option deadlines for charitable pledges

This part of the book will expose you to some of the best fundraising techniques in the conservationist's tool kit, with tips from practitioners who have used them well. Some techniques work better for raising operational revenue, such as annual fundraising. Others are better for acquisition (e.g., capital campaigns) or stewardship (e.g., transfer fees).

Figure 5.1
Protecting sixty acres
of pristine desert with
a $180,000 check from
an anonymous donor
gave the small Castle
Rock Collaboration
credibility and helped
it and its partners
raise $2 million.
(Photo © Grant Collier)

Let's try for stewardship starting with raising money. The first step is understanding the scale and nature of the need. Stewardship, being a perpetual requirement, will ultimately demand the lion's share of the funding. Purchased conservation, as opposed to donated conservation, may require more initial funding because sellers may have less commitment to conservation than donors. (Less commitment means more cost to the land trust).

Even if the land trust intends to transfer the conservation interest to a government agency, there can be a delay during which the land trust must carry the costs of the land. If it requires restoration prior to transfer, the land trust must pay for that too. Added to these costs may come others as concern grows that some public agencies are unable to manage conservation interests transferred to them. At some point in the future, land trusts might be asked to share in that stewardship responsibility.

Often land trusts do not or cannot transfer their acquisitions. They continue to own and manage conservation easements and land for demonstration projects, preserves, and education centers, and because that is how land trusts undertake their conservation missions. On top of the costs that ownership creates are the potentially significant expenses of conservation and conservation easement defense. For one lawsuit that was settled out of court, the Jackson Hole Land Trust had to spend over $200,000 in legal costs. Since perpetuity is a long time, you can see how the costs of stewardship start to add up.

But, you may say, "stewardship is not as sexy as land acquisition, so raising this kind of money will be much harder." I would challenge that notion.

Figure 5.2
Seven thousand children visit the Little Traverse Conservancy's preserves annually. (Courtesy of Little Traverse Conservancy)

We have let acquisition campaigns—the easy sell—overshadow stewardship fundraising. I am as guilty as anyone as I spent twelve years raising money for acquisitions.

With our desire to keep critical land out of harm's way, few land trusts have used the passion and power inherent in stewardship to raise money for it. Yet stewardship is the actual connection we make with the land over the long term, and it is through this relationship that people come to love land. Stewardship is the opportunity for seven thousand children to visit the Little Traverse Conservancy preserves annually, or the chance for a dairy farmer to pass a viable operation into the next generation on land preserved by the Vermont Land Trust. It is the assurance of productive spawning streams that fishers enjoy year after year in Montana after a conservation easement is given to the Montana Land Reliance.

What are the right funding sources for stewardship? For donated easements, many land trusts rely on gifts from easement donors. This technique doesn't work, though, when the conservation interest is purchased. One can make a good argument anyway that the people who enjoy and benefit from conservation—that is, the neighbors and the community—should be asked to foot part of the stewardship bill.

Figure 5.3
Restoration of a
wetlands by
volunteers. (Courtesy
of Jackson Hole
Land Trust)

In this part of the book, we will examine several good sources for stewardship funding. At the top of the list is incorporating stewardship costs into the capital campaign budget for an acquisition project and raising these funds alongside the acquisition costs from all the typical campaign sources.

In addition, land trusts have found alternative approaches to stewardship (and easement legal defense) funding. For example, New Hampshire's Monadnock Conservancy built its Enforcement Fund, which is separate from its Stewardship Fund, by transferring 5 percent of its operating revenue into the fund annually between 1998 and 2004.[1]

As institutions that are also around for the long haul, foundations grasp the importance of a healthy land trust stewardship endowment. The Cissy Patterson Trust gave the Jackson Hole Land Trust a seed grant of $35,000 to establish its stewardship fund. Clear documentation of stewardship costs helps make the case for the need.[2]

Ongoing streams of income, such as transfer fees, can keep revenue coming in for many years. The Jackson Hole Land Trust just passed the $1 million mark for revenue generated by transfer fees for its stewardship endowment. Other long-term revenue streams, such as rental income, can also be dedicated to stewardship.

In the interest of building stewardship and protection funds at every opportunity, some boards split or designate part of windfall gifts, sales of assetss and trade lands, and bequests for these accounts, and over time proceeds accumulate into sizable funds. Boards can institutionalize this strategy with a policy that automatically allocates windfall revenue in this manner.

With operating revenue stable, some land trusts make a concerted effort, as the Society for the Protection of New Hampshire Forests did, to market their stewardship programs to donors and increase their stewardship endowment as a component of a campaign.

The perpetual nature of stewardship can have appeal to donors who have an interest in the land for such uses as environmental education. The upside of a land trust's substantial, perpetual commitment to monitor and defend its conservation easements and land is, if marketed right, that it can help to characterize a land trust as a long-lasting institution. A growing stewardship endowment defines a land trust as such. People like to invest in institutions that will be around for a while—for perpetuity, actually.[3]

Using that contagious passion for land to put the tools described in the following chapters to work will help raise a lot more money, often very creatively, for conservation.

Chapter 6
Traditional Fundraising Methods

Raising cash, stock, or other liquid assets as charitable donations from individuals, foundations, or other donors in ways typically used by nonprofit organizations.

Fundraising skills are the most useful skills for all forms of conservation finance. The first time I asked for a significant amount of money ($5,000), it was from an elderly couple for a young grassroots environmental group I was running. The couple took me to the nicest restaurant in the area. We talked about their land in Montana and their hobby, hydroponic gardening. I awkwardly told them about my efforts to promote land use planning. Delicious food came and went. I didn't eat a thing. Suddenly, the meal was over. I couldn't put it off any longer; I had to ask for the gift. I did, and they said yes. I was exhilarated but hungry. One successful experience like that can launch a fundraising career.

Years later, at another lunch and working for another organization, a board member and two of us on staff were asking a wonderful, generous couple to initiate a very challenging fundraising drive. We planned to have my colleagues set the stage, and I was to ask for $3 million to be donated over multiple years to make the amount seem less daunting. When the time came, I mustered up my courage and asked for $500,000 a year for five years. "Where did I learn math?" my colleagues wondered afterward. To top it off, the response was, "Oh, we thought you were going to ask for much more!" We clarified my mistake later, and a pledge for $3 million arrived by mail. These were very special donors who fully understood our needs.

Over the years, I have learned two things about fundraising. First, it is mostly a science and only partly an art. The art is passion, style, and persistence. The science is everything else. Many people get discouraged because they don't think they can fundraise. If you have the passion and a style that connects with people, and if you are hungry for success (that is, persistent), the other skills can be learned. For starters, investigate the many good books on fundraising. I began with what is now an old book called *The Grassroots Fundraising Book: How to Raise Money in Your Community*, by Joan Flanagan.[1] A myriad of newer books is now available, including *Raise More Money: The Best of the Grassroots Fundraising Journal* and *The Fundraising Planner: A Working Model for Raising the Dollars You Need*.[2] Better even than books is finding a fundraising mentor. Find an experienced fundraiser, and follow that person around until you know everything he or she does.

The driving force for me was stimulated by huge development pressures bearing down on the ranchland of Jackson Hole. Having only a board of directors, a phone, a box of names and addresses, and no furniture or money was also motivating. I began making fundraising calls sitting on the floor with a phonebook.

The second lesson is that fundraising is only partly about actually asking a donor participant for money. It is a continual process during which, once in a while along the way, someone has to actually request a gift. It is much more about building relationships, doing research, making the right introductions, and, most important, telling the stories that make conservation—your conservation program—so appealing. This is how you build the connection between the audience of donors and outcomes on the ground. The money will follow.

Most people who say that they are not good fundraisers and do not like it don't like one specific part of fundraising—the ask. If fundraising is broken down into its many parts, most people in an organization can help fundraise without actually asking for money. Only a few people must solicit the gift. Surprisingly, actually asking for money is the best, not the worst, part of fundraising. A deep sense of satisfaction comes from bringing in the actual check that allows the donor and the organization to achieve their mutual goals.

My colleague for many years at the Jackson Hole Land Trust, Leslie Mattson-Emerson, now executive director of the Grand Teton National Park Foundation, demonstrates daily how fundraising is made of many parts. I went on at least fifty fundraising visits with her in the years we worked together. During all those visits, I don't think she ever made a request for money. Instead, she did all the advance work, came up with just the right amount for the request, briefed the rest of us, and made us rehearse "the ask." She invited the right people, teed up the case, and then was silent. Those of us who volunteered to make the request took it from there.

Of course, Leslie has asked many people for money. But when she knows a more appropriate person (usually and rightly a board member) to do it, she charms that person into it. As someone who has been that person, I can now ask, "What is there not to like about asking for money?" It is exciting. It makes the heart race. It's like driving a car fast or staring over a cliff. It is a true adventure with a very real element of risk. And the rewards to conservation are great. Why not enjoy it? Could there be a more productive adventure for a conservationist?

I got into fundraising not because I wanted to but because I wanted the results. I wanted to conserve land, and I needed money to do it. From my perspective, fundraising is about wanting the outcome so badly that you are willing to fundraise. Then it is so rewarding, you start to love it. Often, that initial discomfort associated with asking for money works to the solicitor's advantage and leads to success. Success is addictive.

I learned how to fundraise by experimenting in the field, watching good lunches go uneaten, failing at times, and trying again. I spent time with very good and very different fundraisers. I learned the mechanics and science of fundraising from Leslie Mattson-Emerson and from books. I learned how natural and enjoyable fundraising could be from fundraiser extraordinaire Peter Seligmann, board chairman and chief executive officer of Conservation International. With thanks to the many who led the way, I offer this chapter and the next as my guide to fundraising.

Why Fundraise?

Seems like a silly question, doesn't it? It is worth asking, though, because there are alternatives to asking for money. A land trust could ask a partner organization to buy the project, it could sell something rather than fundraise to pay for it, or it could just take a pass on protecting that piece of land. But fundraising has multiple benefits, including the following:

- It builds a strong organization and produces cash to pay for operations, stewardship, *and acquisition.*
- It builds valuable relationships.
- It gives an organization credibility.
- It provides a match to public funding.
- It gives supporters another way to help.

- It allows an organization to take risks.
- It provides cash to pay back debt-financed acquisitions.
- It demonstrates that a land trust can succeed at its mission.

The value of building relationships cannot be overstated. Relationships lead to more money, to enhanced skills, and to limitless new opportunities for conservation.

Asking for Money

The technique of asking for money is useful when asking anyone for anything. You can successfully ask a major donor prospect for a gift, a lender for a loan, a realtor to donate part of the commission, or a landowner to give a break on a sale price. Remember that if you don't ask, you'll never get what your conservation program needs.

Fortunately, no one is alone in the fundraising business. The board, the staff, and a group of volunteers should all be working together. As Joan Flanagan says in *Successful Fundraising*: "Fundraising is a team sport. You need a team of caring people to make it fun and profitable."[3]

Understanding a donor's motives for giving money helps structure the pitch and define the nature of the relationship to follow. A donor gives for many reasons, which can be because he or she

- believes in the goals, programs, and activities of the organization
- perceives the cause or organization as successful and wants to be part of something successful
- is directly involved with the organization (or a family member or close friend is involved)
- wishes to receive public recognition for a good deed or wishes to be memorialized or to memorialize others
- seeks a tax benefit
- respects the solicitor or owes him or her a favor
- respects the management of the organization
- has a keen sense of community responsibility
- enjoys the company of the people associated with the organization
- is passionate about conserving land.[4]

Figure 6.1
Coast Dairies is part of Santa Cruz county in California, founded and protected by the Land Trust of Santa Cruz and the Trust for Public Land. (© Paul Norcutt)

Some people believe that they can guilt a donor into making a gift. But guilt is rarely a deciding factor in the decision to give, and tax benefits are nearly always a consideration. The perception that the project can succeed is also a significant motivator. Everyone wants to be part of something successful and enjoyable. It is easy to say that the project will be successful, but the best evidence is past success. "The fact that we were able to buy this property and protect it has made a lot of people believers," says executive director Dale Bonar of the Maui Coastal Land Trust. "The skeptics have realized we are not a flash in the pan, and it will really help us build more support in the future."[5]

Another prime motivator is the particular outcome. What will be accomplished with the money donated either by the one donor or to the campaign collectively? "The number one reason people have trouble asking for money is that they don't know what they need money for," says Donna Fletcher, fundraising consultant with Mission Driven. "I ask people, 'Can you tell your donors what you would do with another $10,000?'" Savvy donors listen for specific needs that they can help meet. "If there is a very exciting project," says Donna, "you'll see people come out of the woodwork who have never made major gifts."

The Solicitor

The solicitor is key. A peer of the donor prospect is the best solicitor. To ask for major gifts, Tom Bailey of the Little Traverse Conservancy in Michigan recruits his solicitors from donors, mostly board members, who have given over $10,000. Other good solicitors are people with stature who are respected by the prospect or who play a key role in the organization. Sometimes these individuals are willing to make introductions or even come to the solicitation meeting, but they don't want to ask for the donation. That is fine in the beginning. They can be there, and a staff person can ask. But the goal should be to eventually reverse the roles so they do the asking, with a staff person at the meeting as support.

Two masters of conservation fundraising have their roots in the same organization: The Nature Conservancy (TNC). The first, Patrick Noonan, who later became president of The Conservation Fund, brought creative fundraising and deal making to the land conservation movement. Pat integrated what are now tried and true fundraising techniques into the culture of TNC. Its staff replicated these techniques, and others watched and learned.

Another master in the new era of land conservancy, which is now heavily populated with conservation groups and successful fundraisers, is Peter Seligmann, former TNC international director. Peter showed me the art of fundraising. Though I am not always comfortable with how and when Peter asks for money, he has been very successful at asking in the moment. Peter has a natural sense of when his audience is sufficiently engaged and excited about a program to respond positively to a request. He senses that moment more clearly than most of the rest of us do. That is why he seems to jump the gun sometimes, and yet it works. Most of the time he gets it right. Is the right time to ask for money right when you meet someone? Probably not. But I have seen Peter do it and walk away with a check.

Peter's style is part of his success. He is compassionate. He has a warm and genuine humor, and his competency shines through. He makes asking for money fun. He always connects his big vision to save global biodiversity with his audience and instills hope based on past success and creative new ideas. Peter is never one to underestimate a prospect's interest and concern for the critical issue of global conservation. He expects the light bulb to turn on. He expects success because he knows that he will be able to spark interest in this issue. These qualities make his requests irresistible.

At Muir Heritage Land Trust in California, executive director Tina Batt has the same philosophy: "Never underestimate people's support for what you are doing." Like many new to fundraising, her staff was at first apologetic about asking for money. "We had to make the transition from feeling badly about taking people's money to being proud to be able to ask for their support," says Tina. "We changed our thinking into 'be bold, be proud of who you are, go out, and ask.'"

Although Peter's sense of when the timing is right is uncanny, I prefer to get a prospect out on the ground or provide an experience that connects the prospect to the land and its people before asking for a gift. An investment of time actually creates commitment or strengthens an existing commitment. Since what conservation is selling is usually beautiful and always interesting, taking a prospect out on the land has the dual effect of creating that invest-ment and letting the land sell itself. While many land trusts take scheduled field trips to their projects, Tina makes a regular habit of informally visiting proj-ects with donors. "There is no reason to sit in a restaurant with a major donor," she says. "You've got something to show them, so why do that when it's much better to take them out on the property and bring a picnic lunch?" Her well-attended hikes on trust-owned properties are a keystone of her major donor program. When Saturday comes, she says, "Grab a board member and some donors and go."[6]

In the end, the solicitor should have passion. As Leslie Mattson-Emerson explains: "It can be very intimidating to sit in someone's office and ask for a gift. What you need to be able to do is key into what the cause or outcome of the campaign means to you as the solicitor. A successful solicitor is passionate about the cause. Once you know the transactional part: how to ask, how to be quiet and how to follow through, it is essential to key into your emotions. That leads to success."

Types of Solicitations

Asking for money can be done in a letter to an individual prospect or past donor, or better yet, in person at a small meeting, reception, or a big event. Let-ters are good for renewing annual support, for introducing new prospects to the organization, and for asking for modest amounts of money. The letter must be carefully composed with these key ingredients: an enticing first sentence; a brief, upbeat explanation; a connection to the donor; an explanation of the broad appeal and popularity of the project; and the ask—all in short, clear sentences with no errors in the spelling of the name or the salutation in the letter or en-velope. The best letters are personalized, though that is not always possible if they are sent to many recipients (see appendix 6.1).

Major gift requests, especially first-time requests, should be made in person at a meeting set up for this purpose. Prospects should be sufficiently cultivated so that the odds are their response will be positive. Some donors move seasonally. If the organization has the resources, visit donors at their primary residences. People would rather vacation where they vacation than spend their limited time being solicited for money. However, they enjoy the excuse to talk about that vacation place when they are at their primary home.

The important thing to remember *always* is that someone in the organization eventually has to ask for money. If you wait and wait for just the right moment and then don't ask, you may never get the money or whatever else it is that you need.

In his book *Nature's Keepers*, Bill Birchard recounts a story of one of the many reasons that Pat Noonan has been such a successful conservationist: "One of Noonan's strongest fundraising traits was other people's weakest. During a weeklong orientation for new employees in 1977, Noonan, curiously, didn't appear for a few days. On Thursday afternoon the group was learning about fundraising (everyone at TNC was encouraged to fundraise) however, and all at once Noonan threw open the conference room door. He glowered from the doorway and said one word: 'Ask!' Then he turned on his heel and walked out."[7]

The remainder of this chapter contains very specific guidelines for each type of solicitation. As Peter Seligmann will tell you, you cannot always plan for the right moment. When it comes, though, seize it and ask. But for the less experienced fundraiser, it is best to have a well-rehearsed request for a meeting, a well-prepared presentation for the project, and a scripted closing with a request for money. Eventually, these strategies will be internalized, and the whole process will become second nature.

Scheduling the Solicitation Meeting

Fear of asking for money is like fear of the dark. The more one knows about what is in the room, the less scary it is. The very first act of asking for money is to request a solicitation meeting with a prospect or donor. Don't be fooled— this request for a meeting can be as difficult to make as making the ask itself. It is your first step into that dark room. Gain confidence from doing it well.

- Identify a prospect whom you are comfortable approaching. (It doesn't have to be the perfect match, just good enough.)

Choose your words carefully. Don't say, "Can we meet so that I can ask you for money?" Instead, say, "Would you have time to hear about a very exciting project for conserving land near where you live and to consider supporting our efforts to preserve it?" Difficult as it is, be clear about the purpose of the meeting, as this will be the first demonstration to the prospect of your competency, which begins building trust. Set up the meeting with full disclosure, if at all possible. A donor once told me that a person she hardly knew asked her for a tour of her new home, which she gladly granted, only to find that the visit ended in a request for money for the woman's charity. The donor, unfortunately, still remembers that misrepresentation.

Setting Up the Fundraising Meeting

Because setting up the meeting is part of the request for money, it should be done right. So guess what? You have to role-play. This can be awkward and no fun, I know, but the request cannot leave your mouth for the first time in front of a prospect. Practice, and the words will roll out more smoothly during the real thing. Role-playing will also make you less nervous. Nervousness is distracting. If you are nervous, you will talk too much and forget to listen—and listening is *crucial*. Follow these steps for setting up the fundraising meeting.

- Be clear about the purpose of the meeting.
- Explain how long the meeting will last and who else might be there.
- Be flexible about the schedule. (Find out the best times for the donor—breakfast, evenings, or another time?)
- Briefly mention your role as a board member, donor, or staff person.
- Don't get deep into content and be careful not to solicit the prospect when setting up the meeting.
- End the conversation quickly—this is not the time for a lengthy discussion.

Getting Ready for the Solicitation Meeting

Once the meeting is set up, prepare for it so that it is as comfortable as possible for you and the prospect. Take the following steps.

- Know as much as you can about the prospect. Gather information; then brainstorm with others, such as with a small group from the board or fundraising committee. These sessions can generate a lot of new and useful information.

- Know how much to ask for or a range (the same group of board members and committee members who know the community or may socialize with your prospect can help with this too). It doesn't hurt to shoot high. The prospect will be either flattered or taken aback. Either way, it will not reduce the size of the gift and it may increase it.
- Make your own gift first (no matter how small it may be) because all solicitors should and because, if the subject comes up, you want to be able to show your support.
- Anticipate questions, and have the answers, even if it is: "I don't know."

The Solicitation Meeting: What to Say

You have to role-play this as well, so that you aren't too nervous, you say the right things, and you listen. If you can, bring someone else to the meeting. That person should either be a friend or an associate or should have some connection to the prospect and be an endorser, someone who is respected in your community. William Ginn, in his book *Investing in Nature*, relates a great story about a difficult meeting between The Nature Conservancy and the Great Northern Paper Company. Only when the individuals realized that they had a personal connection did the meeting turn around. The deal resulted in the protection of 241,000 acres.[8] This can happen at a fundraising meeting too. So pick your team carefully.

Following is a general outline for a meeting.[9]

1. *Start the conversation with a few minutes of small talk about common interests* (but not too much; don't waste the prospect's time). Then briefly lay out what you would like to cover at the meeting. Always be mindful of how long you are talking; don't talk on and on. This is particularly important when you are actually describing the project. It is easy to get carried away.
2. *Speak to your credibility as a solicitor.* The prospect will be more comfortable if he or she can respect the solicitor. For example, you can say, "You know that I have lived in (your town) for X years and am on the (board/ staff) of (your land trust)." Introduce your associate in the same way, mentioning any connections that person has with the prospect. For example, you might say, "My colleague, (colleague's name), like you, loves to fish," or, "I believe that my colleague, (colleague's name), has a child who goes to your children's school." Let the prospect talk (briefly) about any mutual connections.

3. *Draw the prospect in while explaining the project.* Ask some open-ended questions, such as, "Do you ever drive by XX farm?" This can engage the prospect immediately in the project itself—it gets the prospect talking about the project—and builds on his or her own emotional commitment to the land, and dilutes any tensions between the solicitor and the prospect. Then give the exciting details of the project, such as "We recently secured an option for a ranch/farm just down the road from you." This is the elevator speech—a well-rehearsed, clear, and short description of the project that can be said in the amount of time it takes for an average elevator ride. Tom Bailey, of the Little Traverse Conservancy, has good advice on this speech: "Tie the solicitation to *the for* not always *the from.*" What is the project going to be *for*? Don't talk just about the threat that the land trust is saving the land *from.* You can always elaborate later if the prospect shows particular interest, but the elevator speech allows you to get the message on the table.

4. *Broaden the discussion to the greater public good.* For instance, you might say, "Our goal is to support conservation here, because the land is our heritage and economy, good for tourism and wildlife, and quality of life for our community and our children." Mention your commitment as a donor, and remind prospects of *their* commitment if they gave to or did anything for the organization before, including coming to an event or even just buying a T-shirt for a grandchild. (Actions, even seemingly unrelated actions, create commitment.)

5. *Ask for the gift.* There are many ways to do this, some of which are scripted in a later section. Rehearse the ones that feel most comfortable.

6. *Let there be silence.* Don't rush in to fill the quiet, especially right after asking for the gift. Give your prospect plenty of time to answer and time to think and ask questions. You won't learn anything about prospects—and they will become frustrated—if they can't ask questions.

7. *Thank the donor* at the meeting, whether or not you received a commitment. The donor gave you his or her time at least. If you did receive a commitment, ask whether you can thank the donor publicly—most enjoy it. If he or she says yes, then do so (in newsletters, at the picnic, in front of the donor's friends, and so forth). If the donor wants to be anonymous, enter that information in the organization's records. If the donor isn't yet sure about giving, determine a way to follow up.

8. If the donor does agree to give, *confirm* the amount, when you will receive the gift, and in what form. If possible, get a check at the meeting.

Tips on the Meeting

These meetings can be tough but exhilarating. Here are a few tips on how to make the whole process easier.

- Respect your prospect. Again, *listen* to responses carefully. Address every question asked. Don't interrupt. Allow for silences.
- Try to have a good time; fun is contagious. If the meeting is not enjoyable, why would a prospect ever want to do it again?
- Never underestimate the value of humor.
- Ask for a "gift" or, better yet, a "commitment," rather than for "money," as the donation could take different forms, such as a pledge. A "commitment" speaks to a personal investment. Both terms are more general and open possibilities for other types of donations.
- Talk about outcomes, not all about raising the desired amount of money. Use maps, and if possible, locate your prospect's property relative to the land in question.
- If applicable, always mention the donors' previous gifts to remind them of their existing commitment and to thank them for their past generosity.
- If you are asking for an increase in giving, provide a reason. Otherwise, it will sound as if you are upping the amount just for the sake of doing it.
- Don't argue; agree when you honestly can. Use objections to turn the discussion around: "That is a good point; here's how we look at it."
- Be as precise as you can with your answers. If you don't have an answer, say that you don't know but will get back to the prospect with an answer. Then make sure that you do!
- Jot down a name or idea that you are otherwise likely to forget, although taking notes can be distracting and formalizing. The second land trust representative at the meeting can do more. Make more detailed notes right after the meeting.
- Be smart. Give yourself time to answer questions thoughtfully.
- Be a little insistent and firm about your request (see the next section).
- Be ready to respond. Prepare possible objections and your responses.
- Use the meeting to sell your land trust and to *listen and learn* about your prospect and close the deal. Walk away with a check, if possible (see next section).
- Again, say *thank you*. How many ways can you do it?

The Ask

Now I have talked my way around the actual request. Here are some scripted asks to role-play, learn, and execute.

Ways to Request a Specific Amount

- Ask clearly and directly for the amount: "Would you please consider a gift to the (your land trust) of $XXX?"
- Ask the prospect to join a group of donors giving at a certain level (there is comfort in joining a group): "In order to complete the conservation programs we are working on this year, we are going to need XX number of donors to give at the $XXX level. (Number of other donors) have agreed to give already. Would you join those generous donors and make a gift at that level?"
- Ask the prospect to join a formal level of giving that your organization has established: "Our Leadership Council is composed of donors who are giving $XXX annually and has thirty nine members. Would you be willing to join the council as our fortieth member?"
- Ask the prospect to pay for all or part of a specific project, event sponsorship, or operational need: "We are organizing an evening with a special speaker, (name of speaker). We are asking three donors to give $XXX to make this evening program possible." Or, "Our stewardship staff members are driving their own cars for stewardship monitoring on rough roads, which is ruining their cars. Would you be willing to donate $XXX so that we can buy a four-wheel-drive vehicle for this purpose?" Or, "The land costs $250,000. We are hoping that two donors will pay for half of it."
- Ask for a lead gift. Some donors like to be the most significant donor leading the way for others: "We are looking for a lead donor to make a commitment of $1 million to give the project stature and set the stage for our campaign. Our board would like to ask you to be that lead donor."
- Ask for a completion gift: "We need $XXX to complete this campaign and preserve this parcel. Could you make the gift that will complete our campaign?"
- Use a gift table (or gift pyramid) as a prop, and point to the level of commitment you are asking the prospect to make. A gift table is a graphic representation of an organization's planning for large contributions for fundraising, usually for a capital campaign. The solicitor uses a version of

the gift table that does not identify the names of prospects but shows the strategy for reaching the fundraising goal, thus demonstrating the thoroughness of the campaign planning.

Ways to Ask for an Increase in Gift Size over a Previous One

- Use the last gift as a launching pad for this request: "Last year you gave $XXX. This year we are fortunate to have XX new projects and thus must raise $XXX more to complete them. Would you be willing to increase your annual gift to $XXX?"
- Use a challenge or matching grant to ask for an increase: "A generous donor will match every new gift of $500 or more we receive. Would you make a gift that could be matched?" Or, "Would you increase your gift so that we will receive a match?" Or, "Would you match every member's gift that is an increase of $100 or more over their last year's gift?"

Ways to Ask for a Gift in a Range

Keep in mind that the donor will most likely give at the bottom of the range.
- Directly: "Would you please consider a gift of between $5,000 and $10,000?"
- Using a range of specific projects: "A gift of $XXX will help us purchase (need). However, a gift of $XXX will buy (another need), which is our highest-priority need."

Be Prepared for These Questions

- "Can I give stock?" Your organization should be set up to receive stock. Be ready with contact information for your broker and the transfer instructions. Know your organization's policy on selling stock. Does it sell immediately?
- "Is your organization willing to take pledges?" If so, have pledge forms and encourage the signing of them while you are there.
- "Is the gift tax deductible?" Understand what is and is not deductible. Know the meaning of such terms as *quid pro quo, private benefit,* and *inurement* as well as the severe restrictions they impose, remembering that a donor should never rely on you or your organization for specific tax advice.
- "Will my name be published in your magazine?"
- "What will my gift pay for exactly?"
- "Is it possible for my gift to support only (specific name) program?"

Be Prepared for These Responses

- "I can't give that much." Don't offer a lower amount—that is bidding against yourself. Try instead: "Could you give it in two payments this year?" or "Could you give in that range?"
- "I'm not one of those big donors." Follow with "Neither am I, but I am doing what I can because the project means so much to me."
- "I have other priorities." Reinforce what you think are your best arguments based on what you have learned at the meeting: "I understand completely; however, did I mention how many children from the local school are anticipated to use the park?" If you are making no progress, keep the discussion very friendly and see whether the donor can help in other ways, such as by suggesting other prospects.
- "Send me the material, and I will see." Follow with: "Can I call you about this in a week?"
- "Yes, I will give something." To avoid the unspecified pledge, the solicitor should say, "That is wonderful! Thank you! As you know, we have $1 million to raise, so it is very important to know how much we can expect."
- The old favorite: "Yes, of course. Whom should I make the check out to?" Keep cool, and thank the donor!

Following Up

Bring all "intelligence" from the meeting back to the office, and write it down to institutionalize it. Then send a follow-up letter immediately, thanking the donor for the gift if a gift is forthcoming and confirming arrangements for receiving it. If the prospect is still thinking about the request, which is quite normal, the letter should discuss arrangements for a follow-up phone call or visit. If the prospect is not interested, thank him or her for the time.

Congratulate yourself and your fellow solicitors whether your meeting raises money or not. Either way, you have helped spread the word about the organization. This is important, hard work.

How Individual Donors Usually Give

Now that you have asked your prospects for money once and that wonderful check is in your pocket, when do you ask again? There are several rather standard answers. Most supporters think about making gifts towards the end of the calendar year and before January 1 so they can receive the tax benefits of the gift in the current tax year. Therefore asking for money in the fall coincides with the time when a philanthropic person is most likely considering which charities to support that year. Though by all means not the only time, or even necessarily always the best time, to ask for contributions, it is the most popular time. If satisfied with the work of the organization, asked annually, and cultivated, these donors will give annually. These same donors will be the first to participate in a capital campaign for a specific land acquisition project. Then as a donor's commitment to and investment in an organization grows over the years and as the institution itself matures, donors begin to respond to requests for planned gifts.

Of course, there are many other ways that people give to charity, which will be discussed in the next chapter. But usually, the core giving, whether from individuals, businesses, or foundations, comes once a year (annual giving), for special purposes (capital campaign giving), or as part of an estate plan, usually posthumously (planned giving).

Prospecting for Donors

To ask for money, you have to find prospects to ask. If you keep going back to that handful of people who founded the organization, your land trust eventually will run out of money, as it is the very rare person who can or wants to carry an organization for perpetuity.

A land trust must always be looking for donors. The task should be a way of life for anyone closely associated with the organization. This is never truer than when an acquisition project looms on the horizon and more money will be needed.

Again, the first place to look is in the annual donor pool. These are the best candidates for increased gifts because they know the organization, are already invested, and want to see the organization succeed. They are likely to help by suggesting friends and acquaintances who might give, by making introductions, by hosting receptions to introduce new people to the organization, and by signing and writing solicitation letters.

The other great place to find prospects is from the board of directors. For its first twenty-seven years, the Land Trust of Santa Cruz County had very few individual donors and the board was reluctant to fundraise. Recognizing the urgency to protect land in their area, the board made a strategic shift to become more proactive. As they prepared to launch a fundraising campaign, the small staff cobbled together a list of major donor prospects. Then they invited each board member to meet individually with the staff, stressing that the members would not be expected to actually solicit donations. Some board members offered names; others agreed to make introductions. As the directors became more comfortable with the process, they were willing to do more. In the end, each board member arranged for at least one meeting and that land trust raised three times the previous year's contributions.

Other prospects are in all of the obvious places:

- Neighbors adjacent to land trust projects that enjoy and benefit from land conservation;
- People with enthusiasm for the conservation values to be protected. (For example, if wildlife will benefit from a project, then consider wildlife enthusiasts, including bird clubs and natural history associations. If scenic values are involved, then consider the commuters who pass by the project. If public access is in the cards, consider recreationists and other community members who may be interested in using the project.);
- Community leaders who can encourage support among their constituents;
- Published lists of other organizations' donors, magazine lists, and articles;
- Attendees at outreach events, local newspaper readers, and radio listeners;
- Residents of nearby neighborhoods with the means to support land trust projects (use county or municipality GIS records to find specific names).

Barry Banks, of the Red-tail Conservancy in Indiana, tells of a retired English professor who called him up after reading a newspaper article describing how the land trust had only eight days to raise money before a unique parcel was to be sold at auction. The forested parcel had, as it turned out, 428 species of plants, likely the most biologically diverse parcel of land in south-central Indiana. After walking the property with Barry, the professor pledged $200,000. Two more people saw the article and eventually bought limited hunting rights, which also helped the Conservancy pay for the property.

Once you find donors, you have to keep them. A donor doesn't just give money. A donor is an investor in a very special company—your land trust—and is one of your good customers. Treat them as such. Involve them. Reach out to them at every opportunity. Events, small dinners, personal visits, and recognition engage them and instill the excitement and satisfaction of conserving land. Emails keep donors current on projects and build momentum. Collect and use email addresses. A well-cultivated prospect will become a donor. A well-cultivated donor will give regularly and increase giving, if they can.

Annual Giving

Now that you know how to ask for money and how to find prospects, what are you going to do with these valuable tools? First, develop an annual giving program, which is the most important fundraising program a land trust can have. Annual donors can be designated "members" (although that designation rarely implies any governance rights). Often, members enjoy special privileges, such as invitations to special events. While adding a level of complexity to record-keeping, the advantage of having members is that membership can carry with it a special cachet. The Cascade Land Conservancy, for example, gives membership status to supporters who invest a certain number of hours volunteering at the land trust's preserves. Other organizations reward members who sign up the most new members.

Whether they are called members or friends or donors, people who give annually provide the basic revenue for the daily operations for most land trusts. They become an important part of the network from which a land trust can draw its volunteers, leaders, expertise, and donors for capital campaigns. Next to the board, they are the closest and oldest friends of a land trust. They give year after year. They get it.

An annual giving program should have a diversity of revenue sources: individuals, foundations, and businesses. Different types of donors (e.g., businesses or foundations) may require different kinds of encouragement to give every year. If the program is established so that most donors give at the same time of year, the organization can have an annual drive for renewals. Annual donors should be invited to participate in the organization through events, field trips, and receptions. They should be asked for advice on issues relevant to their knowledge and expertise, invited to serve on advisory committees, and encouraged to help at events, with mailings, and in the field. Annual donors keep an organization operating and provide the fiscal comfort that can launch it to new levels.

Capital Campaigns

A capital campaign is a drive to raise money for a specific project. In the case of land trusts, that is usually land or conservation easement acquisition or more complex projects or collections of projects. A campaign asks supporters to make exceptional gifts for an exceptional need. Capital campaigns should not be taken on lightly. They have lots of moving parts and require attention to detail and must be well organized. That does not mean that a small organization can't undertake a capital campaign, however. Many volunteer land trusts successfully raise money for high-profile land projects, but they usually have a strong team of volunteers who have had experience with other capital campaigns.

A cultivated annual donor pool drives a capital campaign. Funding for an acquisition project usually requires larger gifts than for annual operations. But because annual donors already support the land trust and are most interested in seeing it succeed, many will be willing to stretch to make a larger capital campaign gift.

Though most of the revenue for a capital campaign comes from large gifts, smaller donors and other categories of supporters play a vital role. In addition to their financial support, they provide a positive campaign atmosphere in the community.

The classic and prudent steps for developing a capital campaign follow.

- *Project identification.* Ideally, this involves applying the land trust's project criteria to identify priority projects for acquisition. But it often happens the other way around, by applying the project criteria to assess whether a parcel immediately threatened by development meets land trust standards. The cost of the acquisition plus fundraising, administrative, and stewardship costs determine the campaign goal. Some organizations roll their annual operational needs into the campaign goal so that donors are asked only once for a contribution.
- *Assessment of organizational and fundraising readiness.* This includes a fundraising feasibility study to assess whether there are the donors and prospects needed to raise the money required for the campaign. To find this out, ask the donors or, better yet, hire an outside consultant to ask; you will likely get more candid answers with the latter approach.
- *A campaign plan.* This should lay out the steps, cost, and cash flow for a campaign. This is also the time to develop a formal case statement defining the campaign's purpose. Drafting a case statement should involve all the people who will be centrally involved in the campaign. (It is assumed that the project has, by this point, a financial plan spelling out the best strategy for its conservation—described in more detail in chapter 2).

- *Identification of lead donors.* Identify lead donors, many of whom should come from the board as well as peers who are willing to ask them for gifts. Start cultivation immediately.
- *The campaign gift table or pyramid.* Estimate the specific number of gifts at each major level of giving with specific donors in mind. Once estimated, show the levels graphically. Normally, this looks like a pyramid, with one or two major donors giving the most at the top and with many donors making smaller gifts at the bottom. Be cognizant that some donors who you project to give certain amounts will make surprise giving decisions (both good and bad). Taking some variability into account, the total estimated revenue from all of the gifts at different giving levels will generate the bulk of the money raised for the campaign.
- *Quiet stage of the campaign.* This stage occurs before any public announcements and generally allows the organization to raise about a third to a half of its goal, usually from key major donors and all of the board members. A campaign that has strong community support can go public sooner than a campaign that must build support from scratch. Use the silent stage of the campaign to get ready for the more chaotic public stage. Although it is highly recommended, this strategy is not always possible if the project is very visible and the community is monitoring the land trust's efforts to save it.
- *Public stage of the campaign.* This is the time to solicit the general public and small and major donors; strategies to do so include events, newspaper and radio interviews, mailings, Web links, and much more. When the public announcement is made, the campaign should already have the momentum to be successful. Since people tend to rally around a winner, the momentum will stimulate greater community involvement.
- *Celebration.* A celebration is a great way to thank everyone and to have so much fun that even more people want to be involved to help with the next campaign.

Many books, seminars, and consultants are available to help with capital campaigns. If your organization intends to stretch to meet its goal, if the board or staff is not already very well versed in campaign fundraising, or the campaign has complicated elements, a good campaign consultant can be invaluable. Even a smaller organization should consider assistance, because such issues as appropriate board composition for a campaign can be hard to discuss without

Figure 6.2
Protecting the 166-acre Glenwood Open Space Preserve required a multiyear, multiphase effort by the Land Trust of Santa Cruz County. (©Paul Norcutt)

an outside person raising them. Barbara Dye, of the small Palos Verdes Peninsula Land Conservancy, advises engaging a consultant who understands land acquisition campaigns, not just more generic nonprofit campaigns. She opted to spend her trust's money there and saved money elsewhere by soliciting pro bono help developing and publishing valuable informational materials, including a popular DVD.

To get the most out of a consultant, clearly define his or her job. What *exactly* are you hiring him or her to do? Do you need guidance in how to conduct a campaign? Do you think that a person outside the organization would be better helping you plan the campaign? Do you need help with prospecting for donors or writing the case statement? Do you need extra hands-on help for the duration of the campaign? I have worked on campaigns that successfully used consultants for all those purposes, and others that did not.

I can think of many land trusts with great fundraising records that hire fundraising consultants because they know the value of an experienced outside perspective or just another experienced hand on deck.

My tips for a campaign are as follows:

1. Be prepared for it to take more work and time than anticipated.
2. Make sure that it is fun.
3. Test the water with donors to assess your chances of success.
4. But be ready to stretch.

5. Use a compelling case statement to help shape, articulate, and sell the campaign and to build an internal consensus around the purpose of the campaign.

For all organizations, staffed or not, campaign leadership is essential. These leaders will invest a great deal of time asking many prospects for gifts. They will be involved in planning the campaign, writing and editing letters, thanking the donors, and working with the media. This said, "don't be afraid to set big goals, and don't necessarily wait for every one of a project's elements to be in place (i.e., funding)." These are good words of advice from Rich Cochran, president and CEO of the Western Reserve Land Conservancy in Ohio. The commitment of campaign leadership and the members' determination to succeed will keep the team energized and help you reach the campaign goal.

If the land trust is lucky enough to enlist great leadership, as the Foothills Land Conservancy, in Tennessee, did by enlisting U.S. senator and favorite son Lamar Alexander and Governor Phil Bredesen to lead its campaign, the profile of a campaign will suddenly be elevated, attracting unanticipated, new support.

Putting a big challenge in front of an organization leads to amazing results. "I am a believer that you have to challenge yourself. You must take calculated risks, and then more risks," says Mark Ackelson of the Iowa Natural Heritage Foundation.

As the cost of land rises, so do the goals of capital campaigns. Fortunately, there is, according to Glen Chown of the Grand Traverse Regional Land Conservancy, "no trick to moving into the multimillion-dollar realm. You do the same things you do with smaller deals; just bigger numbers."[10]

Certain circumstances, such as the sudden threat of development to a critical parcel, can compress or truncate planning for a fundraising campaign. Brad Chalfant, of the Deschutes Basin Land Trust in Oregon, got a call from senior management at Willamette Industries the day before the company was being bought out in a hostile takeover. The caller said: "If you want to option the parcel we know you are very interested in acquiring, you have to do it today." There was no time for a feasibility study or campaign planning. Fortunately, the land trust was ready with a good staff, board, and product—the largest and most critical parcel of private land in an entire watershed. And they had some good luck. But planning, if you have the time to do it, helps. Brad admits he wishes he had had that time.

Here are a few words of caution. Though a campaign can energize an organization, everyone must move at lightning speed all the time. It is exhausting. It can strain relationships and disrupt daily operations. Good people may unnecessarily burn out. Everyone in the organization, including the board, should be responsible for making sure this doesn't happen. If necessary, take a breather, go out to dinner together, take another year to complete the campaign, and lower the sights. The health of the organization and its people are more important than meeting every goal exactly on time.

Planned Giving

Planned, deferred, or testamentary gifts are gifts made by donors during their lifetimes or through their estates where a significant gift comes to an organization at a later time or when the donor dies. In general, land trusts must be well established (ten years old) to be credible recipients for these gifts. Donors want to know that the organization will be around for a long time, as planned gifts are often large and are particularly appropriate for funding endowments that by definition have longevity. Stewardship endowments are a particularly good match for planned gifts.

As annual donors become comfortable with your organization, you can begin cultivating them for these gifts. Always suggest planned giving on return envelopes, in newsletters, and elsewhere. Be ready for questions by knowing basic information and retaining an estate planning lawyer for the more sophisticated questions.

Donors have various motivations for making planned gifts to land trusts. Planned gifts of land or conservation easements offer donors peace of mind that the land will be protected forever. If donors have assets to give away upon their death, directing those to a charity they love makes good sense (and sometimes generates tax benefits). By planning for this in their lifetime, they can ensure that the gift will be made and that the recipient organization is prepared.

Mark Ackelson, of the Iowa Natural Heritage Foundation, has some good recommendations for developing a planned giving program.

- Don't try to be more sophisticated or knowledgeable than you need to be, but do have knowledgeable experts to help when you need it.
- Start with simple programs. Over time, more sophisticated programs may enter the mix.

- Be willing to accept planned donations in the context of a capital campaign.
- Have planned gift information brochures available on request. Though they usually don't have enough detail to be technically helpful, they suggest options to donors.
- Most important, define the need. How will you use the money?
- To the extent possible, understand the extent of the existing planned gifts to the organization. Donors may have named your organization in their will and you don't know it! These donors deserve to be appreciated in their lifetimes, both because they have chosen to be very generous but also because wills can be changed. So generate as much publicity as the donor will allow.

The Vermont Land Trust, the Iowa Natural Heritage Foundation, the Maine Coast Heritage Trust and other organizations have good sections on their Web sites on planned giving as well as informative brochures that clearly present the various techniques for donors.[11] Some of these somewhat sophisticated tools allow donors to make tax-deductible gifts, often of appreciated stock or real estate, to a land trust and then be paid a stream of income for a fixed period of time or for the donor's lifetime. They allow donors to turn a nonproductive asset into income, often with income tax and estate tax benefits, and then benefit a charity (such as a land trust).

Planned giving is a marvelous thing. You lose a wonderful friend and devoted land trust supporter only to find out that he or she made a significant planned gift to the organization with lasting value. If you are paying close attention, you will have already known the ship was coming in.

Monitoring and Tracking Donors

Just as with monitoring land protection projects, fundraising requires maintenance. Leslie Mattson-Emerson is vigilant about this. She cautions: "If sixty days go by after a solicitation is made with no response, you will have to start over again with that donor." So don't let that happen. Don't be a pest, but keep in touch through letters, invitations, and visits. Whatever the size of your land trust, develop a method that reminds the responsible person when donors need contact. If the land trust can afford it and commit to use it, a computer program such as Razor's Edge will do much of the reminding for you. But an Excel spreadsheet can work very well too, if one remembers to refer to it. Of course, tracking contacts and gifts is equally important. All of this is just basic sales tracking. The key is doing it. That is where the persistence in the art of fundraising comes in.

Thanking Donors

The two most important acts of fundraising are asking and thanking a donor. Think about how many ways you can thank donors from the heart. This should not be hard, because without donors a land trust could not succeed. Thank donors in person. Thank them in front of an audience, such as at an event. Thank them with a personal handwritten note very soon after their gift is received. Make sure the people writing the thank-you notes are creative writers. A note that says, "Thank you for the gift," is better than no note, but adding several lines about the importance of the gift to the organization, what will be done with the money, and something specific about the donor or new developments in the field is better.

Unless they want to be anonymous, also thank donors publicly in newsletters, at events, with small, thoughtful gifts (nothing big or expensive; they don't

Figure 6.3
Every donor, regardless of the size or type of gift made, deserves a thank-you. (Courtesy of Jackson Hole Center for the Arts)

want to see their money go to buying a gift for them), and in other meaningful ways. One example of a creative acknowledgment is a project of Peninsula
Open Space Trust (POST). For its very major, $100,000-plus donors, POST is
building a circular seating area called the Council Circle along a section of the
California Coastal Trail. Each seat bears a plaque engraved with a donor's
name.

A more modest program that serves as both an incentive for giving and a
thank-you is the "sale" of steps by the Central Pennsylvania Conservancy along
the popular 699-acre Thousand Steps Trail. Donors purchase steps for $100 to
$1,000, and the donor's name appears (along with the number of the partic-
ular step the donor helped to protect) on a sign placed on the property.

The Hail Mary Approach to Fundraising

Though I hesitate to close with this approach to fundraising, anyone who has
been in this business for any length of time has stories to tell about the desperate side of fundraising. Desperation occurs when, for one reason or another,
too much has been risked, too little has been raised, and no time is left.

When Brian Steen was with the Big Sur Land Trust, he was working to save
an eighty-acre redwood forest that was slated for almost immediate timbering.
The monks at an adjacent monastery were deeply concerned about the log-
ging. But when approached by Brian for help, their spokesperson, Brother
Gabriel, said they had little to offer financially as the monastery's funds largely

Figure 6.4
Peninsula Open Space
Trust (POST) built a
public lookout deck
and informational
kiosk near its Council
Circle seating area,
which includes
benches that list the
names of special
donors to POST's $200
million "Saving the En-
dangered Coast" cam-
paign. (©2006 Paolo
Vescia/POST)

came from the seasonal sale of fruitcakes. But Brother Gabriel said he would try to find more help. Brian's own fundraising for the parcel was not going well, and time was running out. Two weeks before he had to come up with the money to purchase the property, Brian met with Brother Gabriel again but the monk could offer only his prayers. Before they parted company, Brother Gabriel calmly looked Brian in the eye and said, "Have faith. God will help out, but he won't do anything before the last minute." This is hardly the kind of consolation that can ease the pressure of a fundraising campaign.

With just days until the closing and with only a small fraction of the money raised, Brian managed to get a second meeting with a family foundation that had turned him down earlier on the project. When he entered their offices, he was met with busy faces and piles of grant proposals on the desk. He realized that he had only a few minutes to make his pitch. He hurriedly rolled out the maps and explained the threat, and the board asked about his fundraising efforts to date. Knowing his time was nearly up, Brian decided to tell them about the monastery and Brother Gabriel's prophecy that God would help out but only at the very last minute. As he told the story, a few smiles appeared as the board members realized they had the power to fulfill the prophecy. Then a motion was made and passed to fund the rest of the project.

Chapter 7
Traditional Fundraising Plans and Sources

When you don't have any money, you have to dream. Document your dreams in a fundraising plan. In the beginning, sitting on the floor of my furnitureless office, I found a pad of paper and started to make a list of sources of money for the new organization I was now running. I made a list and then tried to make reasonable estimates of how much I could raise from each source. Then—the really fun part—I totaled the bottom line, and that was what I would have to raise and be able to spend (!) in that first year.

The fundraising plan for the second year has more of a reality check, using the actual revenue numbers from the first year as the starting point. But you can still dream. Think about those new fundraising initiatives, how you will bump up your major donor gifts, and of an event you want to plan celebrating the organization's first year. These become your second-year dreams.

The Fundraising Plan

Now it is time to create a plan to solicit gifts in different circumstances from a variety of people and institutions. Assuming the land trust is organizationally ready to expand its fundraising activities, it should explore the breadth of traditional sources of giving described in the following sections. Then, as the community becomes inspired by the organization's accomplishments and as relationships develop with funding sources, bigger and more innovative opportunities will emerge.

The first step toward expanding fundraising is to develop a fundraising plan for the upcoming fiscal year that briefly and simply lists all revenue sources and projections for revenue for each.[1] The estimates should be based on the previous year's revenue adjusted for anticipated change and aspirations (new initiatives) in the new year, such as hiring another staff person to help with the individual donor program (anticipate more revenue in those categories) or a downturn in the economy (reduce business revenue). The land trust should develop its budget of expenditure in tandem with the development of its fundraising plan, because it cannot spend more operating money that it is able to raise, unless it has a really good reason to borrow the additional funds and a well-thought-out plan for paying them back (see part 3 of this book). All anticipated revenue should be accounted for in the fundraising plan in a brief (one sentence or two) explanation of the strategy to reach the goal for each revenue category. The plan doesn't have to be long. It should, however, have good numbers and be used to guide the fundraising for the year, not just left on a bookshelf.

If a land trust is ready and chooses to leap forward with a bold new vision for the organization or a major capital campaign and is ready to invest the time and money to do so, revenue numbers can increase dramatically. Big, realistic, well-thought-out visions with buy-in and hard work from the leadership, staff, and volunteers will lead to revenue growth.

Sources of Support

The range of sources from which a land trust can raise money is surprisingly extensive because the missions of land trusts are generally popular and their projects benefit their communities in many ways. The question for an organization is more specifically which sources should be approached first. These are the ones that offer a natural fit with the particular land trust and generate a high potential return *as well as* other benefits to the organization such as expanding its base of support in its community. The ultimate goal, however, is to have a diversity of sources of support.

Small Individual Donors

These are individuals who give small amounts of money to an organization. Small donor relationships should be cultivated and cared for regardless of the amount the donors are able to give. Their gifts can be as significant to them as a large gift is to a major donor. Also, they can usually give more often than major donors.

Small donors are extremely valuable to an organization because they create a community of support that is healthy in its own right and very comforting to major donors who like to know that they are not carrying the entire burden of conservation. And, of course, enough small donors can generate a significant amount of money.

Small donors can also increase their giving, even become major donors if they get excited about the land trust's programs or come into wealth or both. The first gift from a donor who went on to be the largest contributor to an organization with which I work was $100. Brad Chalfant, of the Deschutes Basin Land Trust in Oregon, tells a classic story of being in the middle of his organization's first capital campaign. He was leaving the office, typically late, when the phone rang. He already had his coat on and was heading for the door. He hesitated but then answered the phone. It was one of his small donors calling from Tokyo. After forty-five minutes on the phone and many questions, the donor said, "OK, I like what you are doing. I am going to send you a check for $100,000." Brad spent the next two weeks camped out by his phone, hoping for a replay.

Major Individual Donors

These are individuals who give amounts over a certain threshold. For a land trust that generates most of its revenue from small donations, the definition of a major donor might be someone who gives over $100 or $500. For organizations, usually larger ones, that receive much larger contributions, a large donor may be defined as one who gives $1,000 or even $100,000. Major donors are a special breed because their gifts account for the bulk of the private money that most nonprofits receive. Without major donors, most charitable organizations would not survive. So the support, interest, and commitment of these donors should be reinforced and strengthened continually. It takes a significant investment of time to cultivate major donors. For this reason, it is highly unlikely that a nonprofit will have as many major donors as small donors. Some ways to strengthen major donor support follow.

- Take very seriously the role that major donors play in the land trust's success.
- Learn from these donors. Their position of wealth often reflects a set of unusual talents. As a result, they may have wisdom that can benefit the organization. Enjoy their company, too.

- Invite them out for a meal, an individual meeting, or a small gathering to update them on the organization's recent activities.
- Organize field trips or events exclusively for donors. (Donors have been known to make a special donation of the threshold amount just to attend an exclusive event held only for major donors.)
- Recognize them at larger events and in newsletters.
- Send them periodic personalized, informational letters from the board chair or executive director that do *not* ask for money.

As expert fundraiser and the president of Peninsula Open Space Trust, Audrey Rust, says: "Almost anyone today who has the capacity to make a large gift can get more recognition and status from other organizations than from yours. Therefore you have to find a way to set yourself apart, and win hearts and minds. If you can, try something new, something that takes one's breath away. Remember that land can offer a legacy."

Foundations

Foundations have always intimidated me, even when I worked for them. The fancy offices and general well-funded feeling exude confidence. As a foundation staff person, it is easy to develop an air of self-importance when aspiring grantees hang on your every word. Gone are the days when calls are not returned. I often marveled at how my calls seemed to be returned even before I made them. Really good foundation funders work hard to maintain their humility and stick right to the task of foundations: strategically giving money to achieve their mission.[2]

There are two types of foundations: private and public. The assets of a private foundation are mostly from a single source, usually an individual, family, or corporation. Private foundations must make "qualifying distributions," grants of at least 5 percent of the average market value of their assets in a given fiscal year by the end of the following year. This requirement is often called "the payout requirement."

The assets of a public foundation normally come from multiple sources, which may include private foundations, individuals, public agencies, and fees for service, and are raised annually. To retain public status, a public foundation must continue to receive funds from diverse sources.

Family, corporate, and community foundations should be of particular interest to land trusts, because they often support local community efforts. (These foundation types are described in more detail later in this chapter.)

In addition to their commitment to giving money away, foundations have a strong interest in their grantees' success. By making a grant to your land trust, foundations—like individual donors—become investors in your program. Most take that role very seriously and can be very loyal. Like individuals, they want to give to successful projects. Finding a foundation officer who believes in the work of your land trust adds a powerful and effective person to your team. Once committed, foundation staff can help you succeed not only with grants and loans (program-related investments) but also by advocating your project with other foundations and funders. Don't abuse this privilege, though, by asking your foundation officer to make too many endorsement contacts.

People give to people, and foundation people are no exception. Ask your board and donors to search their networks of friends for contacts and introductions. If a foundation is staffed, use the contact for advice but work through the staff member.

Tom Bailey, of the Little Traverse Conservancy, advises careful research before applying for a foundation grant to make sure that the foundation's interest matches that of the organization. Here are a few other tips for finding and approaching foundations that may be most appropriate for your organization.

- Talking to the staff of a community foundation is the best way to find out the foundation's level of interest in land conservation. Community foundations may have donors who have particular interests in conservation and donor-advised funds that support conservation.
- Identify foundations that give only in support of specific species or habitats and match projects that protect those species or their habitats. The Jackson Hole Land Trust received grants from the National Fish and Wildlife Foundation, the Rocky Mountain Elk Foundation, and the Foundation for North American Wild Sheep for a parcel that protected critical elk, deer, and mountain sheep habitat.
- Research answers to as many of your own questions before meeting with the foundation, so that you use the meeting and the foundation's staff time most efficiently.
- Many foundations give regionally and have quite general guidelines tied to regional needs.

If a land trust has done its research, it can usually find a foundation that supports its mission, but that is only the first step. It is more effective to focus on a few likely candidate foundations than to send out inquiries to hundreds. Foundations do not take kindly to mass mailings or casual, informal approaches. They usually have formal application procedures. They meet only at certain times of the year, often quarterly, to approve applications and to decide on the size of the grants. Some, especially larger foundations, do not accept unsolicited applications.

Foundations can offer the kind of support that is hard to find from any other type of donor. Often, their support can be for more than one year, especially in the case of regional, local, or family foundations. Many are interested in new ways to solve problems or grant seed money to start organizations or new programs.

Foundations like a big, clear vision, either geographically or on policy or strategy. For example, several years ago, the Doris Duke Charitable Foundation chose several ecologically important regions of the country in which to make grants. After meeting with organizations in each region, it developed multitiered conservation funding strategies in those areas and funded local and regional conservation organizations with large grants for a discrete period of time.[3]

Foundations can also be interested in helping organizations with acquisitions. The Kresge Foundation is well known for its challenge grants to help stimulate giving at the end of a capital campaign especially for buildings and to build institutional capacity. Kresge, like others, has an extensive application process that encourages applicants to demonstrate support within a community and to clearly articulate the reasons the organization should receive support. The National Fish and Wildlife Foundation more commonly supports conservation acquisitions of important wildlife habitat requiring clear, thorough thinking about the project and proactive initiatives that involve the community.

Foundations can play other essential roles. The Vermont Land Trust is supported by the Freeman Foundation, which pays stewardship-related costs such as title search, property mapping, baseline documentation, and stewardship endowments when easement donors are unable to cover the full costs.[4] Another foundation helps a land trust pay the difference between the purchase price for conservation land and its lower resale price encumbered with a conservation easement. Other foundations support organizational capacity build-ing—recognizing the value of adding personnel to an organization.

All foundations must file a 990-PF form with the Internal Revenue Service, which is a valuable source of information on their finances, board members, and grants. The Foundation Center, which has an extensive Web site (http://www.fdncenter.org), is a great source of information on foundations. The Center has a database of all filed 990-PFs. The Center's Foundation Directory (online or in hard copy) has very useful information on most foundations.

The types of foundations of particular interest to land trusts are described below.

Private independent foundations. These are mission-driven foundations governed by an independent volunteer board. Many independent foundations began as family foundations and evolved into independent institutions.

Family foundations. Private family foundations are funded with the assets of a single family or individual and are often governed by the foundation's benefactor or the benefactor's family. Family foundations are a type of private foundation that can approach giving quite differently than other independent foundations. Family members sit on the board and can have great influence. Small family foundations are harder to research, are more informal, and have broad discretion in giving. Knowing a family member is a good way to get the attention of unstaffed family foundations and to have an advocate for your program at the meetings.

Community foundations. Through a community foundation, community members—including individuals, families, businesses, and organizations—raise and pool financial resources to support programs in a community or region. A volunteer board of citizens and community leaders (who are not necessarily donors) provides leadership for this public foundation. A professional staff that knows the community's needs administers the funds and grant making. The number of community foundations has grown in recent years, creating new opportunities in addition to more funding for land conservation.

Many community foundations offer an assortment of services to donors, such as providing information on local and regional charitable organizations and monitoring charitable gifts. Some donors earmark their gifts to particular areas or organizations through donor-advised funds.

(The recent emergence of large funds sponsored by investment firms, including Fidelity and Schwab, are essentially modeled on the community foundation aggregate of donor-advised funds.) Other donors commit their funds anonymously. For nonprofits, they offer funding opportunities, educational programs, and connections to individual donors.

The Mount Grace Land Conservation Trust makes use of its local Community Foundation of Western Massachusetts's investment services. The community foundation invests a portion of the land trust's savings along with its other funds. The land trust has reaped many other benefits, including greater exposure among the foundation's donors through its annual report and informational video. In 2005, the Community Foundation of Western Massachusetts and the Greater Worcester Community Foundation granted a total of $35,000 to the land trust for specific land protection projects. Leigh Youngblood, the land trust's executive director, says that the grants give her organization another opportunity to build its network because the foundations' volunteer grant reviewers interview the land trust each time it applies and thereby continue to learn more about conservation. In general though, land trusts underutilize community foundations.

Corporate foundations. The private corporate foundation is funded and run by a for-profit corporation with which the foundation is associated. The objectives of these foundations are discussed in the following section.

Business and Corporate Interests

Businesses require a different approach and a different maintenance strategy because they often expect a specific benefit in return for their support. After all, their objectives are very different from those of nonprofits—they are in the business of making a financial return. Businesses can give goods, services, and cash. Corporations can support land trusts with advertising dollars and corporate foundation dollars. Their employees can be a source of expertise, volunteers, and donors who have matching support from their employers. Other examples of successful local business partnerships are described in chapters 8, 9, and 16.

A popular land trust with a good reputation can offer what Rebecca Chapman, vice president for philanthropy of the Peconic Land Trust, on Eastern Long Island, calls "the halo effect." Association with a land trust is a kind of unspoken endorsement for a company—a part of its marketing strategy. If a land trust is able to marry its interests with a company's marketing interests, then it can become part of the corporate marketing strategy, not just a recipient of its charitable giving.

Companies can usually make contributions through advertising more easily than straight, no-strings-attached contributions of cash. A onetime commitment to an event sponsorship or an advertisement in an event's program booklet is a simple first approach. The business will monitor the exposure they get from its investment. If the experience is positive, a longer-term relationship might be possible.

A good example of a simple land conservation–business relationship is the Business Partners program sponsored by the Nantucket Conservation Foundation. Participating businesses display the foundation's logo in their shop windows and in their advertising. The foundation lists its business partners in its annual report. Partners are invited to foundation events, including breakfasts during which the foundation asks for feedback about its program. Gage Dobbins, development director at the Nantucket Conservation Foundation, says that the program is "an education tool that goes both ways." The foundation staff learns from the business members and vice versa. Furthermore, the business partners pass this information on to their customers, thereby helping the foundation's network grow. For example, agents at a partnering real estate firm introduce their new (and likely affluent) clients to the foundation.

Also, major individual donors to the foundation are impressed that it has such vital other sources of revenue. The program has helped connect business partners with one another. Gage says it encourages healthy competition among them in support of the foundation.

Raising money from larger corporations is a different matter. How many times have you heard someone say, "This place is so beautiful. Let's ask Eastman Kodak Company for money." Save the postage. The chances improve, though, if the company does business in your service area *and* a personal connection to company leadership exists. This personal relationship is important. This is not to say that corporations don't support conservation in other instances. In response to consumer concern about health and the environment, corporations are becoming more socially responsible and in many cases are changing the way they do business.[5] Corporate philanthropy is generally trending upward with increases in corporate profits, as has the expenditure of corporate advertising dollars with charitable partners.[6] For a small organization with modest resources, larger corporations are more likely to take an interest if there is a distinctive overlap of service area geography and either a personal relationship with the corporation's board or senior management through a land trust board member or donor, or a corporate officer who takes a particular interest.

To identify appropriate candidate corporations, Rebecca Chapman urges land trusts to stay informed about the business world and local and regional news. She reads the *Wall Street Journal* daily and all the regional newspapers. She wants to know how companies are doing, whether certain ones may be interested in moving into her land trust's service area, how they are perceived, and why they are in the news.

To begin the cultivation process, identify a small number of companies on which to focus that are represented on the land trust's board or to which board members have a direct connection. If there are none, consider putting a person on the board with corporate connections. Some companies have a natural interest in your area or mission. The sporting-life clothing and supply company Orvis picked up on the Deschutes Basin Land Trust's efforts to protect the key parcel in the Metolius watershed—an area world renowned for its fisheries. Through its catalog and Web site, the company urged millions of readers to support the project.

Rebecca Chapman explains that companies are looking for nonprofit organizations that can "become part of their business strategy."[7] They want to know that the land trust has a good reputation and an audience that the company wants to reach, and they want to know how that audience will be informed about the corporate partnership.

The Peconic Land Trust built, over time, a strong relationship with the KeySpan Foundation and its executive director, Robert Keller. KeySpan is a utility company invested in Long Island, New York, where the Peconic Land Trust is located. The Peconic Land Trust recognizes the importance to corporations of return on investment. The land trust has a strong high-quality image in the service areas of a number of companies. If a company is trying to improve its image, associating with a well-known "green" organization is more efficient than associating with an unknown one.

The Peconic Land Trust is a very good example of a land trust that recognizes the value of its logo (a scallop shell) and its brand. The shell is on all of its informational material and publications. The more branding an organization has done, the more attractive it will be to a company.

To succeed with a corporation, Rebecca stresses that a land conservation organization has to rethink the way it generally views corporations. It must thoroughly understand the corporate culture and learn what its funding partner—the corporation—needs. She advises "not to rush to the altar. Start small and deliver big." Develop relationships over time; invite the program officer out on the site, plan and execute public relations activities that showcase the program and the funder, and involve them in any media releases regarding projects they have funded.[8]

As this partnership develops, many opportunities for benefits will arise. Beyond the very real benefits of sponsorships and corporate foundation grants is a myriad of goods and services. More than a third of corporate giving is in kind.[9] Company products are frequently donated. The corporation's public relations department can help develop a media plan and work on the wording and distribution of press releases, the company's planners can help with outcome and vision for a strategic plan, and company vendors can be asked to participate and donate goods and services. In addition and depending on its size, the company has an internal audience for the land trust message. Some land trusts have special days when the employees and families of their corporate sponsors are invited to visit land trust projects.

Finally, ethical questions can arise from getting support from some corporations. So choose your partners carefully. A company that is working against the land trust's mission, whether intentionally or unintentionally, is obviously not a good choice for a partnership. For example, a company that is trying to develop land that the land trust is working to conserve is not appropriate. On a larger scale, a corporation with a high media profile because of a government dispute over emissions standards could damage a land trust's reputation even though the land trust doesn't get involved in clean air issues. Merely by association, a well-respected land trust "greens up" its corporate partner. A disreputable corporation can have the opposite effect on a land trust and diminish the value of its brand. The land trust must carefully consider the benefits and consequences of accepting money or goods or services from a corporation to be sure that the reputation of the land trust is not endangered.

Some nonprofits have policies to help them determine whether they should partner with a particular organization and have set up a procedure for vetting organizations. This is a good idea. Branding is big business, so consult an expert to help your land trust protect (and develop) the value of its brand.

Creating Opportunities for Giving

A perfect way to begin building funding partnerships with corporations as well as others who are unfamiliar with your conservation programs is to involve their employees in your work in the most enjoyable ways. Look for ways to further their interests while furthering yours. Create easy, enticing opportunities for new constituencies to participate. Inviting them to events is one good way because event enthusiasm is contagious. Design these opportunities so that you make your product as accessible and understandable to them as possible. The next sections describe some of the ways to do that.

Events

Hats off to event planners! Can you imagine working for months to lure hundreds of people with high expectations of being entertained to a place—usually outside, if a land trust wants to showcase a project—where one has no control of the weather, the noise, or the temperature?

I have organized events where the lightning was so intense we were certain it would hit the tent pole and we would die, where the culinary centerpiece—a large, roasted pig—was cooked down to just a few white cinders, and where the sound system was so bad that only the very closest tables could hear the speaker, causing the other four hundred people to return to their own conversations, further contributing to the cacophony.

The latest problem plaguing events I have attended is speakers arriving late because of flight delays. I attended an event at which we were given delicious wine while we waited for the delayed speaker. We forgot the time but, sadly, also the speech. At another event, guests were leaving the freezing, windy, and rain-worn tent as the speaker arrived. Event planning is a tough business.

This is why I am always so impressed when I attend a truly wonderful event. There is nothing better than an evening well spent listening to a great speaker at a great venue with wonderful company and decent or better food. Such an event will be successful for fundraising, for prospecting new members, and for generating enthusiasm for an organization or a capital campaign.

And, there are subtler benefits. First, developing an invitation list is a great excuse for board members to get out holiday card lists to suggest names. While those same board members might be reluctant to hand over names for a fundraising solicitation, an invitation to an event is a softer sell. I work with an organization that, at one time, had a very small base of support but an international reach and had sworn off direct mail. It was faced with the challenge of finding new supporters to finance its operations. I suggested events. The first one, held in New York City, was purely for cultivation (i.e., by invitation but free). Thanks to great leadership and a strong dinner committee, an unusual venue, excellent speakers, and a good sound system, the event was such a success that guests paid to come back the next year and brought their friends. Now the organization holds at least three of these a year, raises millions, and has a long list of new prospects (and many, many more donors).

Some other possible benefits of events include the following:

- Involving a spectrum of donors in a variety of fundraising opportunities through graduated ticket prices, table sponsorships, and auctions (silent or otherwise), with donations made amid the excitement stimulated by the event. One cautionary note: make sure the ticket prices and donation opportunities match the audience's means. Also, it is best to presell everything (i.e., tables, tickets, and minimum auction bids), then all of the proceeds from the actual event go to benefit the organization.
- Demonstrating to major donors that a program or project is popular and that peers and others in the community are supporting it.
- Initiating relationships with new sectors of the community, such as the business sector, that might want to advertise in the event program booklet or participate in kind.
- Offering an opportunity to receive in-kind gifts of food, supplies, printing, decorations, and hands-on help.
- Giving smaller donors and volunteers a way, through sweat equity, to raise a lot of money for the organization.
- Generating interest and curiosity among nonattendees.

When organizing an event, even a small one to raise money for that threatened neighborhood property, identify a committed and ideally prominent host and create a reception or event committee since events are logistically demanding. The host and committee should develop a strong invitation list. However, written invitations alone are not good enough. Attendance vastly improves when friends invite friends, even committing to bring a specific number of friends or raise a certain amount of money. Committee members should attract sponsors, sell tables, or do everything if the organization is unstaffed!

Committee members can suggest a convenient event time and venue. A host's home is a good choice for small receptions. Some will attend just to meet the host (and see the house). Recently, I organized an event at the home of a prominent project endorser whose home was near those of the invitees. Attendance was high. A less formal gathering after work might be conveniently held at the host's offices.

The committee should create a buzz about the event. To amplify the buzz, some committee members should be endorsers, lending their names but not time. Regular committee meetings will build enthusiasm. Some organizations invite speakers to meetings to energize the group for the hard work of event planning.

To keep expectations in line with results, be clear about the purpose of the event. Is it cultivation or fundraising or both? A cultivation event is to pique interest in the land trust or project. That event is not likely to make much money, and it may even cost money. The solicitation happens after the event.

A fundraising event raises money at the event itself. Some events are intended to make a targeted amount of money but are mostly cultivation, and vice versa. Gauge whether your prospects and donors will be ready to buy a ticket to a fundraising event; cultivation events may be required first to pique interest. A happy compromise is to enlist a small core of supporters to sponsor the event and then charge a small entrance fee or nothing. Then at least expenses can be covered and some revenue generated.

Find the right "event niche." Consider a theme that is consistent with the mission of the organization. You can check out other successful events in the community and model yours after them. Or, be daring and find an unfilled niche. A particular event may not be hugely successful initially, but if the theme and structure seems to have good potential to generate money or new prospects down the road, keep after it for a few years because most new events start small and build a following over time.

Figure 7.1

What better way to celebrate a profitable recycling program than with a Party at the Dump? The Rattlesnake Gutter Trust's event includes a Dump Kings Coronation, staged "rat" attack, music by the Dumpettes, and other creative festivities. (Rattlesnake Gutter Trust's Annual Meeting)

Box 7.1 Ideas for Events

- Kayak, canoe, or barge trips
- Owling, birding, or natural history field trips
- Field trips to owned or conserved land led by a landowner/biologist/historian
- Campfire talks on the history of the region
- Visiting speakers or panel discussions
- Awards dinners and informal barbeques
- Openings of movies, plays, or galleries
- Auctions (silent and live)—art and others from which all or a percentage of the sale price goes to a land trust
- Small neighborhood receptions
- Tours of wineries, houses, or other interesting venues

Leah Whidden, director of development for the Western Reserve Land Conservancy, describes a new event they sponsored last year that couldn't be more consistent with a land trust's mission. Searching for a different structure that gave guests more time to socialize, they decided to have a very short program to auction off their mission—one hundred acres of conservation for $50,000, at $500 per acre. Guests bid to protect acres in open space. Everyone who bid for acres, not just the highest bidder, donated their bid amount. For example, four guests bid a total of $10,000 for twenty acres. The fundraising part was over in roughly ten minutes, and the organization raised $101,000. Everyone left with a Norway or blue spruce sapling as a party favor.

Except when events are exclusively for existing donors, Joan Flanagan reminds us that eventgoers are not yet donors, even if they have bought a ticket to the event.[10] The real fundraising work around events is the follow-up—asking the guests to give immediately after the event now that it has instilled interest. The challenge is to keep up the energy level so that the solicitors, often the same people who served on the dinner committee, are willing to help with follow-up donation requests. Make sure that this expectation is understood from the onset.

Small events are appropriate for organizations that don't have a lot of hands-on help or that have a smaller constituency. They can be useful for fundraising and great for cultivation or education. Putting on a small event is also the best way to learn the ropes for doing bigger ones later. As an organization grows, these smaller events still have their place as more intimate gatherings for special donors or prospects. However, as another land trust fundraiser says, "if the purpose is raising money, big events can make big money."

Whatever the size, events are nerve-wracking and stressful, and they require obsessive attention to detail. But they should also be fun and should showcase the creativity and strength of the organization. So the trick is to find someone to organize the event who has contagious enthusiasm for the cause as well as nerves of steel.

Anniversaries

An anniversary or birthday is a great excuse to raise money. The anniversary can be the land trust's or the donor's or can mark just about anything, such as a historic occasion or the date the organization received its first easement. While celebrating the land trust's first, fifth, or tenth birthday is very common, supporting conservation as part of the celebration of an anniversary of a business or an individual is less so.

Some donors have been motivated to celebrate these milestones through conservation. The board of the Henry Francis du Pont Winterthur Museum gave a conservation easement over the 908-acre Winterthur estate in celebration of the estate's fiftieth birthday as a museum.[11] The Conservation Fund, and ten partnering organizations, including the Chesapeake Bay Foundation and the National Geographic Society, are working to celebrate the four-hundredth anniversary of the founding of Jamestown and Captain John Smith's monumental exploration of the Chesapeake Bay region by establishing the Captain John Smith Chesapeake National Watertrail. The water trail will be a boating and driving trail that will bring new focus on restoring the bay.[12] By choosing a historic event, the organizations are connecting a special natural place with nationally important historical events and therefore broadening the reach of the campaign through heritage tourism.

Corporations often celebrate anniversaries with gifts as well. The Toyota Motor Manufacturing Corporation made a $25,000 grant in support of the Kentucky Natural Lands Trust Pine Mountain Legacy Project, which promotes sustainable forestry practices, as part of its twentieth anniversary celebration of its plant in Kentucky.[13]

Holiday Gifts and Memorials

Gifts to organizations in lieu of holiday giving are a growing phenomenon. In the winter of 2003, Senator Lamar Alexander of Tennessee and several of his neighbors donated a seven-hundred-acre conservation easement to the Foothills Land Conservancy and The Conservation Fund as a holiday gift.[14] The Potomac Conservancy, which works to protect the Potomac River and its tributaries near Washington, D.C., was part of an alternative gift fair at which visitors could shop for appropriate organizations to support financially in lieu of making holiday gifts. The organizations notify each person that a gift has been made in his or her name. To generate funding from gift fairs, land trusts must make the donations seem "tangible" by strengthening the connection between the gift amounts and the specific benefit they will provide.[15]

Memorial and honorarium gifts are used more frequently. What better way to honor or memorialize someone than through the perpetual gift of conservation? The Iowa Natural Heritage Foundation and the Little Traverse Conservancy have built cultures around these forms of giving. The Little Traverse Conservancy's Web site describes honoring others as "A Living Legacy through Permanently Protected Land." It suggests remembering a special occasion or person while helping conserve land. The program generally raises between $50,000 and $65,000 annually.[16]

The Iowa Natural Heritage Foundation raises $15,000 to $25,000 per year from a similar program. The foundation's president, Mark Ackelson, describes a donor couple who made memorial gifts to the land trust of $7.50 every year for fifteen years. They ended up making a significant planned gift in their will. In another case, a donor's marriage announcement was featured in the *Des Moines Register* suggesting that donations be sent to the land trust in lieu of wedding gifts. A few days later, the land trust was flooded with "in honor" gifts. Another donor periodically sends an envelope of multiple checks from friends, endorsed over to the land trust. As Mark says, "People have so much stuff now. It's more than they need, so they want to make a different kind of gift."

At least twice a year, memorials and honoraria are listed in the land trust's newsletter, thereby recognizing the donor and the honoree publicly. Donors are also thanked personally and sent another "in memoriam" form, which they can use to make another gift. The land trust notifies the honored or, in the case of memorials, the next of kin that the gift has been made, without disclosing the exact amount. A land trust must put in place a modest system so that acknowledgments are processed smoothly, but it is worth it. It provides another way to also start that ever-crucial relationship building.

Special and Community-based Fundraising Projects

The momentum created by a capital campaign to save a well-loved piece of

Figure 7.2
The sign on the Tennessee River Gorge Wishing Well at the Tennessee Aquarium asks passersby to drop in a coin to help protect the Gorge, adding, "Your change will make a change!" (The Wishing Well supports the Tennessee River Gorge Land Trust's land preservation efforts)

land can stimulate amazing acts of generosity and creativity from a community. Often, an entirely new way of raising money emerges from an enthusiastic community. The most creative ideas for financing conservation come from surprising sources, such as developers, business owners, retirees, and elementary school classrooms. For example, children donated birthday money to the Aquidneck Island Land Trust in Rhode Island to ensure that Third Beach, which they used and loved, continued to be accessible to the public as part of a campaign to expand a bird sanctuary. Tennessee schoolchildren donated the cost of one soft drink and thus raised $70,000 for the Foothills Land Conservancy's 4,700-acre Adams Creek campaign adjacent to Great Smoky Mountains National Park.[17] Randy Brown, the Foothills Land Conservancy's former executive director, spoke often at schools throughout the campaign. The Tennessee River Gorge Trust and the Tennessee Aquarium partnered on a coin drop at the aquarium that is designed to look like a tree trunk. The coin drop is particularly popular with children, who like to watch the coins spiral down the trunk.

The small Rattlesnake Gutter Land Trust in Massachusetts sponsors a labor-intensive, community-based recycling program. It has raised over $40,000 and is the pride and joy of the volunteers who run it. If placed end to end, the recycled cans would extend from Massachusetts to the top of Mt. Everest.

On a larger scale, the wrestling coach at the local high school in Marysville, Tennessee, approached the Foothills Land Conservancy about sharing in the revenue from recycling printer cartridges. There are several large factories in the area that manufacture mechanical parts for cars and use large printer cartridges. The coach built a warehouse to store the cartridges and was transporting them to Chattanooga for recycling, passing off the loads to his daughter halfway. During his tenure with the Conservancy, Randy visited the manufacturing plants to invite them to participate in the program. He gave them large white bins for collection with the Conservancy's name and phone number clearly displayed. When the bins were full, the employees called him and he or his volunteers picked them up. In addition to generating money for the land trust, Randy says that it was a great way for him to meet many people, especially in middle management, whom he might not otherwise have met.

Another source of community funding for land conservation is service organizations. This source is underutilized by conservation organizations because it has historically given to other sectors of the community. But when strong community support for conservation exists, these clubs can be meaningful contributors. Most service clubs, such as Rotary, Kiwanis, and Zonta, conduct annual fundraisers and award the proceeds to nonprofit organizations doing important work in their communities. Many service clubs have formed foundations and have established grant programs with standard guidelines and applications. One Rotary Club in Traverse City, Michigan, formed a foundation in 1978 when oil and gas were discovered on land the club leased to the local Boy Scout Council for camping activities. Rotary Charities of Traverse City, a nonprofit foundation, actually helped to form the Grand Traverse Regional Land Conservancy (GTRLC). Since the inception of GTRLC twelve years ago, Rotary Charities has given more than $800,000 to support its startup, land acquisition activities, and operating endowment. Though this particular Rotary collaboration is unusual, many other service clubs have a commitment to land preservation, interested members willing to volunteer, and the ability to provide substantial financial support.

Sales

T-shirts, caps, sweatshirts? Are these the only items that nonprofits can think to sell? No, there are tote bags, calendars, greeting cards, food, and so on. Well-designed items that support a strong program still sell well. Everyone seems to need T-shirts and caps, even though they are sold absolutely everywhere. But why not add a new twist? How about using organic cotton or selling work gloves for habitat improvement projects? Some land trusts are branching out.

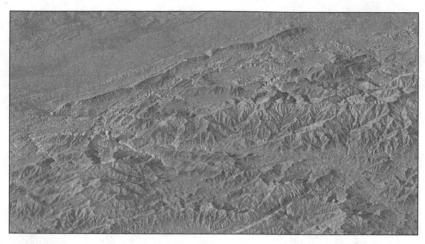

Figure 7.3
The Foothills Land Conservancy offers for sale on its Web site a high-resolution poster of the Great Smoky Mountains. (Courtesy of Foothills Land Conservancy)

For example, the Foothills Land Conservancy has created a beautiful, high-resolution thirty-nine- by twenty-seven-inch poster of the Great Smoky Mountains and foothills made from USGS 30 Meter Digital Elevation models, which it sells for $25.

Sale items are a good vehicle for getting the organization's brand out on the street. The more the public can identify an organization through its brand, the more the organization will be remembered and, the theory goes, supported. Surprisingly, organizations rarely record the names of the people who buy sales items, which would add a third and very valuable dimension of expanding the mailing list. But beware of getting sidetracked with this labor-intensive relatively low-return investment or letting inventory build up.

Obviously, the less it costs to produce the items, the more revenue that will be generated. Ask the printer, the photographer, or the T-shirt, hat, and tote manufacturers to donate or discount the item or service.

Conclusion

Traditional fundraising is the stepping stone to innovation. While land conservation is strengthening its core support and building its capacity to do its important work through grant requests to foundations and solicitations to major donors, it is using that momentum to reach farther—to expand its network in new ways into new places. A small donor talks to a major donor prospect who happens to be a bank president, who loans the land trust money. An art lover attends a land trust–sponsored art auction (remember to meet new constituencies where they are most comfortable), then tells his wife, who is public relations director for a corporation that is planning a celebration of its tenth anniversary. She calls to brainstorm about ideas for sponsoring the land trust as part of the festivities. A volunteer brings her aunt, who serves on the board of the community foundation, to your annual event. The next thing you know you are invited to submit a proposal. Pleased by the success of the grant and at your suggestion, the community foundation establishes a revolving fund for conservation.

Innovation builds off of tradition. So as you develop your annual fundraising plan, if it is solid with a good track record of meeting its goals, push the envelope a little. Plan for something that reaches beyond the traditional—not dangerously beyond but just far enough to attract new thinking and more support to your good conservation work.

Chapter 8
Voluntary Surcharges

A small charge that a business adds to a customer's bill that is given to a nonprofit and that the customer can remove voluntarily.

Ethan Hicks was frustrated with local development pressures. He had watched a developer turn a popular place for hiking, biking, and camping—a mountainside bench overlooking his beloved Crested Butte, Colorado—into sprawling trophy homes. He had no idea his frustration and disappointment would lead him to invent one of the most effective revenue-generating techniques for the local land trusts.

Ethan served on the advisory board for the young Crested Butte Land Trust, which formed in the wake of the development of the bench. As this new land trust was getting established, Ethan saw the huge disparity between the cost of land being developed and the ability of the land trust to raise the millions of dollars needed to conserve it. He thought that the land trust's efforts weren't going to make a difference fast enough. The athletic and intense Ethan wasn't about to give up. Because he was in the clothing business, he was aware that the outdoor clothing company Patagonia Inc. donated 1 percent of its gross revenues to environmental causes.[1] He thought something like that might work in Crested Butte.

When he suggested to the local Rotary Club his idea that local stores request a voluntary gift for conservation from their customers, Ethan was surprised by the lack of enthusiasm. Ethan persevered. "I had a position in the community where I could do it on my own," he explained. As owner of the popular sporting goods store the Alpineer, he decided to try a donation program anyway. "Not as a publicity thing, just to help the land trust," he recalled. When he announced his plan to ask for donations for open space with everything he sold in the store, it made quite a splash. As Ethan tells it: "On the first day we started, a lot of people came into the store just to participate." The local

Figure 8.1
The Alpineer was the first retail store in Crested Butte, Colorado, to add a voluntary 1 percent donation on its sales for the benefit of land conservation. (Courtesy of The Alpineer)

newspaper covered it, and the popular morning radio show did a story. Businesses called in to the station asking how they could sign up. The land trust got calls too, and within a week the land trust had the framework of a program in place.

Ethan's determination to step out in front to preserve Crested Butte set an example and built momentum. "I came up with the idea, and it evolved from there," he says. Over sixty businesses—from restaurants, retail stores, and guiding companies to doctors, attorneys, an acupuncturist, realtors, newspapers, and even an animal hospital—now participate. In 2006, the income from the program was $34,935. Since its inception in 1997, the program has raised over $1.18 million.

The brilliance of the program is in its design. Unlike the Patagonia program (known as 1% for the Planet), businesses participating in Crested Butte's 1% for Open Space program add the 1 percent to every customer's bill. The money comes from the customer, not the business. If, for instance, a customer buys a $300 ski jacket at the Alpineer, a $3 donation is added to the bill. If a tourist stays three nights at a participating local hotel and the bill is $150 dollars, $1.50 is added to the bill.

In all cases, customers have ample opportunity to remove the donation if they don't want to make it. Informational signs are posted, and opt-out procedures are clearly stated. Store staff are trained to explain the program to every customer. Few customers choose not to make the gift, only a very small percentage of the customers—ironically, less than 1 percent. At Ethan's store, only four or five people a year say no. When it happens, he gives their money back, "right out of the till—so the store pays for it. I don't want to get into protracted discussions," he says.

Most businesses use the program's preferred percent method of support, though some give a set amount each year, such as $100, and don't ask their customers to participate. Some real estate companies give a donation from each home sale, basing the size on either a percentage of the broker's commission or a predetermined amount. These variations may be a consequence of philosophical differences in how business owners want to collect the money and whether or not they want to involve their customers in the process.

Early Crested Butte Land Trust board members David Baxter and Glo Cunningham helped Ethan get the 1 percent program going. Ethan was particularly influential in addressing the questions of business owners and recruiting them to join. Other board members helped to work out technical problems, investing many hours dealing with the mechanics and logistics of the program.

Figure 8.2

Participating businesses in the "1% for Open Space" program post signs to inform customers about the program. (Courtesy of 1% for Open Space)

Initially, there was a small but strong negative reaction to the idea. "I got all kinds of hate mail when I first did it," recalls Ethan. "Some said that they weren't going to participate because they thought it would eventually become a mandatory tax. A lot of people had a lot to say about where the program was going to lead us. Now, it's just the way business is done."

The subsequent owner who bought the store from Ethan and continued supporting the 1 percent program said that tourists don't even notice the donation. They are on vacation and aren't really looking at the bill. The locals are very aware of it, but it is in their interest, too, to see land conservation efforts succeed. "That is the beauty of it. Everyone who benefits from the natural beauty of the area contributes to the program," he said.

The 1% for Open Space program gave the Crested Butte Land Trust a tremendous boost.[2] It legitimized the organization. It didn't take long, though, for the board to recognize that it needed staff to administer this quickly growing program as well as to handle many other functions. Now they had the money to pay for staff. They hired Vicki Church to administer the conservation programs that had become more prominent as a result of the 1% for Open Space program and to promote and sign up more businesses. Initially, though, as a volunteer organization, the board designed the materials, set up the program, and promoted it in the business community.

Vicki needed to decide the clearest way for customers to become informed and to note the donation on the bill charged, the best way for them to opt out of the program, and how businesses should submit the funds to the land trust. She had to make sure that the businesses had all of the materials and training they needed to make the program function smoothly. She estimates that in those early years, 1% for Open Space took between 30 and 50 percent of her time. All land trusts that now have voluntary surcharge programs have benefited from the good work of Vicki and the Crested Butte Land Trust's board in developing these mechanisms.

In January 2001, the 1% for Open Space program was spun off into a separate organization that is now run on a part-time basis by Molly Murfee.[3] The land trust created an independent program to make funding available to other organizations working on open space programs. Molly trains business staff, collects the money, solicits new businesses, distributes materials, and, says Molly, writes press releases "every time someone sneezes" (see online appendices at www.conservationguide.com). A volunteer accountant helps new participating businesses set up their systems. The program receives other volunteer support, such as for managing its Web site.

Participating businesses must post signs in two places in their stores or offices. 1% for Open Space Inc. provides envelopes for submitting the money,
which most businesses do monthly. As a thank-you to the participating businesses and as a subtle nudge to stay with the program, 1% for Open Space Inc.
publishes a biweekly thank-you advertisement in the local newspaper. Its five-
person board meets monthly to review applications for grant money. They
have not yet had to choose between competing projects. Grants range from
$5,000 to $35,000 and have resulted in the protection of more than 2,500 acres.

Because the money goes to support land acquisition projects, Crested Butte
Land Trust is still the primary beneficiary. The 1% for Open Space board is
comfortable with the land trust because of the popularity of its projects. It
funded one of Crested Butte Land Trust's highest-profile projects, the Lower
Loop Trail. The land trust bought 193 acres along this popular trail, which links
the town to the national forest and wilderness. A corporation was considering developing along the trail, thus cutting off public access. The land trust
stepped in and preserved the 1.5 mile stretch.[4]

In September 2005, the 1% for Open Space program celebrated passing its
$1 million revenue mark. For Vicki Church, the biggest success of the program
has been its educational value. With over sixty businesses participating and
new ones joining up each year, the program provides a reason to go out into
the business community to talk about the land trust's programs. And, because
the program must be explained to each customer, the business community itself is transformed into a league of ambassadors talking up the value of land
conservation every time a sale is made. You can't buy that kind of marketing.

Jackson Hole Land Trust

In 1998, when I first heard about the 1% for Open Space program, I thought
we could tailor it for Jackson Hole. My colleague took a Jackson Hole Land
Trust board member to ask Ron Harrison, owner of a popular bed and breakfast, the Rusty Parrot Lodge, if he would start up a voluntary surcharge program in support of the land trust's five-year capital campaign. He agreed and
wrote one of the best promotion pieces on the reasons to help conservation by
making a donation through his hotel.

The Rusty Parrot program began with a two-dollar-per-night voluntary
surcharge on each guest's bill. It was later changed to a 2 percent charge, then
increased to 3 percent. It was originally an optional guest donation dedicated
to the Jackson Hole Land Trust. Ron later made it an automatic fee that

Figure 8.3

Ron Harrison, owner of the Rusty Parrot Lodge in Jackson Hole, Wyoming, wrote a stirring appeal to his guests to add two dollars to their room bills for the Jackson Hole Land Trust. (Courtesy of Jackson Hole Land Trust)

supports a variety of community programs, including the land trust. "Over so many years, our philosophy evolved," Ron says. "We don't have any type of lodging tax here in Jackson Hole and our tax rate is low. So we included the donation as a community fee. With our 6 percent sales tax, we wound up with a total of 9 percent. I don't know anywhere that's that cheap."

After Ron started the program at his hotel, he invited other businesses to participate. But the response wasn't positive. He thinks it was due to a combination of factors. Many resorts in Jackson Hole are corporately owned, so finding the right person who can make a decision can be difficult. He thinks that a different promotion strategy might have helped. If a group of supporters had sponsored a meeting for business owners to demonstrate how the program works and how successful it could be, he believes that more would have signed up.

With only thirty-two rooms, the Rusty Parrot generated almost $15,000 per year in its first five years. In the succeeding years, my colleague Leslie Mattson-Emerson persisted and brought in two other bigger, high-end businesses, which have generated more revenue. In an interesting fourth case, a motel owner with whom the land trust had partnered in a high-stakes auction bid of a critical national forest inholding asked to help the land trust by participating in the surcharge program. Even that small, seasonally open, thirty-four-room motel has generated an impressive $12,000 in its first four years. In total, the four hotels and motels have generated well over $170,000 in the last six and a half years for the Jackson Hole Land Trust.

Since 1998, Grand Teton Lodge Company, a concessionaire for most of the commercial properties in Grand Teton National Park, has been running a similar program at Jackson Lake Lodge, independent of the Jackson Hole Land Trust program. The program benefits the Grand Teton National Park Foundation. A one-dollar donation is added to the nightly bill. A small sign at the check-in desk explains the program. If a guest chooses not to participate, there is a check-off box on the registration form.

Jackson Lake Lodge is a large, 385-room hotel in the middle of the national park. It is crowded all summer with park visitors arriving by car or in bus tours. It is closed in the winter. In its five-month season, it has generated between $30,000 and $54,000 per year—a total of over $300,000 since the program began. The manager is not aware of any complaints.

Ron Harrison may be right about the value of a different promotion strategy for broader use of the surcharge program in Jackson Hole. In June of 2006, 150 people attended a kick-off event for 1% for the Tetons, a program sponsored by the local Charture Institute.[5] The program asks businesses to contribute at least 1 percent of their gross income to fund the long-term sustainability of Jackson Hole's natural resources and related essential qualities. Forty businesses have joined, representing at least $20 million in revenue, which promises to bring in at least $200,000 to the program in the first year. The 1% for the Tetons program is designed more like Patagonia's 1% for the Planet than the other voluntary surcharge programs discussed here; the businesses pay the 1 percent however they please, not necessarily by asking their customers for a donation. By joining 1% for the Tetons, businesses automatically become members of 1% for the Planet. However, where 1% for the Planet members contribute their 1 percent directly to approved environmental groups anywhere in the world, 1% for the Tetons members' contributions go into a granting pool, which funds long-term sustainability-related projects in the Jackson Hole area.

One might think that the abundance of nonprofits—more than 130 in the Jackson community, which has an estimated permanent population of 20,000—that besiege businesses with requests for money, auction items, and more would have caused donor fatigue. Apparently not. To help keep intact the qualities of the natural resources of the place they live, and by extension keep it a great place to visit, local businesses are willing to step forward yet again.

Nantucket Green Fund

The Nantucket Green Fund is another example of the business and land trust communities coming together to protect open land. On the small forty-eight-square-mile Nantucket Island, open space is at a premium.

This five-year campaign grew out of the local community's efforts to convince the town selectmen to adopt a bond measure to fund an island-wide open space program. The selectmen rejected the idea, causing three local businesses, working through the Chamber of Commerce, to levy a voluntary surcharge to raise revenue for conservation. Unlike Crested Butte and Jackson Hole, their program had an "anything goes" style to it. To launch the campaign, American Express gave $10,000 in seed money to pay for brochures, mailings, and stickers that participating businesses could display. American Express also committed matching dollars for all money raised by the fund. Participants were invited to donate either a percentage of their sales or whatever sum they chose. Here are some ways that the two hundred participating businesses raised a total of $225,000.

- Some restaurants added ten cents to the price of coffee; others offered special meals and donated all proceeds.
- Some hotels added two dollars onto the bill; others gave all proceeds from lodging on certain holidays.
- One bank gave one dollar on every ATM transaction during the summer, and another gave one dollar from all new accounts opened.
- The newspaper gave a percentage of advertising revenue, plus free ads.
- In addition to its other commitments to the program, American Express gave five cents for all transactions for several seasons.

The program ended in 2001 after five years. About the same time, the town passed a $25 million bond measure to fund open space conservation. The majority of the Green Fund money went into land acquisition projects, although some was set aside for mailings. Local conservation groups were encouraged to submit proposals for open space protection projects for farmland protection, open land, and "pocket parks" in town (small-acreage projects designed to create local awareness about conservation).

When the Green Fund ended, the $50,000 remaining in the fund rolled over to the Nantucket Conservation Foundation, which started its own Business Partners program. The former president of the Green Fund board (who subsequently joined the Nantucket Conservation Foundation board) wrote a letter with a local businessman inviting past participants of the Green Fund and other business owners to join the foundation's Business Partners program. Approximately sixty-five of the original Green Fund participants and fifty additional businesses joined. Donations range from $100 to $5,000 per year.

Gage Dobbins, development director for the Nantucket Conservation Foundation, says that the only problem with the Green Fund campaign was a lack of public understanding about its short-term nature. American Express had agreed to support the fund for only the designated five years. When the fund ended, some members of the public thought it had failed—even though it was actually a tremendous success and was succeeded by a public program now in place.

The Door County Green Fund

The Door County Green Fund, in Door County, Wisconsin, was established in 1999 with the help of the Door County Chamber of Commerce, which supports the fund annually and stays closely associated with the fund, with chamber members always on the fund's board. Designed after the Nantucket Green Fund, the program differs in that it is ongoing and, rather than offering its customers the opportunity to donate, raises money more conventionally through annual contributions. Nonetheless, its scale is significant for a local organization. Approximately 120 businesses participate. All of the money is spent on permanently protecting open space through grants to nonprofits throughout the county.

Ironically, the presence of this successful program may contribute to the difficulties that the Door County Land Trust faces with its lodging fee program.

Some local businesses don't want to give to the land trust's program because they are already supporting the land trust through gifts to the Door County Green Fund.

Additionally, this land trust has not made it a priority to devote the time needed to cultivate participants, promote its program, and respond to the needs of businesses setting up collection systems over this large county. The Door County Land Trust's land program director, Terrie Cooper, also thinks that a climate of misunderstanding about land conservation prevails in the county. A strong, vocal group is promoting more development despite current high levels of building activity. A public referendum for open space failed. Nonetheless, Terrie thinks the idea of a surcharge is a good one, and several well-known bed and breakfasts support her land trust through the program.

The Truckee Donner Land Trust

I stumbled across the Truckee Donner Land Trust surcharge program when a visitor to Truckee, California (near Lake Tahoe), e-mailed me that he had seen their cards on tables in a restaurant where he was eating. Their "Buck for Open Space" program started in October 2004 with two businesses. Less than a year later, it had raised $23,000 with twelve businesses participating. The money is split equally between the land trust and the Truckee Trails Foundation.

Following in Crested Butte's footsteps, the land trust and the Truckee Trails Foundation have built a campaign around the surcharge. Media coverage helped them build momentum. Since the community is small and business owners know one another, the two organizations use participating businesses to leverage additional interest. "It is a partnership of community-minded local businesses who provide a way for their customers to support open space and trails in Truckee by adding a buck. It doesn't cost the business owner anything, which is a good selling point," says Truckee Donner Land Trust development director Kellie Wright. She points out that the program benefits the business too because some customers prefer to patronize businesses that are participating in the surcharge program (see online appendices at www.conservationguide.com).

Because the community is small, the challenge is identifying businesses that aren't frequented by the same customers in the same day. If a customer donates at a restaurant, then a hotel, then a store, and then another restaurant all in the same weekend, there could be a kind of donor fatigue. As Kellie explains: "We have done a good job eliminating this because participating businesses add the

Figure 8.4
Downtown Truckee, California, is a perfect resort community for the Buck for Open Space and Trails program, which asks customers of participating businesses to add one dollar to their bills in support of the Truckee Trails Foundation and the Truckee Donner Land Trust. (© Pattie Lesser)

fee but provide a mechanism for the customer to easily opt out. For example, at Dragonfly Restaurant, the bill says to circle the charge if you'd like to remove it, without embarrassment." There have been a few complaints, so Kellie has tried to make refusing to donate even easier.

Truckee businesses send the income collected to the land trust monthly or every other month and the land trust forwards 50 percent to the Truckee Trails Foundation. All of the participating businesses have figured out efficient and uncomplicated ways to account for their donations, techniques they're happy to share with other businesses.

The Truckee Donner Land Trust and the Truckee Trails Foundation have developed a simple question-and-answer informational sheet that addresses most of the questions that a business owner might have. [6]

Larger Resort Programs

Some of the most financially successful surcharge programs are those that partner with large resorts. This is not an option all land trusts have. But, for those that do, it can amount to one-stop shopping with a big financial return. The St. Simons Island Land Trust's partnership with the Cloister, a consortium of five-star hotels and rental houses run by Sea Island Resorts in Georgia, is a very good example of what is possible.

In 2001, the land trust was approached by the Cloister, a family-owned business, suggesting that they start a surcharge program for the accommodations they own. They settled on a voluntary donation of two dollars per night. The guests receive a beautiful brochure with a full explanation of the program. The Sea Island Company sends the land trust quarterly checks totaling roughly $140,000 per year.

A South Carolina land trust, the Kiawah Island Natural Habitat Conservancy, set up a voluntary surcharge program with four different lodges on the island. The largest is the Kiawah Island Golf Resort's hotel, the Sanctuary. For two years, the resort charged a $25-per-room-per-night "amenity surcharge," of which 2 percent went to the conservancy and the rest covered the cost of other hotel services. In 2005, this hotel's program generated $230,000. The resort paid the conservancy with monthly checks "like clockwork," says Donna Windham, the conservancy's executive director.

Under new management, the resort decided to return to the original voluntary arrangement so as not to hide its fees in an umbrella charge. Because of the way the resort negotiates package rates for corporate business, the revenue to the conservancy has dropped somewhat. Donna looks forward to familiarizing the new management with the significant benefits of the program to the region and is optimistic that, once the benefits are understood, the revenue will increase. The conservancy depends on this revenue to pay for some of its acquisitions.

The other three hotels have slightly different arrangements with the conservancy. From all four properties in total, the land trust received $253,000 in surcharge revenue annually in the past.

The Equinox Resort and Spa in Manchester Village, Vermont, originally set up its own Equinox Preserve Trust to manage nine hundred acres of conservation land owned by the resort with conservation easements held by the Vermont Land Trust and The Nature Conservancy. A $20-per-night resort fee for guest amenities is charged, of which $2 goes to the trust. This contribution amounts to $60,000 to $80,000 per year.

Though all of these programs require some monitoring and reinforcement, the benefits can be tremendous.

Advantages of Voluntary Surcharge Programs

Voluntary surcharge programs have two primary benefits: (1) they can generate a lot of income, and (2) they can be a vehicle for getting the word out about land conservation and a land trust. The revenue is not likely to meet all of a land trust's needs, except possibly in the case of the large southeastern programs. But, as a new source of money, the income can be substantial.

The awareness-building benefit of a surcharge program is very significant. By educating businesses' employees who in turn educate their customers, a land trust builds awareness throughout a community exponentially. Of course, some employees will be better at making the pitch than others. A land trust might even risk the circulation of misinformation. But a simple message coupled with an aggressive training program can keep the pitch on point. Customers are likely to be more attentive because the money is coming out of their pockets here and now. When they understand the purpose, the vast majority of customers are happy to donate. The small amount relative to the size of the purchase probably contributes to customer acceptance.

From awareness building comes relationship building. It is often hard for land trusts and other conservation organizations to build strong partnerships with businesses in their communities. This program, by which the business can help without (in many cases) donating money itself, is an easier sell—and it starts that valuable relationship-building process. In Nantucket, the relationships that developed over the five-year span of the Green Fund carried over to support the Nantucket Conservation Foundation.

Once the idea of business philanthropy for conservation takes hold, other creative ideas often emerge. For example, in Granby, Colorado, where the Middle Park Land Trust has twenty-seven businesses participating in its Business Partners surcharge program, the real estate community is starting to give a membership in the land trust as a closing gift to new landowners. The land trust gives a reproduction of a 1934 map of Grand County along with the membership. This is a great way to reach new landowners at the moment they join the community (see appendix 8.7).

Disadvantages of Voluntary Surcharge Programs

Surcharge programs can require significant manpower to set up and maintain. The land trust must contact all of the businesses, sign them up, produce marketing material and other information, and make invoicing arrangements. One land trust received a foundation grant to develop often extensive promotion materials. The foundation apparently saw the high-leverage value of getting the program off the ground. The Crested Butte program eventually spun off its program partly because of the manpower demands. The Door County Land

Trust when faced with other priorities didn't devote the resources needed to administer a big program. The High Country Conservancy in North Carolina has a backlog of businesses that have signed up, been trained, and still need to integrate the charge into their computer systems. While land trust board members have been very helpful in soliciting businesses, the technical aspects of modifying the computer systems are more than they can be expected to help with.

Middle Park Land Trust, in Granby, Colorado, commented on this challenge of the program. They advise that a land trust make sure that its board is very enthusiastic about the program. It takes that kind of leadership and many volunteer hours to make it successful. Middle Park Land Trust's program, though modeled after Crested Butte's 1% program, varies the donation size; thus it decided to change the name to the Business Partners program. Contractors and other large-scale businesses may choose to donate a lesser percentage, such as one half or one quarter of a percentage point.

Despite the success of the Grand Teton Lodge Company's program, I learned that national park concessions might now be constrained from adding new fees for nonprofits to their bills. (Existing programs are grandfathered.) Federal law governing concessions dictates this. While likely to have been an unintended consequence of new and stricter concession regulations, it prevents these natural partners from teaming up with land trusts, at least for now.

Most successful programs depend on the leadership of at least one prominent businessperson who uses the program and sells it to others. The most successful programs have started where communities are particularly aware of the potential loss of open space valued by that community. Resort communities have had the greatest success. Programs in Crested Butte, Nantucket, and Truckee have all been born out of serious growth pressures with open space values that are the basis of the communities' economies. Not all places where land trusts work fit this profile, and not all business communities are ready to take on the responsibility for conserving these lands.

If a program becomes highly successful, like the Crested Butte program, there may be a saturation point. Vicki Church thinks that the Crested Butte community has reached it. However, she says, it is expanding into neighboring communities; Molly Murphee isn't so sure, saying, "We have new businesses coming in and changing hands, plus new growth on the outskirts of Crested Butte." Molly is also trying to "think outside the box" by pursuing new sources of income, such as a weekly mountain bike race series (offering an optional check box on its entry form), festivals, and ski lessons.

Finally, enforcement issues can arise, though few land trusts mentioned them. Crested Butte's 1% for Open Space program has a "three strikes" system for addressing delinquent businesses. Molly first sends a friendly reminder by mail. If this doesn't produce payment, she makes a phone call, followed by a personal visit. She tries to use a polite, appreciative approach and allows businesses to lapse for three to four months on a monthly payment or a full quarter on a quarterly payment. Still, she says, "every month, I have 'strikes' to send out, phone calls and visits to make." Her approach is firm yet positive.

The 1% for Open Space program has been careful to stay in close touch with businesses. The collection of the money has to be generally self-enforcing, though having the benefiting organizations, such as the land trust, out in the community offers encouragement to the businesses to follow through on their commitment to collect the donations.

Conclusion

The most successful surcharge programs are located in popular tourist destinations. But part of the appeal of these programs is the small size of most of the communities. Perhaps that smallness encourages a sense of personal responsibility for the protection of special lands. There is a "can do" spirit in those programs where the community understands that time is running out for open space.

A pattern seems to develop that pegs these programs to high-end resorts. In these places, two dollars added to a hotel charge doesn't seem like much when the hotel room is costing hundreds of dollars. In less expensive places, a percentage surcharge seems more equitable than a flat charge. Even where the revenue generated might be far less, the awareness-building value of a big campaign such as Crested Butte's has tremendous value in its own right.

On the other hand, other places have chosen to use the program more selectively by identifying a few high-end, high-volume enterprises as their partners. This approach does not require a community to be united and feverish about open space conservation. Instead, working with one or two big establishments can produce plenty of money with less administrative effort.

Chapter 9
Transfer Fees

A revenue generating mechanism that pays a percentage of the price of a parcel of land to the land trust when the parcel is sold.

A transfer fee or assessment is a proven but underutilized way for land trusts to generate ongoing revenue. It is as literal as its name: a fee on the transfer of land from one party to another. It is a voluntary agreement between a landowner and a land trust that the landowner[1] will pay a percentage of the gross sale price of a specific parcel of land to a land trust when the parcel is sold. The fees are especially useful in covering the stewardship costs of owning land or holding a conservation easement. The landowner commits to the fee, requested at the time the land trust receives the conservation easement, in lieu of or in addition to a cash gift to the land trust's stewardship fund. Land trusts apply transfer fees to individual parcels or to multilot developments. Though this tool is not widely used, it is very popular with the land trusts, landowners, and developers who do use it.

Establishing a transfer fee program requires opportunity, technical, and organizational wherewithal. The opportunity is in having a friendly landowner or developer willing to use it, having the legal support to design the program that meets state law, and well-grounded confidence that the lack of law and legal precedent won't undermine the program.

At the closing on the sale of land, one of the parties, usually the seller, pays the transfer fee to the land trust. The amount is based on a percentage of the gross sale price; the fee ranges from 0.2 to 10 percent. Some land trusts have lower percentage transfer fees if the land has preexisting improvements. A transfer fee can apply to a onetime real estate transfer, can continue over a period of years, or continue in perpetuity. While most land trusts prefer a perpetual arrangement, the decision depends more on what can be negotiated with the landowner pursuant to state law. Most land trust transfer fees extend for many years or perpetually.

By agreeing to the fee, the landowner is committing to make a gift to a land trust at the time the property is sold, if it is ever sold. The arrangement is palatable because most people are usually in a better position to be generous when they are receiving income. If the landowner is land rich and cash poor, then he or she is especially better off making a gift in a sale situation when money is changing hands. The fee allows the landowner to defer part or all of a gift or stewardship payment to the land trust until the land value is realized through sale.

This is not to say that a land trust should rely on transfer fees to meet all of its stewardship needs. Years might go by before a parcel of land is sold, and the land trust would be without stewardship resources in the meantime. Though a request for a future fee is more palatable than a request for an immediate cash gift, land trusts must start building stewardship funds, one way or another, as soon as they hold their first parcel of land or conservation easement. However, as a supplemental means of generating stewardship revenue, especially from landowners who cannot afford a large up-front stewardship gift or who benefit from nearby conservation projects (as in the case of lot owners in a development with open land), the transfer fee is an extremely good method of raising money with notable side benefits.

One such benefit is that the value of the obligation rises with the real estate market. In some places rising real estate values may correlate to increasing costs for stewardship. Of course, it falls with the market too, so there is a degree of speculation in accepting the transfer fee arrangement. Another benefit is certain: a transfer fee keeps on "giving" with each subsequent transfer of the land.

There are currently two primary applications of the transfer fee. In the first, land trusts negotiate transfer fees with individual landowners who are giving conservation easements on their property. In the second application, a small handful of conservation-minded developers fund the stewardship of the open space in their developments, associated conservation programs, or new land conservation with transfer fees on lot sales. The fees benefit existing local land trusts, or, in some cases, the developers create new land trusts, homeowner associations, or similar organizations and direct transfer fee revenue to them.

A third application of the fee has yet to receive much use, if any. A landowner could write the transfer obligation into the deed simply as a way of making a future gift to the land trust. The gift need not be associated with the gift of a conservation easement or as part of a conservation development. Like estate planning gifts, the transfer fee gift would generate income to the land trust sometime in the future when and if the property changes hands.

Conservation-minded developers were likely the first to use transfer fees and to use them successfully.[2] A developer in South Carolina created what may be the earliest programs, adapting them from the model of early, publicly levied real estate transfer taxes. (Some government agencies tax land transfers to generate revenue for public programs.)[3] In 1989, Jim Light and his partner, James Chaffin, of Chaffin/Light Associates, instituted a private transfer "assessment" at their Spring Island luxury development in South Carolina. This 3,000-acre development includes 1,200 acres of nature preserves and open space with live oak forests, marsh, and waterways that lie on a protected island on the Atlantic coast northwest of Hilton Head Island. The development's transfer fee funds the Spring Island Trust, which the developers created to manage the conservation land and easements on Spring Island. The fee also funds the Low Country Institute, which offers educational conservation programs to the surrounding communities. Over the first ten years of sales, the 410 lots in the development generated a substantial $3 million from a 1.5 percent fee on all transfers of unimproved lots and a 1 percent fee on improved lots.

Chaffin/Light Associates has continued to use the transfer fee for land and easement stewardship and conservation programs in their other developments. Since conservation is a prominent feature of their communities, fee-for-conservation programs have been well received by lot owners. If there are no local land trusts working in the vicinity of their developments, Chaffin/Light Associates creates them or less independent 501(c)(4) supporting organizations to steward the development's own easements, manage other conservation programs, and undertake conservation outreach within the development and the surrounding communities. The Spring Island Trust, for example, manages specific habitats on Spring Island in addition to stewarding the conserved land.

The transfer fee percentages in the Chaffin/Light developments have ranged from 0.5 to 2 percent of gross sales depending on the scope of the conservation programs, the stewardship requirements, and the scale of the development. The company's Colorado development, the Roaring Fork Club, has a transfer fee on sales of its sixty cabins and suites and on its five hundred club memberships. The proceeds fund the general operations of Roaring Fork Conservancy, which predated the development, and which include river conservation, environmental·education, and watershed research. The conservancy requests additional cash stewardship gifts when it accepts donated conservation easements.

Jim Light was so taken by the transfer fee model that in 1990 he suggested it to a landowner in Jackson Hole. That landowner, my husband, Bill Resor, with his father, had acquired a strip of land between his family's ranch and the ski area at Teton Village in order to buffer the ranch from ski area development. To pay for the buffer, he developed some of the land closest to the ski area into the Granite Ridge Development, clustering homesites along the ski runs and leaving open space along the ranch. As part of the project, the ranch dedicated more open space along the border with Grand Teton National Park. The plan followed Teton County's planned unit development (PUD) regulations, which require that open space in a PUD be dedicated either to the county's Scenic Preserve Trust, which the Board of County Commissioners administers, or to a land trust.

However, Bill was concerned about the county's commitment to conservation over the long term and the political nature of its oversight board (the county commissioners), so he asked the Jackson Hole Land Trust if it would accept and steward the easement instead. The land trust recognized the greater liability of the stewardship responsibilities for open space adjacent to a thirty-seven-lot subdivision. It was also concerned that its usual stewardship request of $15,000 was insufficient to cover future stewardship costs for open space associated with lots with multiple ownership.

At Jim Light's suggestion, Bill offered a transfer fee in lieu of an up-front payment. He proposed an ascending percentage of the gross sale price of each of the thirty-seven lots, starting with one seventh of 1 percent and leveling off after seven years at 1 percent. The fee would be instituted for twenty years with optional twenty-year renewals, due to the limitations of Wyoming state law on perpetual contracts. Because this was uncharted territory for the land trust, the staff ran multiple scenarios of lot sales and resales to ensure that the fees over time would be in excess of the land trust's preliminary stewardship requirements. With some trepidation, it accepted the transfer fee arrangement.

After the first ten years and sixty-one sales and resales, the Granite Ridge transfer fee generated $582,380 for the Jackson Hole Land Trust. In 2005, the revenue to the land trust passed the $1 million mark. Its phenomenal success is due to a combination of happy circumstances: numerous high-end lots in the program, a strong real estate market, and a fee based on a reasonable

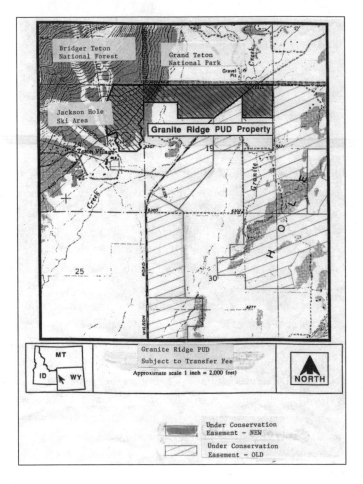

Figure 9.1

The plan for the Granite Ridge development in Jackson Hole included dedicated open space, as required by Teton County's planned unit development (PUD) regulations. A transfer fee is used to pay the Jackson Hole Land Trust for stewardship of the open space. (Courtesy of Jackson Hole Land Trust)

percentage of the gross sale price. Even in a weaker market, the program would have been a strong income generator because of the high inherent value of the lots. The steady construction of new homes further increased that value and thus the revenue (based on gross lot value) during this period.

Across the country, land trusts and developers have created other transfer fee programs on a variety of scales. Prairie Crossing, an environmentally oriented conservation community and development outside of Chicago in Grayslake, Illinois, with 677 acres of open space and 359 house lots, instituted a one half of 1 percent transfer fee at its inception in 1994. The fees are now earning an average of $2,250 per sale. The last of the 359 home sites sold in the second half of 2005. The same transfer fee also applies to thirty-six new condominiums. At build out, the developers predict a turnover rate of approximately 15 percent per year, generating about $133,000 annually.

Prairie Crossing's transfer fees fund a small foundation, Liberty Prairie Foundation, which partially supports the local land trust, Liberty Prairie Conservancy, and other local nonprofits. Similar to the Chaffin/Light developments, the Prairie Crossing developers, George and Vicky Ranney (working with neighboring landowners), established the Liberty Prairie Conservancy to undertake land conservation and stewardship throughout the area.

At Prairie Crossing, Liberty Prairie Conservancy and the Prairie Crossing Homeowners Association split the stewardship responsibilities. The conservancy undertakes major restoration and conservation projects in and around the development. The homeowners association is responsible for annual monitoring and ongoing upkeep. The transfer fee revenue from Liberty Prairie Foundation now covers 30 percent of the conservancy's annual operating budget.

East West Partners, a development company with projects in Tahoe, Denver, and Vail, also collects a transfer fee that it distributes to a variety of environmental and community-based programs. The developers direct the 1 percent fee on the sale of their four developments in Tahoe to three entities: the Tahoe Mountain Resorts Environmental Fund, which helps create proactive environmental solutions (recycling programs, river restoration projects, etc.) in the greater Tahoe area (25 percent of the revenue); the Tahoe Mountain Resorts Foundation, which supports community programs in the arts and

Figure 9.2
The Prairie Crossing conservation community is part of the Liberty Prairie Reserve, located in the heart of rapidly developing Lake County, Illinois. Almost 3,200 of the Reserve's 5,800 acres are legally protected. (Vaughn Wascovich)

education (25 percent of the revenue); and the Truckee Donner Land Trust, which uses the money primarily for acquisitions of open lands (50 percent of the revenue).

In Colorado, a residential golf course development, River Valley Ranch, voluntarily established a transfer fee dedicated to the Carbondale Agricultural Heritage Fund, which is now part of Aspen Valley Land Trust (AVLT), for conservation projects within a seven-mile radius of the town. The development collects the fees and pays the land trust quarterly amounts totaling in the range of $60,000 to $100,000 a year. AVLT's Conservation Technical Assistance Program covers the easement expenses of some easement donors who otherwise would be unable to afford to go through the easement process. In exchange, the landowner agrees to add a transfer fee clause to the easement, which gives one quarter to one half of a percent on the sale of the easement property and/or any lots associated with the easement to AVLT. In addition, AVLT asks for a one quarter to one half of a percent transfer fee from individual landowners donating conservation easements with substantial reserved rights like homesites. The exact terms are individually worked out with each landowner.

The Western Reserve Land Conservancy (WRLC) requests a perpetual transfer fee in lieu of a cash stewardship gift for every property for which it receives a conservation easement. WRLC establishes a 1 percent fee for all land encumbered with an easement, a 2 percent fee for encumbered land with reserved homesites, and a 10 percent fee for all public agency pre-acquisitions. The latter high fee recognizes potentially greater monitoring and enforcement challenges in the unlikely event that the public agency resells the property to a nonpublic owner. It also serves as a disincentive for the agency to resell.

Since the program began in 1999, WRLC (and its predecessor, the Chagrin River Land Conservancy) has instituted transfer fees on sixty of the sixty-one parcels on which it holds easements. Only one easement donor has chosen not to participate; he made a cash stewardship gift instead. Thus far, WRLC has raised about $50,000 from transfer fees on the sale of five properties. WRLC designates the revenue from the fees to its stewardship fund. The fee comes to the land trust as unrestricted revenue, so WRLC has the flexibility to use it for other purposes. According to WRLC's president and CEO, Rich Cochran, WRLC would not consider other uses until it had met its stewardship fund goals.

Figure 9.3
The Chagrin River Land Conservancy requests a transfer fee in lieu of a cash stewardship gift for every property for which it receives a conservation easement. Among its protected properties is the 282-acre Snake Hill Farm, home to these Belted Galloway cattle. (Anne Murphy, Western Reserve Land Conservancy)

The transfer fee is most effective when it is applied to a large number of parcels, because the greater the number the more likely it is that transfers will occur and fees will be generated. Initially, the Jackson Hole Land Trust was concerned that the volume of transactions would create tracking and, thus, collection challenges. These problems did not materialize for several reasons. First, Bill Resor and the land trust kept the title companies informed about the program so they knew to routinely calculate the fee into the closing costs. Second, the lot buyers did not resist paying because they benefited directly from the protected open space that enhances their views, property values, and the community at large. Third, the modest additional acquisition cost is not materially discouraging to buyers eager to purchase in an attractive development in a strong market. The trust reviews all lot sales at the end of each year to ensure compliance.

Mechanisms

The Jackson Hole Land Trust, cognizant of the lack of precedent and limited state real estate law, designed its first transfer fee program as a service contract. By agreeing to accept the fee, the trust obligated itself to provide stewardship services to the area defined in the contract as Granite Ridge's open space, as well as to other conserved lands and easements near the development. The seller pays the fee essentially for benefiting from services rendered—for example, stewarding adjacent or nearby conservation lands. Land trusts and developers in other states have written contracts without such direct stewardship requirements. Though somewhat limiting to a land trust, the service contract method, by tying the funds directly to services rendered, takes a more conservative legal approach.

The transfer fee is incorporated into the conservation easement or into the deed for the land title, whether the land is encumbered by an easement or is a development lot near to encumbered land. For subdivision lots, the developer highlights and documents the commitment to pay the fee in a variety of places, including on the subdivision plat, in the covenants for the homeowners association that are accepted by the buyer when he or she joins the association as a lot owner, and elsewhere. The theory is that the more places the transfer fee is noted, the more likely it is that buyers, sellers, title companies, attorneys, and realtors will be aware of it.

For transfer fees written into conservation easements, the document usually highlights the fee language in a clearly titled section and in the "whereas" section. Since the actual language requiring the fee can get lost in the easement text amid the other often lengthy and complex provisions, the Aspen Valley Land Trust and the French and Pickering Creeks Conservation Trust place a notification of the fee in a box at the top of the conservation easement document to inform title companies (and others) that a fee is involved.

After extensive legal research, the Chagrin River Land Conservancy decided to write its transfer fee into its easement documents. Using the easement document to require fee payments raises a series of legal questions that are worth noting and that may or may not create problems depending on state law. The primary issues relate to consistency with state conservation easement statutes and whether they allow for a land trust to enforce an obligation like a fee through an easement instrument. Under enabling law, for example, can a land trust use its easement to place a lien on a property as a consequence of nonpayment? A conservation easement already has other affirmative obligations, so why not this one? There are other legal issues that may be inconsequential in a given state but should be well researched.

In Ohio, enabling legislation does not address these issues, nor is there case law suggesting whether a land trust can enforce an obligation or not. Without statutory guidance the Chagrin River Land Conservancy chose to use the easement instrument as the vehicle for a transfer fee and is not overly concerned about possible and theoretical future issues. It has built a solid, successful program using this approach. The Lowcountry Open Land Trust in South Carolina has done the same. However, drafting defensible transfer fee language, like all other legal questions associated with these fees, must be carefully researched on a state-by-state basis.

Transfer fee language often, but not always, exempts all real estate transfers where there is no financial consideration for the transfer, such as gifts to nonprofits, among family members or for inheritance, or in cases of foreclosure. Some land trusts are more formal about these exemptions and write them into the text of the documents, while others review each transaction individually. Some land trusts, such as the Central Pennsylvania Conservancy, exempt very little. This land trust has a stewardship fund for monitoring easements to which several easement donors have made significant contributions. However, since many of its easements are with cash-poor farmers, it relies heavily on its transfer fees for stewardship funding. Willistown Conservation Trust has transfer fee language in thirty conservation easements but applies a transfer fee to land already under a conservation easement (see online appendix at www .conservationguide.com). Land trusts should exempt the fee from cumbersome transfers, such as foreclosure sales, or from transfers with little or no real consideration between parties, such as mortgages or deeds of trust transferred for security on debt.

The buyer or the seller pays the fee out of escrow at closing, administered and calculated (along with other closing fees) by the title company conducting the closing. The title company pays the land trust immediately. In some cases, other collection entities pay land trusts at set intervals throughout the year, especially if there is a high volume of sales, though immediate payment is preferable.

Advantages of Transfer Fees

Using transfer fees has obvious advantages. Since stewardship is perpetual and potentially more expensive as time passes, it is valuable to have a means of generating revenue on an ongoing basis. For fees tied to encumbered land, having the land itself support its own management lessens the stewardship liability for the land trust.

The same is true for open space in a development that can sometimes be neglected due to lack of interest in maintaining conservation resources and to lack of funding. Transfer fees granted to land trusts for associated land stewardship provide perpetual care and set resource conservation standards. Lot owners' annual fees collected by a homeowners association can fluctuate and decline if the association becomes polarized or other priorities like road maintenance take precedent. Some homeowners associations tend to want to reduce the cost of assessments, which can shortchange stewardship programs as well. In contrast to standard homeowners association documents, land trust transfer fee provisions describe the amount and method of payment for transfer fees and are set before lots are sold. Homeowners do not have the opportunity to change them except with the consent of the contracting land trust. Additionally, lot owners see the direct benefits of this fee without having to manage the stewardship themselves and are likely to be willing supporters of a program that carries out land and easement management for them. The transfer fee program is particularly well suited for developments that emphasize conservation and have the volume of lots necessary to generate substantial revenue over time. Of course, the greater the number of homesites, the greater the likelihood of use of the open space by larger numbers of people and the potential for greater stewardship costs. Thus, higher revenue is appropriate.

The Chagrin River Land Conservancy prefers transfer fees to cash stewardship gifts because the former builds in land appreciation. It is a kind of savings account for the future, when enforcement is likely to be a greater problem and more expensive. The conservancy also has encountered less landowner resistance to a future fee than to cash now, especially when requesting it from the same individual who has just made a generous easement donation.

Transfer fees can benefit other conservation programs in addition to stewardship. In the case of the Jackson Hole Land Trust's program, the money is dedicated to the stewardship of open space in a specific development up to an amount estimated to be sufficient for an endowment to cover those costs. Revenue above and beyond this amount can cover the trust's general stewardship obligations and the cost of conducting other conservation efforts in the Jackson Hole area that "provide continuing and substantial benefits to the (lot owners)."[4] The transfer fees from the Chaffin/Light developments, for the Western Reserve Land Conservancy, and from others generate general support revenue, but the respective land trusts have chosen to designate it for stewardship programs.

There are advantages to closely tying the use of fees to programs that will benefit the payors in some direct or logical manner. Covering costs of conservation projects near them is in their direct self-interest by enhancing land values and conserving salient features of the area. It strengthens the connection between the payors and the conservation work a land trust does.

The financial value to neighboring landowners of open space conservation was documented in Jackson Hole by an appraisal firm some years ago. The appraiser measured the appreciation of land values when adjacent open space was conserved. It found that, on average, adjacent land and subdivision lots appreciated 21 percent when adjoining land was permanently conserved. Armed with similar information for other communities, a land trust could market the transfer fee as a project fundraising tool to landowners (as well as to easement donors and developers) who are reluctant to make cash gifts but recognize the appreciation in value of their land when a land trust conserves nearby land.

It is even possible to envision a program tailored to less wealthy landowners who wish to financially support a land trust but are limited in what they can give in cash. By incorporating a transfer fee into a property deed, a landowner can make a generous gift when the property is sold.

Overall, transfer fees have thus far proven to be a painless way to raise revenue for conservation. Development lot purchasers have rarely been concerned about relatively minor and legitimate fees associated with selling in the future, the use of which benefit them directly. Buyers coming into an area or a development that has conservation as an objective generally view the fee as a way to further the conservation mission, and so they embrace it. Owners of encumbered land also seem to understand the need to ensure funding for stewardship and have shown little resistance. For a land trust, the transfer fee offers needed revenue and a way of informing subsequent landowners of the responsibilities associated with conserved land. Transfer fees create a wonderful vehicle for making personal connections with subsequent owners of conserved lands or lot owners—relationships that can blossom into greater organizational involvement and financial support.

Disadvantages of Transfer Fees

There is a good argument for obtaining cash stewardship payments to build a stewardship endowment so that it is available when needed. Because transfer fee payments require the land to sell to generate the fee, the timing of stewardship revenue is much less predictable. It is especially hard to predict revenue flow for a small transfer fee program that depends on only a few individual sales. Larger developments have more predictable turnover rates. Even then, unexpected market slumps can affect the amount of money generated. Expectations about the level of funding based on the success of such programs as Spring Island or Granite Ridge may exceed reality in other places and under less favorable market conditions.

Land trusts that are able to collect cash may have less of a reason to consider a transfer fee for stewardship purposes, although the tool can have value as a substantial supplement for stewardship obligations or to meet other needs. A good approach is to build a stewardship fund using both cash and, if possible, transfer fee revenue.

Other risks arise if the real estate market weakens. Buyers may become resistant to paying another cost at closing, especially when the cost can be significant once the land has expensive improvements. If, say, the property is worth $1 million and now has a $2 million house on it, a 1 percent fee amounts to $30,000! Sellers may be less enthusiastic if they are losing money on the sale already.

Transfer fees are not tax-deductible for the original landowner because the time and fee amount is not established until the land is sold. Nor are they deductible for subsequent landowners because future owners are obligated by contract to pay. Cash stewardship gifts, in contrast, can usually be deducted as long as they are not a condition of the easement gift.

Exemptions from the fee could potentially cause disputes with landowners. What if, for example, a lot owner is transferring lot ownership to some construct not anticipated in the transfer fee documents? Certain structures and types of trusts may be exempted from paying the fee, while other trusts understandably may not be. In some cases, these situations can get expensive for a landowner.

In states where a public real estate transfer tax exists, adding a private "tax" on top of the public one might meet with resistance, especially if the public tax is also dedicated to conservation. Lake Forest Open Lands Association in Illinois has some experience with private transfer fees in communities that have public transfer fees, but they have encountered little or no resistance to the program. George Covington, board secretary and practicing real estate attorney in Lake Forest, told me that in his thirty years of practicing law, he has not seen any buyers object to the program.

Transfer fees for conservation are untested in the courts. Enforceability of any legal requirement that remains untested always has risks. While well-researched and well-drafted transfer fee language added to the fee title is likely to be legal (barring prohibitions under state law), enforcement against a resistant landowner carries legal costs and the risk of bad press. Transfer fees using the conservation easement as the enforcement vehicle raise other questions. In some cases, such provisions may not have been contemplated in the enabling legislation. Some lawyers question whether the fees are enforceable in the absence of explicit language authorizing them.

Most other legal questions relating to transfer fees stem from the novelty of the program and the lack of related laws and case law. There are questions in some states about imposing a long-term financial burden on real property in addition to the restrictions of a conservation easement. And there is the bothersome question: can such burdens on titles like this one be perpetual? In some states it seems that they cannot, while others may allow these perpetual commitments absent a challenge in court proving otherwise.

How to establish a transfer fee program will vary from state to state. As a result, the land trust may need the considerable legal expertise of an attorney specializing in local real property law to draft a defensible transfer fee program.

Real estate agents may also offer some resistance. In the case of the Jackson Hole Land Trust, there was resistance from realtors who anticipated that having the fee added to their own 6 percent commission would discourage sales. Bill Resor and the land trust addressed this concern by phasing in the fee over seven years. The Lake Forest Open Lands Association uses a transfer fee that begins at the second sale, probably for the same reason.

The Chagrin River Land Conservancy encountered some resistance from a few landowners who argued that the valuable preexisting improvements on their land should not be subject to the fee. In these cases, the conservancy reduced the percentage. In anticipation of buyer concern over higher fees for improved lots, Chaffin/Light Associates also established a lower percentage fee across the board for all improved lots.

Recommendations

In an informative paper published by the Pennsylvania Land Trust Association, attorney and land conservation consultant Bill Sellers reviews the legal issues associated with transfer fees as applied in Pennsylvania.[5] He makes several cogent arguments for the use of transfer fees with recommendations for how land trusts can strengthen their legal position (in Pennsylvania at least).

He also makes some good practical suggestions worth considering in any circumstance.

The article is generally positive. Sellers writes: "Generally speaking, the courts have shown reluctance to interfere with private covenants." He suggests that congressional and state agency concerns about land trust capacity to perpetually steward conservation easements would suggest that transfer fees support public policy. He believes that the courts and agencies alike recognize the need for land conservation organizations to meet their stewardship and enforcement obligations and that to find a continuing source of funding to do so is essential to meeting the purpose of the easement. This assumes, of course, that the provisions of the transfer fee language meet state and federal law in other ways.

In addition to the legal issues, Bill has some practical advice on establishing and implementing a transfer fee program to support a stewardship program. He recommends that a land trust do the following:

- Quantify the costs of staffing and hiring a consultant to deliver its stewardship program.
- Estimate the minimum and maximum cost of stewardship per easement.
- Determine how much the easement donors will likely contribute toward the stewardship endowment, which might affect the size of the transfer fee.
- If the transfer fee is the sole source of stewardship endowment funds, consider asking how likely it is that the land will change hands and thus generate revenue from the fee. If it is unlikely, then a higher fee may be necessary.
- Ask whether the easement reserves rights or imposes conditions that might increase the cost of stewardship in the future.
- If the transfer fee yields substantially more money than necessary for stewardship, ask how the land trust will use this money in a manner consistent with the fee's intended use.

Sellers rightly suggests that the best way to maintain support for a stewardship program and its transfer fee program is to cultivate good relationships with the easement donors, lot owners, and subsequent owners. Many of his guidelines for stewardship programs will be incorporated into the land trust accreditation process.

Conclusion

Like any fundraising tool, transfer fees are not the single solution to a land trust's financial needs. But they have proven to be a reliable source of revenue under the right circumstances and for the right purposes. In an appropriate area, where buyers are attracted to scenery and conservation and are willing to invest in perpetuating these values, a transfer fee program is likely to succeed, particularly if land values are appreciating. Such a program is also attractive to landowners because it is a future payment. But from the land trust's point of view, it may result in an immediate revenue shortfall if the land trust is solely dependent on the program for stewardship revenue.

With new programs come new obligations. The land trust must monitor the program carefully and be ready to address a new set of questions from realtors, attorneys, and prospective purchasers. Though there have been few problems with private transfer fee programs to date, it is still a sophisticated tool that requires very careful legal consideration and that has potential future consequences that are yet unknown.

All in all, the transfer fee concept is underutilized because land trusts are unaware of the tool, may not have relationships with developers that would facilitate their use in subdivisions, or do not have the legal or organizational capacity to create and monitor a program. Transfer fee use with conservation easements requires significantly greater legal sophistication to ensure compliance with state law. Nonetheless, new developments are built in land trust service areas daily. Surely land trusts could convince more of these developers to establish programs to support land conservation that so often directly benefits their own projects. Other landowners with holdings near land trust projects benefit as well. They might be convinced to contribute, if not with cash then with future transfer fee payments to support the land trust.

The transfer fee concept has been very useful in meeting stewardship obligations for the few land trusts that use it. With realistic expectations and good legal review, an ongoing transfer fee, particularly in multilot developments, has proven to generate substantial funding and could do even more.

Part 3
Borrowing Money

Chapter 10
Borrowing Money

"Let us all be happy and live within our means, even if we have to borrow the money to do it with."

Artemus Ward[1]

I know of a land trust at which the board members and supporters used their credit cards to secure a loan for a land acquisition. To purchase a 252-acre forest, individuals pledged various amounts per month for a nineteen-month period so that the Lake County Land Trust could both borrow from a local bank and pay the interest. The project dragged on longer than expected, and the land trust obtained extensions of the credit card authorizations in diminishing numbers until they could no longer cover the interest payments. At that point, Resources Legacy Fund Foundation, a California-based intermediary organization, stepped in with a lower-interest loan and saw the project through to completion. Credit card borrowing, especially when the takeout is not certain, is definitely not the optimal approach. But you use the tools you have.

If a time gap exists between when land or conservation easements must be purchased and when the money is available, borrowing is necessary. Timing often makes the difference between protection of land and no protection. A landowner chooses to sell or must sell. A land trust or public agency has access to sufficient funds but doesn't have those funds on hand. This is where borrowing money comes in.

Secured borrowing of money is a simple concept. You lend me money, and I give you something of equal or greater value to hold on to until I pay you back. If I don't pay you back, you can sell what I gave you and keep the amount I owe you plus some for the risk of making me the loan. The simplest real estate lending model involves lending cash and holding rights to the land purchased until the loan is paid off, then releasing those rights to the borrower. Someone or some institution (usually a bank) does the lending. If you are

Figure 10.1
While securing funding
from public agencies,
the Lake County Land
Trust received loans
from private lenders
and a local bank to
make the initial pur-
chase of Black Forest,
on the slopes of Mt.
Konocti. (Courtesy of
Lake County Land
Trust)

lucky, a foundation or revolving fund has loan funds available for land protection at a lower interest rate.

Like most businesses, the business of borrowing and lending, otherwise
known as financing, has its own language. The most common financing terms
are explained in chapter 11. Additional definitions can be found in the glossary at the end of the book. It is worth learning to speak the language, or financing will be unnecessarily confusing.

Borrowing money requires real discipline. It should never be entered into
lightly. Many land conservation organizations are not ready to borrow money
because they cannot be sure of paying back the loan. They don't yet have a
track record of reliable cash flow and a stable base of support or funders on
which they can depend. Getting to the point where a land trust knows where
its next dollar and the one after that will come from takes hard work, as described in part 1 of this book. Once there, borrowing allows an institution to
greatly leverage its assets and effectiveness and to grow and mature. When your
organization is finally stable and well funded and thus in a position to expand
its financing resources, you sleep better too.

Without confidence that the land trust can find permanent funding for an
acquisition, borrowing money is risky. That is why some conservationists believe that all other options should be exhausted before an organization takes
on the burden and risk of a loan. I have come to realize that there are many advantages to borrowing money even when there are other options. However,
being highly certain of loan repayment is critical.

When considering borrowing, the organization must understand how to calculate the cost of the loan, the risk, and the organizational exposure. Interest rates, loan terms, fees, and other elements of a loan arrangement determine the loan's actual dollar cost to the borrower. But there are other financial impacts of a loan that are not immediately apparent. For example, paying interest on a loan can get expensive very quickly.

Assessing the risk of taking out a loan addresses the organization's ability to pay back the loan in the allotted time. Will the financial burden of carrying the loan—making interest and principal payments—be manageable? Can the covenants of the loan agreement, such as the administrative reporting requirements or prohibitions against new loans during the first loan's term, be met? Bank loan covenants require more than just a check in the mail. What are the public relations consequences? Some land trusts say that taking a loan to purchase land distracts from the urgency of a protection project and dampens enthusiasm for fundraising.

Does taking a loan put the organization out on a limb? What is the organization prevented from doing because, for example, its unrestricted endowment was used for loan security and therefore cannot be used for other purposes? What if another important parcel becomes available while the organization is occupied raising money to pay off a loan? Are the board and staff members too absorbed with paying off the first loan to work on the new project?

Taking a first (second or third) loan can be scary, but it shouldn't immobilize the organization. If it might, then the land trust isn't adequately prepared to borrow.

Short-term Loans

When sale negotiations are complete, sellers like to close. Sometimes, if the purchase money is not available, an organization can get an extension from the seller, but this is rare. Other circumstances are even less flexible, as in a purchase through a public auction. The money must be paid, or the deal is lost. While bigger organizations like The Nature Conservancy and the Trust for Public Land (TPL) have internal sources of funds to bridge these timing gaps, many smaller groups have to rely on external sources.

Land conservation organizations mostly need short-term or interim loans because of the timing gap between real estate closings and when the money, public or private, is in hand to pay for the acquisition. This form of financing bridges that gap and, thus, is often called bridge financing.

Short-term loans can also pay for the up-front costs of a transaction, such as options, earnest money, or down payments, or to cover legal, appraisal, or planning costs. Restoration projects often have retention requirements (withholding of money until the project is completed), which hinder cash flow for the project. Fronting these expenses can be beyond a land trust's immediate capability but can make or break a deal. In these cases too, short-term financing can make the difference.

The loan is usually for a relatively short period of time—at most three to five years, usually much less. Land trusts have used one-month bridge loans very effectively. Short-term lending or financing by institutions and individuals is increasingly common in the land conservation business, though many land trusts still do not use it.

There are now several types of institutions that will loan money for conservation acquisitions until longer-term, or "takeout," funding is available. These will be discussed in this part of the book. The seller of the land may also be willing to finance the transaction. In addition, conservation-minded individuals are sometimes willing to make a loan for this purpose.

Bridge financing is commonplace in the commercial world, but it has only recently emerged as an essential component of land conservation. Its use has become more common since public agencies started accepting "pre-acquisition" projects from land conservation organizations. The Trust for Public Land was originally established principally to pre-acquire conservation lands for state and federal government agencies. Because it was nimbler and less burdened by the bureaucratic constraints than the government was and could offer tax incentives, TPL could often buy high-priority land or easements for less than their market value. Additionally, landowners usually preferred to negotiate land sales with private organizations rather than with governments. TPL would pay for the land and then resell it to a public agency at closer to market value when the public funds were appropriated. The difference between TPL's purchase price and sale price would help to fund the work of the organization. Many land conservation organizations now serve in a "pre-acquisition" role.

The same funding gap exists when a land trust must close on an acquisition and is using a foundation grant or capital campaign to fund the purchase. The grant might be tied to annual, semiannual, or quarterly foundation dockets, and the fundraising might be tied to year-end or seasonal giving or may extend over several years. Sometimes the magnitude of the fundraising requirement is such that a land trust needs more time to raise the money from many sources.

Loans are most useful and *safest* when borrowing land trusts have solid commitments for repayment. Loans then become merely placeholders until longer-term funding is available (though interest payments often must be raised in addition). If it weren't for bridge financing, many conservation transactions would be lost just because of timing.

Land conservation organizations do use longer-term loans, though they are less common, to finance such projects as education centers or offices. Farm credit associations make long-term agricultural loans. Investments in new environmental technologies are often financed with longer-term loans. However, in part 3 I primarily address places to find short-term loans for land and easement acquisition.

The best thing about borrowing is that it puts a land trust in control of the timing for conservation, because money is available when the land trust needs it. For the more experienced land trust, loans also leverage the land trust's own capital or other less liquid assets. Borrowing money allows an organization to have the use of money without spending down its own.

Who Lends Money?

The obvious answer is banks. Most people and some land trusts borrow from banks. In recent years new institutions have emerged that lend for conservation. Several of these are discussed in this part of the book, notably external conservation revolving loan funds and foundation program-related investments. Sellers lend buyers money as part of a real estate sale. An organization can informally lend itself money using its own internal funds. These lenders are also covered in this part.

Lenders are careful about how and to whom they make loans. If the borrower is a good risk, the lender is likely to offer a better interest rate on a loan and provide a larger loan relative to the value of what is being pledged for security. The more the lender knows about the health and stability of the borrower—its financial profile—the more comfortable it can be about making a lower-cost loan. If a lot of unknowns are involved, then the lender must protect its risk by charging higher rates or by not making a loan. Generally, local lenders or lenders with local representatives can most easily learn about your

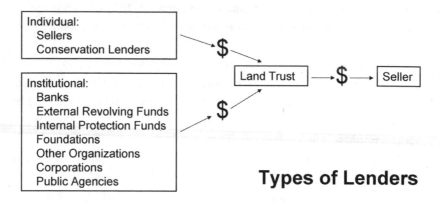

Figure 10.2
Lending can come from a variety of sources, even in the conservation marketplace.

organization and get comfortable with your ability to pay back the loan if indeed you can. It is very helpful if the representative is familiar with nonprofits in general, because nonprofit accounting can cause a regular loan officer pain and reduce your chances of getting the loan in a timely manner—or at all.

Risks of Borrowing and When Not to Borrow

The primary risk of borrowing is defaulting, which means being unable to pay back a loan in the agreed-to time. The borrower loses the collateral put up to secure the loan because it is sold to pay off the loan. If the loan requires security beyond the collateral, the borrower will have to pay any deficiency that remains after the sale of the collateral.

Defaulting on a loan can have many negative consequences, not the least of which is losing whatever the land trust gave the lender to secure the loan. Bad press and a loss of faith by donors may also result. Lenders don't want to deal with a default either and, depending on the lender, will make an effort to resolve a failure to pay off a loan in another way, usually by allowing the borrower more time to pay. But no organization should go into borrowing counting on such leniency.

Beyond paying back the loan, the next challenge of borrowing is finding acceptable collateral. The obvious collateral is the parcel of land being purchased. However, many conservation loan funds and foundations do not accept the acquired parcel as collateral because they don't want to have to sell off important conservation land if the organization defaults. Banks will probably lend on the property as collateral, though many are reluctant to take raw land. Chapter 11 describes forms of collateral that are often overlooked by land trusts. Less-experienced land trusts struggle to find the right type with enough value to suit the lender. Some, for example, find it impossible to obtain third-party guarantees, while others use them routinely.

There are circumstances when organizations can have legitimate unanticipated problems paying back loans. A public agency, for example, having signed an intent to purchase land from the pre-acquiring land trust, may run into a delay getting appropriated funds. Or, in the more extreme case, a natural disaster may prevent donors from making scheduled gifts. If an organization with a strong track record has entered into the financial contract in good faith with good prospects for repayment and an unforeseen situation arises, the parties are much more likely to resolve the problem without default. It is when an organization or individual gets overextended that problems are more likely to arise. For a young land trust, overextension can simply mean that completion of its first capital campaign for the project takes longer than the term of the loan.

The main thing to remember here is communication with the lender. *Before* you miss a payment, get together with the lender to discuss the situation. You will earn valuable credibility by coming forward to inform the lender of your situation. It shows the lender that, though you are behind, you are at least aware of the problem and want to work to fix it. The lender may be able to work with you to avoid default.

How Does a Land Trust Start Borrowing?

The following chapters describe how many land trusts took out their first loans. As you will see, borrowing teaches many valuable lessons and helps a land trust increase competency. If a land trust is well prepared to borrow, it is stronger for it. Yes, borrowing can be scary. But as one foundation executive said, "It is scary to take a loan out on a house or car, but it is done and done with full repayment."

While borrowing is a valuable learning process, change is never easy and it takes time. Even filling out a loan application can be difficult if the land trust is not prepared to respond to the questions and does not have the appropriate financial records. This does not mean that borrowing is off the table; it just means that the land trust has more to do before it is ready to borrow. Keep at it. It's worth it.

There is so much to learn from the stories of land trusts venturing into the realm of borrowing. Here are a few of the lessons.

1. *Get ready.* That is what the first part of this book is about. A stable land trust, even a very small one, that follows the recommendations of part 1 is ready to borrow.
2. *Think ahead.* It is very hard to borrow money in the middle of a crisis. I have done it, and it is not pretty. So start building relationships with creditors and lenders early.
3. *Find borrowing expertise.* Find a person—and there are many—with financing experience, such as a retired banker, an accountant with real estate expertise, or a real estate attorney to invite onto the land trust board. With guidance, the land trust can assess its financing options and get prepared internally.

Choosing an Appropriate Lender

There are two important factors in considering lenders. One is the bottom-line cost of the loan; the other is ease of borrowing, especially on a first loan. For most borrowers, the decision is simple: the lender that offers the lowest cost loan gets the business. For a land trust, particularly one new to the financing business, other considerations follow, such as which lender will help prepare the loan application, manage the loan, have tolerance for nonprofit procedures and land trust goals, or even accept atypical collateral. Try to build a good relationship with your prospective lender. Find a lender who knows the organization or wants to learn about it. This will help you not only to get a loan but also to gain the lender as a member or donor. Give the lender publicity when they make the loan. Keep them informed of your fundraising progress. Invite them to your functions. A good relationship is always important, particularly if things go awry. In many cases, however, especially once borrowing becomes routine, the lowest rate from a credible lender is the best. If you build a good relationship with your bank, it may meet the rate that others quote.

All other things being equal (which they rarely are), for a first loan the seller is the first place to go to for financing. If the seller is willing, this will be the simplest way to borrow money with the least amount of paperwork and the most flexibility. In a hot real estate market, sellers are less inclined to finance. (Why finance when you can get your price in cash?) However, under other circumstances, seller financing may be attractive to a seller. These situations are discussed in chapter 12.

My second choice for first-time borrowing would be to use an external conservation revolving loan fund, discussed in chapter 13. The staffs of many of these funds are helpful to first-time borrowers, assisting with the application and even, on occasion, helping to secure the takeout to pay off the loan. Conservation revolving funds are becoming more abundant in the United States but they still do not reach into certain parts of the country.

My third choice would be a foundation. If the land trust has close ties with a foundation that lends money, its rates arc likely to be very good for reasons explained in chapter 15. Here again, not many foundations make loans. Another consideration when approaching a foundation for a loan is the land trust's bigger relationship with that institution. A novice borrower may not want to risk mistakes with an institution that makes grants to it. Future funding opportunities might be jeopardized while your organization figures out how to get its borrowing act straight. If the organization knows how to borrow money, however, foundations are wonderful sources of low-cost loan money because they share the mission of land conservation. They usually offer lower rates too.

Most land trusts start by borrowing from local banks because they are accessible and for other reasons discussed in chapter 11. However, it is worth looking first for more sympathetic and cheaper alternatives because banks are not usually conservation-minded, or inexpensive lenders.

With any lender, a preexisting relationship makes all the difference. Never go cold to a commercial lender. Even in the most desperate situation (which is not advisable), always ask a board member or another person who knows the institution to set up the meeting and go with you. Particularly with commercial lenders, use the entrées offered by donors and board members who have preexisting relationships to help build a direct relationship for your land trust. Thus my constant refrain: "Take your banker to lunch."

If bank borrowing is your choice, it is a good idea to eventually put a bank president or sympathetic senior officer on your board. The land trust should choose that person carefully, and the bank he or she represents should be one from which you hope to borrow. Before an approach is made, make sure that the land trust has a customer relationship with that bank.

As a land trust becomes more experienced at borrowing, there are real advantages to borrowing from a bank. Banks are well connected with community leaders, land owners and other key players in real estate and finance. They can do a lot for land trusts beyond lending. Remembering that banks will not be as sympathetic as conservation-minded lenders if you are having a hard time coming up with collateral or if your loan payments are overdue, banks, for many reasons, are often the first line of lending for conservation.

Conclusion

The uncertainties of raising the funds for loan repayment should legitimately keep land trusts from borrowing before they are ready. But a land trust that is positioned to finance and that needs financing but doesn't pursue it will be limited in its conservation work to the region's often limited pool of landowners who are willing to donate conservation easements or who can provide extraordinarily flexible terms for selling land or easements. These circumstances will constrain the land trust's ability to proactively conserve land.

The country is awash with financing capital. Investors are scrambling to put their money to use with relatively few really good options. Land conservation organizations are not accessing as much of this money as they could be even though land, even conservation land, is considered a good investment. The current situation may not last forever. For now, borrowing is a good way to access this capital. When carefully and responsibly used, it can increase your land trust's discipline and sophistication.

Chapter 11
Bank Lending

Loans at commercial rates, or sometimes better, from commercial banks established to lend to businesses, institutions, and individuals (and to offer many other financial services).

The Iowa Natural Heritage Foundation first hired Mark Ackelson, its current president, as a short-term employee to negotiate the purchase of a $3.5 million property. After a few rounds of discussions, he was able to option the property for $3 million. When the parties agreed to the price, the seller's lawyer asked Mark what he was going to put down as payment to secure the option. Mark knew that the land trust was barely making payroll and that the seller was sympathetic to the land trust, so he asked whether a dollar would be enough. "A dollar?" responded the lawyer. "How about twenty-five thousand dollars?" Imagining that the whole deal would now unravel, Mark hurried to his board chair to ask him where they could get that kind of money. His chair said, "Go right to the bank and borrow it! I will guarantee it."

Banks, especially local banks, are the most attractive commercial retail lenders. For land trusts, they have three big advantages: they are highly motivated to lend to people they know and trust, they are present in most midsize or larger communities, and they are often willing to take real estate (assuming it has sufficient value and meets certain other criteria) as collateral. Since the land that the land trust is buying may be all that a land trust has to offer as collateral, this can make a good match.[1]

There are other functions of banks that can help with land conservation. Banks are good at assessing risk. They aren't scared of lending to complex projects like multiparty transactions or limited developments if the projects are sound.

Banks are often local in nature. Even some large national banks encourage their local branches to be community-minded. Most banks support local charities with sponsorships and favorable lending terms. Good bank officers

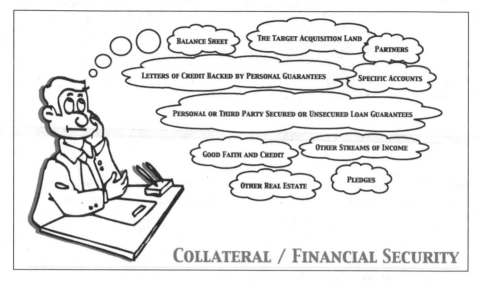

Figure 11.1
Collateral (and financial security) comes in many shapes and sizes.

tend to be well connected in the community. Because there is a bank in prac-
tically every midsize town in the United States, and because lending is their
business, they are generally accessible to land trusts throughout the country.

There are three potential problems with banks for land trusts: (1) because
banks are commercial, profit-making ventures, they aren't always interested in
lending on raw land, the liquidity of which might be less assured; (2) their
lending rates can be expensive; and (3) unlike lenders with conservation as part
of their mission, including certain foundations and conservation revolving
funds, banks are not always as flexible and accommodating to land conservation borrowers. That is why some practitioners recommend using banks as a
last resort and going instead to a conservation-minded, external revolving loan
fund. An experienced staff at a revolving fund will help a land trust with borrowing procedures unique to nonprofits.

Many banks, however, have neither the capacity nor inclination to be helpful within the specialized arena of conservation transactions, unless the problems are easily solvable or the bank has a compelling reason to help. Bankers,
like individuals, can be suspicious of conservation based on inaccurate information in newspaper or magazine articles and hearsay about the meaning and
implications of conservation and conservation easements. In certain parts of

the country, these attitudes are particularly common inside and outside banks. Motivating a bank to be helpful is key. I will discuss how to do this later.

Despite all of these factors, land trusts, large and very small, have overcome the barriers and use banks frequently and regularly, most often for bridge financing. Banks have been instrumental in helping many land trusts protect thousands of acres and become more sophisticated, effective organizations.

Borrowing from a Bank

Every bank has its nuances, and every state has specific banking laws and regulations. That said, I'll start by describing the typical, orderly way that land trusts can borrow money from banks.

In the model situation, a land trust would like to purchase a parcel of land. It has a signed letter of intent from a public agency to buy the property after the land trust acquires it. The land trust needs financing until the funds will be available for the agency purchase—a familiar interim financing story. A director on the land trust's board suggests approaching a local bank. The board member serves on the bank's board as well. Fortunately, the land trust already keeps its funds at that bank. The board member arranges a meeting with the bank president. The bank president subsequently sets up a meeting with a loan officer. The land trust informs the bank of the public agency's commitment. The loan officer, the board member, the land trust's accountant, and the land trust representative work together to fill out the bank's loan application. The land trust submits the application with the fees and all the necessary attachments (purchase and sale agreement, appraisal, environmental reports, financial statements, letter of intent, etc.). The loan officer reviews the information, completes the credit analysis or underwriting, and presents the proposed loan terms to the borrower.

When both parties have agreed to the terms and numerous other provisions, the loan officer presents the loan terms to the bank's loan committee for approval. Once approved, the bank officer drafts the loan documents (the loan agreement, promissory note, mortgage or deed of trust) for the borrower to sign. The loan is funded by recordation of the mortgage or deed of trust when the borrower purchases the property. Though there are significant legal differences between a mortgage and a deed of trust, both forms effect a collateralization for the benefit of the lender. For the purposes of this discussion, I will use the term "mortgage" to refer to both legal arrangements.

When the land trust closes on the property, it gets the loan and gives the bank the signed promissory note and the mortgage for the property. A few months later, when the agency funding comes through, the agency buys the land from the land trust. The land trust repays the bank with interest that it raises from its membership or which the agency agreed to cover.

Of course, it doesn't always happen this way. Rich Cochran, president and CEO of the Western Reserve Land Conservancy[2] in Ohio, and former executive director of the Chagrin River Land Conservancy, tells of the Chagrin River Land Conservancy's first loan. The land trust wanted to conserve two parcels called Harmon and Wellfield. Harmon was controlled by a developer and subject to eminent domain (condemnation) litigation. The Village of Chagrin Falls owned the Wellfield parcel. The land trust arranged to buy conservation easements on both parcels if the village acquired the Harmon parcel. The land trust went to a local bank for a loan to pay for the conservation easements. With the help of a good relationship with the bank's leaders, the land trust was successful in acquiring a loan, and the bank issued a letter of credit backed by pledges to the land trust's capital campaign. The land trust purchased the conservation easements from the village. The loan was repaid with a combination of collected pledges and land trust reserves, which covered the uncollected portion of one pledge made by a donor who reneged on the pledge. The land trust sued the donor, who had left town, and recovered two-thirds of the pledge to replenish its reserve outlay.

Figure 11.2
The Chagrin River Land Conservancy purchased a conservation easement on the Wellfield property with a bank loan. (Anne Murphy, Western Reserve Land Conservancy)

The less-planned approach to bank borrowing is more common. Jane Calvin, the executive director and one of two part-time staff people at the Lowell Parks & Conservation Trust in Massachusetts, received a last-minute call from the local Red Cross telling her that they were selling a key property. The parcel was the Red Cross land and building abutting one of the land trust's projects in downtown Lowell. The land trust appealed for help to a friendly foundation and to Enterprise Bank, whose president had been on the land trust board. Both institutions lent the land trust the money to purchase the building and its one-acre site for $821,000. The land trust secured the $656,000 bank loan using a four-acre developable lot the land trust also owned as collateral. The foundation loan (or program-related investment) for most of the remainder was unsecured.[3] The land trust is seeking permanent funding from the National Park Service for the one acre for a recreational site to connect with other sites in the area, and hopes to resell the building for affordable housing. The loan from Enterprise Bank was essential.

Don't despair if there are too many new terms and details in these examples. I will explain these in this chapter. For now, just note the common threads

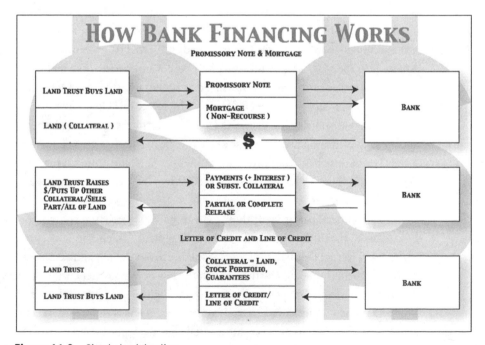

Figure 11.3 Simple bank lending.

of basic practices that helped these land trusts with bank borrowing. The first and obvious one is having a well-positioned connection with a bank before approaching it for a loan. The second is knowing a bank that is willing and able to help. There are many extremely creative and responsive bankers who will help land trusts borrow money and conserve land. The challenge for land conservationists is to find the right banker and bank, make the right connections, and be well prepared.

How Banks Make Money

One way that banks make a profit is by lending money and receiving interest payments from the borrower for the service. Banks also charge fees for costs associated with loans and for a range of other services. There can be other upfront charges for borrowing called "points." Sometimes there is a penalty for paying back a loan before its maturity date (the date when the loan must be repaid) called a prepayment penalty. Many of these costs can be reduced through negotiation of the loan package.

Banks use the money they receive from depositors to lend out to customers to finance buying homes, cars, businesses, and land. Larger banks then package their qualified loans, especially home loans, and "sell" them to investors in the secondary banking market, which is administered primarily by Freddie Mac and Fannie Mae.[4] Big institutions looking for investment, like insurance companies and government and quasi-governmental institutions, generally control the secondary market. Conservation loans are local loans and almost always remain in-house. Smaller banks lend out surplus capital or borrow at wholesale rates from government sources for greater profitability. The more money banks raise from depositors and other services, the more money they have to lend and the more loans they can sell. When the local economy is weak, there are fewer deposits and fewer loans.

Like all lenders, banks want their loans repaid. They therefore structure their loans to maximize the likelihood of repayment, which happens either by the borrower repaying the loan or, if the borrower defaults, the collateral for the loan being liquidated by the bank. If the risk of nonpayment is low, then the bank might be willing to lend more money with lower fees and interest rates or lend on an unsecured basis. If repayment is less certain, and the collateral is excellent (meaning it has substantially greater value than the loan and is liquid), the bank might improve the terms of the loan. If, for example, repayment is expected from a land trust's upcoming first capital campaign, that

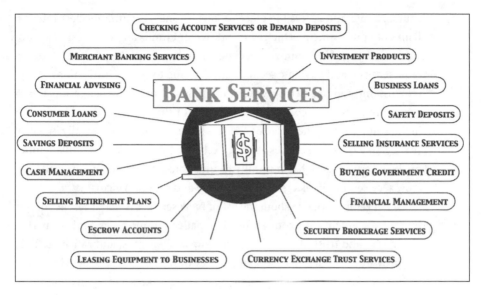

Figure 11.4
Banks provide a wide variety of services and thus have significant networks in communities.

is a greater risk for a bank than expecting repayment from a government agency with a letter of intent to purchase from the land trust. The bank will treat terms and security differently in these two cases.

Banks understand the difference between risky deals and risky loans. They are good at assessing risk if they understand the project (they are often not familiar, however, with conservation projects). They will not make loans with risk profiles that are inconsistent with the bank's underwriting requirements. If they can structure a loan in a manner that reduces the risk of nonpayment to acceptable levels (i.e., with good collateral or strong loan covenants), they will make the loan on those terms. Their concern is more about the safety of the loan than the deal.

Banks can often be creative about how to finance projects because it is their business to be efficient with their money. As a result, if they are squarely on your team and understand your conservation goals and conservation project, they can help you structure financing that will save money and time. If you know the banks in your community well, you will know which ones have a particular interest in charities. A helpful bank can set the standard for other banks. On the other hand, banks can also be very uncreative because they are so risk-averse.

The modern-day bank offers an abundance of other financial services, which can benefit land conservation in direct and indirect ways. Banks are, of course, a safe and accessible place to keep money, earning modest interest. Banks offer investment vehicles for endowment funds and reserves. They provide safe storage for documents, facilitate purchases and sales through their escrow services, and facilitate security and lending for other institutions. Banks are constantly adding new services as the financial markets change and as laws permit. Despite the fact that banking is one of the most regulated businesses in the United States, the range of services has expanded dramatically in recent years. Some of these services are not exclusive to banks; for example, money can be invested through community foundations, and title companies offer escrow services, but banks specialize in these and other services.

What is most notable about the list of bank services is that it reaches deeply into most segments of a community. In smaller communities bankers, particularly loan and trust officers, know landowners, farmers, and ranchers. They can provide introductions, especially if they think a land trust can help a client landowner address his or her financial needs. Bankers can open all kinds of doors and help expand the land conservation network.

I had lunch recently with one of our community's more prominent bankers and every person who walked by our table knew him, shook his hand, and had something nice to say to him. He, tactfully, always introduced me. I have lived in this community for thirty years and knew none of these people. Those are the kinds of introductions that can elevate a land trust's position in the community.

Choosing a Bank

When choosing a bank, the big issues are: Which banks have experience or interest in lending to nonprofits? Do they lend on raw land? Some do it often and well, others only lend on commercial and residential real estate. What is their tolerance for risk? Are they comfortable with the scale and type of loans that the land trust needs?

More quantitative issues are all the details of the loan itself, such as: interest rates, fees, points, loan-to-value ratios, collateral requirements, ease of application, and turnaround time. Some banks are in a position to lend more generously because of the philosophy of the bank ownership or its profitability. Some land trusts have found that a local bank can do better for them than conservation lenders under certain circumstances.

The climate of the community can also affect banks' willingness to loan for conservation land. If the local economy is booming and there is competition

Figure 11.5
The first property that Lake Forest Open Lands Association borrowed money from a bank to purchase was the West Skokie River Nature Preserve, a thirty-five-acre parcel along the Middle Fork of the North Branch of the Chicago River. (Courtesy of Lake Forest Open Lands Association)

among banks for borrowers, then a land trust and other borrowers will get a better deal. Banks usually like a diversity of loans—business, residential, and land. If they are carrying a lot of loans on raw land, they may be less enthusiastic about another one and offer a less attractive loan package.

Many banks don't understand the value of land conservation, or even the meaning of it. When they think of community causes, they think of low-income housing or the arts. This is just another reason to take your banker to lunch. If that first loan goes well, subsequent loans can be processed more quickly and potentially on better terms.

How do you learn about the personality of various banks? Find board members who know and use banks in your community and ask them to set up a meeting with their bank president. Make a case for the land trust then ask for a reaction. Think about which bank can do the most for your land trust in the business it is in. Think about the connections and services you want from the bank. Is it more important for your land trust to have the endorsement of a bank that is well connected in the ranching community, or with charities and possibly donors to charities? If you can't decide, shop and compare terms, rates, and fees. Then you will know which bank really wants your business.

How To Approach a Bank

If there is ever a case for a well-connected board of directors, it is when approaching a bank. Good relationships lead to good access. Lake Forest Open Lands Association in Illinois is a case in point. Its board is integrated into the financial community. Board members know and work with the local banks as a matter of course. Since many of the land trust's projects are expensive and involve limited development, these board relationships have helped it obtain bank loans for these large and complex transactions.

These people are pros. Lake Forest Open Lands has borrowed from banks for at least five multimillion-dollar transactions and now has a $10 million tax-free bond issue that gives it great rates for its current and future borrowing. Most notably, the land trust has convinced several banks to work together to finance one big project.

Open Lands' first bank-borrowing experience was with the Northern Trust Bank, which lent money for the purchase of a thirty-five-acre parcel along the Middle Fork of the North Branch of the Chicago River, secured by the land and personal pledges to the organization's capital campaign. Open Lands designed and sold a limited development with six clustered lots to pay back the bank. It preserved twenty-three of the thirty-five acres as the West Skokie River Nature Preserve (after the colloquial name for the river).

The land trust's second financed transaction is particularly interesting. The project, which was a limited development of two noncontiguous properties, was too big (almost $10 million) for one local bank. Longtime board member Jim Richter, who is in the money management and banking business, approached the community's five local banks to participate in the loan. Four agreed. Lake Forest Bank and Trust was the lead bank and managed the loan with the other banks participating. The willingness of the banks to work together was likely fueled in part by the land trust's strong track record with the community. At the time, more than 20 percent of the Lake Forest families were members of the land trust.

Even with such connections, a land trust must take the right steps and demonstrate its ability to repay the loan. Banks hate surprises.

The Western Reserve Land Conservancy (WRLC) is a master at the bank presentation. The land trust has a longstanding (and very successful) relationship with Sky Bank in Cleveland, Ohio. But it needed more credit to carry multiple projects. The connections through Rich Cochran and a board member who had been an executive of National City led them to Melissa Rowitz, vice president, relationship manager, corporate banking, at the bank whose job it is to connect the potential borrower with all the resources that it might need from the bank.

Melissa described how the land trust's presentation impressed her. Rich introduced himself and the qualifications of the people on his team. The team explained the project they were seeking to finance, its location and financial profile, how the land trust handles its acquisitions, and how it structures the deals so that the bank will be protected. Rich described what he thought were the risks to the bank. "The level of expertise of the group was very evident. Their understanding of these risks made us feel much more comfortable," Melissa remembers.

The bank agreed to lend at 80 percent partly because the term was short and the takeout was solid. More importantly, the bank was comfortable with the risk profile. Rich had successfully explained that WRLC's raw land had inherent value, unlike the usual vacant land the bank worked with that required infrastructure. The land trust had created a very strong financial plan for the conservation of that first parcel that resonated with Melissa and her team. In the end, they structured a more complex, multiple-facility loan. The loan structure gave Rich the ability to borrow for several projects in a similar manner to a revolving line of credit, each with an interest-only draw period. The bank retained the right to reevaluate the risk for each project.

To create this kind of professionalism, encourage community leaders and respected experts in fields related to finance and land conservation to join your land trust's board and advisory committees. Then assemble a strong team to work with the bank. Meet with the right team at the bank well in advance of needing the loan and try to anticipate and address the needs of the bank.

Different banks make decisions in different ways. Loan officers have varying limits on the size of loans that they can unilaterally approve. Certain loans have to go to the bank's loan committee for approval. That committee can be housed at the bank or at a central bank in the same city or far away. Generally, the farther away the decision makers are, the longer the approval process takes, and the more difficult it is for an unusual request to be approved.

Security

Banks want it, but what is it? This is the manner in which a bank ensures that a loan will be repaid. It is the phrase that a banker or any lender likes to hear.

Loans can either be "secured" or "unsecured." A loan is secured if the bank receives an asset that can be cashed in if the loan is not repaid. Loan security can be in the form of real estate or another personal asset, such as a car, or stocks, or bonds, assuming the bank agrees that the security is sufficient and will retain value. For most real estate bank loans, the standard collateral is the land for which the loan is made.

In addition to collateral, there are other forms of security. Say, for example, that a wealthy land trust board member guarantees to a bank that he or she will cover a land trust loan in the case of default. From the bank's point of view, the loan is secure, though the bank will have to work out with the board member how and from where the payment is to be made if the land trust defaults. Of course, preparing and negotiating separate guaranty agreements adds additional transactional costs and fees, which the land trust should not ignore.

If the bank is very comfortable with the financial strength of the borrower, whether because of its assets, cash flow, or credit history, then the bank may not require security, just a written promise to pay. That is an unsecured loan. The lender lends based on the borrower's balance sheet.

Larger land trusts with money in the bank in liquid accounts and a past and present stable cash flow are able to offer their balance sheet as security. The lender is depending on the borrower to honor the promise of repayment without committing specific collateral. This is the most subjective type of security, because it relies on the character and track record of the borrower. It is often referred to as a loan based on the "good faith and credit" of the borrower. This is an unsecured, uncollateralized loan with full recourse (see below) to the borrower. Pledges, though not necessarily enforceable pledges (also discussed below), can endorse the commitment of the borrower and bolster the underwriting for unsecured loans.

Nonrecourse and Recourse Loans

Fundamental to lending is the extent to which the bank can reach into the assets of the borrower for repayment. A nonrecourse loan identifies a very specific source of repayment for the loan, with the borrower having no personal liability. If, for example, a land trust defaults on its nonrecourse loan, the bank can sell whatever security the land trust committed to the bank. If that security does not cover the value of the loan, the bank is stuck. The bank cannot go after the assets of the borrower for more. A secured, nonrecourse loan identifies a specific asset that the bank will sell if the loan isn't repaid. This is a great way to go if the lender will do it. If the security is sufficient, banks frequently make nonrecourse loans.

A secured recourse loan gives the lender the ability to compel the borrower's secured repayment. If, for example, a land trust can't repay the loan, the lender can sell whatever security the borrower gave the bank and, if it is insufficient to cover the amount of the loan, the land trust will have to pay any deficiency that remains after the sale. An unsecured, recourse loan does not identify any specific asset that the bank will sell if the loan isn't repaid. Instead, the bank is satisfied that the borrower has the financial strength to repay. The bank has the legal right to go after its assets without identifying a specific asset up front.

It is very important to understand that the assets of a charitable organization are not like those of other entities that borrow, such as businesses or individuals. The assets of charitable organizations are held in public trust. Their boards have strong fiduciary responsibilities that should constrain pledges of certain assets for recourse and some nonrecourse loans. A land trust must fully consider the consequences of foreclosure, and thus loss of an asset or assets.

The Loan Package

When a borrower arranges for a loan with a bank, there are numerous elements to the loan and to the package that the bank officer assembles for loan approval. Banks have different requirements, so borrowers should internally compare loan packages among the best candidate banks. This requires a sharp pencil, because comparing fees and interest rates and penalties means translating apples and oranges into costs to you. Throughout the process, be careful to respect the confidentiality of each bank's parameters. You should be after a good relationship too, so don't say to one bank: "But X bank is willing to give us such and such. Can you match that?"

A land trust should research its options and know these differences before choosing a bank. In addition to seeking the advice of knowledgeable board members, it helps to talk to other charities that have worked with the local banks, as charities can receive very different treatment (either better or worse) than commercial ventures.

When you settle on a bank and terms, try to think of all the possible circumstances that might arise that could affect the loan during the borrowing period. Cover those in the initial agreement with the bank. For example, is it possible that the land trust might want to pay back the bank before the maturity of the loan? What happens, for example, if a conservation buyer comes along and wants to buy the property? If there is any scenario by which the loan might be repaid early, make sure the loan has no prepayment penalty. Or if ownership of the land used for collateral is expected to change, include a collateral release or substitute collateral provisions in the loan documents. Generally speaking, a conscientious bank officer wants to make the loan and do it right. He or she will help to anticipate these issues, too.

If possible, start with a simple loan. Simple and safe. A safe loan is one that is needed to bridge a timing gap, but with a guaranteed repayment. It is worth taking one out from a bank even if you have other financing options, just to start building a successful business relationship with the bank.

Mortgage or Deed of Trust

This is a conveyance to a lender of conditional ownership of an asset, usually the same asset for which the loan is made. Some states use the term "mortgage" for certain types of assets and "deed of trust" for others. In Montana, for example, a deed of trust may not be used to finance properties over thirty acres. Among the legal differences between a mortgage and a deed of trust are different rights of redemption associated with each type of interest. State law distinguishes these two types of instruments. Because both forms are similar in that they effect a collateralization for the benefit of the lender, I will hereafter use the term "mortgage" when referring to either a mortgage or a deed of trust.

A mortgage has a face value, which is the amount of money that the lender will get if the asset must be sold to pay off the loan. The mortgage or notification of the mortgage is filed in the public land records, as is the release of the mortgage when the borrower repays the loan. Banks can transfer mortgages to other banks, which is common when loans are "bundled" for sale to investors.

Promissory Note

This is a written and legally binding promise made by the borrower to pay off the loan within a certain period of time and at a certain interest rate. It is the actual evidence of the debt. Many banks also have a loan agreement, which contains all of the terms and conditions of the loan. Some banks use a loan agreement instead of a promissory note.

Real Estate or Personal Property Collateral

Collateral is an asset that the bank can access and liquidate to repay the loan if the borrower defaults on the loan. The bank will take an interest in real estate or personal property that it has the legal right to seize and sell. Collateral is that asset, which is held by the bank for the loan period. It can be land or personal property such as a bank account or stock. The procedures for the bank securing an interest and legally filing that interest are different for real estate and personal property.

If the collateral is land, then it is usually represented in a bank loan by a mortgage. For most real estate bank loans, the standard collateral is the land for which the loan is made. It works like this: The land trust wants to borrow money to buy land. The bank appraises the subject land to ensure that it has more than sufficient value to cover the loan if the land trust doesn't repay it. The land trust promises that it will repay by signing a promissory note and gives the bank a mortgage on the property to back up the promissory note. That commonly used phrase "note and mortgage" refers to the promissory note and the land mortgage.

Despite the fact that the land is a common form of collateral, it is not the only form, nor does a bank consider it the perfect security, because the real estate market fluctuates and the parcel can be hard to sell. Further, each state has its own foreclosure and deficiency judgment procedures. Under certain circumstances a defaulting borrower can repossess the land. Borrowers will want to consult with local counsel to understand these procedures.

For typical commercial loans, banks may want both collateral and personal guarantees so the bank has two ways of recovering its capital if the borrower defaults. Because nonprofits aren't privately owned, owner guarantees don't exist, but banks like other guarantees, especially those from their wealthiest benefactors. These individuals can pledge their personal assets, such as part of a stock portfolio or savings account, with the bank to back up the loan if the other collateral does not fully cover the loan value. If the bank is nervous about the real estate collateral, it may ask for personal guarantees. Some land trusts have neither boards nor donors with the capacity to make guarantees or they are reluctant to ask for them. The board leadership can set the tone, and encourage its even modestly wealthy supporters to make personal guarantees, usually from among other board members or donors. Many people do, as in the case of Mark Ackelson's board chair at the beginning of this chapter. Any land trust lacking this caliber of board member or donor should strive to cultivate such prospects for board seats. But often it is just a matter of encouraging board leadership to step forward, as individual guarantees can be small—$5,000 or less. Others, even with little wealth, will follow. Guarantees can be particularly useful in adding incremental levels of security to other collateral.

Land trusts often don't apply for loans because they don't think they have any collateral or any other way to secure a loan. Smaller organizations may have difficulties finding good collateral. Some really may not have any. This can be a real impediment to borrowing. One great advantage to borrowing from banks to buy land is that the land being purchased may serve as the collateral, assuming that the constraints on foreclosure on conservation land are addressed.[5] Even in other situations, more collateral and security options are available than most land trusts believe. Here are some that land trusts might overlook, remembering that if the loan isn't paid back the collateral goes to repay it.

REAL ESTATE COLLATERAL

The target acquisition land

Again, a land trust can often use the land it is purchasing as collateral. If the buyer, the land trust, places a conservation easement or another restriction on the land, then the bank will only loan against the restricted value, which will be a smaller amount, because the bank will likely be required to subordinate its mortgage to the conservation easement (discussed later). Logically, some banks may be concerned about these limitations on the collateral, and may be less inclined to finance.

Other real estate

This should be investment property, not conservation land, again because the bank will sell it if it needs to cover the loan. Collecting these trade lands is useful to raise money through resale, but also for collateral.

Conservation easements *cannot* be used as collateral. A conservation easement is not a marketable asset. Also, a bank cannot hold a conservation easement because it is a for-profit, non-charitable institution. Whether "development rights" can be used as collateral in jurisdictions that recognize them is beyond the scope of this discussion and would require determination by local counsel.

PERSONAL PROPERTY COLLATERAL

Specific accounts

For smaller organizations that have segregated accounts like unrestricted endowments, these can be put up as collateral assuming that the board agree that this is a legitimate use of the nonprofit organization's assets. A land trust should be conservative with the use of its charitably raised funds, making sure they are kept at low risk.

Stock or bonds

Assets in a stock or bond portfolio can serve as collateral. The interest in the stock or bond is assigned to the bank for the period of the loan.

Other streams of income

If the land trust has another reliable source of income, like lease revenue, the bank might be willing to take it as security. Other creative revenue streams might include transfer fee or surcharge revenue.

Legally enforceable pledges

Banks will sometimes take donation pledges from donors as collateral. A
bank's willingness to take pledges will depend to some degree on the legal
enforceability of those pledges, which varies considerably depending on
state law, and the financial capacity of the donors. Campaign pledges can
secure loans for acquisitions made before the land trust receives all of the
campaign funds. The land trust asks its donors to sign bank-approved
pledge forms. From the bank's point of view, these pledges are similar to
personal guarantees as financially capable individuals are putting up their
personal assets to secure a loan. This approach works best when the bank
is familiar with the financial position of the donor. Though some banks
regularly secure loans to charities with pledges, a bank with no exposure
to pledges as collateral will be more comfortable talking to another banker
who uses them. If there are several levels of decision making at the bank,
this may require several conversations.

Other property

This can be other property of value, like inventory or equipment, that is
not that relevant to land trust borrowing, but important collateral to commercial borrowers.

Substitute Collateral

Because the real estate being purchased is so often used as the collateral, anything
else is called substitute collateral, especially if it is "substituted" after the bank has
issued the loan. There are many kinds of collateral that can be substituted for
the original real estate collateral. Substitute collateral is useful when the owner
must transfer the purchased land or a portion of it to another entity before
he or she has paid off the loan. A third party can also provide substitute collateral. When the need for substitute collateral is foreseeable, it is much better
if a land trust prearranges substitution with the bank prior to closing.

Loan-to-value Ratio

This is the amount that the bank will lend relative to the value of the collateral. It is also called the advance ratio. Most banks will lend at a higher percentage of value of real estate for which they are familiar, such as commercial or
residential. These have vested development rights and are more liquid, in most
markets, than raw land. Whereas a bank might lend up to 70 or 80 percent of the

value of a commercial venture, for a first loan on raw land the ratio might be 50 percent. The better educated the lender is about the value and liquidity of the asset, as in the case of Rich Cochran's work with Melissa Rowitz, the better the chances of improving the loan-to-value ratio.

Banks do lend against much higher percentages of the value of the asset depending on other loan terms. A higher loan-to-value ratio, for example, might require a higher interest rate. Other factors matter too, such as the nature of the collateral and the financial strength of the borrower. Well-funded, community-supported nonprofits tend to get better loans.

Interest Rates

Banks don't often give the best interest rate in the conservation arena. However, land trusts have developed very strong relationships with banks, resulting in greater bank confidence and an assessment of lower risk and therefore better rates.

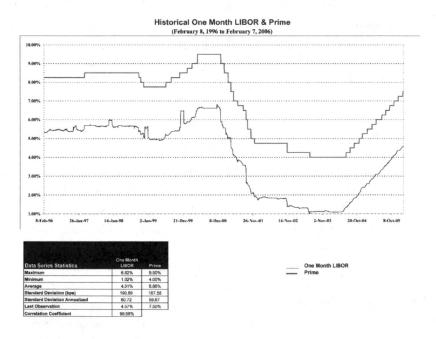

Figure 11.6
The London Interbank Offered Rate (LIBOR) is a benchmark or reference interest rate for short-term interest rates at which banks borrow from other banks. It is usually lower than the prime rate.

Prime rate is the rate at which many banks lend short-term money to their best customers. It is usually indexed to a national prime rate (meaning it rises and falls exactly as prime does) published in the *Wall Street Journal*.[6] There are other regional rates and indexes as well. Prime rate is not necessarily the lowest rate at which a bank will lend, but it is generally the best they will do given normal circumstances. Landowners with very valuable land put up for collateral at a very good loan-to-value ratio, or large entities that frequently borrow, can get better than prime rate for longer-term loans.

The London Interbank Offered Rate (LIBOR) is another benchmark or reference interest rate for short-term interest rates at which banks borrow from other banks, in marketable amounts, in the London interbank market. LIBOR is the most widely used rate in the world, calculated daily by the British Bankers' Association and released to the market at about eleven o'clock every morning. It is usually lower than the prime rate.

A bank and borrower can tie the loan to the prime or LIBOR rate in different ways. A fixed rate picks prime or LIBOR on a particular day and keeps that same rate throughout the duration of the loan. A floating rate is indexed to a commercial rate like prime or LIBOR and moves up or down with that rate. An adjustable rate could be fixed for a period of time and then tied to a commercial rate. A floating rate carries the least risk for the bank. Rates usually have a "spread," that is, a difference between the indexed rate and the borrower's rate, the borrower's rate being higher.

Points

The term "points" has two meanings in bank lending. The first is as a loan fee. *Discount Points* increase the lender's yield from the loan (and the effective interest rate) because the fee is taken out of the loan, yet the bank charges interest on the full amount. One point is one percent of the loan principal. If, for example, the loan is for $250,000 and the bank charges four points, then the bank will charge $10,000 in points. The borrower still pays interest on the full $250,000, but since it only gets the use of $240,000, the yield is higher for the bank. Points can be paid up front to avoid this problem. Either way, know what discount points mean to your bottom line.

The second meaning is banking jargon for "basis points" describing hundredths of a percentage point. If you get a loan at prime plus twenty-five basis points and prime is 7.5 percent, then your loan is at 7.75 percent.

Fees and Expenses

Fees and expenses can add up, but they are also negotiable. A lot depends on what you are buying. If it's a house, there will be more inspections and reports than if it is vacant land. Some of the possible added costs are: credit report, appraisal, legal expenses, document preparation, hazardous materials environmental assessment, field investigation, mortgage insurance recordation fees, survey check, title review, and title insurance. The land trust may already be getting this work done as part of its own due diligence and can sometimes share its reports with the bank. For example, a land trust can sometimes share its appraisal with the lending bank by reassigning it so the bank has a direct client relationship with the appraiser. The land trust might be contracting for a level-one report (hazardous materials environmental study), and will definitely be requesting a title report. These can usually be shared. The bank should absorb other expenses, especially if it is charging points. Ask the bank to itemize all fees and expenses early in the process and discuss each item with the loan officer. What you don't want is to hear about all these other costs after you have settled on an interest rate. Typically, a bank charges a flat fee in the $500 to $1,000 range for simple loans with simple collateral.

Loan Covenants and Other Loan Agreement Provisions

Commercial loans, which land trust loans are, have many provisions that a borrower must negotiate, understand, and then strictly adhere to. Unlike residential loans, which enjoy a high level of statutory protection and are not open to a great deal of negotiation, commercial loans are not so protected. Negotiating all loan provisions is fair game. These provisions need to work for the borrower so that it can fulfill its obligations for repayment and reporting under the terms of the loan. Therefore the borrower must know what those provisions are, which means reading and understanding the fine print in the loan and other agreement documents. The borrower also must have systems in place so that it can comply with the requirements set forth in the loan.

Other Ways to Borrow

Line of Credit

This is a widely used credit instrument among land trusts or anyone dealing in real estate. It is usually called a revolving line of credit because the borrower can borrow the credit, repay it, and borrow it again, up to an established limit, over a certain period of time. A borrower arranges with a bank to have access to a range of funds on which the borrower can draw. As an example, a land trust knows that it will be acquiring a parcel in the coming months, but it is not sure of the exact price or when it will be available. The land trust may have to make a sizable down payment, then close quickly. Then it may make some improvements to the property before reselling it. The land trust has several individuals on the board who are willing to personally guarantee the line of credit up to $1 million. The bank arranges to make $1 million available over the next year, renewable for another year. The land trust draws on the $1 million as it needs it for the transaction.

Foundations use lines of credit in lieu of making a specific loan. The Gaylord and Dorothy Donnelley Foundation has used guarantees creatively to support conservation and artistic vitality, its two areas of interest, in the Chicago region and in South Carolina. It is supporting a project in the Lowcountry of South Carolina to buy a conservation easement from a developer on three thousand five hundred acres. The foundation is backing the acquisition with a large, $10 million guaranty, and a line of credit to Ducks Unlimited. The reason for the line of credit is to provide funds to Ducks Unlimited for payments to the developer if its fundraising does not keep pace.

Letter of Credit

This is a form of guarantee to ensure that an individual, business, or other entity will pay or do what they have committed to pay or do to a third party. A customer secures a letter of credit from a bank and the bank guarantees that, for a certain period of time, it will pay off the obligation if the customer fails to perform. A letter of credit is a credit instrument that is backed by collateral or other security. The letter explains the terms and duration of the guarantee. A borrower provides the bank with collateral and pays the bank, usually a percentage of the value of the collateral, to issue a letter of credit to guarantee a loan or a bond.

If, for example, a land trust gets a permit from a municipality to divide a property on the condition that it build a road to the back lot, the agency might require a bond to ensure that a permittee makes the required improvement. If the land trust has sufficient credit with the bank, it can buy a letter of credit to give to the agency in lieu of a cash bond.

With a letter of credit a bank actually guarantees a loan or another financial commitment. Individuals, foundations, and businesses can secure letters of credit with their own assets. A bank doesn't have to foreclose on a letter of credit because it is liquid, similar to a bank check drawn on a checking account.

In a sense, a letter of credit is a form of currency that banks commonly use. It is like an uncashed check that a third party can keep and return if all goes well, or can cash in if the customer fails to perform. It allows the backer of the letter of credit to be one step removed from the transaction, working out a private arrangement with the issuing bank to cover it.

Personal or Third-party Guarantees

Third parties such as individuals, foundations, or other organizations or businesses can put up their own assets to "guarantee" a loan to a land trust. The third party can identify particular assets or offer a personal, noncollateralized guaranty to the bank. The bank will do its due diligence on the guarantor to confirm capacity and assess risk. If the bank knows the guarantor well because the guarantor has accounts at the bank, the bank's due diligence will be less extensive. Banks like these guaranties if they are familiar with the financial health of the guarantor.

Partners

Land trusts that partner with other organizations, corporations, and individuals on projects may be able to use their partners' assets for collateral. A large land trust, for example, could arrange a line of credit with the bank with which it usually works, or the bank might agree to an unsecured loan based on the good faith and credit (i.e., the balance sheet) of the organization. Conservation buyers working in partnership with land trusts can also put up their assets as collateral. A partnering foundation can guarantee a loan or a letter of credit instead of making a loan.[7] A commercial partner can do the same.

Individuals, foundations, or just about any entity that has assets that the lender will accept to back a loan can offer a guaranty. Many do. Foundations are particularly good sources. Even though a guaranty does not apply towards the foundation's 5 percent payout requirement,[8] it is a simpler way for a foundation to support a project than making a grant. In another fascinating project supported by the Gaylord and Dorothy Donnelley Foundation, the Wetlands Initiative, a nonprofit organization, bought out the farmers in an entire levy district near Chicago, turned off the pumps, and restored the wetlands from cornfields. The foundation and a donor backed with guarantees $6 million of municipal bonds floated by the Village of Hennepen to pay for the project. The federal farm bill, state funding, and private donations will eventually pay off the bonds.

Subordination

Subordination is an acknowledgment by one creditor that its claim on certain collateral is secondary to another creditor's claim or to another instrument burdening the collateral. Usually the oldest claim on collateral is the primary or first mortgage. But this order can be rearranged if the first mortgage holder is willing to take a second mortgage position. Some parcels even have third and more mortgages. Multiple claims usually occur when investors in a commercial project have loaned the purchasing entity money to finance the purchase or improvements. The investors take junior positions even if the investment does not currently have sufficient value to cover the loan. Subordination can also come into play when the acquisition is seller-financed (see chapter 12).

Subordination is a particular issue when a landowner wants to place a conservation easement on land that is subject to an existing mortgage.

Bank Lending and Conservation Easements[9]

Borrowing from a bank to buy a conservation easement quickly gets the bank into unfamiliar territory. Banks don't like to get into a lending situation with unfamiliar elements, so familiarizing the bank with easements is a necessary first step. In addition, a conservation easement is not a bankable asset, so the land trust must substitute alternative collateral.

As the banking community becomes more knowledgeable about land conservation, a new problem arises, and that is misinformation. Bankers may say that they understand conservation easements and be unwilling to hear an explanation of them. But the person might have the information entirely wrong. In this situation, a visit to a conservation project with an opportunity to provide a more informal presentation might help.

Relationships with banks or other lenders can get more complicated very quickly if twists are added to a simple mortgage. One of the biggest complicating factors for a bank–land trust relationship is placing a conservation easement on land that is subject to an existing mortgage. For a conservation easement to be perpetual, it must be immune to any foreclosure process and survive a default and sale of the collateral by the lender. Any unsubordinated mortgage will jeopardize the conservation easement if the land is sold to pay off the loan because the title conveyed to the purchaser is the one that existed at the time the mortgage was originally placed on the land. Transactions recorded in the intervening years are wiped out. This means that a tax-deductible conservation easement gift, or partial gift, must be perpetual and that mortgages must be subordinated. An older mortgage cannot jeopardize the conservation easement if the land is sold to pay off the loan. Therefore, the preexisting lender must subordinate any preexisting loans to the conservation easement or the easement is potentially not perpetual.

A bank will be instinctively reluctant to subordinate. Banks like a primary position. A conservation easement will reduce the value of the land, which is usually the collateral. If the loan is relatively new and large, the land value might fall below the collateral value needed by the bank. Banks typically require an "equity cushion" or a value in the collateral that is substantially greater than the loan to protect against fluctuations in land value (if the land is the collateral) and errors in appraisal. The remaining equity in the land must be sufficient to provide that cushion. Banks also don't like to take a second position because they lose some control over the collateral. But if the collateral has enough value with the easement in place to support the mortgage, then the lender theoretically should be willing to assume a subordinated position.[10]

Many bankers know nothing about conservation easements and don't want to burden their collateral with this unknown, unwanted encumbrance. Even if the local bank officer understands conservation easements, if it is a national bank, the subordination decision may be made on the other side of the country. Or if the bank has transferred the loan and mortgage to another bank, just finding the decision maker can be time-consuming, not to say anything about explaining how an easement works at each step up the decision-making ladder.

Of course if the land trust buys the easement, or the owner refinances the existing loan, he or she should be able to pay off all of the loan or enough to satisfy the bank. In these situations, the lender may need to do additional due diligence to assure that there is sufficient equity to support the loan.

Even when the landowner, whether it is the land trust or a third party, has a good relationship with the lender, subordination can add months for the simplest transaction. I worked with a landowner on a modest conservation easement in terms of diminution in value, and only late in the game did we learn that he was having difficulty subordinating the mortgage on the property. Though he had a good working relationship with his banker, the banker worked for a large bank and could not make the subordination decision himself. It took time to find the bank officer with the authority to decide. At first the landowner insisted on explaining it and then the land trust's attorney met with the senior banker. Land trusts can be alerted to potential issues including those regarding loans early in the negotiating process by obtaining a preliminary title report.

Barring some predisposition against conservation or conservation easements on the part of the banker, with some persistence a land trust should be able to overcome these barriers to subordination if the critical issue for the bank—valuation—is addressed. Still, uninformed bankers will get nervous, and misinformed bankers may be steadfastly opposed.[11]

Other Issues That Complicate Bank Borrowing

Collateral Issues

Financing restricts the use of the collateral for the obvious reason that the lender doesn't want the value of the collateral to decrease or the title burdened in case it must foreclose. In general, the bank must approve any change in the use of the collateral. If, for example, a land trust uses its entire unrestricted endowment as collateral and another project comes along that requires a big option payment out of that same fund, there can be a problem.

A land trust should be certain that the loan documents do not include a "due on sale" clause, which requires the whole loan to be paid back when an interest in the secured property is transferred. Concern about missing unacceptable covenants like this one is just one of the many reasons to have a knowledgeable real estate attorney carefully review all loan documents.

Certain other forms of financing can have other limitations. For example, financing from an external conservation revolving fund might require that the conservation land ultimately be permanently protected. Then, though currently free of any conservation restrictions, the value of the land for use as collateral can only be its restricted value. Another lender participating in financing the project, such as a bank, will be wary of the marketability of restricted land or the restricted value might be so low that there isn't much value to use as collateral.

Partial Release

When a landowner wants to sell a portion of the land that is subject to a mortgage, the bank must issue a partial release from the mortgage. To obtain the release the landowner can pay off enough of the loan (with the proceeds of the sale) to reduce the need for the entire original collateral; or, if the remaining land has sufficient value the bank may be satisfied with that as collateral; or the landowner can substitute other collateral to obtain a partial release.

Condemnation

If a land trust owns land subject to a mortgage that is condemned by a government agency for a road or utility right-of-way or for another government use, then logically, if the borrower doesn't pay off the mortgage, the lending institution would have the right to a share of the proceeds proportional to their interest. If the land trust chose to fight condemnation to protect the conservation interest, the land would become embroiled in a lawsuit. This would be discomforting to a bank but certainly within the rights of the landowner and the land trust unless otherwise stated in the loan agreement.

Appraisals

In most situations in which real estate collateral is used, the bank requires an appraisal to assess the value of the collateral. A new or updated appraisal is usually required if the value of the collateral changes significantly. Often commercial appraisers don't want to share proprietary information contained in an appraisal that is produced for a different client, say, for example, a landowner. But a bank's appraiser is not likely to be familiar with, say, conservation easements or complications involving easements. In some cases, the bank and landowner or land trust can work this out so the bank can obtain an appraisal from an appraiser who is more knowledgeable in this area.

Foreclosure

There are many disincentives for a bank or any lender to foreclose on conservation land. In a community that supports its local land trust and enjoys the benefits of conservation, if a bank must foreclose a conservation project, the community may object. This is why a bank is particularly careful when making a loan where the collateral is associated with a community organization. Still, a well-informed, community-minded local bank knows these risks and likes to work with stable nonprofits whenever it can. It is good for its image and the community.

Banks will foreclose, though, and foreclosure is a messy business. Different states treat foreclosure in different ways. Having bought several parcels that were subject to foreclosure, I know that in Wyoming the borrower has more than one opportunity to repossess the land, but it can be risky, expensive, and time-consuming. For a purchaser of land out of foreclosure, such as a land trust, these redemption rights create uncertainty in the ability to make the purchase.

Conclusion

A strategy for approaching banks should be pretty clear by now. But the lingering concern still may be: Is my land trust ready to borrow from a bank? My answer is: If the land trust is ready to borrow, then it is ready to borrow from a helpful bank—if one exists in the community.

There are so many good reasons for this. Banks can do a lot for land trusts beyond lending. Banks are fiercely loyal to their customers. The stronger the relationship, the greater the benefits. Like donors, bankers judge the institutions by the people who represent them. It is not all about the cut-and-dry numbers. If a banker connects on a personal level with land trust representatives, there are likely to be benefits beyond lending. The bank might even send out a land trust promotional statement stuffer to its customers. Return the favor. Give the bank some publicity when it makes you a loan, keep it informed about your program and fundraising successes, and invite the bankers with whom you worked to join the land trust family by attending events. On the other hand, if a banker gets a bad feeling, a loan can be turned down based solely on that. So it goes without saying that land trust representatives should work to make a good impression. In addition to taking your bankers to lunch, never yell at them.

Competition among banks is good for a community and good for a borrower. A land trust should work to have close relationships with at least two banks because they have different benefits to offer. Sometimes they will work together, as in the Open Lands experience. Sometimes they will fight for your business and you will get better rates.

It can be difficult to find a bank with which to work. Do not be discouraged if the first or second bank you approach will not lend to you. Some banks will not. Some departments of the same bank will not and other departments will. After numerous calls, one land trust executive director found a receptive lender not in the real estate lending department, but in the commercial department. Persevere. If you strike out finding a receptive bank, ask other nonprofits in your community where they borrow from and, once again, get into the banking world with connections at the highest possible level. Take heart that once you are in the door and one loan has gone well, future ones should be much easier.

Most importantly, by building a relationship with the financial sector, a land trust is extending its reach into a very useful part of its community. Those new relationships can lead to introductions to landowners, donors, and other contacts that will serve land conservation well.

Chapter 12
Seller Financing

A loan from the seller that allows the purchaser to pay in installments over time.

Think of yourself as a landowner who is interested in selling land. It's a hot real estate market and you don't care how the land is ultimately used. You hold the cards. You can sell to whomever you want, whenever you want, and however you want. You can wait for a strong cash offer if that is what you want.

But what if you are a seller who wants or needs to sell and the market isn't so hot? Or you want to sell soon to fund your upcoming retirement. Or you care about the ultimate use of the property because you are keeping adjacent land, you like providing habitat for wildlife, or you just don't want to see a subdivision on your land. Sometimes selling to a buyer with a good reputation really matters. In all these cases, if you find a buyer who meets your needs but can only pay part of the sale price up front and the rest of the money later, you might agree to this arrangement to make the deal. Then you become a source of financing for the buyer. That is called seller financing.

Seller financing or installment sales is an often-overlooked form of financing and one of the simplest ways to pay for property over time. It can be great news for a buyer, like a land trust, that may not have immediate, available cash to pay the agreed-to price. Seller financing can sometimes be less expensive than conventional bank financing, too, and certainly less paperwork.

Seller financing is great for a seller in certain circumstances as well, especially if the seller has specific income needs, because it is flexible with negotiable and renegotiable terms.

The great benefit of seller financing is that a seller-financed transaction can be tailored to meet the needs of the buyer and seller and can take unusual forms—anything legal goes. Anything, that is, to which the seller and buyer agree, which leaves a wide-ranging give-and-take between parties. If, for example, the seller is receptive to seller financing and the buyer can only offer a modest payment at first, with more money available later, he or she might propose making a small down payment and then making interest-only payments for a number of years, with the principal due in the last year. The seller, understanding that he or she will be getting very little money in those first years, might insist upon a higher overall price and, if the buyer defaults, the seller would repossess the property and keep the down payment. The permutations only begin here.

Because the structures are infinite, it is important that someone close to the deal is able to calculate the costs of different scenarios to the land trust. For example, 20 percent down and four years of interest-only payments at 5 percent with a balloon payment in year five produces a very different bottom line than 20 percent down and equal payments of the remaining 80 percent over three years at 6 percent. As with any transaction, the land trust must know exactly what these different structures might cost.

A word of caution. Seller financing is not for every seller. If you sense resistance on the part of the seller to financing, or if the conditions and benefits aren't right for the seller, it won't happen. If your seller is reluctant, comfort yourself with this: There are many issues for a buyer and seller to work out in most land sales. Even with one seller involved, all these points—price, terms, title questions, closing considerations—can make the negotiations pretty dicey. As good as seller financing can be for the land trust, why risk the deal by adding financing to the negotiations mix? If your seller is reluctant and the land trust needs to borrow money to buy the land, go to one of the other lending sources described in this book.

First Mortgage/Deed of Trust Seller Financing

The standard structure for seller financing has the seller lending the buyer the money to buy the land by taking less than full payment at closing. The parties close on the purchase with an initial payment. The buyer receives the deed and signs over a promissory note and mortgage or deed of trust to the seller. The buyer then pays the rest of the purchase price with interest over time to the seller.

If the buyer wants to resell or transfer part of the land before the loan is paid off, the seller may want additional security. If a land trust is purchasing a conservation easement, other security must be provided, as the seller cannot sell the easement if the land trust defaults. Also, the easement can't be subject to foreclosure if tax benefits are relevant. More often, the preferred instrument for financing conservation easement purchases is a contract of sale.

Contract of Sale (or Contract for Deed, Land Sale Contract, or Land Contract)

If a buyer pays a very small amount of the purchase price, say under 15 percent, the seller may insist upon a contract of sale rather than a typical financing structure with a mortgage or deed of trust. A contract of sale is a sales agreement that does not transfer the deed to the buyer with the initial payment. Instead, the seller releases the deed of ownership once the terms of the contract are met or when the buyer has fully paid for the property. In some states all seller financing arrangements are handled in this way. The contract of sale spells out all circumstances of the transaction including what happens if the buyer fails to pay the full purchase price.

Typically, the contract of sale is recorded in the public records with a memorandum of sale giving public notice of the sale but not detailing the terms. The seller escrows the deed, and a quitclaim deed or warranty deed from the buyer to the seller until the buyer completes the purchase installments. At that time, the escrow instructions allow for the release of the deed to the buyer. In the event of a default, the escrow instructions would instruct the escrow agent to file the quitclaim deed in the public records, which returns to the seller any property interest that the buyer may have purchased and releases the memorandum of sale. Depending on the type of default, technical or otherwise, the contract would offer appropriate protection to the buyer.

Traditionally, the advantage to the seller of a contract of sale versus a mortgage or deed of trust is the ease with which the seller could repossess the land in the event the buyer defaults. Rather than going through lengthy state-regulated foreclosure proceedings, the escrow instructions allow for the quitclaim or warranty deed to recover the seller's property interests. The courts in some states view these default provisions in which the buyer has made non-*de minimis* payments in the same light as a mortgage and subject to foreclosure rules. In those cases, most contracts of sale are less advantageous to sellers unless the parties agree to a very small initial payment. In this case, the courts may view the commitment of the buyer to not be significant enough to warrant foreclosure.

The basic difference between a contract of sale and a mortgage/deed of trust and note financing agreement is that the seller holds the title in a contract of sale arrangement until the loan is paid off, and with a note and mortgage the buyer holds title. A contract of sale is more limiting in what the buyer can do with the property. Improvements, for example, are less appealing because the buyer does not yet own the property. Though the difference may seem like a technicality because a seller holding a mortgage and note also has control of the property, there are differences. For example, if the parties use a contract of sale and the *seller* goes bankrupt or dies during the loan period, it may be harder to extract a deed than to release the mortgage or deed of trust. States have particular laws to protect the buyer in these instances.

Contracts of sale are useful for purchasing conservation easements. Since a seller can't get back a conservation easement once it has been sold to a land trust in the event of default, a contract of sale permits the seller to hold the easement in escrow until the buyer completes the payments. At that time the easement is released from escrow to the buyer. There are risks to the buyer with this arrangement though. If the buyer fails to complete the purchase installments, there may be fewer remedies that protect the buyer's equity in the conservation easement. Once again, buyer protection in the event of default is determined on a state-by-state basis.

While a contract of sale allows a buyer with a small down payment to begin purchasing a parcel of land or a conservation easement, it is absolutely imperative that the land trust use a good real estate lawyer to draft the agreement, because this structure is not as well understood as more conventional financing and lacks the standard and comprehensive forms of protection.

Second Mortgage/Deed of Trust Seller Financing

There are at least two situations in which a seller would assume a second mortgage position. In the first, a seller can provide additional financing when the buyer can only borrow a limited amount from a bank and needs more to close the deal. If the buyer receives bank financing for 50 percent of the value of the land, has 40 percent, and needs another 10 percent to close, the seller could finance that 10 percent, taking back a second mortgage. Because sellers are less constrained by rules and regulations than banks and usually have greater confidence in the value of their own property, they may be more willing to finance if motivated to make the deal.

In the second situation, the seller may have a preexisting long-term mortgage on the property. If the loan is for a small amount compared to the overall value of the property or the seller has substantially paid down the loan, then the seller might make a loan to the buyer to make the purchase, secured with a second mortgage on the remaining value of the property. The other option would be for the buyer to refinance the earlier loan and then give a second mortgage to the seller.

When Do Sellers Finance?

Put yourself again in the shoes of a seller. When specifically would you be willing to finance? A seller is likely to finance when motivated to sell and doesn't want to lose a sale just because the buyer needs financing. Even in a hot market, a seller might be motivated to sell for conservation purposes. Since there aren't many buyers willing to buy land for conservation, the seller will want to work with the land trust and be as flexible as possible with the structure of the deal.

The land trust might be in a position to make a down payment, pay interest while it is raising the money for the purchase over the next five years, and make a balloon payment of the balance at the end of the five-year campaign. This is a pretty ideal purchase structure for a land trust, but not bad for a motivated seller either.

When the competition in the real estate market is for buyers, a motivated seller might attract a buyer by offering competitive terms such as a financing interest rate that is lower than the bank's. This might also meet the needs of a buyer if his or her own conditions for payment do not qualify for a bank loan.

The second type of seller likely to finance is one with particular reasons for wanting to receive the proceeds from the sale over a period of time or after a certain date. It may be that the seller wants to avoid a large capital gains tax payment or is purchasing another asset and wants to match its payment schedule with the sales schedule. In a high-tax environment, he or she may have significant other income for the next few years and doesn't want to move into a higher tax bracket with the income from this sale.

Some sellers understand that at certain periods of time installment payments will generate a higher return than what the seller could get investing a lump payment in a money market account at the same interest rate. (Because the interest rate is paid on the pre-tax amount rather than the after-tax value.) These sellers may also trust the inherent value in their land more than other investments, such as, say, in the stock market. They know and understand land, while investments like the stock market are often less predictable. A seller knows that if a sale falls through he or she can recover the land.

In an unusual but interesting situation, one land trust told me about a purchase transaction in which the seller, for tax reasons, wanted the tax deduction for the bargain sale in that calendar year. But the land trust could not complete its due diligence on the property in time to receive the state funding to pay for it in that year. The seller suggested that they close on the sale with no money down and a promissory note from the land trust. The parties were so far along in the negotiations and the state money was pretty well assured, so the seller did not require a mortgage. They closed on the sale at the end of the year and the land trust took title. Early in the next calendar year, the land trust completed the due diligence, received the state money, and paid off the 100 percent loan.

There can be other more psychological reasons for sellers to self-finance. I have seen sellers who are reluctant to sell an option for the sale of their property because they want more assurance that the buyer will in fact make the purchase. They prefer to close the transaction and then finance it themselves. Alternatively, they enter into a contingent sales agreement (or purchase and sales agreement) even if it has numerous conditions. In a sales agreement, a seller might accept a modest down payment with a condition that the payment is refunded if the due diligence turns up title problems with the property. Both are common deal structures for developers who don't have funds on hand or don't want to risk their capital and must get zoning approvals or raise capital to develop the property or sell lots to pay for it. In the former case, the transaction closes with a small amount of money changing hands and the seller financing the rest. In the latter case, the transaction doesn't close until the parties meet the conditions of the contract. Either way, the buyer doesn't pay the full amount for it for a period of time, often many months, even years, while, for example, the permitting process is underway. Sometimes the schedule of payments by developers to sellers is tied to revenue from the development so financing can continue for many years.

Motivated or conservation-minded sellers want to be flexible, just as a land trust would be if the right buyer came along to buy land that it was trying to sell. Sellers can provide financing and de facto financing in a variety of ways through extended sales contracts, lease options, long option periods, and phased or installment sales, or sometimes a combination of several of these. Thus creative financing structures can result from motivation by either party given their own unique requirements.

Here is another interesting case. A seller wanted to sell to a conservation-minded buyer, but his family wanted him to get a big per-acre price for the sale, though they were in no hurry to actually receive the money. The family had another reason to defer payments on the sale because the land was held in a C corporation that must pay taxes before distributing income, which is taxed again when the stockholders receive it (a double-tax structure). The family was in the process of restructuring the corporation[1] and didn't want to receive significant income before the restructuring had eliminated the tax problem. The buyer at the other end of the transaction was trying to exchange the seller's land with the U.S. Forest Service for another parcel. But the exchange was initially speculative, so the seller didn't want to risk a lot of money in case the exchange was not approved.

The parties agreed on an arrangement that served all their interests. The seller sold a long-term option to the buyer. The buyer exercised the option when the family had restructured the corporation and the Forest Service had approved the exchange. The seller financed the purchase and the buyer made small payments over ten years with a balloon payment when the exchange actually occurred. The buyer resold the land transferred from the Forest Service.

Because the transaction was heavily back-loaded, meaning that most of the payment for the land was made several years after the parties made their agreement, the buyer had the use of the money for all that time and thus could pay more in the end. Even though the present value of the purchase price was about the same, the family was able to enjoy a big payment, and the price held up well even in light of the future market.

Learning (Again) from Developers

Sometimes we will not know why certain sellers like financing and others insist on cash. It can simply be that a particular seller is more comfortable with the buyer who wants financing. I remember being bewildered when a landowner didn't want all the good things we were offering in a deal that involved seller financing. It seemed like the more we explained the benefits, the less he wanted to hear them. Then a developer came along with an extended financing offer, of no greater cash value than what we were offering, and the landowner took it.

Sellers have agreed to some pretty strange deals, apparently because, at some level, it felt right. This may be the reason why some landowners give generous terms with small down payments and endless contingencies to developers—deals they would be unlikely to make with a different buyer, especially a conservation buyer like a land trust.

How do developers do it when the rest of us have to pay cash? Because the sellers get other benefits or perceived benefits. Here are a few specifics of these benefits and why they result in seller financing.

First, developers often offer high purchase prices in exchange for financing. The seller enjoys receiving a high per-acre price for the land, and the developer gets to extend payments. A land trust can only do this to the extent that its total payment (cash and financing) is the appraised value of the land, as it is a charitable nonprofit. By both satisfying the seller with a high per-acre price and tying him or her to the financing arrangement, the developer can build a useful long-term relationship with the seller. Because financing extends over a period of time, connects the seller to the transaction, and involves them inadvertently in a kind of seller-developer partnership, the fortunes of the seller become inextricably tied to those of the developer. By putting the seller squarely on the team, he or she is more likely to support the developer with the permitting approvals during the potentially politically charged county- or city-approval process. Developers even offer sellers an upside for taking the financing risk if the pro forma for the business plan (i.e., the profit estimates) is met.

Second, some sellers like to see their community grow and like being a catalyst for growth while at the same time making money. If sellers want development and the developer wants financing, they finance.

Third, and this is more subtle, certain communities need and welcome developers. Other communities go through phases during which certain developers gain respect and social status for being agents of growth. When a real estate market is coming out of a slump, developers are welcome in town. Certain landowners are attracted to the social groups that include developers. In addition, clever developers know the value of entertaining landowners and making it easy and comfortable for these potential sellers to associate with them. Like good land trust negotiators, developers can further ingratiate themselves by meeting as many of the desires and needs of the sellers as they can. While seller financing is not the only benefit to the developer of addressing a seller's needs, it is a big one.

On the other hand, a young land trust, with a small following and possibly not yet any deep cultural connection to the more conservative, often

Figure 12.1
At the Teton County
4-H auction the
community bids
alongside the
agricultural sector.
(Jackson Hole News &
Guide)

agricultural, landowning community, is at a disadvantage. Even a land trust that has been very successful with its donated easement program may find it hard to build on that reputation as it moves into purchasing conservation interests.

As a result, there may be landowners who remain out of reach to land trusts for many years. But actions speak louder than words. After a few large land trust purchases, more effort to reach into the community and stronger branding, the land trust's reputation will start to change. By taking the right steps, the land trust can increase a seller's level of comfort with a land trust buyer. A seller who is comfortable with a buyer is more likely to finance.[2]

Local Practices

Whether or not sellers will finance sometimes depends on local practices. A place to start understanding whether seller financing might work is to ask the questions: What is the norm in our community? Is it seller financing or does everyone finance through the bank? Whatever the current situation, sellers often have their own reasons for the way they want to structure sales. Often deal making is not all about the money; it is about something else that the seller wants or needs, which may be intangible. In the case of seller financing, the need can be very subtle. You don't always need to know what those reasons are. Just remember that achieving their desired outcomes should ultimately drive how you approach the deal.

Chapter 13
External Revolving Loan Funds

A conservation-friendly source of short-term loans, primarily for use by land trusts to purchase land and conservation easements, and to cover associated costs.

At first blush, Ann Hooke seems like an unlikely person to have led a small land trust through several complicated land acquisitions. Ann came to the Island Heritage Trust on Deer Isle, Maine, because, as she says, she "likes to tromp around in the woods." As an exercise instructor for older adults and an avid hiker, assisting a land trust steward its lands was the perfect way for her to help.

In 2002, the Island Heritage Trust was small, with an annual budget of $35,000 and one part-time clerical staff person. Ann was vice president of the board of trustees. That year, the developer who owned most of the nearby, small Carney Island was willing to sell to the land trust for a bargain price. Not only is the scenic fifteen-acre island just offshore from Deer Isle, but it is a refuge for ospreys and eagles that nest there. The water around the northern part of the island is rich in marine life, and a feeding ground for raptors, wintering ducks, and migratory shorebirds. "The land trust had to buy it," she explained. "It was just too important to Deer Isle, right in everyone's view. So many people wanted the island protected. We just couldn't let the chance to save it from development get away."

Over the coming months, the land trust raised almost $70,000, but needed $155,000 more to close on the purchase.[1] Ann was quite confident that eventually the rest of the money could be found because the project was so popular, but not in time for the closing. She approached the Maine Coast Heritage Trust (MCHT) for a loan from its revolving loan fund. While MCHT was receptive to the application, they required collateral to secure the loan. Neither MCHT nor the land trust wanted to use the island as collateral because, if the land trust couldn't raise the money for repayment, the island would have to be sold. MCHT suggested that the land trust instead collect personal guarantees from board members and other land trust supporters. In 2004, Ann and her husband guaranteed $5,000 themselves, knowing that if the land trust did not raise the $155,000, they would have to honor their $5,000 commitment or a portion of it. But Ann was confident that the support and money were there.

Collecting the personal guarantees gave the Island Heritage Trust new confidence that they could raise the money. If people were willing to guarantee the money, they reasoned, then surely donors could be found to close the funding gap. The guarantees helped bring around some board members who were "still going through that sand-under-the-skin discomfort of borrowing money," says Ann. Securing the loan invigorated the volunteer workforce to raise the money to pay it off, which they soon did.

The Island Heritage Trust went on to collaborate with MCHT and a community group to acquire several related parcels. MCHT helped the land trust with negotiating the contract to purchase the properties, training on due diligence research, and fundraising. Energized by the Carney Island loan and by the success of a similarly ambitious campaign by a neighboring small land trust, Island Heritage Trust raised over $2 million. Ann says that the land trust could never have considered borrowing money or taking on the larger collection of acquisitions without the help of the staff of MCHT and its loan fund.

MCHT's external revolving loan fund is like others around the United States in that it loans out money to land trusts for bridge financing. These funds have been established mostly with the help of foundations in many parts of the country to make financing readily available to constituent land conservation organizations. They fill a gap in conservation financing because land trusts often don't have other places to go for low-cost loans and may need assistance in setting them up and paying them off. The advantage to these funds over other sources of lending is that they share the land conservation mission with the borrowers they serve. The staffs of most are eager to help a novice land trust apply for a loan, and to do what they can to ensure that the borrower and the conservation project for which the loan is made are successful.

Maine's Conservation Revolving Loan Fund

MCHT has one of the most user-friendly conservation revolving loan funds in the United States. Under the leadership of Jay Espy, MCHT has designed a lending program that encourages small land trusts to do great things. MCHT staffs its large region, the coast of Maine, with locally based project managers.

Figure 13.1
With the help of loans from the Maine Coast Heritage Trust, land trusts including the Island Heritage Trust (its Carney Island project shown here) (above) and the Quoddy Regional Land Trust (shore-line project shown) (below) are protecting Maine's coast. (Courtesy of Island Heritage Trust and Quoddy Regional Land Trust)

Each manager becomes intimately familiar with the land trusts in his or her region and is available to help the land trust with technical support to use the loan program and to impose the discipline essential for successfully borrowing and paying back loans. MCHT's core staff supports the loan program with legal, programmatic, and financial assistance (see appendices 13.1 and 13.2).

The project manager for the Island Heritage Trust's area, Ciona Ulbrich, is very involved with land trusts in her region. "On the coast of Maine, each harbor has its own culture, not just its own wildlife and scenic resources. MCHT feels that it is important to tailor its projects to meet the needs of each community," says Ciona. "If there is a local trust working in an area, MCHT will often partner with that trust on a project at a range of levels and ways. Sometimes project managers even suggest projects to a local land trust, or more often we offer help through the process or with certain steps along the way. On the other hand, some land trusts need very little help and project managers have little to do with the project except provide a loan." When Ann Hooke became board president of Island Heritage Trust, Ciona helped her with everything she needed to oversee the organization. "She would come to board meetings and could tell the board what other land trusts were doing and reassure them," Ann explained.

MCHT is committed to the success of the one hundred land trusts of Maine. It makes loans, helps raise money, advises, and holds hands. MCHT has made forty-one[2] loans from its $3 million loan fund[3] since 1994. The fund made twenty-five loans to other land trusts. The rest were internal to MCHT, mostly for pre-acquisition projects for government agencies. The fund now averages three to four loans a year to land trusts. In addition to the support given by its project managers, MCHT's financial associates and legal counsel carefully review each loan application. Other staff members review the programmatic aspects of the proposal, and MCHT's board or executive committee (depending on the timing of the closing) signs off on the loan.

On certain occasions, MCHT shares in the risk of the loan. In the case of the Carney Island loan, MCHT made the no-interest loan because the island's protection was a high priority for MCHT as well. For another parcel, MCHT partnered with Island Heritage Trust because protection was, again, such a high priority.

Even with MCHT's help and partnership, Ann still thinks that taking out loans can be a little daunting. For the Carney Island loan, part was to be repaid using grants that had not yet been approved, though Ann had received favorable feedback from the foundations. But the land trust was definitely farther out on a limb than they had been in the past, and for more money.

Other land trusts use the MCHT loan fund more conservatively. Robert Miller, a founder and current board chair of the small Great Auk Land Trust in the easternmost corner of the Maine coast, says that they use MCHT's loan fund exclusively to bridge timing gaps between a project closing and when the takeout money will be in hand. This land trust had a budget of $3,000 and no staff when it made its first purchase and received its first loan from MCHT. Great Auk Land Trust wanted to buy two hundred acres for $120,000. The state had approved a grant for $45,000 and the land trust had raised the rest of the money through smaller grants and gifts from individuals. But payout of the state grant extended past Great Auk Land Trust's closing date. MCHT made a loan to bridge the six-month gap.

Robert prefers that the repayment money be guaranteed before taking a loan. He does not like borrowing in anticipation of raising the money. "We like to know where all the grants and funds are coming from and have everything budgeted and programmed in. In other words, we don't like to go out on a limb." Unlike its namesake, the large and extinct coastal bird, this land trust intends to stay in business for a very long time by managing its acquisitions carefully.

Other groups are more flexible with their MCHT loans. Nancy Perlson, executive director of the Rangeley Lakes Heritage Trust, is particularly creative. When the land trust was quite small, with an annual budget of $100,000, it took out its biggest loan from MCHT. Nancy draws on her previous experience administering community development block grants and in real estate to help meet the conservation objectives of her land trust. "The primary problem with acquisitions," she says, "is that land deals usually close quickly and at the year end, and grant making and even fundraising cycles have different timing." Her biggest fundraising season is the summer, when the population of the small community of Rangeley swells with wealthier seasonal residents. If a project comes up after the summer, she is hard-pressed to raise the money for a year-end closing. She has also found that there is a significant lag time between when pledges and grants are made and when the payments are received.

In one project, the Rangeley Lakes Heritage Trust contracted to buy the 1,100-acre South Bog for $1.2 million with a December 17, 2004, closing. Most of the parcel was habitat-rich wetland and forested upland. The land trust split the property into two parcels. It put permanent conservation restrictions on a one-thousand-acre portion, and a one-hundred-acre portion was left unrestricted to serve as equity for loans. Rangeley Lakes Heritage Trust was prepared to sell the one-hundred-acre parcel with restrictions for limited development because of its location and limited natural resources, if it could not pay off its loans any other way. With the property split, the land trust qualified for a loan from MCHT for conserved lands. MCHT requires that loans only be made on projects where conservation is guaranteed. Having an exit strategy through the sale of the hundred acres allowed the land trust to borrow enough money to finance the project. It was a realistic and smart way

Figure 13.2
With creative planning
and a loan from Maine
Coast Heritage Trust,
Rangeley Lakes Her-
itage Trust protected
the 1,100-acre South
Bog property.
(Courtesy of Rangeley
Lakes Land Trust)

for the land trust to structure the project, given that the land lent itself to these opportunities. Conserving most of the land rather than none of it is the best result in many circumstances.

The Rangeley Lakes Heritage Trust secured a bank loan for $250,000 and a $250,000 line of credit with a first mortgage on the one hundred acres without burdening the rest of the one thousand acres. It then secured a loan for $250,000 from MCHT's revolving fund using the line of credit from the bank as collateral. The land trust borrowed another $300,000, which was unsecured, from a fund set up in conjunction with a Federal Energy Regulatory Commission (FERC) dam relicensing settlement agreement[4]. In total, this $100,000 organization borrowed $800,000.

How does the land trust intend to pay off these loans? Nancy has a plan. Since MCHT requires a thorough repayment plan, the discipline of knowing where those dollars will come from is instilled in Maine's land trusts. Rangeley Lakes Heritage Trust is using traditional sources, including a major capital campaign, and some innovative ones. Fortunately, the land trust has a good track record with individual fundraising and is less concerned than it might be about its ability to fundraise for a significant portion of the repayment. It has already received $300,000 from a wetlands mitigation project funded by the transportation department and has paid back its MCHT loan, thus freeing up its bank line of credit for other projects. It also expects to receive a $300,000 grant from the FERC licensing settlement fund. And the land trust has its fallback of selling the one hundred acres if the planned revenue sources come up short. "It always helps if you have a terrific project with multiple values, such as river preservation, fisheries habitat protection, and recreation," says Nancy. But before taking on any project, she wants to be confident about where the money is going to come from, usually by conducting an informal feasibility study.

Despite Maine's two bond issues funding the state program for conservation, Land For Maine's Future, many land trusts find ways to buy properties and pay off loans using nongovernmental sources. Obviously the wealthy resort communities along Maine's coast have a lot to do with land trusts' success in fundraising, but it goes beyond this. Maine land trusts far north near the Canadian border, with far fewer affluent communities, have managed to fund their projects creatively. MCHT's assistance with bridge financing is usually a big part of their success.

The Shapes and Sizes of Conservation Revolving Loan Funds

Conservation revolving loan funds take the traditional bank-lending model and infuse it with conservation goals. They share the missions of the land trusts they serve. In many cases, they do more than loan money; they "go to the mat" for a project, working out favorable loan terms and even securing takeout funding.

Conservation revolving loan funds come in a variety of shapes and sizes. Internal loan protection funds (covered in the following chapter) lend only to their own programs. Those that lend primarily or frequently to outside entities are external revolving loan funds.

This chapter considers state and regional external loan funds (e.g., MCHT) that are primarily administered by regional land trusts, coalitions of land trusts, and conservation intermediary organizations. National conservation organizations such as The Conservation Fund also loan externally. There are other loan funds with capital from mitigation or re-licensing agreements, regulatory approvals or legal settlements administered by land trusts, community foundations and public agencies; some public agencies lend out of their own conservation programs.

State and regional external loan funds discussed here serve such borrowers as the Island Heritage Trust that do not have cash reserves to close an acquisition before receiving the take out funding for it. Like almost every source of conservation financing, loan funds fill this interim financing niche.

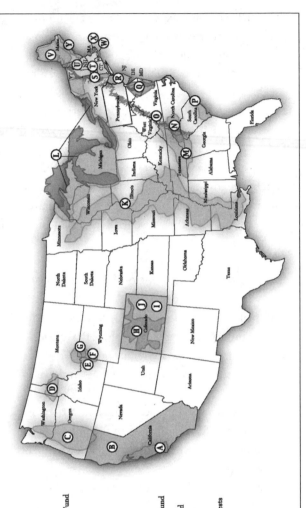

Regional Internal / External Conservation Revolving Loan Funds

A. Central Coast Opportunity Fund
B. Preserving Wild California
C. Pacific Forest Trust's Conservation Capital Fund
D. Avista Revolving Trust Fund
E. West Hill Foundation for Nature, Inc.
F. Greater Yellowstone Ecosystem Revolving Loan Fund
G. Greater Yellowstone Loan Fund
H. Colorado Conservation Loan Fund
I. Colorado Tax Credit Revolving Loan Fund
J. Colorado Open Lands Revolving Loan Fund
K. Mississippi River Revolving Loan Fund
L. Great Lakes Revolving Loan Fund
M. Southern Appalachian Loan Fund
N. Conservation Trust for North Carolina Land
     Acquisition Revolving Loan Program
O. Appalachian Trail Conference Land Acquisition Fund
P. Lowcountry Conservation Loan Fund
Q. Chesapeake Bay Foundation Revolving Loan Fund
R. New Jersey Conservation Loan Fund
S. New York Conservation Loan Fund
T. Western Massachusetts Loan Fund
U. Society for the Protection of New Hampshire Forests
     Environmental Loan Fund
V. Northern Forest Protection Fund
W. Buzzard's Bay Lands Revolving Fund
X. Cape Cod Land Fund
Y. Maine Coast Heritage Trust Land Acquisition
     Revolving Loan Fund

Figure 13.3

Nongovernmental external revolving loan funds that support conservation in the United States.

The source of the loan capital and restrictions, if any, on its use can affect the flexibility of the terms of its loans. Funds capitalized with grants or capital campaign proceeds have more latitude than those capitalized with loans—usually foundation loans (program-related investments)—absent supplemental funding.

Loan funds like MCHT's with experienced staff on the ground invested in each project's success can meet many of their borrower's needs. They can, for example turn around a loan in short order, or spend the time and effort to work with a borrower to come up with security for the loan that meets both parties' needs.

Another condition that can improve the success of a loan fund is the availability of takeout money. There is a theory that conservation revolving loan funds can only thrive where there are significant sources of public takeout money. This is not entirely true. Land trusts have become very adept at raising takeout money. In areas where there are wealthy full-time or seasonal residents, this is much easier. In other places, though, land trusts have mixed and matched funding sources to pay back even substantial loans with little or no public money.

Changes in the levels of state funding can slow or even shut down loan demand, by flooding the market so loans aren't needed or drying it up completely. One previously active foundation loan program didn't make a loan for nine months during one such period, and the regional Open Space Institute had a similar drought for a while in New Jersey.

Lack of public money can have an impact. The Greater Yellowstone Ecosystem Revolving Loan Fund program experienced lower demand for loans than it initially expected because of an unexpected reduction in federal takeout funds. This was partly due to high expectations by all participants for funding, based on a history of federal investment through the Land and Water Conservation Fund in the area around Yellowstone and Grand Teton national parks. While the land trusts in the ecosystem have, in the past, undertaken governmental pre-acquisition projects, they are now adapting to new circumstances and finding new sources of money, public and otherwise, as the traditional public sources dwindle.

State and Regional External Revolving Loan Funds

There are at least twenty-five nongovernmental regional external revolving loan funds in the United States.[5] Most of these lend to their own programs and to land trusts, though a few also lend to landowners and public agencies. There are likely more regional loan funds than those discussed here. Since there is no central clearinghouse it is difficult to obtain information on all existing funds.

All of the regional external revolving loan funds are relatively new (the oldest ones are ten to fifteen years old) and thus have limited track records. Nonetheless, the vast majority of these are frequently and successfully lending money for conservation transactions.

State and regional external revolving loan funds are scattered across the nation and vary in their origins, sources of funding, and level of support. State or regional land trusts or intermediary organizations administer most of them, though the national Conservation Fund sponsors three funds (see online appendix at www.conservationguide.com) and at least one community foundation sponsors another.

Intermediary-Administered Loan Funds

Some loan funds are run by conservation intermediary organizations, which are a new breed of conservation institution offering a variety of services to land trusts and donors. These organizations have emerged to support large foundations with regional lending and grant making. They help foundations and other donors to "outsource" some of their philanthropic functions to organizations with soulful expertise.

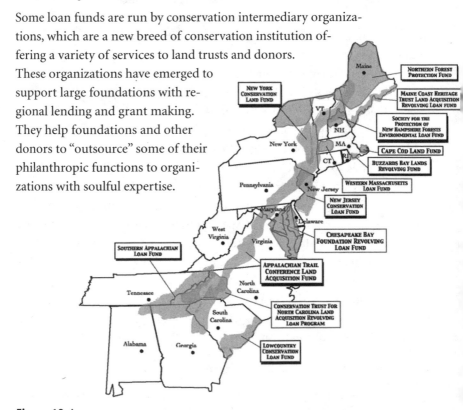

Figure 13.4
Nongovernmental external revolving loan funds that support conservation in the eastern United States.

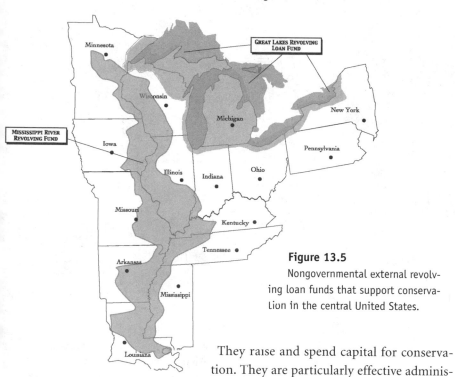

Figure 13.5

Nongovernmental external revolving loan funds that support conservation in the central United States.

They raise and spend capital for conservation. They are particularly effective administrators of loan funds because they are knowledgeable and professional about lending and helpful to their clients.

Loans from intermediary organizations are usually exclusively external.[6] Their mission is to support other organizations. Because intermediaries do not engage in their own land acquisitions, they do not compete (and are not perceived to compete) with their borrowers for projects. A sampling of these intermediary organizations include: Colorado Conservation Trust, Resources Legacy Fund, the Chesapeake Bay Foundation, the Coastal Community Foundation of South Carolina, the Compact of Cape Cod Conservation Trusts, Inc., and the Coalition for Buzzards Bay. The two latter organizations, the Compact of Cape Cod Conservation Trusts and the Coalition for Buzzards Bay, are small associations of land trusts with the primary functions of providing technical assistance to their member land trusts and administering loan funds. Some other larger land trust programs act like intermediaries to the degree that they invest large amounts of money into projects in highly leveraged and nuanced ways (see online appendices at www.conservationguide.com).

One model for an intermediary organization is Resources Legacy Fund in California, which was initially established by the David and Lucile Packard Foundation and is now primarily funded by twelve foundations and private

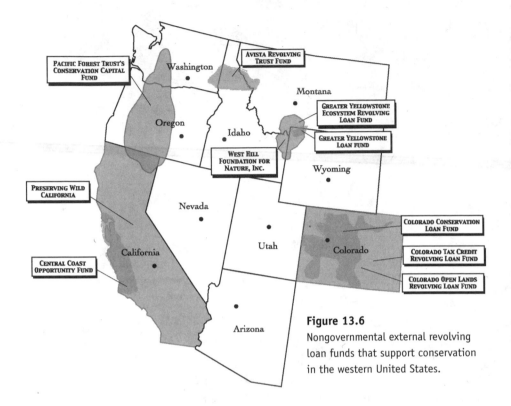

Figure 13.6

Nongovernmental external revolving loan funds that support conservation in the western United States.

donors. Resources Legacy Fund (RLF) and its supporting organization, Resources Legacy Fund Foundation (RLFF), initially helped to manage a large, $175 million initiative of the Packard Foundation, Conserving California Landscapes Initiative (CCLI). This program funded California land trusts and land conservation and leveraged the protection of more than 400,000 acres of California lands (and attracted over $700 million in leveraged funds) over five years. RLF does a sizable volume of lending. It also grants (or regrants, since most of its money comes from foundations) to projects all over the state and recently to projects elsewhere in the United States and the world.[7] In 2004, it regranted approximately $50 million and was involved in the lending of some $30 million in loans.

RLF runs several large grant and loan programs, including Preserving Wild California and the Greater Yellowstone Ecosystem Revolving Fund (GYERF). In California, land trusts are familiar with incurring debt because of the big state conservation programs that have invested billions of dollars in the system in recent years. RLF and RLFF have been substantial funders of capacity-building in land conservation organizations. With RLF's young GYERF in

Montana, Idaho, and Wyoming, it is taking whatever steps are necessary to assist land trusts new to borrowing. As one associate of RLF advised, the land trusts can "get practice by taking these friendly loans."

Intermediaries must make a special effort to understand and meet the needs of land trusts because they are not directly "in the game." This can be a disadvantage, but also an advantage in that they aren't in competition with their borrowers and they can dedicate more of their time to attracting new funding to land conservation and conservation organizations in other ways.

In order to stay close to its far-flung Greater Yellowstone Ecosystem Revolving Fund, RLF contracted with a well-respected conservationist in the area. It also carefully chose a local advisory committee that has the regional knowledge needed to assist in vetting the loan applications, but is not conflicted by direct involvement with any of the land trusts of the region. The advisory committee meets whenever loan applications are submitted. It rates the projects against evaluation criteria and assesses their biological and regional attributes.

RLF and the land trusts in the Greater Yellowstone Ecosystem have faced several challenges to using RLF's loan fund to conserve some of the most threatened and dramatic landscapes in the country. The borrowing experience of the land trusts of the region varied widely; takeout funding was less readily available. The fund itself was capitalized with a loan (program-related investment) from the Packard Foundation and had relatively little operating capital. When commercial interest rates were low, it was more difficult for RLF to offer loans at competitive interest rates because it had to pay back its own loan from the Packard Foundation at a negotiated interest rate, and was challenged to use the revenue from the slightly higher rates it charged to land trusts to cover its lending expenses. Despite these barriers, the loan fund made three loans in its first year, including one to a smaller land trust. While working with a loan (as opposed to a grant) may constrain RLF in some ways, it also motivates it to get loans out the door, as the interest paid by its borrowers helps to cover its costs. With interest rates rising, its lower-interest loans have become more attractive.

Regional External Loan Funds

The following three funds demonstrate the breadth of loan funds, ranging from the Colorado Conservation Trust's modest, narrow-purpose Colorado Tax Credit Revolving Loan Fund, to the very independent, self-sufficient, and appropriately capitalized Cape Cod Land Fund, to the large, independent, highly capitalized Open Space Institute with its multiple loan funds. Two other less active loan funds, Pacific Forest Trust and West Hill Fund for Nature, offer different and potentially promising models.

1. *Small and Targeted: Colorado Conservation Trust's Tax Credit Revolving Loan Fund*: The Colorado Conservation Trust (CCT), an intermediary organization, has capitalized two loan funds, one of which, the Colorado Tax Credit Revolving Loan Fund, offers small loans to land trusts. The money is targeted to help landowners defer the transaction costs of donating conservation easements that produce state tax credits in anticipation of revenue from the sale of those credits. The Colorado Conservation Trust loan program advances funds and is paid back with the tax credit proceeds. The other fund, the Colorado Conservation Loan Fund, provides bridge financing to land conservation organizations for land conservation transactions.

   The Colorado Tax Credit Revolving Loan Fund addresses a cash-flow problem for landowners that prevents them from taking advantage of the state's tax credit program. Imagine one of Colorado's many ranchers who is land rich but cash poor. He cannot afford the upfront costs of protecting his ranch with a conservation easement or the costs involved in applying for a state tax credit—costs that can amount to as much as $25,000 for such expenses as appraisals and legal costs. Without upfront capital, his beautiful pastureland edged with critical riparian and winter habitat for elk or sage grouse will go unprotected.

   Rather than making a loan to the landowner, the CCT loan program relies on the local land trust that will eventually be holding the landowner's easement. The land trust identifies the landowner as someone truly in need of a loan to cover transactional costs. It then documents the extent of the costs and why the landowner cannot pay them, and submits a promissory note from the landowner stating that the loan will be paid back at the closing on the sale of the tax credit. The land trust secures the loan with a recourse note (or personal guarantee). CCT evaluates the proposal with preference for projects with high conservation value, public benefit and imminent threat of development. Based on that evaluation, CCT then makes a no-interest loan of up to $15,000 for up to one year to the land trust, and the land trust re-loans it to the landowner. As a general rule, a single organization may not have more than two outstanding loans at any given time; however, CCT reserves the right to make exceptions.

This loan program is interesting because it has targeted a specific problem: the cash-flow barriers to utilization of the state tax credit program. Because a relatively small amount of money is needed to solve the problem in the individual cases, the fund does not have to be very large.

2. *Medium-sized and Independent: Cape Cod Land Fund (Administered by the Compact of Cape Cod Conservation Trusts, Inc.)*: The Cape Cod Land Fund shows what a group of land trusts can do to create their own loan fund. The mission of the Cape Cod Land Fund is to provide its member land trusts with low-interest loans on a timely basis.

The Cape Cod Land Fund was established in 1992 by the Compact of Cape Cod Conservation Trusts, Inc., a coalition of twenty-five local and regional land trusts working in Barnstable County, which encompasses the peninsula of Cape Cod in Massachusetts. The Compact, a small, nonprofit service center, delivers expertise and loans to its member land trusts. Representatives of the member land trusts serve on the 250-person board of the Compact bringing, Executive Director Mark Robinson says, capacity resources and energy to the cause of land protection. The land trusts determined in 1992 that, with the intense development pressure on Cape Cod, they needed a loan fund in order to compete for land. But to do so the Compact had to raise money in the same county of its member land trusts. This was a delicate issue. To avoid conflicts, the Compact made up a list of potential donors and gave the land trusts the power to veto solicitation of any of the prospects. Because the land trusts wanted the loan fund to succeed, this strategy worked well. In many cases, the Compact was able to raise funds from donors with whom the land trusts individually had had no success. The Compact also tried to raise funds through foundations, but Mark Robinson says that very few private foundations were interested in building a revolving loan fund, though he has had some success with family foundations. In addition, each member land trust contributed $1,000. In total, the Compact raised $600,000 to launch the loan fund. It is now capitalized with $650,000.

The terms offered by the Cape Cod Land Fund are unusual. They require no security. Mark says that the Compact trusts its member land trusts. He develops strong relationships with them, attends their meetings, and participates in projects. So he feels familiar enough with their boards and staff to know if they're capable of repaying loans. Some land trusts use loans to bridge pledges that donors want to give in the following tax year.

Others are waiting for town meetings to authorize expenditures to buy a property. On Cape Cod, the town governments are committed to protecting what they can of their varied landscapes of white sand beaches, salt marshes, pine forests, intriguing cranberry bogs, and startlingly blue kettle ponds. They are very good about following through on their promises to pay land trusts. Mark does not see the no-security requirement as a great risk and instead believes that it cuts down on paperwork and turnaround time.

The Cape Cod Land Fund's interest rate varies from 1 to 4 percent, and the loan-to-land-value ratio ranges from about 0.5 percent to 100 percent. Loans are primarily used for land acquisition, though at least one loan has been used to pay for an appraisal. The application is an uncomplicated two-page form and the approval process is simple and quick. Loans are reviewed and approved within days and money can be paid out within a week. (See online appendix at www.conservationguide.com)

Of the twenty-seven loans made by the Cape Cod Land Fund between 1992 and 2006, all have been repaid or are on schedule. The Cape Cod Land Fund hasn't made any loans greater than $300,000, but Mark says they would be open to lending more if a land trust requested it. He is very keen to have the money in the fund used. Three hundred forty acres, worth $11.55 million, have been protected with Cape Cod Land Fund loans.

The Cape Cod Land Fund has guidelines for prioritizing projects based on environmental significance, location, size, and development threat. Other factors considered include public support, partnerships with other groups, the applicant's funding history from the Cape Cod Land Fund, and the perceived capability of the project's eventual success. Mark tries to help land trusts get takeout money pledged before agreeing to a loan. "The land trusts have found it much easier to create a sense of urgency to generate takeout funding when the property is still unprotected," he observes.

So far, the Cape Cod Land Fund hasn't had to worry about prioritizing projects, because competitive applications have never been submitted simultaneously. Should this happen, the Cape Cod Land Fund would try to divide the funds evenly, helping all applying land trusts as much as possible, rather than making a judgment call on which project is more worthy.

Mark Robinson has a full-time staff of three. When he receives a loan application, the Cape Cod Land Fund board of managers votes on it. The fund board, elected by the board of directors of the Compact and including members of three land trusts, a bank president, and a former county commissioner, directs investment, grant, and loan decisions. Most of the Compact's land trusts don't have many technical staff, so the Compact staff serves as technical advisors for the loans. Mark helps to fill out the loan applications for most of the land trusts, and then personally submits them to the loan board.

In 1998, the Cape Cod Land Fund began using the interest income from its corpus to make mini-grants ($1,000 to $7,000) to accompany the loans or as stand-alone grants for land purchases. The grants are not to exceed 10 percent of the purchase price of the property or 25 percent of any amount being borrowed, and can only be made where the land trust will be the ultimate owner of the property, or where the land trust is a formal partner with a public or nonprofit conservation agency. These mini-grants have been useful in building confidence for land trusts to start capital campaigns and to persuade other donors of a project's viability.

A distinguishing quality of the Land Fund is the close connection between the Compact's leadership and the client land trusts. The land trusts work together to guide the Compact, which creates a high level of trust and interchange. The commitment to shared risk developed through an awareness of the work of each trust, and the governance role that these land trusts play in the Compact, allow the loan fund staff and board to feel comfortable offering generous, flexible loan terms.

3. *Large: The Open Space Institute*: One of the most active and largest external revolving funds is administered by the Open Space Institute (OSI), the largest land trust in New York State. OSI was founded in 1964.[8] Its reach as a land trust was greatly expanded in the 1970s by the generosity of DeWitt and Lila Acheson Wallace, who founded the *Reader's Digest*, the most widely read periodical in the world. The Wallaces endowed OSI with *Reader's Digest* stock. The stock was later converted to other assets, which has since appreciated. OSI's endowment is now worth $210 million.

OSI has protected over one hundred thousand acres in New York State, originally focusing on the Hudson River Valley. In 2002, after a strategic planning process, OSI's trustees decided to establish the conservation finance program and to commit $20 million of its own assets for use as loans to other land trusts in selected regions of the eastern United States. OSI acts as a hybrid intermediary–land conservation organization that does its own projects only in New York State. Elsewhere (primarily in the Northern

Forest of New England), it grants and regrants money from other foundations.

Its primary function outside of New York State is to make low-cost loans for sizable regional transactions and a spectrum of smaller transactions. Using its own capital and loans from foundations, OSI has established several regional "branch" loan funds: The Northern Forest Protection Fund for New England in 2000; the New Jersey Conservation Loan Fund in 2002; the New York Conservation Loan Fund in 2004; the Southern Appalachian Loan Fund in 2005; and the Western Massachusetts Loan Fund in 2005. These intermediary functions are modeled after the Resources Legacy Fund in California, described above.

Each of OSI's funds has a field coordinator or loan officer who acts as OSI's eyes and ears on the ground and is responsible for assessing the conservation merits of the potential loans. Its three-person credit committee approves all loans.

OSI works closely with several foundations that not only capitalize certain of its loan programs (with almost $6 million in loans[9]), but both the Kohlberg and the Geraldine Dodge Foundations have made operating grants to OSI to defray the expenses of due diligence on their loans. The Kohlberg Foundation also granted OSI $75,000 to regrant to its borrowers for transaction costs. This is a very significant benefit, as these costs can be prohibitively high. These grants offer a meaningful incentive for borrowing.

With its substantial endowment and big vision, OSI plays in the big leagues, protecting large tracts of land in partnership with the large conservation organizations. It invests in and has made loans to some of the largest domestic land acquisitions for conservation, particularly in the Northern Forest region of New York, New Hampshire, Maine, and Vermont. Its Northern Forest Protection Fund has made sixteen grants and three loans totaling $15 million and protecting over 1.5 million acres. It is an involved funder and grantor that supports the protection of large forested landscapes and integrated management of working forests and forest reserves.

As a lender, OSI has fewer conservation criteria, relying on the local knowledge of its field coordinators. It uses a "green screen" to assess the conservation merits of its loan applications. As an example, it made a $3 million loan to the Appalachian Mountain Club for a $14.2 million, 37,000-acre parcel in the heart of Maine's 100-Mile Wilderness, traversed

Figure 13.7
A $1.5 million loan from the Open Space Institute's New Jersey Conservation Loan Fund to the New Jersey Conservation Foundation facilitated the purchase of the 9,400-acre DeMarco Cranberry Farm (now the Franklin Parker Preserve), which connects five state-owned properties within the 1.1-million-acre Pine Barrens. (©M. Hogan/hoganphoto.com)

by the Appalachian Trail. The Katahdin Iron Works property has important ecological and recreational resources and will be made available for multiple compatible uses including protection of natural areas, sustainable forestry, and low-impact recreation.

Altogether, in the Northern Forest and elsewhere, OSI has made twenty-three loans since 2002, totaling $24.365 million, for the permanent protection of 910,910 acres with an aggregate real estate value of $208 million. OSI has not had any defaults on its loans. Their average loan is $1.06 million, with loans ranging in size from $200,000 to $1.5 million, primarily to midsized land trusts.

An interesting new feature of the program is an internal loan loss reserve, which is designed to cover losses from its lending program. With this cushion, OSI will be able to make riskier loans, which will allow it to experiment with the way that loan money can be used. OSI is committed to growing its lending programs so that it can maintain at least ten to twelve million dollars in outstanding loans. It continues to expand its services as an already substantial intermediary organization to help strengthen the financial capacity of land trusts through loan counseling and technical assistance. It also seeks to build on its growing track record to assist foundations with regranting and reloaning services. Foundations often avoid the business of lending because they lack the expertise to screen, underwrite, and monitor loans. OSI hopes to offer these services to foundations and encourage them to become involved in the conservation lending business. (See chapter 15 on program-related investments.)

It is difficult to discern the scale and breadth of OSI's activities because it does so many things, and is growing and changing so rapidly. While OSI seeks out larger, more complex transactions with substantial conservation outcomes, it also has made smaller loans to smaller, regional land trusts in some of its geographic areas of interest.

With the strength of its large capital reserves and the creativity of its leadership, OSI plans to continue to innovate in conservation bridge financing. As its revenue from lending grows, it will commit more money to research and information dissemination about conservation finance. "We want to be the 'go-to' institution for financial information and support in the Eastern United States," says Peter Howell, OSI's vice president and director of conservation financing. The growth in OSI's lending program and its new initiatives are evidence that it is committed to this approach. This organization is one to watch in the coming years, as it will likely create important new opportunities in the area of conservation finance for all types and sizes of conservation borrowers.

4. *Two Noteworthy Models: Pacific Forest Trust and West Hill Fund for Nature:* These two loan funds are interesting in their unusual approaches—one for its target borrowers, and the other for its capitalization. Though neither are often used, it is the structure and purpose of the funds that offer potential for broader application. The Pacific Forest Trust (PFT), a land trust working to conserve critical forestlands in California, Oregon, and Washington, lends to landowners. It looks for conservation-minded landowners who are on the verge of selling out because of the high cost of their commercial debt. PFT steps in, buys out and restructures the debt to make it more affordable in exchange for a legally binding conservation commitment such as a sale or gift of a conservation easement. PFT meets its objectives by keeping a conservation-minded landowner on the land (which

promises good stewardship) and by receiving a conservation benefit. In one case, that benefit came from the sale of a conservation easement, the proceeds of which were used to pay off the debt.

West Hill Fund for Nature accesses a significant but little-used source of capital. This relatively inactive loan fund is capitalized through the portfolio of a conservation-minded businessman who wanted to put it to work for conservation, but at minimum risk. Although the Trust for Public Land and The Nature Conservancy have used this loan fund on occasion, it is now somewhat dormant as the focus of the foundation has evolved away from loan making. Nonetheless, the idea that investment portfolios of conservation-minded people could be working for conservation through loan funds is a potent concept.

Regional Loan Funds Nuts and Bolts

Mechanics: Applying to an external revolving loan fund is fairly straightforward. But meeting its requirements can be problematic for a novice borrower. A typical application asks for information that can help the fund evaluate an organization's ability to repay a loan and to identify where the loan fund can go to recoup its loan if the land trust fails to repay. Evaluating repayment goes beyond an oft-required repayment plan. The loan fund wants assurances that the land trust is entirely committed to repayment, through a corporate or board resolution; that the land trust is well run and can raise the money for repayment, by reviewing its financial reports and its certificate of good standing from the state; and that the property is a sound purchase from a programmatic, real estate, and legal point of view. By reviewing title reports, evaluation criteria, and often by visiting the site, the loan fund can determine how important the purchase is. Loan funds strive to minimize turnaround time on the loan. Some can pay out a loan in one to two weeks from application. Others need more time. If a land trust has borrowed before or has been prequalified by the loan fund, turnaround time can be quicker.

Loan Terms: The terms offered by loan funds are standard with a few notable exceptions. In general, the loan period is one year, often with provisions for limited extensions (usually no more than one year). The interest rates are below prime, or indexed to prime or LIBOR, or at fixed rates between 1 percent and 3 percent (in 2005), though these rates will change as interest rates fluctuate. Repayment plans and collateral are usually required. First mortgages on the targeted conservation properties are rarely accepted as collateral because the loan fund does not want to be forced to foreclose on a high-resource parcel.

The Maine Coast Heritage Trust and others have been willing, on occasion, to take a first mortgage if they want to take a second crack at protecting the property if the borrowing land trust fails and must default. When OSI wants security for a loan, it prefers financial security (i.e., security other than land). However, it is often prepared to take a first mortgage on an undeveloped or minimally developed property at its "conservation" or restricted value.

Variations on collateral arrangements are found at two very flexible loan funds in Massachusetts: the Cape Cod Land Fund and the Coalition for Buzzards Bay's Land Revolving Fund. Both offer very generous terms. Because the loan funds are so closely connected to the land trusts that established them, they are particularly user-friendly. This may be a luxury of knowing your client base so well. Buzzards Bay has no security requirements for loans under $100,000. The Cape Cod Land Fund has no security requirements, no specific repayment plan requirement, and charges 1 to 4 percent interest. Unsecured loans offer an added opportunity in that they can be used to help secure bigger loans from third parties. Larger lenders like OSI routinely secure their loans to larger borrowers with recourse notes against organizational balance sheets.

Mark Elsbree, the director of the Northwest Office of The Conservation Fund, administers the Greater Yellowstone Loan Fund (a second revolving fund operating in the Greater Yellowstone region). Because the fund is capitalized with a *grant* from the Doris Duke Charitable Foundation, Mark can price his loans with less focus on the fund's sustainability. Mark has been creative with his use of interest rates to meet the acreage and land-value conditions of the grant that created the loan fund. He initially kept rates very low (often 1 percent) to attract borrowers. If the borrowers intended to keep the loans for more than the minimum amount of time, he would increase the subsequent rate to encourage them to repay more quickly. Because his fund is relatively small, Mark managed the size of the loans to maintain a fund balance so other land trusts could access the fund. Early in the loan fund operations, Mark could have loaned out the entire $1 million corpus to one borrower. Tempting as it was to see the loan fund used completely, the conditions of the capitalizing grant and

Mark's own interest in spreading the money around argued for only partially lending the corpus early on. Taking this approach, Mark increased the impact of the fund on conservation in the region and created a model of lending flexibility that demonstrated a significant demand for a well-managed fund.

Several other funds will, on occasion, reduce their interest rates to as low as 0 percent. The Colorado Tax Credit Fund makes all its loans with no interest.

Despite the generally favorable terms offered by loan funds, it is always worth doing a little comparison shopping. Comparing terms—including interest rates, repayment periods, collateral requirements, ease of application, fees, and turnaround time—some land trusts have found that a local bank can do better for them under certain circumstances. For the very novice borrower, however, the benefits of working with a sympathetic lender should weigh heavily into the choice.

Advantages and Disadvantages of Borrowing From, Starting, or Investing in a Loan Fund

Advantages: Some of the many benefits to borrowing from a conservation revolving loan fund are:

- Working with a lender with a shared mission
- Borrowing in a safe environment that encourages borrowing and increases chances of success
- Help with the technicalities of borrowing
- Good loan terms
- Flexibility with loan terms
- Quick turnaround
- Supplementary advantages of capacity-building and financial and organizational maturity
- Support to help foreclosure
- A "shared risk" approach in which the fund participates in one way or another in making the project successful

If a land trust is an inexperienced borrower and has a choice of lenders, a conservation revolving loan fund should be near the top of its list.

The benefits to a funder of investing in a conservation revolving loan fund are leverage and the corollary benefits of capacity-building. The great

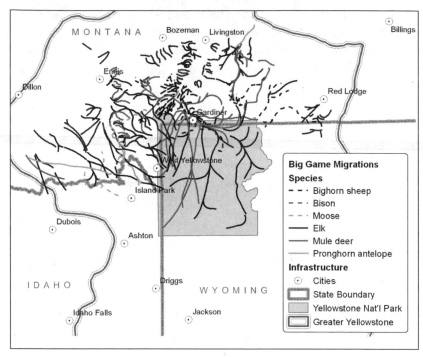

Figure 13.8
Protecting land within the Greater Yellowstone Ecosystem is critical for maintaining migratory routes of large mammal species, such as bighorn sheep, bison, moose, elk, mule deer, and pronghorn antelope. (Courtesy of Wildlife Conservation Society)

leverage value of a loan fund is derived from the money being recycled over and over again in loans. Again, the Greater Yellowstone Loan Fund (GYLF) is a case in point. The Doris Duke Charitable Foundation funded the GYLF with a $1 million grant and grant conditions that required that the recipient, The Conservation Fund, leverage the modest $1 million into ten thousand acres of protected land with a cumulative value of more than $12 million over a four-year period. Mark Elsbree met the challenge. At the end of year three, the foundation's grant had helped to protect an impressive 9,107 acres. The initial $1 million has thus far produced $47 million of protection. How often can a foundation see its money go that far?

Other funds have also had very good records. The Cape Cod Land Fund has leveraged its $650,000 into $11 million in land protection. The leverage value of the fund should be a statistic that all loan funds routinely track, as it makes a compelling case for philanthropic investment.

The corollary value of increasing land trusts' sophistication not only in borrowing so they can take on bigger, more sophisticated projects, but in project and organizational management, cannot be overstated. A funder may invest in a conservation revolving loan fund because of the high leverage of his donation, but he or she gets the added satisfaction of watching all the client land trusts become stronger, more capable organizations. As the director of Maine Coast Heritage Trust's land protection department puts it, "MCHT, through its revolving loan program, has helped land trusts grow stronger and has helped them reap the benefits of that growth."

Loan funds that are closely supporting their land trusts are also able to meet the needs of their borrowers more directly and quickly. They can go to bat for takeout money, argue alongside neighboring constituents for appropriations with congressional representatives, and call up state agency contacts for information on the status of funding applications.

Disadvantages: Borrowing from a conservation revolving loan fund carries the same obligations as other debt, the largest of which are finding acceptable collateral and takeout funding. There are few disadvantages to borrowing from a conservation revolving loan fund that are unique to these funds. One possible problem might arise if an inexperienced lender encouraged an inexperienced land trust to borrow. Some of the limited number of outstanding loans still on the books may be the result of simple inexperience. Awareness of the risks to both sides of financing a transaction unprepared minimizes these occurrences.

Still, not every story of land trusts borrowing money from loan funds is glowing. Loan extensions are needed and given on occasion when scheduled repayments from grants are delayed or denied, or anticipated donations have not yet met the fundraising goal. Extensions for large loans will curtail the ability of a loan fund to make future loans. These and other problems midway through a loan term can be stressful for both parties and strain relationships. Land trusts can have rough bumps in the road when a seemingly secure grant for permanent funding does not come through or collateral is hard to come by. Conservation revolving funds try to be flexible. I know of funds that have taken the land as collateral just to make sure that a land trust had the money to take a threatened parcel off the market, or provided a loan extension while the land trust reapplied for funding. Although the borrowing process does not always work out exactly as was expected, land trusts look back at the benefits as a learning experience and are grateful that the loan fund was there to be a helpful lender. Loan funds themselves have challenges. For MCHT, it is the high cost of a labor-intensive operation. For Resources Legacy Fund's Greater Yellowstone Ecosystem revolving fund, it is successfully operating under the constraints of the foundation loan that funds it. For the Lowcountry Conservation Loan Fund in South Carolina, it is getting more money out the door, and for the Cape Cod Land Fund, Buzzards Bay, and The Conservation Fund's GYE loan fund, it is having enough loan money to meet the demand.

Conservation revolving loan funds require relatively large amounts of money to fund them. If they are capitalized from in-region sources, there can be competition for money with the local land trusts. The Cape Cod Land Fund handled this by discussing specific prospects with the land trusts, which quelled fears. But as landscape-scale funds emerge, the dynamics of trust building with local land trusts will be more difficult and more effort will be needed to coordinate, and even share, donors.

Establishing a loan fund requires financial and legal expertise, and then continual due diligence. Loans, promissory notes, and collateral must be legally secured. The due diligence on each loan can be extensive, often involving legal and financing expertise. Other aspects of the fund require an allocation of time. Staff members must be accessible to inquiries from constituent land trusts and from others. There is a public relations component to any loan fund. To facilitate inquiries, there should be enough written material available so that the basic questions can be answered in writing. Several well-organized funds have question-and-answer handouts that save the staff time addressing all inquiries. (See online appendix at www .conservationguide.com)

If the loan fund is capitalized with a foundation program-related investment, there is the question of who takes the risk. The loan fund administrators may be entirely on the hook if there is a default on a loan, and unable to offer extensions or other remedies because of the need to repay its own loan to the foundation. Nonetheless, a loan from a foundation to start a loan fund is not unusual and puts new and needed money into conservation transactions.

A very small number of funds have actually stopped operations due to insufficient capital or outstanding loans that tied up that limited capital. But most have had few or no loan defaults and have been able to generate enough capital to support pretty significant loan programs.

Since loan funds revolve slowly at first, the interest income from the early loans is never sufficient to offset the start-up and operational costs, especially if the fund intends to offer technical support to its clients. Some foundations have recognized the need for accompanying grant money for administration and due-diligence costs for the funds.

Conclusion

The future of conservation revolving loan funds comes down to two issues: money and scale. The availability of money to capitalize these funds and pay operational costs will depend to a great degree on foundations' continuing interest. Foundations have been the primary source of capital through grants and loans (program-related investments) for the loan funds that exist today. The most compelling reason that foundations should continue to support loan funds is the very high leverage offered by well-used loan funds. Each dollar invested is used over and over again.

Several large foundations fund loan funds. Foundation loans have been a major source of loan fund capital to OSI, for example. Foundation grants, because the capital can be spent without payback, give a loan fund even more flexibility to attract borrowers with low interest rates and serve specific outcomes. Loan funds also build land trust borrowing experience in the relatively safe environment of a lender with a shared mission. The big land trusts have the knowledge to borrow from the less user-friendly loan funds. But if the goal is to increase the capacity of the hundreds of land trusts that know little or nothing about borrowing, then technical assistance and other support really matters.

The other driving money issue is the necessity for permanent or long-term funding to pay off debt, which largely depends on the presence of publicly funded programs and the capability of land conservation organizations to raise private funding. The existence of large public funding programs can create a demand for bridge funding of all kinds. Loan funds do and should move into areas where there are large public programs as they can facilitate more efficient and strategic use of public funding. Loan funds can also meet the diversity of needs of land conservation organizations pre-acquiring land or easements for the public agency. Even without abundant public funding, many land trusts successfully capitalize their acquisitions and benefit from bridge financing.

The question of scale—both geographical and financial—is more complex. Loan funds that have strong connections with their constituent land trusts have proven to be among the most successful. Their risks are lower because they know and work frequently with their client land trusts, often just a town away. A loan fund that works very locally in a small region, however, runs the risk of not serving enough clients to create an active program. This is especially true with a new program. An active program in which the loan money turns over often with interest is more sustainable. There must be at least one entrepreneurial land trust in the service area to get the loan fund revolving and to lead the way for other land trusts.

If the land trusts are either inexperienced in taking on debt or face other barriers to borrowing, then a geographically small loan fund can have a hard time building momentum. This has been the case with the Lowcountry Conservation Loan Fund. Generously capitalized in 2002 with grants from the Gaylord and Dorothy Donnelley Foundation and the Merck Family Fund, this loan fund has been used infrequently and mostly by national organizations. There are smaller land trusts in the Lowcountry region but, because they do not often acquire land, they haven't used the loan fund.[10]

So is a bigger region better? The land trust community has discussed sponsoring loan funds that serve very large regions in the way that the Open Space Institute has expanded its region to cover the eastern part of the country. There are challenges to this model as well, especially if the intention is to reach smaller land trusts that might not have access to other capital. A centralized loan fund is far removed from its clients, which can limit its ability to work closely with the smaller land trusts. The Great Lakes Revolving Loan Fund hired a "circuit rider" to travel through its eight-state region to strengthen its connection with and knowledge about the local land trusts. The Resources Legacy Fund's local consultant puts a face on this California-based organization in the Greater Yellowstone region. The Open Space Institute has local field coordinators who administer and assess each of its regional funds. This model has greater administration costs.

A strategic benefit of a larger fund is the ability to diversify risk. A loan fund with a broad reach can make loans to more experienced and therefore generally safer land trusts, and mix into the portfolio a few higher-risk, maybe smaller loans.

Another argument for larger-scale conservation revolving loan funds is the opportunity to attract out-of-region funding. The Greater Yellowstone Ecosystem through the Resources Legacy Fund attracted a $7 million program-related investment from the Packard Foundation. The Conservation Fund has been considering a national loan fund, but it is not so easy to get traction with funders when the geographic focus is virtually unlimited. OSI has shown that region-specific funds have more potential as they can follow the service areas of regional foundations.

Because these loan funds are so new, and have limited track records, it is hard to say which is the best model. The very active, localized loan funds like Cape Cod Land Fund, Buzzards Bay, Maine Coast Heritage Fund, and The Conservation Fund's Greater Yellowstone Fund have been the most effective to date with smaller land trusts. In a four-year period between 1996 and 2000, the Cape Cod Land Fund made fifteen loans to its small member land trusts. Through 2005 it had made twenty-seven loans. The Maine Coast Heritage Fund has made twenty-five loans to other organizations since the fund's inception in 1994. OSI has also been active, making twenty-three loans, in a huge region with field coordinators.

In general, loan funds have been surprised that they have not made more loans in their first few years. With limited data, it is difficult to determine whether it's the structure and size of loan funds, the lack of lending expertise among the land trusts themselves, difficulty raising takeout dollars, or competition from other lending vehicles. The low-interest environment in which many of these funds started is definitely a contributing factor. Land trusts could do as well or almost as well with interest rates from local banks or loans from donors. And many banks are willing to take the land as collateral. As interest rates increase, external revolving loan funds look more attractive. It is definitely the case that the learning curve on borrowing among land trusts is still very steep, and most land trusts are just starting the climb. The turnover among land trust staff necessitates that this learning be repeated often. Turnover among loan fund staff, some of whom are themselves new to lending or to the region, is another hurdle.

Conservation revolving loan funds are not plentiful and are particularly absent in some of the fastest growing areas of the country where they are most needed. The southwest and the southeast have very limited access to loan funds. With the spectacular leverage benefits of an effective fund, one would think that funders would be clamoring to establish and support them. Because these loan funds are particularly beneficial to novice borrowers, it is possible that land trusts that could use them the most don't know it and therefore have not placed sufficient demands on the philanthropic community to establish more.

One experienced conservationist suggested that land trusts that administer conservation revolving funds might, at some point, get into a situation where their own programmatic interests in conservation projects might con-flict with those of their borrowers. This is a potential problem that interme-diaries do not have because they don't undertake their own conservation projects. It suggests that intermediaries might, in the long run, be more suit-able for running conservation revolving funds. I did not find evidence that land trusts are experiencing this type of conflict with their lenders, but these funds are young. Instead, I found that "parent" land trusts redoubled their efforts to help a borrower when they had a particular interest in the project, as in the case of the Maine Coast Heritage Trust offering particularly good loan terms when it had a strong interest in the parcel. Although this demonstrates some subjectivity in lending practices, it has not resulted in conflicts of which I am aware. With the shortage in conservation lending options in many parts of the country, I believe that new lenders, both land trusts and intermediaries, should be encouraged to offer their services. But the question of conflict should not be forgotten. It should be addressed in the policies under which future land trust loan funds are established.

Despite their recent emergence, conservation revolving loan funds have al-ready had an impressive impact on land conservation in the United States. The loan funds working on large transactions with sophisticated land trusts have changed the course of conservation, particularly in the northeastern forests. The loan funds that reach out to smaller land trusts have not only been cata-lysts for significant land conservation, but have helped those land trusts be-come more professional and more capable of increasing the scale of their own conservation programs. Brian Price of the Leelanau Conservancy in Michigan sums up his point of view, which is shared by many others: "There is a differ-ence between working with a bank and working with people who share the same goals. These are people who understand our business." When a loan fund makes a loan, it joins the team and becomes a partner in conservation success.

Chapter 14
Internal Protection Funds

A fund established within a land trust to buy or otherwise support the acquisition of land or conservation easements.

It is very comforting to have money in the bank. It is also a good idea. In the business of buying land or easements, having even a small savings account is the best way to get a leg up, since the timing of finding money can be unpredictable and funds may be needed quickly to save or at least secure threatened lands.

Like most land trusts during their early years, the Jackson Hole Land Trust had to struggle just to meet its small payroll. But its vision was big and the idea of raising money to buy conservation easements had appeal. Looking ahead, executive director Jean Hocker (who later became president of the Land Trust Alliance) approached a sympathetic family foundation to establish what the board optimistically called an opportunity fund. The foundation awarded the land trust a $50,000 grant for that purpose. But, with so much interest among generous landowners in conservation, the land trust stayed focused on accepting donated easements on some of the most magnificent ranchland in the United States. The opportunity fund sat untouched, though knowing it was there must have been a great comfort to Jean and her board.

As the organization grew, the opportunity fund grew. By 1989, two years after the fund was established, it had enough money ($100,000) to make a showstopping option payment and secure the 137-acre Hardeman Meadows. With its back against the wall and the community clamoring for its help, the land trust risked its entire savings on a three-month option to buy the ranch. After completing the Hardeman Meadows purchase, the land trust used the opportunity fund (now twice its pre-Hardeman size) occasionally for earnest money and to fill the gap when project fundraising fell short. But it didn't leverage it the way some land trusts did, because in spite of its success, the land trust was a little traumatized by the risk it had taken earlier on the Hardeman Meadows project.

Even when the land trust finally had a significant amount in the fund, the board didn't want to spend it. Like many boards, it was risk-averse. It liked having a big cushion and wanted to hide behind the safety of all that hard-earned money. At a board retreat in 1997, the staff forced the issue: are we just going to let this fund grow or are we going to risk it again, get into the real estate conservation business, and stay there? As Audrey Rust, executive director of Peninsula Open Space Trust, said about her land trust's approach, "If we don't take risks, why are we hanging around?"

Later that year, when what the Jackson Hole Land Trust now called the protection fund was at $525,000, the board finally agreed to risk it on a small "triple critical" wildlife parcel south of the town of Jackson. Bordered on three sides by U.S. Forest Service land and critical winter habitat for elk, deer, and bighorn sheep, this parcel had been named the most important and threatened parcel of land for wildlife in the state by the Wyoming State Game and Fish Department. Like its unappealing name, Poison Creek, the parcel wasn't much to look at: a sagebrush-covered hillside with a small spring and one solitary stand of aspen trees. But it provided critical wildlife habitat. It also abutted a major highway approach to Jackson Hole.

The land trust had tried to buy the parcel two years earlier, but to raise the money (so as not to risk the protection fund) the land trust concocted a complex deal involving a forest service exchange and more. Given the development potential of the property, the owners thought the price was too low. But now these same owners had the Internal Revenue Service at their door demanding back taxes. They needed the money. Armed with the protection fund, the land trust moved quickly, and boldly offered them the whole fund, a price that was $200,000 less than our previous offer. While I was negotiating the price and terms, others on staff were diligently fundraising from wildlife-oriented foundations, wildlife enthusiasts, neighbors, and supporters. At the completion of the project and with the help of a $200,000 loan from a conservation lender, we had to spend only $250,000 of the protection fund. The goodwill created by the land trust's willingness to take a chance on protecting Poison Creek helped quickly to replenish what the land trust spent. With the taste of what money could do still fresh, we plunged into planning for a $25 million capital campaign for the protection fund. Now the Jackson Hole Land Trust was in the game to stay.

Mark Ackelson built the Iowa Natural Heritage Foundation's fund in a more systematic way. "In the end it's all about discipline. Put away money whenever you can, and then you will have it when you need it," Mark says. "It's the way I have always lived personally, too. I divide my unexpected income: one-third to savings, one-third to operations, and one-third to personal use." Early in the Iowa Natural Heritage Foundation's (INHF) history, it had a grand vision of protecting Iowa's prairies, woodlands, wetlands, streams, trails, and key watersheds. Since several of its founding board members had been affiliated with university fundraising, "their first thought was: let's raise an endowment, so we never have to raise money again," Mark recalled. So off they went, in true university-fundraising fashion, and came back with $1 million. "This was before the land trust even had any hides on the wall! No projects or even members" he tells. The lesson here is: Put university fundraisers on your board. No one can raise money like active alumni-association fundraisers.

Mark successfully grew INHF's discretionary endowment using his disciplined approach. If the land trust receives an unexpected, unrestricted, or planned gift (it raises about $250,000–$300,000 a year in planned giving), Mark puts the gift in this discretionary endowment unless specified otherwise by the donor. Memorial gifts[1] are allocated to the endowment, as well as one third of other unexpected gifts (the rest to programs and operations).

A challenge grant and a corresponding bequest initiated the Columbia Land Conservancy's protection fund. In upper New York State, where the Hudson River borders one side of the county, Judy Anderson, then Columbia Land Conservancy's executive director, and her staff saw the value of having ready cash to act quickly to secure projects at risk. After a number of years of discussion with two potential donors, Judy secured two gifts totaling $200,000 to establish the fund. Over the past several years, the funds have been used for various projects. However, because of the difficulty of finding permanent funding to replenish the fund, the organization has used it sparingly. This land trust is very active in other ways, however, the lack of guaranteed public money to pay back the fund has dampened the board's enthusiasm for using this fund.

As in the case of the Jackson Hole Land Trust, the reluctance of the Columbia Land Conservancy resulted from a combination of a risk-averse board, lack of familiarity with acquisition and takeout strategies, and a very real limitation on available money to replenish the fund. In contrast, on Long Island in New York State, the Peconic Land Trust's fund is constantly in use with strong state and local public programs repaying the land trust for its acquisitions. "This year, it has been a virtual revolving door. The fund has been used six or seven times already and it is only June!" says its president, John v.H. Halsey.

Many land trusts have learned to live with the risk of no immediate source of payback. As Mary Anne Piacentini of the Katy Prairie Conservancy in Texas tells it, "with the development pressure we have, we need the money now. We know we can pay it back eventually."

Partly because of repayment uncertainties, some land trusts don't formalize their acquisition dollars in a protection fund with a targeted monetary goal. They spend their money as they need to and replenish it when they can. For the small Katy Prairie Conservancy, it is all about having working capital. Mary Anne speaks of the immense development pressure west of Houston threatening the Katy Prairie, where millions of migratory birds, especially waterfowl, spend the fall and winter: "Without the money today two things will happen: the price of real estate will only go up, and we are going to lose out on properties because people are going to buy them for development." Katy Prairie Conservancy spends its working capital as fast as it can raise it. Sometimes there is $250,000 in the fund, sometimes $4 million.

For the much larger and older Peninsula Open Space Trust (POST) in central coastal California, the urgency is the same. Audrey Rust and her staff are well-known for their fundraising acumen. POST raised $200 million from more than ten thousand donors' gifts and pledges for working capital to purchase and conserve twenty thousand acres in many projects along the central coast of California.[2] The account revolves because POST buys public acquisi-

Figure 14.1
Every year, millions of migratory birds use the Katy Prairie, on the Texas Gulf Coast, for winter habitat or as a staging area before migrating south. (©Michael Morton Photography)

tion priorities, resells them to government agencies, and uses the proceeds to buy more land.[3] In this way, POST's capital account builds over time, allowing them the opportunity to own a ranch for a period of time without making interest payments to a lender. Though POST's working capital account is very large by most land trust standards (in the tens of millions), the ranches it buys are big and expensive. Audrey says that the size of the account is less important than its use. "The money must be in play. You have to be prepared to show that it is in play," she says. Actively conserving conservation land then becomes the best way to build a capital account or protection fund. "Once you have some working capital, you are taken more seriously by everyone by whom you want to be taken seriously," Audrey says. This includes landowners, donors, agencies, and other lenders.

Marin Agricultural Land Trust (MALT) in Marin County, California, is often described as constantly being in a capital campaign. MALT doesn't have a static goal for its protection-fund. The goal changes based on the price of the projects it targets for the next three to five years. "Right now, we couldn't buy anything, but in six months we could," says executive director Bob Berner. That is because MALT has just spent down its fund of the last three years and is getting ready to raise money for its targeted projects for the next five years.

The Piedmont Environmental Council (PEC), a ten-county land trust covering three thousand square miles of northern Virginia, uses protection funds more expansively than most land trusts. Here, in the rolling piedmont that extends from the Blue Ridge Mountains to the plains of the Tidewater River, farms are being gobbled up by suburban development advancing from Washington, D.C. In an attempt to keep pace, PEC has created eight regionally based protection funds, seven of which are very active. Each fund covers a county or a watershed, has a local advisory board, and raises money for its own local protection projects. The Piedmont Foundation, a 509(a)(3) supporting organization, with its own four-to-five-person board controls these funds. PEC must apply to the foundation for the release of any payment over $5,000.

Like other land trusts, PEC chose to establish these protection funds so that it could have liquidity to buy land and easements.[4] Originally, they were intended to revolve by buying land, restricting it with a conservation easement, reselling it, and fundraising to cover the difference in value. The protection funds are now also used to buy land targeted by county agencies for conservation that then partially compensate PEC for purchasing them. The PEC advisory boards raise the rest locally.

Figure 14.2
Over the last thirty-five years, the Piedmont Environmental Council and the Virginia
Outdoors Foundation have worked cooperatively with landowners to preserve this
viewshed just west of Washington, D.C. To date, 50 percent of this landscape is under
conservation easement. (Courtesy of the Piedmont Environmental Council)

The protection funds have also proven to be successful vehicles for
fundraising, appealing to the enlightened self-interest of donors who have a
greater awareness of conservation of land close to where they live. Fundraising for each fund focuses on specific projects. PEC tells donors that if it fails to
exercise its option to buy a parcel, the money will go into their local fund. If
donors are uncomfortable with that arrangement, they can make a pledge to
be paid at closing. But most people are content with the local fund as a default.

An example of a PEC local fund is the Bull Run Mountains Land Conservation Fund, which successfully raised the money to purchase conservation
easements on a historic dairy operation composed of two farms, the Fox Den
and Mountain Home. These farms, which have been in operation since the late
1700s, form one of the last dairy operations in northern Fauquier County, Virginia. Projects such as these give PEC another opportunity to distinguish its
regional activities.

Catherine Scott, director of land conservation for PEC, believes that on
balance the individualized funds have been hugely successful. They revolve
with 100 percent repayment and have raised well over $5 million collectively.
But they have some drawbacks. They are labor-intensive because each fund,
advisory board, and transaction requires staffing. She says that each transaction requires approximately 30 percent of a staff person's time for six months.
Since some owners of important conservation lands in the area are still willing to donate conservation easements, the success of the protection funds and

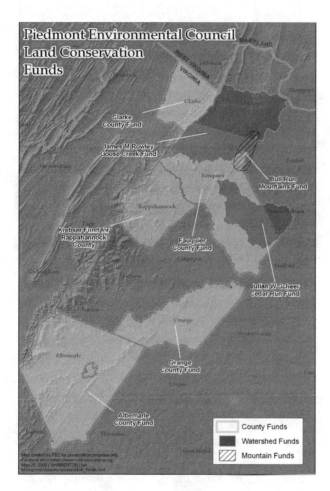

Figure 14.3
In order to protect especially sensitive or threatened lands with significant scenic, natural, historic, or agricultural resources, the Piedmont Environmental Council has established seven regional funds for land conservation. (Courtesy of the Piedmont Environmental Coucnil)

the associated acquisition programs may infringe upon time dedicated to these less-expensive conservation methods. Additionally with so many local residents serving on the multiple advisory boards or participating in other ways, the chance for real or perceived conflicts of interest exists. PEC can be prevented from buying a farm because it is owned or abuts land owned by an advisory board member or a major donor to a fund, and the perceived conflict of interest from a purchase would create potential public relations challenges for the organization.

Of greater concern is the increase in the cost of land in this area. Some of the targeted properties are now in the $25 million range. The funds' resources are becoming inadequate to acquire key parcels. Catherine is using other tools such as the Virginia tax credit program and conservation investors to conserve the higher-priced parcels.

Figure 14.4
The Peconic Land Trust has used its internal protection to protect vineyards on Long Island's North Fork. (Dawn Haight, Peconic Land Trust)

Raising the Money for a Protection Fund

At the east end of New York's Long Island, a supporter of the Peconic Land Trust suggested that he was willing to help the land trust build an acquisition fund. To get started, he convinced a foundation on whose board he served to make a challenge grant of $3 million to the land trust. The first million had to be matched by $500,000 from Peconic Land Trust's other fundraising. The second million required a dollar-for-dollar match, and the third million, a $1.5 million match. When all was said and done, the land trust would have $6 million in its protection fund to get into the game of buying conservation on the coastal lands, salt marshes, and potato farms that have become some of the most popular and expensive second-home real estate in America.

Peconic's president, John v.H. Halsey, emphatically defends the value of his protection fund in meeting his land trust's objectives. "Having that available cash so that if you have to jump, you can jump, can make a land trust competitive in a strong real estate market. You don't have to go to a bank and go through the process of identifying land as collateral or drawing up letters of credit. You can move faster after, of course, having weighed the risk very carefully."

For the Land Trust of Central North Carolina, it was another farsighted donor whose challenge gift catalyzed the creation of the land trust's protection fund. As Executive Director Jason Walser tells it, the land trust wanted to buy a parcel of land and had applied for and received a grant of $500,000 to pay for it. But when the appraisal came in, the value was unexpectedly $400,000 higher due to the marketability of the timber. Jason went to his mentor and land trust donor to ask him to help make up the difference. The donor said he would fund the acquisition, but told Jason to think bigger. "Don't just let me give you a check," he said. Instead he offered the land trust a $500,000 challenge gift.

Without a farsighted donor or years to squirrel away funds, how should such a fund be raised? The most typical way is with a capital campaign. The Vermont Land Trust provides the classic example. It had had small funds in the past, which had been very useful, and it had been considering creating a large protection fund for many years. It decided to create a $4 million revolving protection fund for land acquisition as part of a bigger $25 million campaign. The campaign took six years and was successfully completed in the fall of 2005.

Using its capital campaign as a match, the McKenzie River Trust in Oregon negotiated a $1 million donation from the Eugene Water and Electric Board (EWEB), the local utility and water provider for the Eugene/Springfield metropolitan area. The utility board obtains most of the city's drinking water and some hydropower from the McKenzie River, and dam relicensing discussions had raised awareness of the value of the river to its customers. To help protect water quality and critical fish and wildlife habitat, EWEB granted the land trust $500,000 outright and a $500,000 matching grant, which the land trust met through its capital campaign. The monies were to be spent on fee-simple purchases and easements on at least four hundred acres of riparian lands over a ten-year period.

Figure 14.5
The wildlife-rich ponds, wetlands, and cherry orchards of Green Island, near Coburg, Oregon, have been permanently protected by McKenzie River Trust.

To get the most out of the EWEB's grant, the McKenzie River Trust creatively used this money for internal bridge loans and option and escrow payments, with the understanding that if other sources of permanent funding fell through, it would still acquire the property with the utility board's grant money. An ad hoc committee representing the land trust, the utility board, and the McKenzie Watershed Council reviewed each project for consistency with the grant goals and objectives. The land trust exceeded the goals for the program by acquiring over one thousand acres in four years. The EWEB funds provided leverage for three to four times as much funding from other sources, and the Trust continues to recapture that initial investment in its internal revolving McKenzie Conservancy Fund—a very healthy track record for such an investment. Though the McKenzie River Trust has completed the program, the McKenzie Conservancy Fund continues to provide leverage for acquisition and stewardship work in the McKenzie River basin.

Other creative strategies have built protection funds. For example, Mary Anne Piacentini of the Katy Prairie Conservancy raises her capital account with the help of a county flood-control district. The Katy Prairie is the headwaters of four Texas streams that flood seasonally, and when they flood, they flood everywhere. The district buys flood-conservation easements from the land trust and the landowners with whom it works. Katy Prairie replenishes its fund with payments from the flood-control district.

Management of Protection Funds

For a land trust contemplating establishing a protection fund, a written board policy must govern its expenditures and its sources of revenue. A policy can encourage discipline in fund expenditure and in building and maintaining it. Many land trusts allocate funds to their protection fund whenever feasible, and thereby grow the funds. Land trusts designate part or all of windfall revenues, such as bequests or sale of *trade lands,* to permanent funds like protection and stewardship. On the spending side, a policy can streamline decision making about the purpose and use of the fund, creating spending thresholds for board review and approval.

If the fund is not in constant use, it should be responsibly and professionally invested. An investment policy sets investment strategies, which should include diversification. A conservative strategy is a good one. No one wants to witness the loss of hard-earned assets to poor investing. Boards often have small investment committees made up of experienced finance people to monitor the health of the fund.

The Land Trust of Napa County has thirteen funds, one of which is a protection fund. Its fourteen-page investment policy thoroughly covers the different purposes and investment strategies for each fund. The language pertaining to its land protection fund is clear and succinct. Interestingly, the investment policy has a "social criteria" section that requires the assets of the land trust to be invested primarily to promote the goals of the land trust, consistent with fiduciary responsibility, prudent diversification, and stewardship, *but also* "to promote environmental and social responsibility, specifically to encourage the conservation and preservation of agricultural and open space resources, as well as other natural resources, including the protection of water and air quality." The types of investment to be excluded and included are described. Excluded, for example, are "investments in the securities of companies that . . . pollute the air and water, or consistently and flagrantly violate regulations of the U. S. Environmental Protection Agency (EPA)," and included are investments that "enhance and preserve the natural environment, agriculture and open space lands, including companies that . . . reduce negative environmental impact by eliminating or reducing the use of hazardous or toxic chemicals."[5]

The policy is worth reading, but something less extensive will do in most cases. The Jackson Hole Land Trust's early protection fund policy (see online appendix at www.conservationguide.com) and the Vermont Land Trust's policies are online in the Land Trust Alliance's *Land Trust Standards and Practices* appendices.

Drafting a policy for a land protection fund gives a board and staff an opportunity to build consensus on protection fund management. To ensure that the assets are liquid when needed, the project and financial staff should meet periodically to estimate how much money should be available for projects in the next six to twelve months. Treasury bonds, CDs, and other investments mature at different times, and the financial staff or a board committee must always be making informed decisions as to where to invest and for how long.

Some land trusts keep each of their funds in separate accounts, sometimes in separate banks, to spread the goodwill. The Iowa Natural Heritage Foundation (INHF), while maintaining the distinction of its funds on paper, invests them collectively for maximum efficiency and return.

Advantages of Protection Funds

Protection funds offer ready cash for options, transactions, and associated expenses. With such a fund, land trusts can avoid the burdens of institutional borrowing. Of course, a protection fund won't last very long if it is misused. Expenditures should meet high standards similar to those set by banks. Some land trusts manage their funds like a bank, paying back the money with interest. Others are less concerned about interest. The Little Traverse Conservancy has lent money interest-free to a government agency just to accomplish time-sensitive conservation.

In addition to having the money already raised to make a purchase, internal protection funds have other benefits, which include:

- Easy access to money for acquisition expenses
- Lower-cost loan funds than commercial loans because less paperwork, no institutional fees, or commercial profit
- Absence of the requirement for collateral
- The competitive edge of ready cash
- Access to matching funds often required for public acquisitions
- Collateral for institutional or other loans
- Backup source of money, enabling land trusts to undertake riskier deals (if carefully assessed and knowingly undertaken)
- A cash-flow buffer or reserve if the land trust has no other
- Payout of interest to support land trust operations or protection expenses
- Service of multiple purposes at once, as in addressing cash-flow needs, providing collateral, and paying out interest to operations

In some cases, organizational dependence on interest revenue from a protection fund is a disincentive, intentional or not, to draw it down. Reluctance to reduce interest income is one of the reasons why the Land Trust of Napa County doesn't use its protection fund as much as some land trusts. Mark Ackelson of INHF addresses this by keeping his fund in place so that it can bear interest to support operations while committing some of it as security for bank loans. Thus he has working capital without spending down the protection fund for this purpose. As loan security, the corpus of the fund is, of course, obligated by the loan in case it is not repaid. Interest payments on the loan are sometimes paid out of a protection fund as well. So this approach is not without its costs, but it increases the functions of a protection fund.

To maintain its funds, PEC strives to set up simultaneous closings so the protection fund only serves as backup if there are unanticipated delays. Having a quick turnaround is one criterion used by PEC for choosing projects to finance internally.

Disadvantages of Protection Funds

While seemingly a great idea, these funds can have some drawbacks. If the real estate market is strong and prices high, a protection fund must be well endowed to be useful. Raising money for a fund can siphon time and energy from other worthy causes, such as building a solid annual base of giving, or even fundraising for a particular project. One land trust had a large protection fund but was $400,000 in debt for operations.

Protection funds are wasted if they are not used. The Jackson Hole Land Trust and the Columbia Land Conservancy are not the only land trusts that didn't always use their protection funds because, for one thing, common sources to replenish them, such as public funding programs, were scarce. But in this business where money in general is scarce, every conservation dollar should be put to work.

Some land trusts aren't motivated to raise money for a protection fund because they make do in other ways. Some have access to other capital. Fred Ellis, director of government and community affairs for the Hill Country Conservancy outside of Austin, Texas, says that he hasn't needed a protection fund because the city of Austin is very responsive to land trust requests for reimbursement for conservation acquisitions. (Given the growth rates in that area, it is surprising that the city can keep up.) Other land trusts have other fundraising priorities. Tall Timbers Research Station and Land Conservancy,[6] dedicated to conserving the Red Hills region of northern Florida and southwest Georgia, including the last remnants of the longleaf pine region in the United States, is building internal staff capacity first. It is looking for a financial institution to serve as a source of capital. Some land trusts have developed effective relationships with banks and have lines of credit that substitute for or extend the reach of a protection fund.

For some, it is a matter of time. One land trust executive told me, "Who wouldn't like to have a kitty? But we don't have it, so we are flying by the seat of our pants." For many land trusts, a protection fund of any size is simply not attainable at the early stage in its development. Making budget is enough of a fundraising challenge. But regularly meeting operational needs is founded in a strong base of annual support, which creates the level and stability of giving that prepares a land trust to build a protection fund. Have patience.

Once a land trust has raised a fund, there can be an inherent conflict between spending it and using the interest to pay for acquisition or operating costs. Since operational costs are harder to raise than project costs, building up a big protection fund can pay out interest to cover operational expenses. Clarity in the fund's policy about the purposes of the fund helps to ease this tension. Also, since the fund is so easily accessible, it is tempting to spend it more liberally than if the money had to be raised or borrowed from a lending institution. Strict adherence to project criteria and fund policy can, again, instill discipline.

Using the fund to secure a loan invades the fund for both interest payments and as a liability against the corpus until the loan is paid off. A land trust should be fully aware of these "costs" to the fund. On the other hand, if the land trust can borrow elsewhere at a lower rate than the interest generated from investing the fund, or if the acquisition will generate a return, then securing the loan has very low risk, if any, and meaningful financial benefits.

Conclusion

It will seem daunting to a land trust that is trying to make ends meet to even consider saving money for anything. It may not be possible to raise a protection fund in a land trust's first few years. But as soon as it can save even $1,000, a land trust will see how comforting and useful it can be. Whether it is called an emergency, opportunity, land protection, land acquisition, revolving fund, capital account, discretionary or board-designated endowment, or just cash on hand, having money in an acquisition account can make a big difference primarily by giving a land trust the ability to act quickly and buy time. As John v.H. Halsey of the Peconic Land Trust says, "Before we had a fund, we had to carefully glue each project together at the closing. Now, with the fund, we can secure a deal and keep working."

A land trust can build a fund through disciplined fiscal management as Mark Ackelson did, or through an all-out fundraising drive either for a specific project or for the fund itself. Most land trusts initially build a fund as a by-product of one or more project-specific fundraising drives; either overshooting the fundraising goal or, as in the case of POST and others, raising project money and being reimbursed with public funding, thus getting the fundraised money back to use again. Whether the fundraising is for a project, a collection of projects, or to build a fund for future use, the pitch to donors must focus on the land-saving outcomes, not the building of a big fund. People want to know what conservation the money will buy.

If the fund revolves or is paid back over time, spent down again, and then replenished, the land trust has developed a true revolving fund, which has significant additional leverage value. The Nature Conservancy's land preservation fund, which is now in excess of $250 million, has "rolled over" more than four times in the past five years.[7] Even at much smaller fund levels, this kind of leverage value is attractive to donors in search of ways to see their philanthropic dollars go farther.

Most land trusts have absolutely no regrets about the hard work and the austerity in certain other programs required to raise a protection fund. Many raised it the same way we did, in fits and starts, and by sticking to their protection fund policies.

Chapter 15
Foundation Program-Related Investments

An investment or a loan made by a foundation with terms that are more favorable than those of the commercial market or an investment that must be used for charitable, qualifying purposes.

"We backed into it." That is how Norcross Wildlife Foundation's managing director, Richard Reagan, describes the creation of their program-related investment (PRI) program. A new land trust had hastily formed to buy the last piece of open land about to be engulfed by the shopping malls surrounding Freeport, Maine. The land trust had secured a $50,000 grant from Norcross for the purchase. Now they were back asking Richard for more: $185,000 to complete the purchase. Richard Reagan suggested to his board that they loan the land trust $185,000 rather than grant it.

From that first loan, which was paid back in full, the Norcross board immediately recognized the value of small loans to small land trusts. Because a landowner often has to make an immediate decision to sell, it helps to be ready with a bank line of credit or a buyer in the wings. But when is a small, overworked land trust ready?

Norcross's PRI program, called the No-Interest Loan Fund, may be the most active in conservation in the United States. In the first years after 1999 when the fund was created, no one knew about it. Now the word is out and the fund is processing loans as fast as it can. The foundation has made over fifty-five loans to land trusts, ten of which are currently outstanding, totaling over $8 million and protecting 15,500 acres. None have defaulted. Ninety percent of the loans go to "the little guys," as Richard calls them. Small land trusts always need money for closings, he says. They may not have access to other low-cost financing because they are located far from lending institutions willing to lend for conservation projects, or they may be handicapped by lack of borrowing experience. A small land trust anywhere in the United States can get a small (up to $250,000) loan from Norcross, "and they have a habit of paying us back" Richard says. "It is so satisfying to help these grassroots groups," he says. "For us, it is a great way to preserve capital and help save land."

Norcross fills a unique niche. It provides small loans for one year to any local land trust or nature center in the United States, "only for the purpose of acquiring land for wildlife habitat conservation." Norcross does not follow the conventional PRI model in that it does not charge interest. Though Norcross is losing a small amount of capital on its PRIs relative to the market, it is not sufficiently significant to warrant internal concern about the sustainability of its corpus.

"A land trust shouldn't be afraid to pursue the possibility of a loan from others or us," Richard says. "We've made loans as low as twelve thousand dollars. Our lawyer will look at the situation, and help them see what they need, no matter how small they are. They have to have a little courage, because asking for a loan is scary, like taking out your first mortgage on your house—scary but you get over it. Norcross is not in the business to make money, we are a foundation dedicated to helping grassroots organizations. That means doing it the way it works for them, not us."

Norcross's No-Interest Loan Fund makes what seems like a daunting process simple. By now, they know what questions to ask and how to best help their applicants. Norcross's biologist and director of land protection and stewardship, Dan Donahue, consulting real estate attorney Hal Poster, and Richard Reagan work as a team, and seem to love every opportunity they have to put loan money in the field.

The Norcross experience demonstrates that modest PRIs need not be complicated, and that they typically support significant conservation, organizational capacity and confidence building, and generate additional public- and private-sector interest and investment. PRIs create opportunities for conservation that banks and other lenders cannot. They have their limitations as we shall see, but for most land trusts looking for financing, PRIs can be the right answer.

The application procedure is simple and clearly spelled out on the foundation's Web site.[1] Norcross, like most conservation-oriented lenders, prefers not to secure its loans with the conservation land in question. The foundation prefers other forms of security, like unrestricted funds, marketable securities, or third-party guarantees. So for some applicants, finding collateral can be a challenge.

PRI borrowing from foundations is like borrowing from banks, only much better. Foundation PRIs or loans usually have lower interest rates and other more favorable terms than banks. They are more willing to lend for remote parcels of raw land. They can help prepare the documentation for the loan and work out security issues. Some even assist with finding takeout financing and, if all else fails, may be willing to share the risk (though counting on a bailout is definitely not advisable). So what is the catch? Not many foundations make loans for land conservation, and for those that do, it is rarely the focus of their program.

While land conservation PRIs are less common, many foundations have been making PRIs in other sectors of the nonprofit world, most notably community development, for over thirty-five years. By doing so, they have been able to increase the value of their own effectiveness and expand the ways that they can assist nonprofits and support their outcomes. But, with the exception of certain national conservation organizations, a few regional organizations, and now Norcross, foundations as lenders have been absent from the land trust toolkit.

PRIs are not always loans, though typically in the land conservation arena they are structured as such. Foundations use other types of PRI instruments, including linked deposits by which a foundation makes a deposit in a bank for

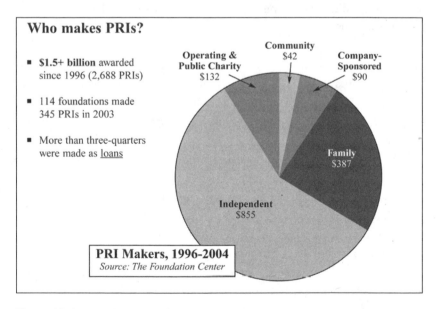

Who makes PRIs?

- **$1.5+ billion** awarded since 1996 (2,688 PRIs)

- 114 foundations made 345 PRIs in 2003

- More than three-quarters were made as <u>loans</u>

Operating & Public Charity $132

Community $42

Company-Sponsored $90

Family $387

Independent $855

PRI Makers, 1996-2004
Source: The Foundation Center

Figure 15.1
Program-related investment (PRI) makers by type of foundation, 1996–2004. (MacArthur Foundation tabulations of unpublished Foundation Center data)

a lower-than-market interest rate of return. The bank then agrees to make a lower-than-market loan to the designated borrower.

Importantly, foundations also make equity investments in ventures that further their program objectives (thus the name program-related investments). Foundations have invested in businesses or venture capital funds with socially responsible missions and in nonprofit loan funds. In the environmental sector, equity investments support new, environmentally friendly businesses and investment funds. These investments allow a foundation to preserve its capital and put it to work in a mission-related manner, in the same way PRI loans (and lines of credit) to land trusts for land acquisition can. In addition to making PRIs, foundations support conservation finance by providing guarantees that secure conservation loans.

Background

In the 1960s, private foundations were challenged to find enough money to address low-income housing and community development problems. They were discovering, however, that these same problems could be handled by charitable investments such as loans to finance housing construction paid back over time with rental revenue. The investments could leverage limited resources, as well as attract other funding to these worthy projects.

The Ford Foundation first used this investment model in 1968 to help finance affordable housing projects that were denied financing by conventional lenders. Then, in 1969 the U.S. Congress was considering penalizing foundations that made risky investments that could jeopardize their endowments. At the same time, more foundations were recognizing the value of these investments, risky or safe, to expand their reach. Congress chose to allow investments by foundations, even high-risk investments, as long as they were consistent with the mission of the foundation and met certain other requirements.[2] The law offered an incentive, which allowed PRIs to be counted toward the 5 percent distribution payout requirement for foundations (more on this requirement later). When the loan is repaid, the repayment increases the foundation's current distribution obligation.[3]

Because of these advantages, over 255 foundations have made PRIs, mostly to community development projects.[4] In the environmental sector, the David and Lucile Packard Foundation has a large PRI program,[5] the John D. and Catherine T. MacArthur Foundation previously made conservation PRIs in the

United States and abroad, and a handful of other foundations have more limited and less formalized ongoing PRI programs. The Norcross PRI program is best known among land trusts, but even Norcross is unknown to many in some areas of the country.

As loans or equity investments, foundations in many sectors use PRIs both domestically and internationally. A paper on PRIs by GrantCraft prepared on behalf of the Ford and MacArthur foundations offers examples of how PRIs are used in other program areas, which include community development, affordable housing, and health care.[6]

Interestingly, a PRI can be made to a charitable or non-charitable organization or venture, as long as the intent and use is for charitable purposes. This provision has led to some very interesting loans by foundations in ventures that strive to stimulate market-based conservation. In making investments, a foundation can generate income but the investment must differ in other ways from investments that would attract commercial investors, such as having a lower rate of return, higher risk, or more favorable collateral or repayment terms.

For our purposes, PRIs address a growing need for short-term capital for the undercapitalized business of land acquisition. But conservation-oriented foundations also are looking for a broader array of loans and investments for different time periods to stimulate innovation and investment and to further their mission.

The 5 Percent Rule

To understand the perspective of foundations and their motivations for making PRIs, it is helpful to look at how foundations are regulated. Foundations must distribute 5 percent of the net value of their investment assets for charitable purposes. These are called "qualifying distributions." Foundations that drop below the required 5 percent distribution must pay an excise tax.

A foundation must also pay a tax if it "invests any amount in such a manner as to jeopardize the carrying out of any of its exempt purposes."[7] An exception to the "jeopardy investment" penalty is provided for PRIs because, by definition, they further the carrying out of proper exempt purposes.

When the PRI is paid out, the amount is counted as if it were a grant for the purposes of the 5 percent rule, thus permitting the foundation to make fewer outright grants in that year. When the PRI is repaid, the foundation must count the repayment negatively against the 5 percent; that is, the repayment amplifies that year's distribution obligation. Though the 5 percent rule is a rolling average, for the sake of clarification, if the foundation had made grants that year totaling exactly 5 percent of the net value of its investment assets and a PRI was repaid during that year, in part or in whole, it would have to make additional grants equivalent to the PRI amounts repaid to meet the 5 percent threshold, or it must pay an excise tax penalty.

A foundation is more likely to make PRIs when its assets have risen sharply and there are unprogrammed funds that must be spent to meet the 5 percent requirement that is now a larger actual dollar amount. A foundation might be more comfortable loaning the newfound money as it will likely be repaid. When asset growth is flat or declining, PRIs can cannibalize existing grants budgets, and program officers are understandably reluctant to recommend them.

One might ask how a foundation like Norcross manages its numerous PRIs to stay at or above the 5 percent level on average. Richard Reagan admits that it could be a challenge if the foundation's goal were to adhere precisely to the 5 percent minimum. The loans often go out and back within one year, and the foundation gives substantially more than the 5 percent minimum, so falling below the threshold is not a concern. The foundation has segmented $3 million of its $60 million endowment for PRIs in addition to creating a line of credit if it needs more loan money.

Parameters for Land Conservation PRIs

The style, formality, and scale of foundation PRIs varies widely within the laws governing program-related investments and loans. Here are some of the parameters of PRIs and how they apply across a selection of PRI-making foundations.

Requirements

Foundations that make PRIs are required by law to use them to further one or more of their charitable purposes. The primary purpose of a PRI cannot be income generation. Ensuring that the terms and conditions are more beneficial to borrowers than what would be available on the commercial market generally satisfies this requirement. Like foundation grants, PRIs cannot be made to foundation board or family members, and they require tracking of the funds to ensure they are used for charitable purposes.

Finally, PRIs cannot be used to support lobbying or political campaign activities. Furthermore, a PRI may not be motivated by the foundation's desire for income or gains.

Size

PRI amounts range widely. In general, smaller PRIs are made to smaller organizations and larger ones to large organizations because smaller organizations tend to do smaller deals. Even large PRIs, when made to intermediary organizations, are redistributed as smaller loans to specific projects. The smallest PRI I heard of was a Norcross loan for $12,000. At the other end of the spectrum, Packard's PRIs to all sectors have ranged from $150,000 to many millions.[8]

Programmatic Focus

Certain foundations have a specific geographic or resource focus for their PRIs. Others, such as the Geraldine R. Dodge and Kohlberg foundations, are more interested in reaching a certain type of land trust within their service areas, in their cases, midsized land trusts that have less access to low-cost capital. Norcross lends for wildlife habitat conservation and also prefers to lend to smaller groups.

Interest Rates

PRIs are made at low-interest rates relative to commercial lending markets. Most PRI loans currently are loaned at 0 to 3 percent. As commercial interest rates rise or fall, foundation-lending rates do the same. PRI lower-than-market rates are the best evidence of a foundation's philanthropic motivations for lending.

Loan-to-value Ratio

Foundations vary in the percentage of PRI investment relative to the total value of a conservation acquisition they are willing to finance. Generally foundations will lend up to 100 percent of the appraised value. When lending for other than land transactions, such as to establish a revolving fund, the amount is set in a similar manner as a grant.

Security and Underwriting

Foundations prefer to have general recourse to the borrower's balance sheet (i.e., total assets), assuming it is strong enough to support loan repayments or to obtain a guaranty from a third party who has the financial strength to support repayment. When loaning to smaller organizations for land acquisition, with balance sheets that are correspondingly small, foundations will look for other security, preferably not marketable securities or real estate that might fluctuate or the targeted conservation property.

There are exceptions. The Bullitt Foundation in Washington State takes a collateral interest in the conservation property and has yet to require any other type of collateral. One assumes that Bullitt's reasoning is that it wants to support small organizations that don't have, or can't afford to offer, anything except the real estate they are buying. Other foundations are reluctant to lend against conservation land, but will on occasion. Understandably they don't want to foreclose on conservation land. Denis Hayes, Bullitt Foundation's president, explains why they take land as collateral: "Obviously, this approach makes very little business sense, but we are not a business. Our board chose this course, with its attendant risks, with its eyes open, because we believe it is the best way to advance our philanthropic mission."

Loan documentation is in line with that of a commercial bank, including a loan agreement or promissory note or both and a mortgage or deed of trust.

Term

PRIs for land acquisition are usually short- or medium-term: one to five years. Foundations work to set loan terms to be consistent with the timing of borrowers' takeouts. Norcross's loans are for one year, while Packard's generally range between three and five years. Packard has made land acquisition PRIs for shorter and longer terms. There are land trusts that have benefited greatly from very short-term (one to two month) PRIs that bridged very small time gaps between closing and takeout.

Repayment Plan and Schedule

Some foundations require a detailed repayment plan and schedule. Where government takeout is the method of repayment, most foundations defer the payment of principal and interest until the takeout money is available, on the assumption that the organization doesn't have the money for repayment of the loan until that point. When the property is resold by the organization, the PRI is then repaid in one lump sum at the end of the term. Repayment in this manner is one of the characteristics of PRIs that make them not commercially attractive. When the takeout is a capital campaign or another higher-risk eventuality such as an as of yet unidentified conservation-buyer takeout, the foundation may require some interest and principal to be paid throughout the loan term.

Use of Funds

In the land-conservation arena, PRIs are mostly loaned for bridge financing for land acquisition or to capitalize revolving funds primarily administered by intermediary organizations. In the latter case, the foundation lends to the intermediary and the intermediary lends to land-conservation organizations. The foundation delegates certain of the relending due-diligence functions to an intermediary that has the expertise to do this work. The intermediaries often carry a significant amount of the risk. Thus, a funder is doing a lot more than just outsourcing the due diligence.

Other Costs

Foundations do not typically charge fees or points for their PRIs as banks do for their loans. Borrowers are still expected to pay their own costs, such as attorneys' fees.

Risk

As with banks, the risk of a PRI to a foundation is a function of two elements: takeout and security. A foundation might be willing to take more risk in repayment, as long as the security is very good. A loan based, for example, on a takeout with a capital campaign, the fortunes of which can be uncertain, but with a solid guarantee, is a relatively risk-free loan. Like most lenders, foundations like to minimize the risk that they will not get repaid one way or the other, preferring to be paid with the takeout, as it is more straightforward. They like documented assurances of repayment. Often they will independently confirm land trust representations regarding sources of repayment, typically with a written letter of intent or some level of comfort from, for example, the public agency intending to purchase the property.

Unlike banks, conservation-motivated lenders such as foundations are most concerned about the quality and success of the project for which they are lending. Regardless of the quality of the security, foundations don't want to see these projects fail. Their mission is land conservation, too, not just protecting their loans.

Foundations and intermediaries prefer to make PRIs when the takeouts are solid, such as from government funding or private fundraising by an organization with a strong track record. But foundations, especially through intermediaries, do make higher risk PRIs. Funders are less inclined to finance controversial projects. Foundations have supported complex transactions with PRIs.

The Application Process

Foundations for which PRIs are a major part of their charitable program usually have a formal application process. The Norcross Wildlife Foundation, for example, requires strict adherence to relatively simple guidelines and forms.[9] Other foundations handle PRIs more informally, without standard application forms.

The Approval Process

Some foundations have a threshold amount for board approval, and others take all PRIs to their boards. Both Norcross and Packard PRIs that are recommended by the staff go to the full board for approval.

Foundations and PRIs

As one might expect, foundations often make PRIs as an outgrowth of their grant-making program. After working on a particular issue or with a particular grantee for a period of time, a lending opportunity emerges. For example, each program area drives PRI activity for the Packard and MacArthur foundations. So one would expect that the funding for PRIs would come out of the program budget as well. This is rarely if ever the case with conservation PRIs. PRIs of this sort would compete with grant making out of the same budget. A PRI budget is usually separately segmented from the endowment, usually comprising no more than 1 to 3 percent of the endowment.

The Bullitt Foundation is an example of a foundation that allocates its PRI funding directly from its asset base. The foundation had a history of making large grants for land acquisition, and wanted to do so while maintaining its assets. So it granted $1 million to the Trust for Public Land to establish the Puget Sound Open Space Fund, an internal revolving fund, and segmented part of its endowment to lend as its own internal revolving fund. Bullitt recently segregated an additional $1 million to allow partners to acquire urban land adjacent to the path of public transport before it escalates in value. In return, the partners will construct super-efficient, "green" housing for low-income residents.

President Denis Hayes has had good experience making PRIs. His foundation has conserved $50 million worth of property on a $3.5 million annual PRI budget in twelve years.

As enthusiastic as the Norcross Wildlife and Bullitt foundations are with their smaller PRI programs, the larger Packard Foundation is strongly committed to its much-larger PRI program. Three percent of its $5.8 billion endowment[10] is set aside for funding PRIs.

The Packard Foundation made its first PRI in 1980 to the Yosemite Natural History Museum for the book manuscript entitled "Discovering Sierra Nevada Birds." In the land-conservation area, Packard has made large PRIs to the national organizations, including The Nature Conservancy, to help them acquire the Baca Ranch on the eastern edge of Colorado's San Luis Valley. The Nature Conservancy later resold the ranch to the federal government and it is now part of the Great Sand Dunes National Monument. As of December 31, 2005, Packard has loaned $309 million in 146 PRIs collectively across all of its program areas, and $102 million is currently out in 34 active loans.

To streamline the underwriting and loan due diligence, big foundations will often outsource some of the due diligence to specialized law and consulting firms, as the Packard Foundation does to Resources Law Group, a California-based law and consulting firm with expertise in land conservation. They also outsource their PRI and grant programs to intermediaries (see the intermediaries section in this chapter).

Mary Anne Rodgers, the Packard Foundation counsel, considers PRIs to be "a big win" for both sides. The Packard Foundation is trying to get the word out about the benefits of PRIs to attract more interest among other funders. The foundation is supporting the development of the PRI Makers Network[11] and internally has hired a writer who researched and interviewed borrowers to chronicle PRI stories for the foundation to use on its Web site and elsewhere. Rodgers says that PRIs present challenges for foundations and nonprofits, several of which are described later in the chapter. But these challenges can and should be overcome.

Other foundations that use PRIs also seem comfortable with their use. Few speak of problems with borrowers. Endowment performance has been hardly affected by these lower-than-market rate loans, probably because the percentage of endowments used for PRIs tends to be small.

The PRI Makers Network organized a conference in January 2006 that offered support to foundations considering getting into the business of making PRIs. GrantCraft published a twenty-five page guide on program-related investments that offers good guidance on the early stages of PRI making on such threshold issues as staffing.[12] In lieu of this, seasoned PRI makers at Packard, MacArthur, and elsewhere have the following advice for foundations new to PRIs:

- Start the process at the top with the board of directors setting direction to the foundation to develop a PRI program.
- Partner with a foundation that has the lending mechanism in place. The William Penn Foundation, for example, partnered with the Geraldine R. Dodge Foundation, which had already created a PRI mechanism, when making its first PRI. Partnering in a "PRI pool" also increases and leverages funder participation in the PRI.
- Look for experienced intermediary organizations that can relend the PRI under a set of mutually agreed guidelines (see the intermediaries section in this chapter).
- Look within the foundation for people with financing skills who might be on the other side of the corridor managing the foundation's assets, but have the ability to assess financing options and undertake the due diligence for PRIs. The KHK Foundation in St. Paul, Minnesota, for example, is a family foundation operated out of the family's investment offices. Attorneys and investment managers who work for the family in other capacities worked on that foundation's first PRI.
- In the absence of internal resources, hire a good outside real estate lawyer. The Norcross Wildlife Foundation hired a skilled real estate lawyer, Hal Poster, in New York City who manages all of the legal, financial, and real estate due diligence for its PRIs.
- Try it! Start small and in a program area that is very important to the foundation. The first PRI may take more time and be more expensive, but foundations can gain experience that may provide them with a new and valuable tool.

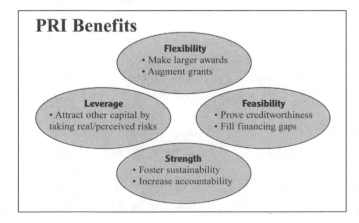

PRI Benefits

Flexibility
- Make larger awards
- Augment grants

Leverage
- Attract other capital by taking real/perceived risks

Feasibility
- Prove creditworthiness
- Fill financing gaps

Strength
- Foster sustainability
- Increase accountability

Figure 15.2
Benefits of program-related investments.
(Courtesy of the MacArthur Foundation)

Land Conservation and PRIs[13]

Most land trusts do not have access to PRIs because they don't realize that foundations can be lenders, or they aren't working with foundations that make PRIs. A land trust may be working with a foundation that makes PRIs, but the size of PRIs made by the foundation may not match its needs, or there may be problems with security requirements, or an apparent or real lack of capacity to borrow at all.

For conservation organizations that have used PRIs, the experience has been mostly positive. For any nonprofit, there are few things better than a sympathetic, well-funded supporter who is willing to lend money. As in the case of foundation grant making, an organization receiving a PRI can receive ancillary benefits, such as the endorsement of a prominent institution, assistance in structuring the transaction, advice, and sometimes even help generating other funding. A foundation or its intermediary lending organization can help in many ways, from drafting the loan agreements to making a call to move along agency takeout funding. As with a grant, a PRI is an investment by a foundation in an organization that puts the investor, the foundation, squarely on the team.

Like an external revolving fund loan, the fact that a foundation shares the goals of borrowers and has the capacity to help them succeed substantially distinguishes a foundation PRI from, say, a bank loan. Of course the less the foundation has to do for the organization, the better. But they can and will help if they need to.

The endorsement of foundation support through a PRI can have benefits. Phil Wallin of the Western Rivers Conservancy in Oregon tells how he had to buy out a landowner five months earlier than previously agreed. The Bullitt and Packard foundations jointly committed to making a short-term PRI to the conservancy. The foundations' endorsements of the project through the PRIs so assured the landowner that the takeout was likely that he decided to finance the sale himself. In another case the willingness of those same two foundations to step forward gave the landowner confidence to take only a short-term promissory note from the land trust until the closing. "Our partnership with the lenders [Packard and Bullitt] enabled us to make the deal and gave the landowner confidence that we could perform our end of the bargain. Without those two foundations, we wouldn't have had the nerve, or the ability, to move forward,"[14] says Phil. He believes that foundations can use this tool to increase

the chances of success of their grants in the same area, expand their reach beyond their granting program, and thus increase their level of investment in
conservation.

For land conservation organizations, there are many other benefits to PRIs.
Friendly foundations can help build both land trust confidence and credit to use
with banks or other lenders. Essex County Greenbelt Association in Massachusetts had received only one other loan in recent history and it was from an individual. A PRI from Norcross was its first institutional loan. Essex borrowed
$70,000 for the fee acquisition of fifty acres of salt marsh mixed with upland.
For the year that the land was on the market, Essex had made several offers for
it, each of which the landowner considered lowball. Then suddenly Essex had
a deal. Though Essex had enough money in its new land protection fund, its
board only intended to use the fund for very high-priority, threatened emergency projects. It decided to approach Norcross, with which it had a preexisting relationship through Norcross's grant program, for a loan instead.

Essex had expected to quickly flip the marsh to the state fish and game department, but the agency lost its funding for this specific project. Essex purchased the property with a loan from Norcross, and a conservation buyer
bought and dedicated it to his wife as a memorial reservation. Dave Santomenna, the land trust's director of land conservation, said that the experience was incredibly positive. Norcross's turnaround time was quick. The staff
was responsive and helpful. The application process was fast and easy. Essex
had an appraisal of the property at $90,000 and was purchasing it at $70,000,
which made Norcross comfortable.

"It gave us the breathing room to find a donor—we had a few months.
Talking the board into going for the PRI did not take a big amount of persua-
sion. The fact that staff had done a diligent job of negotiation and that the
property had high resource values was persuasive." Though Dave hasn't found
another project that fits Norcross's requirements quite as well, the message
from this project is that, although it was not a blockbuster, it was an important, good-sized project for the organization. It built their confidence and
credit. "Right for us and right for Norcross," he says.

Much smaller land trusts have used PRIs from Norcross because it is a
friendly lender and may be more receptive to rural projects. Nancy Ailes of the
Cacapon & Lost Rivers Land Trust in the eastern panhandle of West Virginia
is the only staff person for the land trust, working out of her living room with
an annual budget of $35,000–$45,000. Nancy's land trust has received two PRIs

from Norcross (for a total loan value of $400,000). Nancy says that she would have lost both parcels without Norcross PRIs.

Unfortunately, aside from small PRIs made by Norcross, not all land trusts have access to PRIs. The requirement of matching mission and geographic focus of a foundation and a land trust, and then hoping that the foundation makes conservation PRIs, can leave many land trusts high and dry. While almost every midsize town in the United States has a bank, few have PRI-making foundations, especially with an interest in conservation. That is another reason why Norcross's program is so valuable to conservation. It loans nationwide.

This is not to say that a foundation can't be convinced to make a PRI even if it has never done it before. Several foundation staff with whom I spoke said they made their first PRI for this reason, and that they would seriously consider making another PRI to a trusted nonprofit if a well-packaged proposal was brought to them. Foundation staff also told me the low demand for PRIs was one of the reasons that they didn't make PRIs, or have made so few.

Only a few years ago, one enterprising land conservationist called a foundation with which he had a good relationship and asked if he could get a loan to save a piece of land from development. The immediate answer was, "No, we don't make loans." But two weeks later an enterprising member of the foundation staff called back and said, "Yes we can." So began a new conservation PRI program. A smattering of private, family, and community foundations are making PRIs on an opportunistic basis. More could follow suit.

An issue not unique to PRIs is the fact that the loans require active management. The accounting and security issues can get challenging, especially if an organization is carrying more than one PRI. Foundations tend to monitor loans more carefully than grants. In the community development sector, foundations have been known to withdraw a PRI if the organization is not strictly adhering to the terms of the loan. Such a response is easier with a loan than a grant, but it is good warning to a land trust to be extra diligent about adhering to PRI conditions.

One veteran conservation PRI borrower explained that securing PRIs can be "such a scramble." Foundations change their priorities and their programs, and their interest in lending can shrink overnight based on the fortunes of their portfolios or the presence of multiple outstanding PRIs. With the exception of the bigger PRI programs, most foundations have not allocated large amounts of money to their PRI programs. Thus a few loans can max out their funds and PRIs can be suddenly unavailable to borrowers when they need money.

"Foundations have been very helpful, but you can't always count on them," says this same practitioner. "What is needed is a clearinghouse for PRIs and borrowers." Several people spoke to me about similar ideas by which PRIs and other loans could be made available nationally.

Intermediaries

Because the job of lending is so different from that of granting, foundations making PRIs have historically looked to intermediary organizations to do the due diligence and often the retail lending to nonprofits. For large foundations that make multiple simultaneous PRIs and respond reasonably quickly, intermediaries serve an essential purpose. These organizations have developed expertise in performing the due diligence needed to make safe and successful loans. In the community development sector, numerous skilled intermediaries play a central role in PRI lending. Even in the nascent conservation PRI market, intermediaries are playing a growing role. In California, Resources Legacy Fund is a major relender for the Packard Foundation and others. Open Space Institute oversees a relending program in New Jersey capitalized with PRIs from the Geraldine R. Dodge Foundation and the William Penn Foundation (first conservation PRIs for both foundations). The Kohlberg Foundation in western Massachusetts has a $4 million PRI program with OSI. Nationwide, The Conservation Fund, for which lending and granting are only two of its functions, lends from its regionally based external conservation revolving funds (see chapter 13 on external revolving loan funds) and from its own internal revolving fund, both of which are partly funded by PRIs. Other land-conservation organizations have, from time to time, served as intermediaries for foundation PRIs. The Maine Coast Heritage Trust, for example, originally established its regional revolving fund in 1982 with a modest PRI from the MacArthur Foundation, which it paid off, replenishing the fund with private contributions.[15]

The Packard Foundation made a substantial $7 million PRI to Resources Legacy Fund in 2004 for five years for relending to conservation organizations in the Greater Yellowstone Ecosystem in Wyoming, Idaho, and Montana. In 2005, it expanded the lending area to include the Crown of the Continent, the northern extension of the ecosystem into Canada.

Foundations usually make PRIs to intermediaries at low, wholesale rates (1 to 2 percent in the 2005 market), so there is room for a small markup for relending as the costly retailing of loans to multiple organizations is borne by the intermediary, not the foundation. Under a commonly used business model, the foundation makes a large PRI—usually several million dollars—to an intermediary. The intermediary then lends out the money at a higher rate, usually 3 to 4 percent. The interest-rate differential helps to cover the costs to the intermediary of administering the loans including: working with the lending foundation to develop criteria for its lending program, outreach to borrowers, conducting due diligence, often assisting the borrowers with their loan application, preparing and negotiating loan documents, and monitoring the loan to ensure adherence to mission and repayment.

I heard from some, though certainly not all, intermediaries that this interest differential of 1 to 2 percent between the rate of the received PRI and the interest rate on the loans lent by the intermediary is rarely enough to cover these costs. This would be true even if the entire PRI amount were lent out all the time so that the intermediary is earning interest from borrowers on it, though that rarely happens. Though naturally the costs are higher when all of the money is at work, there are high base costs whether or not all the money is out in loans. In some cases, the foundations make grants to defray these expenses. The Geraldine R. Dodge Foundation made a $100,000 grant to Open Space Institute (OSI) to cover some of the expenses associated with its PRI of $2.5 million. The Charles Stewart Mott Foundation granted $225,000 to The Conservation Fund to provide technical assistance to the borrowers working with its Great Lakes Revolving Loan Fund, funded by a much larger grant (over $6 million) from the Mott Foundation.

The problem of the carrying costs of PRIs for intermediaries may speak to a need to refine the model. PRI programs, including Norcross's, require subsidy. Higher loan volume should reduce costs, though it may still not result in sustainability. PRI programs that are relatively "programmatically agnostic" (in that the lending entity does less research into the quality of the land being protected) require less overhead. Greater costs for a lender, though, are the administrative and due-diligence aspects of the loan. The more work that the foundation or intermediary must do, the more expensive the loan will be for the lender. As conservation borrowers become more experienced at packaging loan applications, these costs should drop.

Scale is also an issue. A small intermediary staffed to help its borrowers, and living off the rate differential on, say, a $1–2 million PRI may struggle. This is the case of some of the smaller external revolving funds. But I understand from one expert in the business that there is a scale of operations at which a program could be self-sustaining. But would that serve the best interests of conservation or just be the most efficient use of capital? When lending to inexperienced organizations, more support is needed, and that carries costs. Even with grants to intermediaries for these costs, the map of external revolving funds in the United States (figure 13.3) (most of which are run by intermediaries and many funded by PRIs) shows that there are parts of the country not served. For now, the economics of relending PRIs in multiple loans to organizations that need them can be tight.

Why Don't More Foundations Use PRIs?

We do not know how many foundations are making PRIs to conservation. There are small, private foundations and community foundations offering a very limited number of PRIs on an informal basis. The Abell Foundation in Baltimore, Maryland, for example, has made numerous PRIs in Maryland for bridge financing to local organizations for pre-acquisitions of public parks. Community foundations all over the United States are making similar bridge loans. And a handful of foundations have made *grants* (and PRIs) to intermediaries and external revolving loan funds, which in turn are lent out for conservation. Nonetheless, with the exception of a few foundations, most notably Packard, Norcross, and Bullitt, most foundations with which I spoke currently

Figure 15.3
Program related investments (PRIs) have some characteristics that would place them under the responsibility of a foundation's program department and other characteristics that would put them under the responsibility of its investment department.

make very few conservation PRIs, if any. Why? I found five main reasons why foundations are hesitant about their future role in PRI making.

- Foundations perceive that the demand for PRIs is limited. In most areas the big conservation organizations have their own funds and the small ones aren't doing a lot of borrowing, so demand is low. It is also episodic and apparently hard to predict, causing foundations to conclude that there really isn't much demand. However, in other parts of the country, land trusts need loans and are looking everywhere for sources of capital. I think of southern Texas around Houston, where the land trusts are so busy they hardly have time to breathe, but had never heard of PRIs. Or Florida, where one land trust struggled to cobble together campaign pledges only to have the bank decide it couldn't loan against pledges. I can name ten land trusts that would use PRIs if they understood them and knew foundations willing to make them. As land trusts grow more successful at borrowing in general, demand for PRIs should increase.

- Foundations are set up as grant-making institutions and PRIs fall between the program and investment arms of a foundation since they are neither grants (the expertise of the program arm) nor financial investments (the expertise of the investment arm). There is push-back from the investment side because of low returns and from the program side because of a perceived and real need for different expertise. Because they are not usually funded out of a program budget, the investment side has to buy in. As one experienced PRI maker said, "There is a bright line in a foundation between grant making and financing. There can be tension between the program and the controller, who must learn to work in a counter intuitive manner—not in a traditional investment manner." In addition, some foundations don't know where to look for available nonprofit lending expertise. As Jon Jensen of the George Gund Foundation says, "PRIs require a very different mentality. A whole different set of questions is asked—more of a banker's mentality." Often that expertise is within the organization in the investment department. But even without it, using Norcross as a model, the expertise can be found in the legal real estate community.

- Conservation foundation program officers understandably aren't well acquainted with lending and how it can help achieve their programmatic objectives. Program officers are often recruited from the conservation world, a field not well versed in finance, and don't fully appreciate how PRIs could extend its reach. Not yet.

- Loans have to be underwritten differently than grants. One knowledgeable PRI consultant suggested that there is a tendency to push programs through loans the same way as through grants. Since the money comes back, the requirements may not need to be so stringent.

- PRIs have a real element of risk. Foundations want to *avoid* risk, where banks *manage* risk. There are certain factors that make that risk seem greater than it is, such as the perception that a recipient will consider the PRI as a grant, concern about lack of solid takeouts, and general land trust naiveté about taking loans. If anything, land trusts are too cautious. In reality very few conservation PRIs have caused problems for foundations. However, if this concern prevails, foundations could ask their intermediaries to share risk, as Penn, Dodge, and Kohlberg have done with OSI.

Other issues that play into the lack of PRI deal flow from the foundation side. The size of PRIs currently available may not meet land trust needs. A survey of land trust financing would shed further light on this. Packard makes relatively large PRIs—in the million to multimillion-dollar range. These go to the larger organizations, or to intermediaries. Where intermediaries are retailing loans to land trusts, size is less of an issue. But intermediaries don't operate everywhere.

Then there is Norcross, routinely making fifteen to thirty small PRIs a year with no hesitation. Other foundations might argue that Norcross, though filling a niche, is not acting in a geographically strategic way. It is likely though that duplication of the Norcross model of a small, informal, highly service-oriented organization would generate more demand. That model does have costs, subsidizing loans at 0 percent interest rates and offering other support. It may not be the 0 percent interest rates, however, that are as much of a draw as the small loan size and simplicity of the application process.

Foundation staff, whether they offer PRIs or not, recognize their value in the field. But of those that currently do not make PRIs, few seem ready to make a big shift to formally invest in them. One foundation had been at the consideration point of whether to establish a PRI program for five years.

Ted Smith of the Kendall Foundation in Boston is also looking into PRIs. Even without a formal PRI program, Ted would consider recommending a PRI if a solid nonprofit came to him with a high-quality package. He says that he doesn't have time to prospect for one. "Most foundations should be understaffed and overworked if they are doing their job. It is very hard to spare the time to break into a new area, especially with something like a PRI that requires the attention of the CEO. This is a threshold issue for a small foundation like ours."

Ted suggests that, for small foundations, the due diligence for conservation PRIs must be farmed out to organizations with expertise. This is a critical point. Could it be that the primary barrier to making PRIs lies in the lack of intermediaries? The experience in the community development field suggests that intermediaries were critical to the success of those PRIs, both on the policy side and to moving capital. Land trusts don't help the situation by not urging partner foundations to offer PRIs. But many land trusts are not familiar with PRIs, some have other acceptable borrowing options, many don't borrow at all, and others prefer not to push their foundations.

Recommendations For Land Trusts

If a land trust is a novice borrower, the application process can be time-consuming for both parties regardless of the type of lender. As one seasoned lender said, "You simply can't draft in an infinite amount of flexibility. The document gets too complicated and becomes an unwieldy thirty-page loan agreement. It is better to keep it simple." Mary Anne Rodgers, the Packard Foundation counsel, agrees that borrowers or nonprofits need a better understanding of borrowing, "to develop experience and credit." But what better place to learn the ropes than with a foundation that shares your mission and wants to help you leverage your position as borrowing can do?

Foundations, however, are generally not the best first line of borrowing for the reasons given here and in chapter 10. Norcross is the notable exception. Foundations want assurance of a land trust's capacity and commitment to repaying the loan. That is best achieved with a track record of successful borrowing. Land trusts shouldn't risk a relationship with a foundation by learning to borrow from them. A successful borrowing experience with an intermediary or an external revolving loan fund or even a bank starts to build that credibility and experience. Still, with an eye to interest rates, foundations often offer the very best. An inexpensive loan from a sympathetic lender is worth the crash course in borrowing that might be needed to apply.

It's the same old story. Land trusts are not beating down the doors of foundations for loans because many lack expertise, but also because of the perceived or real lack of takeouts.[16] Setting those bigger issues aside, here are some tips for land trusts when approaching a foundation for a PRI.

- Have a good preexisting relationship with the foundation before approaching it for a loan. Being a successful grantee is optimal, so the foundation already knows how the organization operates. Even a lesser relationship through a board member or staff helps.
- Alert the foundation that your request might be coming in weeks if not months before the loan is needed.
- Structure the PRI (bank loan, etc.) so the lender is protected. You won't get anywhere without providing real security to the foundation.
- Demonstrate knowledge of and commitment to capital and financial planning. Organizations that don't show this are unlikely to impress a foundation with their ability to repay loans.
- Make sure the package of information submitted is what the foundation needs to know and is as complete as possible. It should contain the following information:

  - How much is the application for and why? Make clear qualitative arguments (e.g., why, without this loan, the project will be lost).
  - If the loan is for multiple projects, what is the turnover or utilization rate, or how well and often will the PRI be used?
  - Be sure that your organization has followed *Land Trust Standards and Practices.*
  - Demonstrate specific board oversight.
  - How important is the parcel to the public, to the mission of your organization, and to the mission of the foundation? How much of the appraised value will the loan and purchase price represent?
  - What is the collateral and how much is it worth?
  - How compelling is the case to the public to make the purchase?
  - What is the expected source for takeout, what is the timetable, and what are the assurances of permanent funding?
  - How well does the purchase fit into the takeout entity's acquisition priorities, particularly if the entity is a public agency?
  - In the case of an agency takeout, what kind of assurances have been made by the agency that it will buy the land?

- What is the backup plan if the primary source of takeout funding falls through?
- What is the worst-case scenario if both plans fall through?

Once you develop a relationship of trust with a foundation, they are often receptive to multiple PRIs. Phil Wallin of the Western Rivers Conservancy used four PRIs and loans from repeat lenders for the acquisition of a $6 million parcel on the Hoh River on the Olympic Peninsula.

Gene Duvernoy, executive director of the Cascade Land Conservancy in Washington State, another veteran of several PRIs, reminds land trusts that PRIs are business transactions and should never be thought of as complete philanthropy, though one might get lower rates. Substantial collateral and other requirements similar to those of a commercial bank must be presented. The details of these vary from foundation to foundation. And, like other loans, PRIs must be repaid.

Conclusion

Despite the apparent barriers that discourage foundations from making PRIs, it is surprising that more don't use them for conservation. PRIs are very well suited to land conservation where access to capital is a necessity. The PRI Makers Network is working to increase the use of PRIs in all charitable sectors; this momentum may encourage more conservation PRI making.

Foundations do seem to be trending slowly toward the use of PRIs probably because of growing demand. In the community development areas, MacArthur's PRI program is in great demand. In land conservation, land trusts are becoming more adept at financing, which will eventually lead to more demand for PRIs. Debra Schwartz, director of program-related investments at the MacArthur Foundation, speculates that PRIs may appeal especially to newer philanthropists and foundations with an interest in social enterprise. PRIs demand a higher level of financial sustainability and sophistication than regular grants. Unlike regular grantees, PRI recipients that successfully repay their obligations demonstrate their creditworthiness and the viability of their organizations from a business standpoint.

If foundation interest in conservation PRIs were to grow, where could it make the most difference? A comprehensive look at the conservation lending landscape might quantify the issues and help foundations align their resources.

Foundations are in an unusual position because they can lend and they can give. Solely using grant money the Doris Duke Charitable Foundation undertook a variation of this concept by strategically packaging regional grants for revolving funds and organizational capacity development. By combining approaches, organizations staffed up as flexible (because its source was grants) loan money became available. Focusing on specific outcomes, say conservation of a river valley, a foundation could build organizational expertise in financing and offer PRIs and a cushion of capital so that PRIs could be used for more difficult but critical land transactions. None of the foundations with whom I spoke (other than Norcross) mentioned combining functions, though other experts in the field did.

High-value conservation land is lost daily because some takeouts require more than two or three years to assemble. These projects are riskier for lenders. Foundations could be lending for longer periods of time or capitalize loan-loss reserves, thus creating more flexibility to make riskier, often very important loans.

In speaking with a small, highly outcome-driven foundation, I was impressed by their willingness to be flexible to achieve their geographically based conservation outcomes through no-interest loans. It is this kind of foundation that could pioneer new financing models, working with a creative financial advisor and with an eye to the good work of foundations in the community development sector.

Providing successful PRI models might encourage greater PRI use. Norcross, unique as it is, has elements that would be valuable to replicate. Community foundations in particular might pick up on the Norcross model instituting low or 0 percent loan programs subsidized by donors. Community foundations are a tremendous source of yet untapped capital in local communities nationwide.

PRIs offer a unique opportunity for foundations to reach beyond their current program. By directing a fraction of foundation endowments, PRIs or other mission-related investments (MRIs), financing for the conservation landscape has already been increased. Imagine the impact if foundations increased even slightly the small portion of their endowments that they were to dedicate? The F. B. Heron Foundation has an essay on its Web site written by its vice president of investments, Luther M. Ragin, that speaks to a future for foundation investment, including PRIs.[17] He asks whether a foundation could do more to achieve its mission by using its endowment to work for its mission while still maintaining its value.

Mr. Ragin ends his essay with a call for mission-related investing: "The approach is not without risk. But if taking well-considered risks for public benefit is not the role of philanthropy, then what is?" In the next two years, the Heron Foundation will pursue four mission-related investment initiatives.

Mission-related investing is really what PRIs are all about. PRI-making foundations are using their endowments to do more than throw off interest to fund their programs. They are putting their assets to work for that mission. It is tempting to speculate about what a modest increase in the use of the billions of dollars held in the collective endowments of the conservation foundations could do for conservation.

For land conservation, the real benefit, the public benefit, of PRIs is to get loans to organizations that don't have access to other capital. This is where foundations and their intermediaries have and will continue to do their best lending work. There is always the temptation to make the easier, lower-risk loans. But, for the most part, foundations and the conservation community should work together to assess where, geographically and strategically, foundations can do the most good. Is that by getting cheaper money (at a lower interest rate) to the big conservation groups for the really big land transactions, or is it getting financing to organizations that don't have access to other sources of funds, or is it to start a land trust up the learning ladder of finance?

If increasing PRI activity interests the land conservation movement, then it is absolutely incumbent upon conservationists to make a safe place for this kind of money to be invested and then argue for its use. Many of the foundation directors with whom I spoke said that the primary reason that their conservation PRI program was small or nonexistent was because of the limited demand for loans from land trusts. Yet here is abundant inexpensive money. Land trusts can't complain about not having it, if they aren't asking for it. So ask for it!

Part 4
Looking Ahead

Chapter 16
Reducing Costs

"It was so much fun I want to do it again."

Mrs. Ethel Theriault, bargain seller to D&R Greenway[1]

A land trust has many benefits to offer the seller, only one of which is cash. As nimble, flexible, and, most importantly, charitable as land trusts are, as payment for an acquisition they can offer sellers many options and usually reduce their own costs in the process. To put together the package that best suits the seller and is workable for the land trust, the land trust must understand what outcomes the seller wants to achieve. Often these are subtler than just getting the biggest check, and not immediately revealed. He or she may not know that there are ways to generate higher *after-tax* income or to buy out a disgruntled partner or acquire the adjoining farm while keeping the family property. By searching for those deeper interests and then assembling the right team to package the elements of the transaction to meet those interests, the seller and land trust benefit in new and unexpected ways.

Part of finding efficiency in a transaction involves being flexible about what the land trust must accomplish—its desired versus its bottom-line conservation outcomes. Ideally, it may want to keep the land entirely wild; however, selling a corner with little conservation value to the town for a playground may make the project financially viable, much more popular and thus sustainable over the long term. Or, it may have been planning to do the project single-handedly, and now needs partners. These are usually good changes. More of the community participates and the land trust increases community interest in land conservation. A land trust reduces costs by thinking about the deal differently.

As Pat Noonan, one of the great conservation dealmakers of all time, former president of The Nature Conservancy and a founder of the American Farmland Trust and The Conservation Fund, tells it, "There is no challenge to buying land if you have all the money in the world. The challenge is in making the deal with what you have and doing it tax efficiently."

The easiest way to put this different mind-set to work is to change the dynamic of the classic, somewhat adversarial relationship between buyer and seller to a team approach.

Starting down the team-building road benefits from the right introduction. Cold calling is not a good approach. Starting down the team-building road benefits from the right introduction. However, finding someone who has both good relations with the landowner and with the land trust can be difficult. When connections were particularly thin, I have even engaged a realtor with strong landowner connections to help make appropriate introductions.

Eventually though, building that personal relationship takes one-on-one time with the landowners, visiting the property and having coffee in their kitchen. If the dynamic changes, and a team approach develops (and sometimes it does not), doors open and together you and the seller can explore different deal structures to meet the seller's needs (and yours). Then when you get to the details of the transaction, when you start discussing numbers, it helps to have a second land trust representative in the room with a different set of skills. That person can help in many ways, by bringing different knowledge to the table and asking those questions that might be awkward for you, now with the personal relationship with the seller, to ask. This second person can help you address the details and document progress.

What Outcome Is the Landowner Really Seeking?

Nothing could be more important than learning what the landowner wants to accomplish. That takes getting to know the seller and his or her values and culture. Even the seller, especially a longtime landowner, may not be able to articulate these goals. Just to sell the land for the highest possible price has always seemed like a good enough reason to sell. As the landowner–land trust relationship develops, other considerations usually become clearer. The landowner, for example, may want enough cash to pay pressing bills; create a nest egg for emergencies or a rainy day; receive a lifetime stream of income; buy the farm next door; or, simply, it may be that family conflicts or fear about financial insecurity are forcing the sale. Selling at market value seems like the best way to achieve these goals.[2] Many problems can be resolved and goals achieved without selling for top dollar or, sometimes, even selling at all.

Getting to these underlying issues can take a long time, years even. How-

ever, once that point is reached, the land trust must be prepared to help put together the right package. This may require sophisticated expertise, partners,
and a lot more time. Pat explains that making a good deal for both the seller
and the land trust requires a set of skills that include negotiating savvy; a
knowledge of the financial, legal, and community context; and a solid understanding of the conservation values, whether they are agricultural, ecological,
scenic, or other. Skillful negotiators don't have to have all or even many of these
skills. Instead, they must uncover what the seller really wants then work with
the right team to structure the offer to meet those needs.

Linda Meade, executive director of the D&R Greenway Land Trust in New
Jersey, is a pro at putting together the right team to get to core issues with the
seller and to create an attractive package that works for all participants. Most
of D&R Greenway's projects are acquisitions and most of those are bargain
sales. Linda works with an investment advisor to offer landowners the full
range of tax and financial options. In the case of Mrs. Ethel Theriault, quoted
at the beginning of this chapter, she sold a conservation easement at a bargain
price to the land trust that allowed her son and daughter-in-law to continue
to farm. D&R Greenway purchased an annuity for her with part of the proceeds of the sale, which pays her an income for her life. She also received a lump
sum to pay expenses and buy a hybrid car.

Working with the Landowner

Persistence and Patience

Persistence and patience can sometimes substitute for abundant funds. Land
deals can be very tough. Just sticking with them, despite serious legal, title, and
personal issues, can make the difference. Linda tells how the D&R Greenway
has gained the reputation of being a problem solver for projects very small (half
an acre) to much bigger (two hundred acres). What they start, they finish. If a
survey or title report comes back with problems or any of a myriad of other
issues emerge, they solve them.

The patience to wait for the right moment—not to push when it doesn't
feel right—is greatly appreciated by landowners who may have their hands full
with other issues. Be sure to remember to keep checking in on those projects
that seem to be going nowhere. Suddenly they can spring loose. Many of a land
trust's proudest accomplishments take years to complete. I talked to one land
trust board member who said that, after twenty years of pursuing a 205-acre,

$24 million parcel of land, they had a tiny opening with the sellers. Success was still so unlikely that this very experienced board member gave it a 3 percent chance. A combination of new representatives for the sellers and more experience on the part of the land trust paid off, and, two and a half years later, over twenty-two years after the land trust first identified the project, the land trust acquired it for $16 million.

I spent eight years on one of my favorite projects, working with a third-generation rancher who was committed to conserving his family's ranch. Originally, the ranch was embroiled in a family dispute that ended up in a lawsuit for partition. The court couldn't equitably split the ranch and ruled that it must be sold and the proceeds divided between the parties. I spent a year walking potential conservation buyers through beautiful riparian forests and spring creeks, almost losing one in a very deep irrigation ditch. That same buyer made a strong offer to purchase the ranch. At the last minute the young rancher was able to buy out the disputing co-owner himself. He was eager to protect the ranch immediately, but there were many other hurdles. Just to mention one, we spent a year on a land exchange to align an irregular, unworkable boundary in the area he wanted to conserve. At last, we sat down together to articulate his vision and draft the conservation easement. However, a rancher's days are very long with not much time to study documents, so this process took another couple of years. With a draft finally in hand, we set about developing a plan for an easement-for-fee exchange. Not surprisingly on this complex parcel, valuation was complicated. We assembled a team of an appraiser, a lawyer, and a sympathetic developer to piece together the legal and valuation elements. Meanwhile older-generation family health and estate issues slowed progress. The rancher persisted. I left the land trust in 2001, and finally in 2005 the land trust and rancher completed the first phase of conservation, fifteen years after our efforts first began.

Seller Transforming into a Donor

With persistence, patience, and a good team, Pat Noonan urges conservationists to create an offer that involves full donation of the conservation interests. Then there is no financing, and only stewardship costs to raise. Despite sounding too good to be true, this does happen. Some landowners decide to sell their land and then run into family resistance or discover the depth of their own attachment to it. Unless there is a compelling financial reason to sell, it can be psychologically difficult to do so.

I have seen sellers become donors. Landowners change their minds about selling and decide to donate the land or a conservation easement instead. Landowners' attitudes can also change as they learn about conservation, the land trust program, and the alternatives to outright sale. Would-be sellers are surprised to find that they share something with land trust people: a love of land. The characteristic flexibility of land trusts is appealing, too.

A donation request sets one end of the negotiating spectrum and market value sets the other. Raising the idea of donation can move discussions off of the market-value end of the options and gives an organization room to discuss alternatives to cash.

Maximizing Return

Nonetheless, circumstances are not always appropriate for asking for a full donation. The land trust must recognize that, in certain situations, it will be paying for conservation. A landowner who needs money to pay burdensome estate taxes or to retire debt is obviously not a good candidate for a full donation. On the other hand, the landowner may not be familiar with how a charitable organization can save them money, reduce estate taxes, and help to refinance debt. Even when the seller wants to maximize return, there are still options that can save both parties money. One of the common ones is the bargain sale.

A bargain sale is a sale of property or an interest in property such as a conservation easement to a qualified charitable organization, such as a land trust, at below the fair market value. The transaction has two parts, a gift and a sale. The gift constitutes a charitable gift and the sale is subject to capital gains tax (in most cases). The seller must obtain an independent appraisal to document the market value of the property. Then the charitable gift becomes the difference between the appraised value and the lower sale price. The seller usually saves on taxes because the gift component of the bargain sale qualifies for a tax deduction. The land trust benefits from the lower sale price.

The other important advantage of a bargain sale is during negotiation. The parties need not negotiate the *value* of the property, only the sale *price*. Different perspectives on the value of land can polarize negotiations. A bargain sale changes the conversation. If the land trust is comfortable with the legitimacy of the landowner's valuation through appraisal,[3] the issue is not the market value of the land, but what the land trust can pay.

Other useful money-saving, tax-related techniques include:

- Purchase of options, which give the buyer time to raise the funds for the purchase and frequently have beneficial tax consequences for the seller.
- Like-kind or 1031 exchanges, which allow landowners to exchange land or conservation easements for land and defer the capital gains tax.
- Retained life estates, by which a landowner can continue to live on the property after selling it, reducing the purchase price for the land trust.

Charitable remainder trusts and charitable gift annuities are two "life income" planned giving techniques that have financial benefits for the buyer and seller. They create an income stream, tax deduction, and future reduction in estate tax liability for the seller (and other beneficiaries), and a frequently significant payment to the land trust.

Finding comfortable ways to talk about these concepts is half the battle. An outside expert, like an investment advisor or attorney from a reputable firm known to the seller, can often explain these details more credibly than a member of the land trust staff despite the staff's knowledge. While a land trust should never give tax advice on which a seller or donor relies, it should be able to explain generally how these techniques work.

Nonetheless, the appraisal, the market, and the seller's expectations will influence the buyer's thinking about what should be paid. With simple real estate listings such as subdivision lots where the seller has set the price through numerous similar sales and has no interest in conservation, there may be little opportunity for a land trust to offer alternatives. The land trust pays what it must. But whenever possible, make paying market price the exception, not the rule. Otherwise our donated dollars will simply be stretched too thin.

Outside the Box Thinking

To offer a little optimism, prices set at market value or higher often get unstuck when:

- A financial advisor (the buyer's or seller's) makes a creative proposal that sparks the seller's interest.
- A member of the seller's family is conservation-minded and insists that the family work with the land trust.
- A smart realtor is motivated to make a deal and willing to be educated.
- A seller's situation changes over time.

- The land trust reexamines its information about the seller's objectives and puts a proposal together in a new way.

On this last point, this new thinking about the seller's circumstances sometimes takes new thinkers. So reach out for advice. A new idea or approach can be just what is needed to make the deal. So leap outside the box. Here are some suggestions from my own experiences:

- Don't get greedy. If the winter wildlife habitat is at the center of the parcel, let the seller mine gravel for a summer on another part of the property. It brings the price down and doesn't affect the wildlife.
- Deal with the thorn. Find a conservation buyer for that adjacent parcel that may be developed. With the neighborhood stabilized and the future neighboring land uses known, your targeted landowner will be more willing to be generous.
- Take half the loaf. If one family member is the only one who wants to deal now, deal.

There are less dramatic ways to structure a proposal to make it less expensive. All things being equal, extending payment out into the future saves money. A land trust may be able to pay the seller to keep the land off the market for a period of time (thereby buying time, reducing risk, and often saving money). Purchasing an option will be less expensive and less of a risk than entering into a full sales contract. Purchasing a right of first refusal will be even less expensive. Purchasing in two phases, with an option securing the second phase, will at least postpone making a full payment if not save money.

As we have seen in earlier chapters, financing is another way to save money. Of its many benefits, one is the opportunity for the land trust to borrow at a low rate from a conservation-minded lender, and another is postponing a large outlay of cash.

The Seller's Response

Complex deal structuring requires sophistication and can throw inexperienced sellers for a loop. Match deal complexity with seller tolerance for it. If a seller is expecting a simple cash payment, then explaining a complex new deal structure becomes a delicate process. In general, the more complicated the transaction is, the more terms the parties must negotiate, and the tougher it is to reach an agreement. Much depends on the negotiator's relationship with the seller and the level of trust between them. That is one good reason to move slowly on an acquisition project: to make sure that the seller is moving along with you.

If the seller seems overwhelmed by the complexity, encourage him or her to bring a professional advisor, such as a lawyer, to the meeting. Sometimes a seller is unwilling to do that because of the cost, but may be reluctant to give this reason. Offer to pay.

Longtime rural farmers and ranchers are used to people coming into their living rooms to tell them what they should do with their land. They tend to be very polite and patient. Insurance brokers, government agents, zoning administrators, and now conservationists all have ideas to which generations of ranchers have listened. Just because they are gracious and offer coffee and are willing to host a second visit doesn't mean that they agree with you. It is easy to think that negotiations are progressing when they are not. This is where being ultrasensitive to the landowning culture of your area is important. This is another good reason for the land trust to choose its team very carefully and to ask questions, not just talk.

A complex deal requires creative solutions. If you don't have several years of negotiating experience, find a more experienced land conservationist or a good real estate lawyer to negotiate for you, always joining them at the meetings. But remember that you are likely to know your seller best. No matter how much your advisors can improve the deal structure, you are probably better able to assess the seller's tolerance for complexity and sense when too much is too much.

Someone Else's Money

Another way to bring down the cost is to use someone else's expertise and resources. It is worth bringing in people with specialized skills who can perform tasks more efficiently or become more formal, longer-term partners, or both. Partnerships can bring money and many other benefits and services to a transaction. They can exponentially increase effectiveness. Partners use overlapping interests to achieve common goals. However, healthy, useful partnerships take time, patience, and compromise.

Though the reasons to engage in partnerships go far beyond reducing costs, successful collaborations often save money in ways that are usually unattainable by a single organization.

The most important partnership for a land conservation organization is with landowners. Landowners control what we value most: land. Whether the land trust holds a conservation easement on the property or is working to conserve one parcel, or a landscape with multiple landowners, developing a good, helpful, trusting relationship with the landowners will facilitate sustainable conservation like no other strategy. In addition, there is a tremendous amount to learn from owners about their land. If it is good enough to continue, then the owners must have managed it pretty well and for its resource values. At the same time, a land trust should learn how to bring value to this partnership by developing the skills to help problem-solve and provide useful information, funding, or access to funding. The more mutually beneficial the relationship, the more sustainable, and ultimately less costly it will be.

Here are a few examples of other types of land trust partners:

- Other land conservation organizations: If another organization has skills or resources such as technical mapping, stewardship, negotiating skills, or even a larger donor base, a partnership can bring those resources to you. The national and regional land conservation organizations partner with smaller, more local groups. Local organizations share resources with each other, which saves money and builds powerful coalitions. Program management contributes greatly to success here.
- Other nonprofits: To reach out to the community, to broaden political appeal, to expand into new program areas and to find manpower and money, land trusts partner with schools, with community groups dedicated to trail building, cycling, birding, hunting, fishing, greenways, agriculture, community gardens, smart growth, and many other nonprofit organizations.
- Public agencies: I cannot talk about partnerships without highlighting the robust partnerships between land conservation organizations and public agencies that fund conservation, recreation, agricultural or historical preservation, and land protection to meet municipal needs such as water supply and electricity. In the last twenty-five years, public acquisition programs have grown and multiplied billions of dollars to work for conservation putting through enduring land conservation partnerships at all levels of government.[4]
- Businesses: Businesses partner with land conservation in many traditional and innovative ways. Corporations sponsor events, make donations, and,

importantly, share valuable expertise. They generate funding for conservation from their customers through matching giving programs and with specific campaigns, as in the case of the Orvis Company advertising the threat to the fisheries of the Metolius watershed in Oregon in its catalog or Petzl Corporation advertising the threat to Castleton tower in Utah on the back of climbing magazines. With the growing interest in "greening up," and in some cases with overlapping missions, many corporations have and want to become advocates for conservation. Both conservation groups and businesses are looking for new ways to partner.

• Developers: Land trusts bring developers in to a deal when the project is too expensive for the land trust to do alone, when development is appropriate, or there is some other incentive. If a developer buys or develops part of a parcel of the land, it can save the land trust the cost of paying for that portion of the property. But it can also be problematic for the land trust to associate with developers. These partnerships must be managed carefully, but with the right partner (and there are many) land trusts can reduce their own costs and leverage protection. Not all developers are out to destroy natural resources; some are simply landowners who need to generate income for their family.

• Other individuals: These partnerships run the gamut. Land use arrangements, such as agricultural or timber leases, create partnerships between land trusts and landowners or those leasing land who can generate revenue and save a land trust maintenance and other stewardship costs. Land trusts participate as the landowning partner. Land trusts frequently partner with individuals interested in conservation as buyers, lenders, and investors. Though not discussed in this volume, conservation buyers are a major contributor to private land conservation.[5] Conservation investors, though still very limited in number, are starting to bring significant funding to conservation transactions. At another level, artists, musicians, and writers offer their talents to raise money through art auctions and sales, concerts, readings, books sales, and limited edition broadsides.

Another option is to partner around a big vision. Whether with other land trusts or a group with a broader coalition of interests, these collaborations can significantly elevate the importance of the campaign and advance conservation through a coordinated team approach.

Figure 16.1
The Jackson Hole Land Trust found commercial partners to purchase the Hatchet Motel and the open meadow at auction. (Courtesy of Jackson Hole Land Trust)

One of my favorite ambitious and visionary partnerships is the Chicago Wilderness consortium, which is an alliance of more than 180 public and private organizations with the mission of restoring ecological cohesiveness and recreational value to over 225,000 acres scattered around and within Chicago. However most collaborations are much smaller.

A functioning partnership doesn't just happen. It takes constant work. If the following factors, not all of which are controllable, are present, the partnership will have a better chance of success: strong and flexible leadership; active participation by all participants; adequate and shared funding; common goals; clear, consistent, and regular communication; shared risks, rewards, and credit; trust; consensus decision making; local authority for decisions; and commitment.[6]

Before a land trust enters into a partnership it must have adequate organizational capacity to take on the added demands of collaboration. It should not be distracted by budgetary or personnel concerns. Partnership demands pay off, but "the organization has to be in a position to take care of its own core functions before it is in a position to partner with other organizations," explains Heart of the Rockies Initiative Coordinator Paul Sihler.

The *Land Trust Standards and Practices* addresses partnerships: "Successful partnerships are more than two or more entities working side by side. Partnerships succeed when the partners share fundamental goals and visions of success; when each partner brings, and is willing to use, skills and resources that the others don't have; and when the results of working together are likely to be better than any partner could achieve alone."[7]

Here are helpful tips from seasoned partners about forming and keeping partnerships strong:

- Sign a memorandum of understanding to clarify and agree to the elements of a partnership.
- Scarcity creates competition, which causes conflict. On the flip side, it creates opportunity. If money is scarce, prepare to avert problems by strengthening lines of communication and addressing the issue up front. On the other hand, when the old ways are no longer effective, groups are forced to find new, often better ways of doing business.
- The right personalities make all the difference. As an example, extreme variation in the size or expertise levels of the partners can stress relationships as smaller groups sometimes fear that their voices will not be heard. The leaders can create that comfortable atmosphere of mutual respect.
- The right dynamic begins with identification of the strategic contributions of each participant. They are not always obvious.
- Even if the vision for the partnership is big (which it should be), bite off small, doable pieces at a time. Early success strengthens partnerships.
- Look for those projects where the costs are lowest and the benefits highest, and that cannot be achieved by the individual organizations alone. Admit it or not, each partner is thinking: What's in this for my organization? To make a partnership function over the long term, partners have to see a benefit.
- With unfamiliar partners, especially for-profit or commercial ones, it is best to proceed carefully. Identify future decision points and address them up front in writing. Then keep as much control of your interests as possible because the choices made by new partners can be surprising, and at odds with the land trust.

In-kind Services

There are other places to save money. Pulling off an acquisition takes professional assistance from lawyers, real estate brokers, surveyors, title companies, hazardous material specialists, land planners, and engineers. If they support the land trust's mission, some will discount their services if asked. By doing so, they associate themselves with a cause they support, in a manner that helps their reputation and saves the land trust money. In a small town, community members often want to help. Learn how to tap community knowledge and individual skills that the land trust needs by asking for discounts everywhere. Our local title company has, for example, budgeted $10,000 of office time for title research for nonprofits. These funds can run out before the end of the year, so we always try to ask them early in the year.

Some realtors are willing to reduce their commissions for a community organization. Owners of real estate firms can donate part of the firm's commission. This is particularly true if the land trust is selling property and there is competition among real estate firms for listings. It can't hurt to ask when purchasing, too. We have had real estate brokers and firms offer to donate part of their commissions to our land trust. Then they use their contribution, legitimately, as a marketing tool.

When developing a financial plan for the project, think about where donations might most likely come from and how best to ask for them. Consider these factors early in the transaction, then use a simple approach: "Thank you so much for helping us conserve the X Ranch. Might you be willing to donate some of your services to this important project?"

Figure 16.2
At the Glenwood Green Acres community garden in North Philadelphia, the Neighborhood Gardens Association partnered with community members to replace an abandoned warehouse with more than eighty individual garden plots. (Pennsylvania Horticultural Society)

Figure 16.3
The New York State endangered black tern feeding its young at Salmon Creek Preserve, protected by the Genesee Land Trust (© Elinor Osborn)

Providers of in-kind services are donors to your organization, just like cash donors, and should be treated as such and involved in whatever ways you involve your other donors. Make sure to give credit to anyone who donates. Do so publicly and often. (Thank-you's help their marketing, too.) The more they feel like they are part of the land trust family, the more they will give and talk up the organization and your valuable network will expand.

At the Core: Your Relationship with the Landowner/Seller

When all is said and done, it is the relationship with the seller that ultimately gets a land trust to a successful agreement at an affordable price. In deal making, as in fundraising, listening to the seller is paramount. If the seller is struggling to pay the up-front expenses of the transaction, find a way to help cover those for reimbursement later, or help to cover them from a fund established for this purpose. Make the seller as comfortable as possible; take the time to figure out what he or she needs. An older seller, for example, might prefer working with an older land trust representative or financial advisor.

Linda Meade of D&R Greenway Land Trust has a great philosophy. She embraces all sellers as members of the D&R Greenway family, despite the fact that the majority of her acquisitions are by purchase or bargain purchase. She holds an annual celebration for them and all the other participants in the transactions. They talk to their friends about their good experience, spreading a positive word about the land trust. She keeps them close because the goodwill of a landowner is priceless.

Chapter 17
Putting It All Together

It is almost time to examine your expanded toolkit for new financial tools for conservation. But before you do, let's address two more issues: how to be sure you have all the information you need to get going, and what to do if you run into problems.

To master the techniques described in this book, there are many resources. Fortunately, the conservation community has a vital and growing support system. The Land Trust Alliance (LTA) provides numerous resources. Its Web site and its annual conference are good places to start. There are also many other organizational management nonprofits, conferences, and consultants. For fundraising, again go to LTA, and the Foundation Center, read the *Chronicle of Philanthropy*, the *Grassroots Fundraising Journal*, and other publications mentioned in this book's bibliography. Hundreds of skilled practitioners, board members, and landowners, many of whom I interviewed for this book, are willing to share their experiences, too. I used every one of these resources and know they work well.

The Land Trust Accreditation Commission, which is an independent program of the Land Trust Alliance, will soon offer an accreditation program for land trusts. The Commision plans to accept applications in 2008. The Commission website explains its progam in detail.[1] To help land trusts prepare for accreditation, LTA will offer fifteeen courses in a new Standards and Practices Curriculum available by the end of 2007. Each will be accessible online, in self-study workbooks, and in traditional classroom settings. As course workbooks become available, LTA members can obtain electronic copies free of charge.

LTA's new online learning center creates a network for land conservation and offers current information on important issues. Land trusts, land trust service centers and coalitions, and others who sponsor their own training sessions will be able to use the high-quality and accessible materials being produced by LTA.

Many of the topics covered in this book will be explored in more depth in the new curriculum. One of the first courses, for example, will offer guidance on running a land trust ethically. Later courses will include topics such as raising stewardship funds, project planning, selection and evaluation, and financial management.

In the meantime, I hope this book has whet your appetite for more learning and connected you with where to get it. I encourage you to reach out to the programs reviewed in here for advice. A knowledgeable staff member might be willing to join a conference call with your board to talk about their surcharge program. Or, if it is borrowing you are after, suggest to your board chair that both of you call a land trust executive director who borrows from banks to ask about his or her first bank loan and what to do if your banker is reluctant to lend on raw land. Or talk to managers of those terrific small external revolving funds about their effective no or low-interest lending programs. If you are interested in the use of pledges to secure a loan, you might ask a land trust that uses them for an introduction to its banker and refer your banker to that person.

For more complex projects and techniques, there are emerging intermediaries, consultants, and partners to help.

Then add a day to your next trip to one of the areas of the country where land trusts are successfully financing transactions. This book is filled with

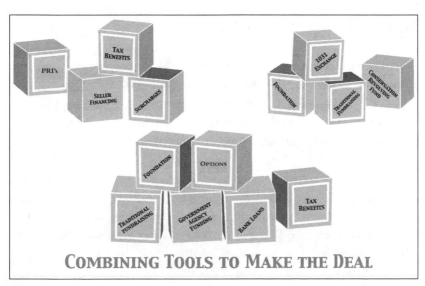

Figure 17.1
Combinations of funding and lending sources often support single projects.

people, places, and land trusts to visit for firsthand learning from those who have worked through the same issues you are dealing with, and now are experts. Just looking around another land trust's offices can be an education. At the next LTA National Land Conservation Conference (Rally), schedule a breakfast to get those questions answered about how to encourage your partnering foundation to start its own PRI program.

The land trust community has just begun to benefit from what conservation finance has to offer. If we want to expand its use to leverage our money more efficiently, each and every one of us has to join the dialogue. For example, why isn't your local university teaching conservation finance to its environmental studies students? LTA and others are developing curricula in this area. Hand a course outline to your friend in the environmental studies department, or offer this book.

How about your board members with financial expertise? Are they using their experience to refine your financial systems or develop new models for conservation finance? Engage them in these new ways.

Take responsibility for expanding the use of one of the methods in this book, or even invent a new way to bring free enterprise into the important work you do. Reach into that parallel universe of for-profit finance, expand the dialogue, harness the power of the dollar.

Backup Plans

As we all experiment, we will be taking more risks. With those risks comes the potential for serious missteps. How do we prepare ourselves for those? No one likes to talk about falling flat on one's face. Frankly, it doesn't happen very often, because the conservation movement is so careful. But as we step into unknown territory, gain confidence, and experiment a little more, difficult situations will arise.

We must create an environment in which it is okay to experiment and, occasionally, fail. We have to find a way to reward risk because with risk comes innovation. The Open Space Institute recognizes the value of risk and is able to budget for it with a risk-loss fund. But few other organizations have the wherewithal, expertise, or vision to think that way about risk. Ultimately, we are going to have to build the costs of risk into our programs.

Mishaps and how to dig out of them is kept pretty quiet in the land trust community, but I have run into a few. Without exception, the groups I interviewed that got in hot water on risky deals survived because they had the fundamentals right. They had positioned their organizations well with redundant layers of support. They had done their organizational assessments and filled in the gaps. They had donors who were willing to step up in an emergency, and accounting systems that tracked financial health so board members could carefully monitor risk. Some even had backup plans so they could retreat gracefully from trouble. The organizations that can't get out of serious trouble are the ones that aren't solid at the core.

You may be one of those readers who skipped the Positioning Your Organization section of this book to get to the fun stuff. You might not own LTA's guide, *Assessing Your Organization*,[2] or believe you have time to consider whether the composition of your board gives you maximum protection and reach. Do yourself a favor: before trying any new, aggressive tools, read that early section of this book. Then use a self-assessment tool. Both will help to ensure that you can withstand the stress of experimentation.

I know one land trust that, after launching its capital campaign, realized it wouldn't be able to meet its well-publicized fundraising goal. What did it do? It scaled back the campaign goal and added a year to it. Not the end of the world, especially because when they were done, they could celebrate success.

Another very small land trust had borrowed to buy a remote parcel. Then the adjacent parcel came on the market and the land trust reasoned that it might be able to sell the two parcels as one and eliminate a home site in a particularly sensitive area as the real estate market in the nearby town was hot. It incurred more debt to buy the second parcel. All summer, it marketed the two properties as one. Lots of lookers, but no buyers. Major upcoming interest payments loomed. After a careful assessment, the land trust sold the second parcel to a neighbor without further restrictions. The sale generated a modest gain, which reduced their original debt. The whole endeavor cost time and money, but telling the land trust's story as part of marketing the two parcels expanded its network. They changed the way they did business, had more contacts and a stronger base of support.

If you are a vital land trust, you have friends. If you think there is trouble ahead, ask them for help and keep your cool.

Still, you may wonder, since we in the land conservation business live so close to the edge already just making our annual budgets and bringing in precious donations for those tight acquisition closings, why do we want to push the envelope further? Because these new tools buy us so much. They leverage our limited dollars, get us out working with new sectors of the community, and start teaching us how to speak the language of finance so we can expand our learning indefinitely.

Just consider the benefits to the Crested Butte Land Trust of those hundreds of thousands of new dollars of revenue from the 1% for Open Space program, not to mention the marketing value to the organization. The people of Crested Butte own that program and, as a result, take a real interest in what are now community-based land conservation projects that they help fund every time they buy merchandise locally.

Choosing the Right Financing Mix

Now let's match financing tools to the task at hand. The first rule is: Play to the strengths of your project. If it is a highly visible farm or ranch, consider a capital campaign and a fundraising event, and reach out to partner with other organizations that support agriculture. If it has significant wildlife resources think about foundations that support wildlife conservation. If the project will create public space, approach the government leadership for parks, greenway, or bikepath funding, and appeal to "friends" groups and clubs that support these activities. Just because we are focusing here on private financing doesn't mean you should not look for public funding. Always investigate public funding programs. There are many of them on all levels of government. If your community doesn't have one, read Trust for Public Land's (TPL) *Conservation Finance Handbook*[3] about initiating a bond and talk to the TPL about organizing a bond initiative. Public takeout money drives most conservation acquisitions.

The second rule is: Have a plan and then a backup plan. Consider the financing for two very different Jackson Hole Land Trust projects—not unlike many done by land trusts throughout the country. Hardeman Meadows (the first story in this book) was a high-profile project funded through a classic mix of sources. Another project, described in the Internal Protection Funds chapter, is a small, unknown parcel with an unappealing name, Poison Creek, with a very different mix of revenue sources.

The Hardeman Meadows was a 137-acre portion of a ranch along a highway approach into Jackson Hole. The Jackson Hole Land Trust found $1.958 million to purchase the land. All of the sources (listed below) reflect the broad community support for the project. (A remote project could not have been funded this way.)

Figure 17.2
The triple-critical habitat of Poison Creek. (Courtesy of Jackson Hole Land Trust)

- Capital Campaign ($855,000): The ranch was very visible, and, because of controversy around the threat of its development, it had a high profile politically and in the media. The community was ready to support it.
- Events ($40,000): Organizing and attending these events gave everyone a role in the project, built momentum, and raised money.
- Bank Loan ($350,000): The delay of the county funding to purchase a conservation easement forced us to borrow.
- Resale of Part of Ranch ($600,000): A donor became a conservation buyer and bought most of the ranch, which was restricted with a conservation easement.
- Ten-year Lease of Barns ($100,000): A major supporter, a donor to another nonprofit, paid up front for a ten-year, triple-net lease to relocate that nonprofit to this beautiful site.
- Interest ($13,000): Several early and large donations generated meaningful interest revenue.

Poison Creek is a small, thirty-five-acre national forest inholding with critical winter habitat for bighorn sheep, deer, and elk. The Jackson Hole Land Trust used $600,000 to purchase the land. Revenue sources highlight the parcel's outstanding wildlife resources and our special relationships with donors who stepped forward because they understood the importance of the property. We kept the requests modest, in keeping with the cost of the project and the funders' capacity.

- The National Fish and Wildlife Foundation ($25,000): This foundation's rigorous application process, which required project endorsements from local agencies and resource experts, helped to articulate arguments and generate support for the target property.
- Foundation for North American Wild Sheep ($25,000): This was a perfect match since the parcel was critical habitat for wild mountain sheep.
- Rocky Mountain Elk Foundation ($20,000): The unusual circumstances of this highly threatened parcel and the foundation's interest and commitment in our region helped get us this grant.
- Two Local Family Foundations ($50,000): The documentation prepared for the National Fish and Wildlife Foundation grant proposal and these families' strong, preexisting relationship with the land trust convinced them to support this project.
- Individual Donations ($30,170): We appealed to the generosity of land trust supporters who had a particular interest in wildlife. We led several field trips to the site.
- Loan/Donation ($200,000): A board member brought in a new donor, who loaned us money, became more knowledgeable about the trust, and changed the loan to a gift.
- Land Trust Protection Fund ($249,830): Success breeds success. If there was ever a time to use the protection fund, it was for this low-profile and important project. Demonstrating that we could do it paid off with new gifts that replenished the fund.

Everyone has their own stories about creatively seeking the right mix of financing. That is why group thinking about each project and laying out a road map with a budget and revenue sources (what I call a financial plan) ensures that the most logical resources are identified and used—not that there won't be other funding opportunities that come up along the way. Here are some strategies for the finance matchmaking process:

Look around you. Tap into the motivations and interests of the people, beyond the obvious, who might want to see the land protected. I know of one community garden project for which the gardeners *and* the consumers of the

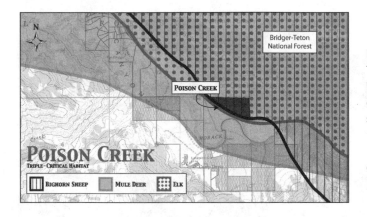

Figure 17.3
The overlapping habitats—for mule deer, elk, and bighorn sheep—in this small parcel made protecting Poison Creek a top priority for the Jackson Hole Land Trust.

produce invested hundreds of hours in fundraising to keep the land open. In another project donors lined up because hunting would be allowed. In more than one project, the chance to honor a loved one was motivation to participate.

Carpe diem (Seize the day). When the Land Trust for the Mississippi Coastal Plain witnessed the devastation of Hurricane Katrina in Mississippi and Louisiana, they used the strong corporate interest in helping the relief efforts to raise $100,000 from the Home Depot Foundation for a massive live oak restoration project.

Push the envelope. When you have the urgency of a threat and the momentum of a strong project, try something new or more aggressive. Add a stewardship endowment to the capital campaign for the project; approach a new group of donors or a new foundation (maybe your town's community foundation) for funding; solicit local businesses that you have never approached before. This might be the time to start asking for loan guarantees from board members and donors, or for leadership to set up a friends group to raise stewardship money for a new park and to be responsible for its upkeep.

Ask and you will receive. Caught up in the spirit of an important campaign, land trust supporters will give you more time, money, and expertise than ever before. Ask for it and you will get it.

Break the nut into small pieces. I believe that almost every real estate problem has a solution. It is just a matter of creating many options and then spending a lot of time with people with the right skills to find those solutions. Usually it is many small solutions that add up to success. To have many options, you have to start making them available early. They won't just

Figure 17.4
When the lot in which they had been gardening since 1973 was under threat of development, residents of southwest Philadelphia raised $15,000 and borrowed $20,000 from the Neighborhood Garden Association to buy the three-quarter-acre property. The Warrington Community Garden is now divided into sixty-two plots tended by individual gardeners.(Courtesy of the Neighborhood Gardens Association)

appear by themselves. That is what the Positioning Your Organization section is all about.

Where's the Money?

The following scenarios will give you some practice in thinking about the best options for financing projects. (Changes in federal and state tax code can offer new tax benefits that may increase net proceeds to certain sellers.)

Case Study One

A rancher has approached your land trust because one of his two sisters wants to sell her undivided interest in the ranch and the rancher can't afford to pay for it. He would like your land trust to buy out his sister and trade it for a conservation easement on all or part of the ranch (depending on how the values work out). The ranch is worth one million, is near a major metropolitan area, and in an important international bird flyway. The sister who is selling does not want to make trouble for the family but she needs income. She has a 33 percent interest in the ranch. Several of your board members have business connections in the city. What should you do?

This is a typical and difficult situation because purchasing a 33 percent or "minority" interest limits the buyer's ability to control the property, there is less certainty about its value, and to get full value the sister could ask a court to divide off or partition her share of the property, which she could theoretically sell for more. Alternatively, the rancher could buy out his sister with part (or all) of the proceeds from your purchase of a conservation easement on the ranch (assuming the values work out right). Talk to the rancher about this option, which would be simpler and less risky for you. Approach the local chapter and state office of the Audubon Society (because of the flyway) or other appropriate (and well funded) organizations about partnering to raise money for the project. Draft a memorandum of understanding to clearly define partnership roles. Research foundations in the metropolitan area with an interest in wildlife or agricultural preservation (don't forget often overlooked community foundations). Ask your board for suggestions of foundations and other donor prospects, too.

Once your initial feasibility analysis is complete and the conclusions indicate you can be successful at raising the funds, suggest that the rancher option his sister's 33 percent interest to buy time for you to pursue fundraising and partnership opportunities. The family and you, working as a team, should draft the conservation easement and work with a knowledgeable, state-licensed appraiser to value the easement and the sister's interest. Draw up an agreement outlining the transaction with the easement as an exhibit. Ask that a transfer fee be included in the agreement to generate additional revenue for easement stewardship in case the ranch is sold. Build the base stewardship costs into your fundraising goal. Schedule a simultaneous closing so the rancher has the money (from your easement purchase) to buy out his sister. If possible, seek an arrangement with the family to purchase the easement at a bargain price. Since steady income is what the sister wants, she might be willing to finance the sale to her brother then he and his other sister could finance the easement sale to you if you need more time to fundraise. (You may need substitute collateral.) Best to leave this option out as the transaction is already pretty complicated.

Case Study Two

Your land trust wants to conserve a very high-profile farm worth $750,000 owned by an older couple. The couple loves the farm and is thrilled that their favorite nephew wants to buy it. Unfortunately, he can only pay $400,000 and over five years. They need more money for it. A developer is developing the highly sought-after adjoining land and will do just about anything, short of buying the property, to help you keep the farm open. You know a banker sympathetic to your situation. What should you do?

Approach the couple and the nephew about creating a plan that works for everyone, including their advisors. The plan could involve the couple selling a conservation easement on the farm to you at a bargain price with easement terms that are acceptable to the nephew as the ultimate owner of the land. With all or most of the development value eliminated, the farm will be more affordable for him. The nephew might consider seeking seller financing from his aunt and uncle, though he may want to work out something privately with them and doesn't want or need your advice.

Appraise the value of a conservation easement for the farm. Good news! The easement is valued at $350,000. Contract for a fundraising feasibility study to see if you can raise the $375,000. If the results are positive, approach the couple about discounting the easement price to $250,000, explaining the potential tax benefits to them, and that you will still be raising $350,000 to pay them for the easement and to create a stewardship fund of $100,000. (The last $25,000 may be a good estimate of the costs of the fundraising campaign and your other expenses.)

Then approach the developer about making a cash contribution to your land trust. Of course, the developer's gift cannot be earmarked for the easement if he intends to receive a tax deduction for it. This is particularly important to note because he stands to gain financially from adjacent open space. You might suggest that he establish a transfer fee program for his lots to augment the $100,000 stewardship fund. An attorney familiar with local real estate law must carefully structure the transfer fee, because covenants imposed on property to run with the title must conform to very specific rules to be enforceable. If your organization is experienced with capital campaigns, you may or may not want to hire a fundraising consultant to help you develop a multi-year capital-campaign fundraising plan. Approach your board to sign guarantees for a loan from your friendly banker to buy the conservation easement secured by the transfer-fee revenue and capital-campaign pledges.

Case Study Three

Your land trust is very interested in a large property with very important resource values that is highly valued in your community. The parcel is worth $5 million. The landowner, who is on your board, will give you a four-month option to purchase it for $3.5 million. As much as you want the property protected, you have never raised more than $500,000 before. What should you do?

Because the seller is an "insider" and conflict of interest and the appearance of conflict of interest are serious concerns, you will have to be especially careful with this transaction. Make sure the project meets your project criteria and is a high organizational acquisition priority. Consider hiring an outside professional to confirm its resource values. Knowing the property's specific resources will also help in targeting institutional and individual donors. The landowner/board member can have no role in any board discussions or decisions regarding the project, and should not be present when such discussions/decisions are conducted. Talk to your board about procedures to recuse the board member from discussions and decision-making on the project, and other strategies to address the appearance of a conflict of interest. Contract with a well-respected, state-licensed appraiser (and maybe a review appraiser) to appraise the property to confirm that the discount the board member is offering is substantial (this helps build a case for the purchase price in an otherwise sensitive buyer-seller relationship). Since the board member will likely also get an appraisal for his gift of value, be aware that if the two appraisals are significantly different, you might have issues regarding signing IRS Form 8283.

After careful consideration with the board and its attorney, it may be advisable that the board member leaves the board for a generous period of time. All board meeting minutes should reflect the timing of board actions on the recusal and the project itself. Be ready with thoughtful answers to questions about the board member-land trust relationship, and how the organization is protecting the public interest.

Because of the organization's inexperience in fundraising, hire a consultant with experience with land conservation capital campaign to do a feasibility study and to help design the fundraising campaign. See if you can negotiate a six-month, or even longer, option as well as seller financing. As a board member (or now a former board member), she should be sympathetic to your financial limitations. It might be possible to find a conservation-minded buyer to purchase some or all of the property from the former board member and give, bargain sell, or bargain trade a conservation easement to you. Working through a third party purchaser would further separate the land trust from the former board member though it has its risks. Remember that currently the IRS, due to Notice 2004-41, precludes any pre-existing agreement with the buyer and thus there is the risk that the buyer might not conserve the property.

Case Study Four

Your land trust is interested in conserving a $2 million parcel that, despite having dense urban development on three sides, is valued for its scenic qualities and high agricultural productivity. It is also near a popular recreational area. A young farmer is inheriting the property and wants to grow organic produce. But the estate has a substantial estate tax bill. There is already a small amount of debt on the property. What should you do?

Immediately talk to the farmer about giving a postmortem conservation easement on the property, which must be recorded by the due date of the return (including extensions) and could reduce the estate tax bill significantly, fully explaining the financial and physical ramifications of restricting property. Be sure your organization is comfortable that the farmer can afford to carry the restricted land without undue financial hardship. The bank holding the mortgage will have to agree to subordinate the mortgage to the conservation easement. This could take some time and education. Use your board member contacts with the bank's officers to help with this process. With the easement in place, the estate may be eligible for a Section 2031(c) exclusion, which could reduce the value of the restricted land by as much as 40 percent (up to $500,000 per estate). Thus if the easement reduces the farm's value by 50 percent to $1 million and the exclusion brings the value down to $600,000, the estate tax will be more manageable, even nonexistant if the estate has few or no other assets. If this is the case, you might be able to rework the easement draft so the farmer reserves more rights/value. If the farmer needs more money, she might consider selling a bike path between the development and the farm to the county or developer, or a community garden to the subdivision residents and approaching neighborhoods to contract for her crop of organic produce. The land trust should also research agricultural lending programs for a long-term low-interest loan to the farmer. Solicit the neighbors for contributions and to institute a transfer fee on their lots with the proceeds going to the Land Trust's stewardship fund for the conservation easement. Consider working with the farmer to offer educational programs to build awareness (and support) for the farm and its products.

Case Study Five

Your land trust is very interested in protecting a remote parcel of land in the state forest that is critical wildlife habitat. A modestly wealthy widow owns the parcel but doesn't live on it. She cares deeply about its wildlife, but must sell it immediately. She has two young adult children who are eager for the family to buy a small store in the town worth $200,000. The parcel is worth $500,000 and you only have $300,000 raised. What should you do?

Assess the likelihood of the state purchasing the parcel. If public acquisition is likely or could become likely, identify a partner organization with expertise in working on acquisition projects with the state. Request a letter of intent to purchase from the state agency. (It will be important to have a solid backup plan in case the state doesn't come through.) Because the widow cares so much about the land, and may give you a discount on the purchase price if you conserve it, her conservation interests must be considered and she must be comfortable with your backup plan. If the state can't buy the parcel, and you can't raise the remaining funds for the purchase, will the property be offered for sale on the open market with certain restrictions or will you look for another conservation-oriented buyer, either another agency or individual or does the land trust want to own it indefinitely?

As an alternative backup strategy, you might be able to buy a partial interest with the money that you have, getting the widow to grant you an option to purchase the remainder in the future, or at her death, for a bargain price. This arrangement should include a provision in which the widow waives any right she may have to seek partition of the property, or variations on that. This would generate money to her over and above what she needs to buy the store, and could also be structured as a like-kind exchange. Or you might buy a discrete portion with an option on the rest to simplify the deal and to give you insurance that you can protect at least some of the property.

Propose buying the land at a substantial bargain sale, such as for the price of the store in town. The widow may be able to use the charitable deduction in the bargain purchase to shelter some of her income. If she is willing, then undertake a like-kind exchange for the store in town ($200,000) and hold the land until you can sell it to the state, or must resort to the backup plan.

If the widow is not willing to sell for that very discounted price, work with her and her advisors to develop a plan that meets her needs. This plan might still involve a smaller discount on the sale price that shelters her income and involves exchanging interests for the store, and meeting her conservation goals for the land. Whatever the final arrangement is, the land trust may be committing to raising more money and must consider its stewardship responsibilities and costs under the different scenarios.

Again, there must be a solid backup plan. Without all the funds for purchase on hand, the land trust will have two difficult decisions: what to do if the state doesn't come through; and how to cover the difference between what it has raised and what the widow is willing to sell the property for. Because of the widow's timing issues, the land trust will need bridge financing. This would be the time to approach an external revolving loan fund for a loan or a foundation for a PRI. These institutions are more likely to understand the vagaries of public agency funding and the value of a remote parcel of land. The lender still may request substitute collateral. It is also possible that the widow might be willing to finance the sale. In situations like these, with numerous moving parts, it is a good idea for the land trust to have a backup plan for the backup plan.

Now It's Your Turn

Ready to go? Start with an organizational assessment to determine if you are ready to step out of the comfort zone. Then brainstorm on what tools are most appropriate for your project, your community's culture, and your collective expertise. Get the help you need, get your questions answered, and give it a try.

Conclusion: How It *Could* Come Together in the Future

From where I sit, the current state of conservation finance has both good and bad news. First the good news. Existing funding is advancing conservation on the ground in significant ways. The annual number of acres conserved by privately funded conservation organizations and by public agencies (many of which fund projects designed and led by private organizations) exceeds the annual number of acres lost to development.[1] In the years leading up to 2003, the amount of money being spent annually on permanent land conservation grew and is estimated at $2.7 billion, which does not even include private support to land trusts.[2]

Now for the bad news. The annual current deficit to capitalize a system of conserved lands is already in the billions of dollars.[3] Thus conservation is starting out far behind development in the race to either conserve or destroy valuable and sustainable networks of conserved land. In addition, developed acreage is increasing more than three times (maybe as much as seven times) faster than the United States population, and that population is growing significantly.[4] It is estimated that by 2050 the development (roads, parking lots and buildings) will cover an area about the size of Texas.[5] Compounding these problems is the destructive tendency to develop the most important ecological, agricultural, and scenic lands first. For example, the rate of conversion of prime land was 30 percent faster, proportionally, than the rate for non-prime rural land from 1992–1997.[6]

Though public funds account for the vast majority of expenditures for conservation,[7] as we have learned, privately supported conservation organizations use it strategically and nimbly. Privately raised acquisition dollars protect conservation resources in many, many places where there is no government money, it is insufficient, or is not targeted at the highest priority conservation resources, including in some of the most ecologically and agriculturally important areas of the country. While greater efficiency—both biological and economic—may be likely within existing conservation funding, development is clearly very efficient at moving into those places most in need of conservation. Private conservation organizations and their ability to move quickly to identify threats to critical resources and to secure these lands have been and will continue to be absolutely critical to conservation. Without this key player, the conservation outcomes from public funding will not be as effective.

There are political, cultural, legal and fairness issues limiting the government from regulating for meaningful land conservation. Thus we must pay, one way or the other, to protect the country's most critical lands.

Despite the fact that Americans give over $240 billion annually to support nonprofit work, philanthropic capital is dispersed over many causes in many sectors and, in the conservation sector (as in others), it is profoundly limited.[8]

Clearly, conservation needs access to more capital, both public and private, if we are to maintain a critical mass of agricultural, scenic, wildlife and ecological services that support and benefit life.

Fortunately we are finding more capital, though not nearly enough, in many new sectors. In addition we are using existing capital more effectively by refining conservation strategies through strategic planning, better science, GIS, and community engagement as well as through better management of our finances, including use of debt. We are learning that financing allows us to be more flexible in how we use what acquisition capital we have.

Still, conservation financing is not nearly as streamlined as it is in the for-profit sector. Some areas of the country have very limited access to low-cost loans. In communities with no conservation lenders and where banks won't lend on raw land, land trusts are challenged to borrow money. If the source of takeout money is not known or if a project takes years to assemble funding, finding lenders will be difficult. Riskier projects don't have a ready source of support, as many do in the commercial capital markets.

If you are new to the business of credit and debt, you still may be wondering how you can possibly use these options when more long-term and takeout sources aren't anywhere on the horizon, and conservation land rarely generates enough income to pay off the debt. In the last several years, conservationists have demonstrated an impressive ability to find new capital from public and private sources despite growing competition for those dollars. To a great extent, conservationists make their own luck. With the right tools, they are successful at raising money, and get better at it each year. Note how many communities have taken the initiative and approved local and state bond issues that invest billions of dollars in open space programs. Public funding at these levels is increasing, despite the fact that (or maybe partly because) traditional federal funding (particularly from the Land & Water Conservation Fund) over which local communities have less control has decreased significantly. Look too, at the increasing size and number of land trust capital campaigns.

In addition, conservationists are experimenting with new ways to use private capital to protect land and water. They are developing markets for ecological services such as carbon, clean water, wetlands and more: creating revenue streams by sustainably harvesting timber; restoring and enhancing areas that add value and generate return from recreational markets; developing local markets for locally grown products; finding conservation-minded buyers to purchase critical areas and protect them; creating conservation developments that truly preserve critical areas and allow very limited development; and teaming up with new and surprising partners from diverse sectors that are helping to capitalize conservation. These innovative approaches give me hope that as land and water resources grow scarcer, markets will give them greater value.

What Each of Us Can Do

Help is on the way, but you can do a lot to help yourself. Based on almost three hundred interviews with people mostly associated with small to midsized land trusts, I learned that successful conservationists working with relatively small organizations are advancing conservation finance. Here are some of the strategies in use and new opportunities suggested to me.

1. *With conservationists making clear connections between human desires/ needs and land conservation, communities are understanding the value of conserving land.*

Clear, simple language and actions are making strong connections between community health and functioning intact landscapes that provide ecological, agricultural, economic, and cultural services.

Land trusts connect with people by the projects they do. Since action speaks louder than words, land trusts that integrate bike paths, community gardens, education centers, outdoor laboratories, agriculture, hunting and fishing uses and even graveyards into their projects demonstrate the value of conservation to people. Communities must value conservation to pay for it.

2. *Small land trusts are effective at expanding the dialogue.*

With small or nonexistent staffs, local land trusts draft bankers, storeowners, and real estate experts for voluntary service. Out of necessity, land trusts put local talent on the team. Not only do these people become part of the financing conversation for conservation, but these multiple points of engagement with many sectors of a community lay valuable groundwork for calling in help when the inevitable conservation crisis emerges.

While the large, well-trained land conservation organizations are generally the most sophisticated, American ingenuity works in surprising ways at small land trusts in rural counties, suburbs, and in the inner cities. As the stories in this book demonstrate, small land trusts have little outside support in the area of finance (or anything else, really). They find their own.

3. *More learning opportunities are on the rise and getting used more regularly.*

A limiting factor is lack of know-how. I remember more than one organization burdened by high interest rates from a bank, with nearby friendly foundations, that had never heard of foundation program-related investments. Another buys large wetlands and did not know of seller financing. Land trusts with greater expertise in finance are finding and leveraging funds, despite seemingly limited external opportunities.

Training and information are becoming more available. LTA's programs are addressing the components of conservation finance. Graduate schools like the Yale School of Forestry and the Environmental Studies and others are offering new programs in conservation finance. New literature points practitioners to places where creative fundraising and financing techniques are in use.

4. *Loan money is available at conservation revolving funds, as well as at some foundations, community foundations, corporations, farm credit unions, and among individual donors and investors.*

Foundation directors told me that the primary reason that their program-related investment programs were small or nonexistent was because their constituents were not demanding loans. Any nonprofit would, of course, prefer a grant, but a loan, as we have learned, can facilitate remarkable conservation results. Few land trusts ask for loans. Out of all of my interviews, including with almost thirty conservation revolving loan funds, fifteen foundations, many banks and donors, I spoke to one, just one, lender whose substantial loan fund was tapped to the max.

5. *Highly-committed donors and other philanthropic entities will participate in multiple financing programs, by lending money, securing loans, investing in property.*

Though the techniques these donors use will be further explored in volume II, suffice to say, land trusts that encourage greater donor involvement, receive it.

6. *Certain financing tools are particularly attractive to donors, with significant side benefits.*

Loan guarantees, for example, are a relatively simple and flexible means for individuals and foundations to secure financing for conservation projects. Take Ann Hooke and her husband on Deer Island in Maine (discussed in chapter 13). They put up a $5,000 guaranty for the Carney Island project. Few donors are asked to make this kind of modest commitment, yet small individual guarantees add up.

7. *The value of that first philanthropic dollar is immeasurable.*

The psychological value—not to mention the real value—of a donor stepping up on a deal attracts other philanthropic and nonphilanthropic participation. Part of that first dollar's value is getting the buyer into the game. Having funding earns a seat at the table from which more funding follows. Donors are stepping up.

8. *Aggregation of philanthropic, investment and public capital is emerging not only as a strategy for the mega-conservation deals, but as one for variously sized projects undertaken by organizations of all sizes.*

Big-thinking land trusts like the Cascade Land Conservancy and some foundations are participating in transactions with multiple financial partners.

9. *The for-profit world is participating to a increasing degree in financing conservation.*

As the financial benefits of conservation are quantified (enhanced property values, revenue from timber and ecological services and limited development) and more widely known, land trusts are offering a number of new investment opportunities for philanthropic and private investors.

Motivations for investing in conservation are expanding, too. The growing interest among businesses to "green up" creates tremendous new business partnership opportunities. Take Wal-Mart's announcement to engage in environmental practices. Or on a smaller scale, consider local businesses that are signing on to the voluntary surcharge programs discussed in chapter 8.

Many conservationists are still hesitant to make alliances with business and developers because of the potential for conflicting goals and it adds reputational risk. Fortunately, organizations are learning how to manage these partnerships. As they do, huge benefits to conservation emerge.

What We Should Do Collectively

As I listened to conservationists around the country, it became clear to me that we need more information to organize our next steps in this field. Here are some of what we need to learn.

1. *Understanding demand.* The unmet demand for capital is infinite. However, scarcity has forced the conservation community to be disciplined, to establish and use rigorous criteria, and to prioritize projects. Making smart choices about protection hierarchy must continue, or it will be hard to make credible arguments for money. The unmet demand for other financing—such as borrowing money for bridge loans—is more finite. Conservation lenders suggest that demand is less than they would like to see. But it may seem deceptively low. Most foundations and conservation revolving loan funds work in a fairly narrow geographic area, with the bigger players, such as The Nature Conservancy having access to their own interim capital. If viewed regionally, demand might be greater. It is likely that if ample low-cost interim capital were available, demand might increase even more dramatically.

Timing affects demand. If new public funding was available, and interim financing could be immediately deployed, the public money could be better leveraged. In addition, matching any major source of capital, such as a major conservation capital campaign, with immediate low-cost financing would make better use of all of the money. On the flip side, anticipating upcoming acquisition opportunities might allow time to assemble appropriate capital and financing.

All this assumes a collective approach to low-cost capital and a collective response to need as in the case of the work by conservation organizations in New England's northern forests.

There are regional issues limiting funding and financing. Certain areas could use low-cost capital of all sorts, including PRIs, however, many foundations are regionally focused. Getting capital to those locales can be difficult.

The cost of borrowing affects demand. A more refined pricing structure for loans might attract more borrowers. Paying interest on top of loan repayment is a burden for conservation when most or all of the cost of the property must be raised from philanthropic sources. For a big loan, this is a big burden. Lowering rates would encourage borrowing, but it might also create an incentive to take on the tough deals that require more time to structure. Conversely, increasing rates would encourage turnover and greater use of the loan fund dollars. Of course below-market rates of any kind have their costs to lenders. Evaluating the benefits produced by these incremental costs might better articulate their value and attract new donors to pay for them.

2. *Collectively quantifying desired outcomes for conservation finance.* The conservation community does not have a shared understanding of where it wants conservation finance to be in ten years. It has not thought collectively about the set of strategies needed to advance conservation finance. A few questions: Are we sufficiently knowledgeable about models to even make choices? As we strive to develop new sources of revenue, where are the specific opportunities and weak links in our primitive system of finance? To whom and how will solutions be sheparded and who will pay for them? Should we leave innovation to the large organizations such as The Nature Conservancy or intermediaries such as the Open Space Institute that are better equipped to spread the risk? Or are there ways and reasons to encourage smaller players to enter the game?

3. *Creating a clearinghouse for information, thinking and support for conservation finance.* So much good information is currently siloed in different places. Some of this is briefly shared at the Land Trust Alliance's Rally, but then it is gone again. The Nature Conservancy, the Lincoln Institute, graduate schools, and ad hoc sessions discuss these issues, but until we break down the barriers between institutions and create collective wisdom, we underutilize our own talents and are not sending a clear message to funders as to what we require to leap forward in this important field.

In Patrick Coady's insightful chapter in *From Walden to Wall Street*,[9] he outlines some of the major challenges to leaping forward in this field and accelerating conservation outcomes. He discusses such issues as the need for research and development, human and organizational capacity, collaboration across landscapes, and the diversification of capital sources. Informal gap analysis should be reviewed, expanded upon, quantified, and acted upon. The conservation community should take an organized and deliberate look at these issues and potential solutions. By understanding how outcomes would be different if needs and potential needs were met, funders might be attracted to funding change, then work together to move this good thinking from talk to action.

4. *We have good models. We should figure out how to scale them for the need and duplicate them.* Take the successful Norcross Wildlife Foundation, described in chapter 15. Could they encourage replication, expand their own program

or provide outsourcing services to other foundations? Another good model is the conservation intermediary organization (discussed in chapter 13), which pools philanthropic dollars and delivers them to conservation programs where they are needed. Could intermediaries be scaled up? Expanding their reach, while maintaining local sensitivity, could facilitate greater investment in conservation.

Some models should be scaled down. We have much to learn from the big guys: The Nature Conservancy and others. Their dollar amounts are so big, they can be intimidating, but many, though not all, of the techniques they use work at a small scale, too.

We could be offering more low risk opportunities such as the West Hill Fund for Nature model described in the external revolving loan fund chapter.

All of these thoughts may be debated daily in the halls of the largest conservation organizations, but elsewhere the discussion is disjointed at best and certainly has not reached the conservation masses, many of whom are struggling with the same challenges just at a smaller scale.

To my knowledge, only a handful of people across the conservation movement are thinking collectively about how to advance conservation finance. Few have the resources to do more, even to experiment or innovate. The larger organizations have the capacity to work on the big financing issues, but the smaller organizations are innovating too, and their creativity should be brought into the mix.

I hope that this book will broaden and enrich this collective conversation. The land trust community—large organizations and small—must take the discussion to the next level, quantify its needs, and act on them.

Appendix

*This appendix is for illustrative purposes only and may not be the most current in use by the organizations. To assure use of the most current documents, please contact the organizations directly or visit the Land Trust Alliance Web site, which has many sample documents and relevant articles as appendices to *Land Standards and Practices* and is researchable through LTAnet.

Regional Internal/External Conservation Revolving Loan Funds

Revolving Loan Fund	Administering Organization	Geographic Area	Size of Fund	Description of Fund (All funds are primarily external unless otherwise noted.)	Administering Organization Web site	Contact Person
Appalachian Trail Conservancy Land Acquisition Fund	Appalachian Trail Conference	Land along the Appalachian Trail	$500,000	Short-term loans made exclusively for land acquisitions and costs of such. Primarily internal, but very receptive to applications from groups helping conserve land along the Trail. Application process and terms are flexible.	http://www.appalachiantrail.org	Caroline Dufour (304) 535-6331 cdufour@appalachiantrail.org
Avista Revolving Trust Fund	Inland Northwest Land Trust	Coeur d'Alene/ Spokane River corridor	$60,000	Funded by Avista Utilities to aid in conservation of lands with high ecological, scenic, and/or recreational values near Avista's hydroelectric facilities. Available for external use but has not been used externally yet.	http://www.inlandnwlandtrust.org	Roger McRoberts (509) 328-2939 rmcroberts@inlandnwlandtrust.org
Buzzards Bay Lands Revolving Fund	Coalition for Buzzards Bay	Buzzards Bay watershed, Massachusetts and Rhode Island	$735,000	Loans available to land trusts in Buzzards Bay watershed for costs associated with land or conservation easement acquisitions: deposits, options, purchases, appraisals, and so forth. User-friendly, short turnaround. No security required for loans below $100,000. Coalition for Buzzards Bay provides technical support when necessary.	http://www.savebuzzardsbay.org	Allen Decker, land protection director (508) 999-6363 ext. 204 decker@savebuzzardsbay.org

Revolving Loan Fund	Administering Organization	Geographic Area	Size of Fund	Description of Fund (All funds are primarily external unless otherwise noted.)	Administering Organization Web site	Contact Person
Cape Cod Land Fund	Compact of Cape Cod Conservation Trusts, Inc.	Cape Cod, Massachusetts	$650,000	Available only to members of the Compact for emergency loans, short-term options, and down payments for land purchases. Simple, quick application process. Loan turnaround time as short as a week. No security required. Income of the fund corpus used to make small grants ($1,000 to $7,000) to accompany loans or as stand-alone grants for land purchases.	www.compact.cape.com	Mark Robinson, executive director (508) 362-2565 compact@cape.com
Central Coast Opportunity Fund	The Nature Conservancy (TNC)	Central Coast, California	$11 million	Created by Resources Legacy Fund (RLF) as part of the Conserving California Landscapes Initiative program. Primarily internal, but external grants and loans are available to land trusts and local and state governments for land and conservation easement acquisition, and subject to RLF approval.	http://www.nature.org	Wendy Millet (415) 777-0487 wmillet@tnc.org
Chesapeake Bay Foundation Revolving Loan Fund	Chesapeake Bay Foundation	Chesapeake Bay watershed	$500,000	Loans available to land trusts and individuals within the Chesapeake Bay watershed for options, down payments, and conservation purchases. Conservation of property must be guaranteed in perpetuity.	http://www.cbf.org	Fay Nance, vice president of finance (410) 269-0481 FNance@savethebay.cbf.org

Revolving Loan Fund	Administering Organization	Geographic Area	Size of Fund	Description of Fund (All funds are primarily external unless otherwise noted.)	Administering Organization Web site	Contact Person
Colorado Conservation Loan Fund	Colorado Conservation Trust (CCT)	Colorado	$4.15 million	Loans available to national and statewide land trusts and public agencies for bridge financing and associated costs. Local land trusts may be eligible for loans in partnership with other organizations or with other forms of security at CCT's discretion.	http://www.coloradoconservationtrust.org	Lise Aangeenbrug, program director (720) 565-8289 liseaa@coct.org
Colorado Tax Credit Revolving Loan Fund	Colorado Conservation Trust	Colorado	$165,000	Zero-percent interest loans available to land trusts for relending to landowners who will receive funds for sale of their state tax credits and want to donate conservation easements but cannot afford the transaction costs. Land trusts responsible for establishing agreements with landowners for repayment to fund simultaneous with sale of tax credit. Loan period not to exceed one year.	http://www.coloradoconservationtrust.org	Lise Aangeenbrug, program director (720) 565-8289 liseaa@coct.org
Colorado Open Lands Revolving Loan Fund	Colorado Open Lands (COL)	Colorado	$110,000*	Fund principally designed to help land-rich, cash-poor easement donors cover transaction costs. Loans are to be repaid from the proceeds of tax credit sales. The land trust makes individual decisions and does not have specific criteria.	http://www.coloradoopenlands.org	Daniel Pike (303) 988-2373 dpike@coloradoopenlands.org

*(COL has until the end of 2005 to raise an additional $25,000, at which time the Gates Family Foundation will give an additional $25,000.)

Revolving Loan Fund	Administering Organization	Geographic Area	Size of Fund	Description of Fund (All funds are primarily external unless otherwise noted.)	Administering Organization Web site	Contact Person
Colorado Open Lands Revolving Loan Fund, cont'd				Loan provisions are part of a larger Project Coordination Agreement the landowner signs for COL to coordinate the easement process for a fee. Under the loan provisions, specific costs are loan eligible (appraisal, title insurance, baseline, mineral reports, etc.). Landowner submits invoice to COL, and COL pays bills directly. Interest on unpaid balance accrues (interest is calculated as the median between the prime rate and the IRS imputed interest rate). COL also coordinates the sale of the conservation easement tax credit for the donor; terms call for COL to be paid the outstanding loan balance out of the tax credit sale proceeds. Loan agreement is an unsecured personal contractual commitment. Total funds advanced to an individual borrower are usually less than $15,000.		
Conservation Trust for North Carolina Land Acquisition Revolving Loan Program	Conservation Trust for North Carolina (CTNC)	Mostly dedicated to the mountain regions of North Carolina	$1.6 million	Accompanied by a Land Protection Assistance Program, which offers grants to cover land acquisition or easement transactional costs, including surveys, appraisals, and legal and and other closing fees. CTNC also offers technical, educational, and professional assistance.	http://www.ctnc.org	Wendy Howard (919) 828-4199 wendy@ctnc.org

Revolving Loan Fund	Administering Organization	Geographic Area	Size of Fund	Description of Fund (All funds are primarily external unless otherwise noted.)	Administering Organization Web site	Contact Person
Great Lakes Revolving Loan Fund	The Conservation Fund (TCF)	Freshwater and coastal sites throughout the U.S. portion of the Great Lakes Basin	$7 million	Loans available to land trusts and public agencies for land acquisition and conservation easement financing. TCF also provides technical assistance.	http://www.conservationfund.org	Mike Kelly, TCF field representative (989) 662-6024 kellym@conservationfund.org
Greater Yellowstone Ecosystem Revolving Loan Fund	Resources Legacy Fund	Greater Yellowstone ecoregion	$7 million	Loans available to nonprofit conservation organizations within the region for land and conservation easement acquisitions. Minimum loan size is $300,000 for terms not exceeding three years. Eligible applicants must have adopted and be actively implementing the Land Trust Alliance's Standards and Practices.	http://www.resourceslegacyfund.org	Sue Haderle (916) 442-5057 SHaderle@resourceslegacyfund.org
Greater Yellowstone Loan Fund	The Conservation Fund	Upper Snake River watershed	$1 million	Loans available to specific land trusts within the region for land and conservation easement acquisitions.	http://www.conservationfund.org	Mark Elsbree (208) 726-4419 melsbree@mindspring.com

Revolving Loan Fund	Administering Organization	Geographic Area	Size of Fund	Description of Fund (All funds are primarily external unless otherwise noted.)	Administering Organization Web site	Contact Person
Lowcountry Conservation Loan Fund	Coastal Community Foundation of South Carolina	South Carolina's Lowcountry region	$1 million	Loans available to land trusts and other nonprofit conservation groups for conservation easement, fee and development rights purchases, closing, and other associated expenses. Local organizations are preapproved to be borrowers through a screening of borrowing histories, balance sheets, missions, boards, and so forth.	http://www.CCFgives.org	Richard Hendry, vice president of programs (843) 723-3635 RHendry@CCFgives.org
Maine Coast Heritage Trust Land Acquisition Revolving Loan Fund	Maine Coast Heritage Trust (MCHT)	Coast of Maine	$3.345 million	Loans available to Maine land trusts for land and conservation easement acquisitions. Very service-oriented fund; offers support to member land trusts through the borrowing process.	http://www.mcht.org	David MacDonald, director, Land Protection Division, MCHT (207) 729-7366 dmacdonald@mcht.org
Mississippi River Revolving Fund	The Conservation Fund (TCF)	Ten states along the Mississippi River: Missouri, Illinois, Minnesota, Wisconsin, Iowa, Kentucky, Tennessee, Arkansas, Louisiana, and Mississippi	$2.8 million	Established by TCF. Makes loans throughout its ten-state region to land trusts based on several established priorities, such as water quality and recreation (focusing primarily on wetlands). Prefers a phone call or e-mail prior to filling out application. Minimum loan size is $25,000.	http://www.conservationfund.org	Upper Mississippi (five states): Tom Duffus (218) 722-2393 tduffus@conservationfund.org Lower Mississippi: Ray Herndon (703) 525-6300 rherndon@conservationfund.org

Revolving Loan Fund	Administering Organization	Geographic Area	Size of Fund	Description of Fund (All funds are primarily external unless otherwise noted.)	Administering Organization Web site	Contact Person
New Jersey Conservation Loan Fund	Open Space Institute (OSI)	Throughout New Jersey but recognizes certain ecologically critical areas defined as the highest priorities by New Jersey's conservation community: the Highlands of the northwest; the Pinelands; the Barnegat Bay watershed; and the Delaware Bay Shore area	$3.5 million	Priority given to projects that provide habitat for rare or endangered species or protect unique water or land features. Loans available for interim financing for eligible land transactions. The fund also seeks to facilitate complex transactions with multiple partners and multiple funding sources, such as the Garden State Preservation Trust, the New Jersey Department of Environmental Protection's Green Acres program, and the State Agricultural Development Committee. Bridge loans of up to three years, with a minimum loan size of approximately $150,000.	http://www.osiny.org	Michael Catania (908) 879-7942 michael@ conservationresourcesinc.org
New York Conservation Loan Fund	Open Space Institute	The Greater Hudson Valley, from the Capital District to the Hudson Highlands just north of New York City	Funds available from OSI's general conservation loan program. $20 million	Priority given to projects that protect scenic open spaces and enhance public recreational access. Although unsolicited applications for loans will be accepted in this region, the majority of loan projects are identified by OSI's land acquisition staff stationed in the Mid-Hudson Valley and the Capital District. Bridge loans of up to three years, with a minimum loan size of approximately $150,000.	http://www.osiny.org	Abigail Weinberg (212) 629-3981 aweinberg@osiny.org

Revolving Loan Fund	Administering Organization	Geographic Area	Size of Fund	Description of Fund (All funds are primarily external unless otherwise noted.)	Administering Organization Web site	Contact Person
Northern Forest Protection Fund	Open Space Institute	The Northern Forest—a 26-million-acre region spanning the northern tiers of New York, Vermont, New Hampshire, and Maine	Funds available from OSI's general $20 million conservation loan program.	Priority given to projects protecting large-scale working forest lands. Goal is to promote sustainable forestry, protect ecosystems, and secure opportunities for public recreation. Bridge loans of up to three years, with a minimum loan size of approximately $250,000.	http://www.osiny.org	Jo D. Saffeir (207) 688-4191 saffeir@rcn.com
Pacific Forest Trust's Conservation Capital Fund	The Pacific Forest Trust	Working forests in the Pacific Northwest (primary focus on California, Oregon, and Washington)	$7 million	Loans available to landowners who need money to manage their forests while public funds are raised to acquire a permanent conservation easement. Fund can also provide working capital at below-market interest rates for forest owners to refinance high-cost loans. Fund can provide specially structured loans for owners who are moving to forest management certified by the Forest Stewardship Council.	http://www.pacificforest.org/services/index.html	Connie Best, managing director (415) 561-0700 cbest@pacificforest.org or pft@pacificforest.org

Revolving Loan Fund	Administering Organization	Geographic Area	Size of Fund	Description of Fund (All funds are primarily external unless otherwise noted.)	Administering Organization Web site	Contact Person
Preserving Wild California	Resources Legacy Fund Foundation (RLFF)	California	$30 million/ year for five years	Invests in systematic acquisitions of land and fosters supportive policies, organizations, and constituencies. Makes grants, offers low-interest bridge financing, and enters into contracts for acquisition, policy, capacity building, planning, and stewardship and restoration. Submit brief letter of inquiry to RLFF.	http://www.resourceslegacyfund.org	Sue Haderle (916) 442-5057 SHaderle@resourceslegacyfund.org.
Society for the Protection of New Hampshire Forests—Environ-mental Loan Fund	Society for the Protection of New Hampshire Forests	New Hampshire	$235,000	Loans available for land and conservation easement acquisitions.	http://www.spnhf.org	Tom Howe, director of land conservation (603) 224-9945 thowe@forestsociety.org

Revolving Loan Fund	Administering Organization	Geographic Area	Size of Fund	(All funds are primarily external unless otherwise noted.)	Administering Organization Web site	Contact Person
Southern Appalachian Loan Fund	Open Space Institute	The Southern Appalachian mountain region: western North Carolina and South Carolina, northern Alabama and Georgia, and eastern Tennessee (In some cases, the fund may also accept proposals from other Southern Appalachian states, including Virginia and Kentucky.)	Funds available from OSI's general $20 million conservation loan program.	Priority given to projects under immediate threat of being developed, that abut adjacent conservation lands, and that help channel or redirect development away from sensitive natural areas. Bridge loans of up to three years, with a minimum loan size of approximately $200,000.	http://www.osiny.org	Marc Hunt, Asheville, North Carolina (828) 278-0134 mhunt@osiny.org
West Hill Foundation for Nature Inc. (Affiliated Funds)	Independent	United States with Greater Yellowstone ecosystem focus	Over $500,000	Loans available to land trusts, particularly national conservation organizations, with excellent security.	None	Chris Sawyer, attorney for lender (404) 881-7000
Western Massachusetts Loan Fund	Open Space Institute	Region west of Worcester, Massachusetts	$2 million	Low-cost loan fund aiming to further conservation through the protection of working and biologically important landscapes in western Massachusetts. Bridge loans of up to three years, with a minimum loan size of $150,000.	http://www.osiny.org	Richard Hubbard (413) 625-9151 rkhubbard@verizon.net

Glossary

The terms defined below are used for purchasing and financing real estate and conservation easements. Generally, these are layman, not legal, definitions and should not be relied upon as legally accurate. For more precise definitions, please consult the Internal Revenue Code, *Black's Law Dictionary*, or other definitive sources.

Adjustable Rate Mortgage (ARM): A mortgage with periodic adjustments in the interest rate, usually every six months. ARM rates are calculated against a money index, such as the six-month Treasury bill rate index.[1]

Amortization: The process of loan payment over time by regular payments of interest and principal. The amortization period refers to a fixed period during which regular loan payments are made. The payment includes interest due each period, plus a gradually increasing amount of principal.

Annuity: An investment contract often purchased from a life insurance company that makes guaranteed payments at some future date, usually after retirement.[2]

Appraisal: A defensible opinion of value. For land trust and land conservation purposes, appraisals should be written by a professional, state-licensed appraiser with familiarity and experience valuing conservation land.

Balloon Payment Mortgage: A mortgage repaid by small payments until a given date, when the balance is due in a single, large payment. Borrowers get lower rates and payments for a specific period of time, which usually is anywhere from three years to ten years. Owners often sell or refinance before the balloon payment is due.

Bargain Sale: A sale to a land trust (or other qualified charitable entity) at less-than-market value. The difference between the price paid and the fair market value determined by a qualified appraisal can constitute a tax-deductible contribution to the seller.[3]

Basis: A taxpayer's cost in an asset such as land, including the original purchase cost and certain improvements.

Borrower: The person, organization, or entity that receives money (a loan) usually from an institutional or individual lender, that is expected to be paid back normally with interest. Most lenders, especially institutional ones, ask for a written promise for repayment from the borrower, usually with a registered lien on property to secure the loan.

Bridge Financing: Temporary or short-term financing to a borrower who is waiting for more permanent funding and usually is reasonably assured of that funding in the next months or few years. Also called interim financing.

Capital Campaign: An organized effort by a charitable organization to raise money for one or more projects.

Capital Gain (or Loss): The difference between an asset's sale (or exchange) price and its original price paid by the owner, plus the cost of certain improvements.

Charitable Donation: A gift or contribution to a charitable organization, with charitable intent, the value of which is deductible pursuant to federal and state income and estate/inheritance tax laws.[4]

Charitable Remainder Trust (CRT): An independent trust that is used for charitable planned giving purposes by which a donor transfers certain assets (usually appreciated property) into the trust, receives an income interest to one or more beneficiary (the donor or other persons), and a charitable deduction for a portion of the transfer. Upon the death of the beneficiary or end of the term, a designated charitable organization receives the remaining assets of the gift as the remainder beneficiary, and the trust terminates.

Closing: A specific time when a real estate transaction is consummated and the buyer and seller, or borrower and lender, sign final documents and transfer funds and real estate.

Collateral: A security interest or guarantee (usually personal or real property of value) pledged by a borrower to assure repayment of a loan.

Conservation Easement: A legal instrument by which a landowner limits, without relinquishing ownership, some or all of the development potential of property with significant natural resource, open space, or habitat value, and grants the right to conserve those values. The original owner and subsequent owners are bound by the restrictions of the easement. The executed easement document is recorded in the public records.[5]

Contract of Sale: An agreement to transfer the title to real property or tangible assets at a given price.[6]

Conventional Mortgage: A fixed-rate or adjustable-rate mortgage. (See Mortgage)[7]

Conveyance: A written instrument, such as a deed, used to transfer (convey) title to a property.[8]

Covenant: A loan agreement provision in which the borrower agrees to meet certain requirements (affirmative covenants), such as to maintain adequate property insurance, make timely loan payments, and keep the business in sound financial condition and/or refrain from taking certain actions, such as selling or transferring assets, defaulting, or taking specific actions that would diminish value (negative covenants) while the loan is in place.

Credit: The arrangement of a lender granting a loan to a borrower with assurance that it will be repaid. *Credit risk* is the risk to the lender of the loan not being repaid and losing principal and interest.

Debt: An amount owed for funds borrowed, generally secured by a promissory note, bond, mortgage, or other instruments that also state the repayment provisions.

Debt Service: Principal and interest payments to the lender usually made monthly or annually.

Deed of Trust: (Similar or equivalent to a mortgage in some jurisdictions.) An instrument by which a borrower conveys title to the property to be held as security to a trustee for the benefit of the lender. The transfer is accompanied by a trust agreement setting forth the terms of the security arrangement.

Default: Failure to fulfill a contractual obligation, such as repaying a loan.

Discount Rate: Percentage rate used to express future payments, receipts or value in present value.

Discounted Cash Flow Analysis: A method to determine the present value of future cash flow by discounting it using the appropriate cost of capital, and a method of evaluating a capital investment by comparing its projected income and costs with its current value.

Donation: A gift to a nonprofit organization, with or without charitable intent, that may or may not result in a tax deduction to the donor.

Due Diligence: The process of evaluating the opportunities and risks of a particular investment, including confirmation of all critical assumptions and facts.

Earnest Money: Funds paid by a potential purchaser as an expression of intent to complete the purchase. The money is usually held by the listing agent or attorney and credited towards the purchase price.

Easements of Sight: Uses of a property that are not recorded, but are visible on the land or are acknowledged by the landowners, such as unrecorded access trails or utility easements.

Eminent Domain: The right of a government or agent of a government to appropriate private property for public use, with just compensation to the owner.

Encumbrance: A burden or limitation on a land title or an interest in land other than ownership, including an easement, mortgage, lease, or lien.

Equity: An investment interest by owners, developers, or other investors typically represented by owners' share (or stock) in a business and share in the return. Equity can also be a property's market value, minus outstanding liens or mortgages.

Escheat: When property or an estate is transferred to the government because the owner died without a will or heirs.

Escrow: A legal arrangement under which legal documents or property or sale proceeds (from a real estate transaction) are delivered to a third party (called an escrow agent) and held until a condition or series of conditions as outlined in the escrow agreement or instructions are met.

Escrow Agreement: A written contract authorizing the holding of an asset, often in a real estate transaction, by a third party.

Exchange: A means of trading two or more real properties. "Like-kind" or 1031 exchanges are exchanges of similar trade, business, or investment property for which certain taxes are deferred in accordance with the provisions of Section 1031 of the Internal Revenue Code.

Exposure: The extent to which a lender has committed credit to a borrower.

Fair Market Value (FMV): An unbiased appraisal based on an estimate of what a buyer would pay a seller for a piece of property.

Fee Title: A legal instrument that is evidence of ownership of land.

First Mortgage: A commitment that creates a primary lien against real property, having priority over subsequent mortgages (junior or second, third, etc., mortgages). If a borrower defaults on the loan, the mortgage holder has the first right to the real property.

Fixed-Rate Loan: A loan with an interest rate that does not vary over the term of the loan (as opposed to a variable-rate loan or adjustable-rate mortgage). Fixed rate loans generally are constant-payment, fully amortizing loans.[9]

Floating Interest Rate: A loan interest rate that changes whenever an index rate, or base rate, such as the bank prime rate, the London Interbank Offered Rate (LIBOR), or Federal Home Loan Bank index rate changes. The loan rate is said to "float" on top of the specified index by a set amount.[10]

Foreclosure: A legal proceeding initiated by a creditor to take possession of collateral securing a defaulted loan.[11]

Full Faith and Credit: The commitment by an institution to repay the principal and interest on outstanding debt. The institution is usually sufficiently large and creditworthy to be able to make repayment.

Fully Amortizing Loan: A loan that can be fully repaid by regular payments of principal and interest by the maturity date.

Goodwill: An intangible asset representing the difference between the purchase price of an asset and its fair market value.[12]

Guarantor: An entity (person, corporation, bank, or foundation) that guarantees loan repayment to a lender and assumes liability in event of default.

Guaranty: A pledge by a third party or a borrower to cover the payment of debt or to perform some obligation if the borrower defaults.

HAZMAT: Hazardous materials in or on the ground or water subject to cleanup requirements by federal or state law.

Imputed Interest: Interest rate required for tax purposes by the IRS when the loan agreement uses a rate that is below the legal limit. Tax law will impute a higher interest rate and less principal, which will result in higher taxes paid.

Index: A statistical representation of an economic condition tracking performance relative to past performance. One example is the consumer price index.

Installment Sale: A sale made over a period of time (usually several years), as in the case of a seller-financed sale.

Interest: Payments for the use of (loaned) money, expressed as a percentage rate for the period of time in use, generally an annual rate. Bank interest is both an amount paid to attract deposit funds, and a finance charge for money loaned to borrowers.[13]

Interest-only Loan: A debt for which the periodic payments only cover the interest with the principal due at maturity.

Interest Payment: The portion of each loan payment that is allocated to accrued interest.

Letter of Credit (L/C): A credit instrument issued by a bank, upon an agreement with a borrower, guaranteeing payment on behalf of its customer for a stated period of time and when certain conditions are met.[14]

Letter of Opinion: A brief estimate of property value by a professional appraiser particularly useful when valuing simple parcels, such as subdivision lots. It is not as accurate or useful for complex parcels or valuations.

Lien: A creditor's legal claim against property to have debt repaid out of a specifically identified property owned by the debtor, which guarantees the right to collect through legal means. There are four primary kinds of liens: monetary (mortgages), mechanics (for work not paid for), tax (for unpaid taxes), and judgment (for determination of rights through legal actions like divorce).[15]

Like-kind Exchange/1031 Exchange: An exchange of investment property for which the capital gains tax is deferred until the exchanged property is sold.

Line of Credit: An arrangement by which a lender agrees to make funds available to a borrower for a period of time at a certain rate of interest and under certain other conditions. The borrower can continue drawing funds up to a certain limit.

Linked Deposits: An arrangement by which a foundation or other entity deposits money in a bank and accepts a below-market interest rate on it. In exchange, the bank makes below-market-rate loans to nonprofit ventures, most notably to low-income housing and other community development projects.

Loan: Money or another asset advanced to a borrower, with the intent that it will be repaid, usually with interest.

Loan-loss Reserve: A fund account established to cover estimated potential losses in a loan portfolio.

Loan-to-value Ratio: The percentage value of the principal amount of a loan to the value of the asset securing the loan.

The London Interbank Offered Rate (LIBOR): The benchmark interest rate for creditworthy borrowers for many adjustable rate mortgages, business loans, and financial instruments traded on global financial markets. It is based on the rate that most banks are willing to lend to each other. It is usually lower than prime rate.

Memorandum of Sale: A notice in the public records of a sale. Unless mandated by state law, this notice need not provide particulars of the sale such as price.

Mortgage: An instrument giving conditional ownership of an asset to a lender that secures a legal right to repayment of debt. Usually, a promissory note creates the obligation to repay the loan in accordance with the terms of the mortgage. The mortgagor is the borrower; the mortgagee is the lender.

Mortgage Subordination: An agreement by the mortgage lender to place its claim on the asset below or junior to another obligation, as in the case of a bank subordinating its mortgage to a conservation easement. The lender is more likely to be willing to change position when enough value remains in the property to pay off the loan in case the landowner defaults on the loan.

Nonrecourse Loan: A loan where the source of repayment is only the collateral securing the loan or the cash flow generated by it.

Note: A promissory note. A legal agreement expressing a commitment to pay a debt or obligation.

Points: An abbreviated term used in lending with two distinct applications and meanings. (1) *Discount points,* often simply called points, is a fee charged by a bank for a loan, payable at the loan closing. Discount points are a percentage of the principle amount of the loan. One point is one percent of the loan. A bank's fee of two discount points on a $100,000 loan is $2,000. (2) *Basis points,* also often called just points, describe the difference between an interest rate and a standard rate such as prime LIBOR, measured in hundreths of a percent. A bank's interest rate of fifty basis points above prime rate is a rate of .5 percent above prime. If prime is 7 percent, then the bank's rate is 7.5 percent.

Prepayment: Paying a loan or mortgage before maturity. A prepayment clause in a mortgage gives the borrower the option of retiring the mortgage indebtedness without penalty.[16]

Prime Rate: A reference note that banks use in pricing short maturity commercial loans to their best, or most creditworthy, customers.[17]

Principal: The face amount of a loan evidencing the amount repayable, exclusive of interest, according to the terms of the note securing the obligation.[18]

Promissory Note: A legally enforceable notice of debt that spells out how much is owed and on what terms. This commitment is the central component of any loan agreement.

Quitclaim Deed: A document in which title, claim, or ownership of property or an estate is relinquished to another, without representing that such title is valid.[19]

Recourse: The right to take assets to satisfy a loan if a borrower defaults. In a full-recourse loan, the lender has the right to take any assets. In a limited-recourse loan, the lender's rights are limited to the particular asset financed by the loan.

Remainder Interest/Reserved Life Estate: A conveyance of fee title by grant deed with a life estate reserved. The right of lifetime tenancy for some certain person.[20]

Repayment Terms: The conditions and circumstances that the borrower must follow when repaying a loan (interest rate, timing of repayment schedule, etc.).

Right of First Refusal: An agreement between the seller and a specific potential buyer that allows that buyer to meet the terms of an offer made by other potential buyers and acquire the property.

Second Mortgage: A mortgage (see Mortgage) that is subordinant to a first mortgage, but senior to subsequent liens. In the event of default the lender holding the second mortgage is paid off only if there are sufficient funds remaining after the lender holding the first mortgage is paid.

Secured Loan: A loan that is collateralized by the assignment of rights to property and a security interest in personal property or real property taken by the lender.[21]

Security: Personal assets pledged to assure the performance of an obligation or the repayment of a debt. Examples of security on a loan include real estate, personal property, stocks, and mortgages.

Seller Financing (also known as *vendor take-back mortgage*): Financing for the purchase of property provided by the seller, the collateral usually being the property being sold.

Short-term Financing: A loan or other form of credit that is usually due (matures) within three years or less.

Simple Interest: Interest computed only on the principal balance, without compounding. For example, simple interest for a year on $100, borrowed at eight percent interest, is eight dollars.[22]

Simultaneous Closings: Several closings completed back-to-back, as in the case of a purchase and immediate resale.

Subordination: The order in which loans are paid off, which is chronologically in order of precedence with senior or first mortgages being paid off first. Thus senior mortgages are always more likely to be fully paid off.

Substitute Collateral: Alternative property used as security for a loan instead of the property for which the loan is originally secured.

Tax Benefits: Income and estate tax deductions and inheritance tax benefits derived from qualified charitable donations as well as other opportunities for tax savings and deferral, such as like-kind exchanges, available through federal or state tax codes.[23]

Term: The length of time until a loan or other obligation is fully repaid.

Title: Indicates "fee" position of lawful ownership and right to property; "bundle of rights" possessed by an owner. Combination of all elements constituting proof of ownership.[24]

Title Insurance: Insurance against losses resulting from a title defect discovered after property has been conveyed from buyer to seller.[25]

Title Insurance Policy: One-time payment that protects the new owner of fee land or conservation easement from any loss due to defects in title covered by the policy and explained in the title report.

Title Report *(preliminary title report, title commitment, title abstract)*: A report that is the result of a detailed investigation into the recorded documentation concerning title, including ownership, easements, covenants, liens, clouds on title, and all associated defects. The report also explains what the insurance company that prepared the report is willing to cover in the title insurance policy and what it will exempt from coverage.

Trade Lands: Land donated or acquired in some other manner that usually does not have significant conservation resources and can be sold to generate revenue for a land trust. Trade lands with conservation resources are conserved before sale.

Underwriting: The analysis of credit strength preceding lending money.

Unsecured Loan: A loan granted on the strength of the borrower's credit history or reputation in the community, earnings potential, and other assets owned, even if unpledged, rather than a pledge of assets as collateral.[26]

Warranty: A statement, whether written or implied, that assertions made in completion of a contract are true. For example, a seller's claim in a warranty deed that the property being sold has a marketable title.[27]

Warranty Deed: A conveyance of real property that is certified to be free and clear of defects, liens, and encumbrances except those known to all parties and usually insured with title insurance.

Notes

Introduction: A Field Guide

1. James N. Levitt, ed., *From Walden to Wall Street* (Washington, DC: Island Press, 2005).
2. William J. Ginn, *Investing in Nature* (Washington, DC: Island Press, 2005).
3. Patrick Coady, "Conservation Finance Viewed as a System: Tackling the Financial Challenge," pp. 22–36 from Levitt, ed., *From Walden to Wall Street* (Washington, DC: Island Press, 2005).
4. William Cronon, "Saving the Land We Love: Land Conservation and American Values," closing plenary speech for the Land Trust Alliance National Conference: Rally 2005, October 17, Madison, Wisconsin.
5. Land Trust Alliance, "About LTA," http: //www.lta.org/aboutlta/ (accessed June 2006).
6. Land Trust Accreditation Commission, http: //www.lta.org/accreditation/ (accessed July 2006).

Chapter 1. Organizational Readiness

1. Most of the organizational concepts discussed in this chapter are described in Land Trust Alliance (LTA), *Land Trust Standards and Practices,* rev. ed. (Washington, DC: LTA, 2004), available online at http: //www.lta.org/sp/index.html. These are also basic tenants of land trust accreditation. For more information on land trust accreditation, see http: //www.lta.org/accreditation/.
2. Land Trust Alliance (LTA), *Assessing Your Organization* (Washington, DC: LTA, 2005). Available at the LTA bookstore at http: //www.lta.org/publications/index .html or download it online from http: //www.ltanet.org/objects/view.acs? object_id=4574 (accessed August 27, 2006).
3. With special thanks to Marc Smiley for emphasizing this point.
4. A land trust's transition from a volunteer organization to a staffed one is a big subject with much literature written on it. The bibliography at the end of the book offers some reading suggestions.
5. Joan Flanagan, *Successful Fundraising: A Complete Handbook for Volunteers and Professionals,* 2nd ed. (Lincolnwood, IL: Contemporary Books, 1999).
6. Michael McKee, "Care and Feeding of Volunteers," *Grassroots Fundraising Journal,* September/October 2005.
7. Land Trust Alliance, "LTAnet," http: //www.lta.org/resources/infoaccess.htm.
8. It is tempting to give large photographs of land trust projects as thank-you gifts. However, people who have other art may have competing uses of wall space.

Something smaller is often better. One land trust gives small photographs; another gives plexiglass serving trays; others, small signed plaques.

9. Land Trust Alliance, "Land Trust Accreditation Commission," http: // www.lta.org/accreditation/.

Chapter 2. Financial Readiness

1. Quasi endowments are accounts that can be invaded for specific uses set by board policy, such as legal defense of conservation easements.
2. Some land trusts have worked out arrangements with public agencies to cover some of the pre-acquisition costs.
3. See Marc Smiley, "What I Do," http: //www.marcsmiley.com/what/index.html# fundraising.
4. See Standard 6D, *Land Trust Standards and Practices* (June 2006), available at http: //www.lta.org/sp/index.html.
5. See Standard 6, "Financial and Asset Management," and associated appendices, in Land Trust Alliance (LTA), *Land Trust Standards and Practices,* rev. ed. (Washington, DC: LTA, 2004), available online at http: //www.lta.org/sp/index.html.
6. With thanks for assistance in articulating this concept to Pat Coady: Patrick Coady, "Accelerating the Pace of Open Space Conservation: The Role of Finance," *Exchange: Journal of the Land Trust Alliance* (Winter 2005); James N. Levitt, ed., *From Walden to Wall Street* (Washington, DC: Island Press, 2005); personal communication with Patrick Coady, April 3, 2005; e-mail communication with Patrick Coady, April 5, 2005.
7. Conservation buyers are defined and briefly discussed in chapter 4. The subject will be covered in more detail in volume two.

Chapter 3. The Deal

1. See the Land Trust Standards and Practices Web site at http: //www.lta.org/ sp/index.html.
2. Trust for Public Land, *Doing Deals: A Guide to Buying Land for Conservation* (Washington, DC: Land Trust Alliance; San Francisco: Trust for Public Land, 1995). This very useful book addresses the basics of project purchase.
3. Per the American Land Title Association, Plain Language Commitment, Schedule B, Section II, "Exceptions," standard exceptions include: 1. Rights or claims of parties in possession not shown by the public records; 2. Easements, liens or encumbrances or claims thereof, which are not shown by the public records; 3. Discrepancies, conflicts in boundary lines, shortage in area, encroachments, and any facts which a correct survey and inspection of the premises would disclose, and which are not shown by the public records; 4. Any lien, or right to a lien, for services, labor or material heretofore or hereafter furnished, imposed by law and not shown by the public records; 5. a) Unpatented mining claims; b) Reservations or exceptions in patents or in Acts authorizing the issuance thereof; c) Water rights, claims or title to water, whether or not the matters excerpted under a), b) or c) are

shown by the public records; 6. Ownership or title to any mineral interest, and the effect on the surface of the exercise of the mineral rights.

4. An opinion of value is a researched estimate of value by an appraiser without the report and its supporting information.

5. If a land trust pays a price that is significantly over the appraised market value, it runs the risk of financially enriching the seller, which is illegal. However, there are circumstances in which paying modestly over appraised value is necessary and legitimate. If the land trust is in this position, it should get very good legal advice and document the reasons for buying the property (e.g., critical public values) and for paying the higher price (e.g., last holdout purchase in a series of parcels). See chapter 4 for more details.

6. A good reference on how conservation easements are appraised is Land Trust Alliance (LTA), *Appraising Easements: Guidelines for Valuation of Land Conservation and Historic Preservation Easements*, 3rd ed. (Washington, DC: LTA, 1999).

7. Roger Fisher and William Ury, *Getting to Yes*, 2nd ed. (New York: Penguin Books, 1991).

8. Fisher and Ury, *Getting to Yes.*

Chapter 4. Legal and Ethical Considerations

1. If the transaction offers any tax benefits, then the taxpayer usually prefers to take those benefits as quickly as possible. If the transaction doesn't close until after December 31, the taxpayer must wait another year to claim the benefits on the tax return and benefit from the tax savings.

2. "Ethics," *Webster's Third New International Dictionary* (Springfield, MA: Merriam-Webster, 2002).

3. Stephen J. Small, "Land Trust Ethics," *Exchange: Journal of the Land Trust Alliance* (Winter 2004).

4. Steven T. Miller, commissioner, tax-exempt and government entities, Internal Revenue Service, plenary speech at the Land Trust Alliance National Conference: Rally 2005, October 17, Madison, Wisconsin.

5. David Ottaway and Joe Stephens, "Non Profit Land Bank Amasses Billions," *Washington Post*, May 4, 2003, A1 (first of three articles); "Landing the Big One: Preservation, Private Development," *Washington Post*, May 6, 2003, A9 (second of three articles); "Nonprofit Sells Scenic Acreage to Allies at a Loss," *Washington Post*, May 6, 2003, A1 (third of three articles).

6. Land Trust Alliance (LTA), *Land Trust Standards and Practices*, rev. ed. (Washington, DC: LTA, 2004), available online at http: //www.lta.org/sp/index.html.

7. *Land Trust Standards and Practices* Definitions: "Insiders: board and staff members, substantial contributors, parties related to the above, those who have an ability to influence decisions of the organization and those with access to information not available to the general public."

8. Land Trust for Tennessee Web site, http: //www.authpro.com/cgi-bin/auth.fcgi? user=landtrust (This site is password protected, but it is easy and free to register.)

9. Elizabeth Byers and Karin Marchetti Ponte, *The Conservation Easement Handbook*, 2nd ed. (Washington, DC: Land Trust Alliance; San Francisco: Trust for Public Land, 2005); Stephen J. Small, *The Federal Tax Law of Conservation Easements*, 4th ed. (Washington, DC: Land Trust Alliance, 1997); see Internal Revenue Code and Regulations cited in above and at http: //www.law.cornell.edu/uscode/html/uscode26/usc_sec_26_00000170----000-.html. Other good resources are Bruce Hopkins, *Law of Tax-exempt Organizations*, 7th ed. (New York: Wiley, 1998) and other references listed in the bibliography for this book.

10. For more information on inurement and private benefit, see "Staying within the Bounds of the Income Tax Code and Public Perception: Private Inurement and Private Benefit," *Exchange: Journal of the Land Trust Alliance* (Spring 1999). In addition, the Internal Revenue Service explains these terms and others in "Life Cycle of a Public Charity," available at http: //www.irs.gov/charities/charitable/article/0,,id=122670,00.html, with a specific explanation at http: //www.irs.gov/charities/charitable/article/0,,id=123297,00.html. Other sources of information are available through LTAnet, http: //www.lta.org/resources/infoaccess.htm.

11. Darby Bradley, ethics plenary session, Land Trust Alliance National Conference: Rally 2003.

12. Michael Whitfield, "Ethical Challenges in Land Conservation" workshop, Land Trust Alliance National Conference: Rally 2005, October, Madison, Wisconsin.

13. The good Jossey-Bass book by Robert D. Herman and Associates, *The Jossey-Bass Handbook of Nonprofit Leadership and Management*, Jossey-Bass Nonprofit and Public Management Series (San Francisco: Wiley, 1994), suggests another set of descriptive terms to characterize ethical behavior: integrity (honesty), openness (transparency), accountability, service, and charity (goodwill).

14. Hopkins, *Law of Tax-exempt Organizations;* Small, *The Federal Tax Law of Conservation Easements.*

15. The curriculum is in development, with fifteen courses scheduled for completion by the end of 2007. For more explanation, see chapter 17 as well as the LT Accreditation Commission Web site, http: //www.lta.org/accreditation/.

16. Prepared by BoardSource and the Independent Sector in 2003, "The Sarbanes-Oxley Act and Implications for Nonprofit Organizations," gives a thorough and practical review of the provisions of the act and how they should be applied to nonprofits. Available through LTAnet (http: //www.lta.org/resources/infoaccess.htm), http: //www.boardsource.org, or http: //www.IndependentSector.org.

17. Stefan Nagel and Konrad Liegel, "Land Trust Ethics: Exploring Nonprofit Accountability," *Exchange: Journal of the Land Trust Alliance* (Fall 2005).

18. Sec Land Trust Standard 4: Conflicts of Interest.

19. IRS 1997 EO CPE Text: "Community Board and Conflicts of Interest Policy," http: //www.irs.gov/pub/irs-tege/eotopicc97.pdf.

20. Ottaway and Stephens, "Non Profit Land Bank Amasses Billions."

21. Summarized from Land Trust Alliance, *Land Trust Standards and Practices,* Appendix1D3: Jo Davies Conservation Foundation, Code of Ethics. Also see *Land Trust*

Standards and Practices 4, "Conflicts of Interest," and appendices for Standards and Practices 1 and 4, particularly.

22. Steven T. Miller, plenary speech, Land Trust Alliance National Conference: Rally 2005, October 17, Madison, Wisconsin.

23. The Internal Revenue Service's revised Form 8283 is available at http: //www .irs.gov/pub/irs-pdf/f8283.pdf with new instructions that require additional information from conservation easement donors. Any donor of a conservation easement in tax year 2006 should use the new form and follow the new instructions.

24. IRS revised Form 8283.

25. Adapted from Lawrence Keuter, "Land Trust Ethics: Reviewing Appraisals," *Exchange: Journal of the Land Trust Alliance* (Winter 2005).

26. *Land Trust Standards and Practices,* Practice 10D.

27. In what may be the first decision of this kind, in 2006 the U.S. Tax Court disqualified a conservation easement donated by a real estate company to a county government for a tax deduction for not meeting specific standards of the law; see http: //www.lta.org/publicpolicy/turner_decision.htm. Interestingly, the county government did not sign Form 8283.

28. Internal Revenue Bulletin 2004-28; Notice 2004-41, "Charitable Contributions and Conservation Easements," http: //www.irs.gov/irb/2004-28_IRB/ar09.html (accessed July 2006).

29. *Land Trust Standards and Practices* 10C advises that the duty of land trusts is not to make assurances concerning the deductibility of a particular land or easement donation or the accuracy of the appraisal.

30. E-mail from Michael Whitfield, Teton Regional Land Trust, March 10, 2006.

Chapter 5. Raising Money

1. Brenda Lind, "Conservation Easement Costs and Funding" workshop, Land Trust Alliance National Conference: Rally 2005, Madison, Wisconsin, October 17; information from Brenda Lind and Richard Ober, Monadnock Conservancy.

2. Useful handouts from Brenda Lind's "Conservation Easement Costs and Funding" workshop, Land Trust Alliance National Conference: Rally 2005, October 17, Madison, Wisconsin, are available on LTAnet (http: //www.ltanet.org/), including the *Land Trust Standards and Practices:* appendix 11A, written by Brenda Lind.

3. My thanks to Peter Helm, of the New Hampshire Conservation Land Stewardship Program, for his response to my listserv request that kept the question of funding stewardship front and center (Peter.Helm@nh.gov).

Chapter 6. Traditional Fundraising Methods

1. Joan Flanagan, *The Grass Roots Fundraising Book: How to Raise Money In Your Community* (Lincolnwood, IL: NTC/Contemporary Books, 1995).

2. Kim Klein and Stephanie Roth, eds., *Raise More Money: The Best of the Grassroots Fundraising Journal* (Oakland, CA: Chardon, 2001); Terry Schaff and Doug Schaff, *The Fundraising Planner: A Working Model for Raising the Dollars You Need* (San Francisco: Jossey-Bass, 1999).

3. Joan Flanagan, *Successful Fundraising: A Complete Handbook for Volunteers and Professionals* (New York: McGraw-Hill, 1999).

4. Thank you to Jim Kitendaugh, of The Wayland Group, and Leslie Mattson-Emerson, of the Grand Teton National Park Foundation, for contributing to this list.

5. Catherine Kolkmeier, "Making The Big Ask: How to Find, Cultivate and Keep Donors," *Exchange: Journal of the Land Trust Alliance* 23, no. 4 (Fall 2004).

6. Kolkmeier, "Making the Big Ask."

7. Bill Birchard, *Nature's Keepers* (San Francisco: Jossey-Bass, 2005).

8. William Ginn, *Investing in Nature* (Washington, DC: Island Press, 2005).

9. Thank you again to Jim Kitendaugh, of The Wayland Group, and Leslie Mattson-Emerson, of the Grand Teton National Park Foundation, for contributing to this discussion on the structure of the solicitation meeting and tips for the meeting.

10. Jennifer Andes, "Stepping Up to the Big Deal," *Exchange: Journal of the Land Trust Alliance* 20, no. 4 (Fall 2001).

11. Vermont Land Trust, "Tax Wise" section of the Web site, http: //www.vlt.org/Tax-Wise.html; Iowa Natural Heritage Foundation, "Planned Gifts" section of the Web site, http: //www.inhf.org/plannedgifts.htm. The Maine Coast Heritage Trust also has a comprehensive booklet, *Conservation Options, A Guide for Maine Landowners,* http: //www.mcht.org/mchtnews/pdf/mchtconsoptions.pdf, that explains planned giving and other ways for landowners to conserve land.

Chapter 7. Traditional Fundraising Plans and Sources

1. Land trusts receive significant funding from local, state, and federal agencies, particularly for acquisition. However, since the focus of this book is on nongovernmental conservation finance, I will not discuss strategies for fundraising from public sources.

2. For much more information on foundations, visit the Foundation Center's extensive Web site at http: //www.fdncenter.org; visit the Center's five locations or extensive network of Cooperating Centers, or use its excellent Foundation Directory (available in hard copy at many libraries or online).

3. The foundation's environment program has since changed focus.

4. Articles on the Vermont Land Trust Web site explain more about the land trust's productive partnership with the Freeman Foundation. See http: //www.vlt.org/freeman-support.html (accessed July 2006).

5. Holly Hall, "Globalization Could Erode Corporate Giving in U.S., Expert Warns," *Chronicle of Philanthropy,* July 22, 2004.

6. Suzanne Perry, "Giving by Companies Rose 14% Last Year, Study Finds," *Chronicle of Philanthropy,* June 15, 2006; Center on Philanthropy at Indiana University, "Giving USA 2005" (Glenview, IL: American Association of Fundraising Counsel Trust for Philanthropy, 2005).

7. Rebecca Chapman and Robert Keller, "Making the Corporate Connection a Success for Land Trusts" workshop, Land Trust Alliance National Conference: Rally 2005, October 2005, Madison, Wisconsin.

8. Chapman and Keller, "Making the Corporate Connection a Success for Land Trusts."
9. Center on Philanthropy at Indiana University, "Giving USA 2005."
10. Joan Flanagan, *Successful Fundraising: A Complete Handbook for Volunteers and Professionals* (New York: McGraw-Hill, 1999).
11. "Land Trust Gleanings," *Exchange: Journal of the Land Trust Alliance* 21, no. 4 (Fall 2002).
12. The Conservation Fund, Captain John Smith Chesapeake National Historic Water Trail, http://www.conservationfund.org/pagespinner.asp?article=2766&back=true (accessed July 2006).
13. Kentucky Natural Lands Trust, www.knlt.org press release (accessed July 2006). http://www.knlt.org/Docs/KNLT-Toyota-Release.pdf (accessed July 2006).
14. "Land Trust Gleanings," *Exchange: Journal of the Land Trust Alliance* 22, no. 1 (Winter 2003).
15. "Tips and Talk: Seasonal Fundraising Ideas," *Exchange: Journal of the Land Trust Alliance* (Fall 2005). Also, the Center for a New American Dream facilitates these fairs; see http://www.newdream.org/holiday/altgift.php (accessed September 1, 2006); e-mail communication: Christine Iffrig, director of development and communications, Potomac Conservancy, July 25, 2006
16. The "Memory Of" section of the Little Traverse Conservancy's Fall 2005 newsletter had 146 donors honoring 55 individuals and "a beloved retriever, Jackson."
17. Jennifer Andes, "Stepping Up to a Big Deal."

Chapter 8. Voluntary Surcharges

1. Since 1985, Patagonia Inc. has donated at least 1 percent of sales revenue to one thousand organizations. It now pledges at least 1 percent of sales or 10 percent of pretax profits, whichever is more. Since 1985 it has given away $25 million to environmental organizations. See http://www.patagonia.com/web/us/contribution/patagonia.go?assetid=1960). In 2001, Patagonia helped to start "1% For The Planet," which now has over 375 participating businesses, donating at least 1 percent of their annual sales and contributing over $10 million thus far for environmental protection worldwide; see http://www.onepercentfortheplanet.org.
2. The 1% for Open Space program initially funded the Gunnison Ranchland Conservation Legacy as well.
3. The Gunnison Ranchland Conservation Legacy, which withdrew from the program in January of 2001 when 1% for Open Space was established as a separate organization.
4. Crested Butte Land Trust still takes great pride in the stewardship of this trail. In October 2005, they organized seventy-five volunteers to plant five thousand trees to complete the reclamation of a parcel along the trail and immediately adjacent to the one they had purchased.
5. "1% for the Tetons" Web site, http://www.onepercentforthetetons.org; Charture Institute, http://www.charture.org/.
6. To obtain a copy, contact Kellie Wright, Truckee Donner Land Trust: 580-582-4711.

Chapter 9. Transfer Fees

1. Under some conventions, when real estate is sold subject to a transfer fee, the buyer may technically pay the fee.

2. The Brandywine Conservancy and probably other land trusts had agreements with developers for fee contributions in the 1980s, before this integrated transfer fee mechanism was developed.

3. The state of Maryland and local governments in states including Colorado, Massachusetts, and Pennsylvania have been taxing land transactions to fund general and capital expenses since the late 1970s and early 1980s. In 1983, the Nantucket Land Bank combined that concept with a land conservation program and became the first land acquisition program in the nation to be funded by a dedicated real estate transfer tax. The 2 percent transfer tax was operational by February 1984. It raised $1.6 million in its first year.

4. Declaration of Covenants, Conditions, and Restrictions for Lots One Through Thirty-Eight of Granite Ridge, A Subdivision of Teton County, Wyoming. Recorded: Teton County Clerk, September 7, 1994.

5. H. William Sellers, *The Use of Private Transfer Fees for Conservation Easement Endowment,* a research monograph for the Pennsylvania Land Trust Association, 2005.

Chapter 10. Borrowing Money

1. John Bartlett, *Familiar Quotations* (New York: Little, Brown, 1992).

Chapter 11. Bank Lending

1. Later in the chapter I will discuss the restrictions on the use of land for collateral that is held by a land trust for a public purpose or subject to conservation restrictions. Not all land owned by land trusts make appropriate collateral.

2. The Western Reserve Land Conservancy was formed by the merger of the Chagrin River Land Conservancy, the Bratenahl Land Conservancy, Firelands Land Conservancy, Headwaters Land Trust, Hudson Land Conservancy, Medina Summit Land Conservancy, Portage Land Association for Conservation and Education, and Tinkers Creek Land Conservancy.

3. The land trust received a third, smaller loan for $50,000 from a local housing and development agency. The foundation loan was subordinant to both of the other loans.

4. Freddie Mac is the nickname for the Federal Home Loan Mortgage Corporation, which is a quasi-governmental agency that buys and sells residential loans on the secondary market. Fannie Mae is the nickname for the Federal National Mortgage Association, which is a private corporation that purchases residential mortgages in the secondary mortgage market.

5. See below subsections: Real Estate Collateral, and Bank Lending and Conservation Easements.

6. The *Wall Street Journal* defines prime rate as "The base rate on corporate loans posted by at least 75% of the nation's 30 largest banks" and is a benchmark for many loan programs.

7. See chapter 15, Foundation Program-related Investments.

8. See chapter 15, Foundation Program-related Investments.

9. Special thanks to Ann Taylor Schwing, of counsel, Mcdonough, Holland & Allen, PC, and trustee, the Land Trust of Napa County for much of the thinking for this section.

10. The reader can find more information on subordination in Laurel Florio, "Mortgage Subordination: Why and When It's Necessary," Land Trust Alliance *Exchange,* Spring 2002 (Vol. 21 No. 2), pp. 19–20; and Dennis Bidwell, "Negotiating with Lenders on Mortgage Subordination," Land Trust Alliance *Exchange,* Spring 2002 (Vol. 21 No. 2), pp. 17–18.

11. Negative misinformation about, for example, The Nature Conservancy, and the whole concept of conservation easements periodically circulates in such magazines as the western *Range Magazine.* As an example, here is the opening line from an article in the Winter 2005 issue featuring land trusts: "Anyone who would put a conservation easement on their property must hate their children, grandchildren, all of their heirs forever, or think that they are stupid and all of their offspring will be stupid forever." Wayne Klump, "A Rancher's View."

Chapter 12. Seller Financing

1. Restructuring to an "S" corporation, for which there is currently a ten-year wait to eliminate the double tax.

2. It should be noted that laws for developers, as dealers in real estate, require that the developer pay taxes on the full value of the sale in the first year, even if income is received over more than one year. Other sellers pay tax as the installment payments are made.

Chapter 13. External Revolving Loan Funds

1. The purchase price included a second 1.5-acre parcel, Bowcat Point.

2. As of May 2006.

3. As of December 31, 2005.

4. This is a fund established as part of a settlement agreement with the Federal Energy Regulatory Commission (FERC) license associated with upper and middle dams in Maine.

5. This includes five Open Space Institute regional "branch" funds, three regional funds sponsored by the Conservation Fund, and two funds sponsored by the Colorado Conservation Trust.

6. Resources Legacy Fund has, very infrequently, invested in transactions with government agencies, but the vast majority of transactions are grants or loans to land trusts (Michael Mantell, personal communication, May 10, 2005). The Coalition for Buzzards Bay does, on occasion, engage in their own land transactions.

7. RLF's national and global programs primarily focus on the Sustainable Fisheries Fund, which is a regranting program established by the Packard Foundation in the Pacific and Indian oceans and an ocean conservation program.

8. Incorporated under the name of the Open Space Action Committee; incorporated as the Open Space Institute in 1974.

9. Capitalized by program-related investments loans from the Penn, Dodge, and Kohlberg foundations.

10. A small land trust, the Edisto Island Open Land Trust, has borrowed from the Low-country Conservation Loan Fund. The executive director, Marian Brailsford, thinks that the small geographic focus of her land trust on an island with extremely valuable ecological resources forces the land trust to be more aggressive with its protection program than some other land trusts may need to be.

Chapter 14. Internal Protection Funds

1. See chapter 6, Traditional Fundraising.

2. For more on POST's capital campaign see: http://www.openspacetrust.org/pressrelease06–01.htm.

3. POST never sells land for more than it paid for it, except when the land is donated.

4. See the Piedmont Environmental Trust Web site for more information about their protection funds: www.pecva.org.

5. The Land Trust of Napa County Investment Policy. Adopted by the board of trustees on December 12, 1999, revised August 24, 2000, May 15, 2002, and November 20, 2002.

6. Formerly the Red Hills Conservation Program.

7. "Achieving Our Conservation Values through the Land Preservation Fund." Pamphlet of The Nature Conservancy, Arlington, Virginia 2001.

Chapter 15. Foundation Program-related Investments

1. The Norcross Wildlife Foundation: http://www.norcrossws.org.

2. Christine I. Baxter, *Program-Related Investments: A Technical Manual for Foundations* (New York: John Wiley, 1999).

3. Internal Revenue Code, section 4942.

4. The Foundation Center, "PRI Financing: Trends and Statistics 2000–2001," PRI directory: http://www.community-wealth.org/_pdfs/articles-publications/pris/book-fdn-center-excerpt.pdf (2003).

5. Packard's PRI program also serves the woman's reproductive health, children, and community sectors.

6. GrantCraft, "Program-Related Investing": http://www.grantcraft.org/index.cfm?fuseaction=Page.viewPage&pageID=821 (2006).

7. Internal Revenue Code, title 26, section 4944: http://www.law.cornell.edu/uscode/search/display.html?terms=4944&url=/uscode/html/uscode26/usc_sec_26_00004944——000-.html (June 2006).

8. Packard did make a $14 million PRI commitment, by far its largest. It has not yet been paid out in full as it is being paid out over multiple years.

9. http://norcrossws.org/Loans/LOAN2.htm.

10. As of December 31, 2005.

11. PRI Makers Network Web site: http://www.primakers.net/home.

12. GrantCraft, "Program-Related Investing: Skills and Strategies for New PRI Funders": http://www.grantcraft.org/pdfs/pri.pdf (2007).

13. Foundations such as Myer Memorial Trust and Packard have extensive and useful Web sites with information on PRIs: www.mmt.org/grants_programs/pri/prilist/.

14. Phil Wallin, "The Case for Expanded Use of Conservation PRI's," Environmental Grantmakers Association "News and Updates," Fall 2001, Vol. 5, Issue 2.

15. Other U.S. conservation intermediaries that received MacArthur PRI support during the 1980s and 1990s include: The Trust for Public Lands, The Conservation Fund and Corlands, an affiliate of the Chicago-based Openlands Project. During the 1990s, the foundation also awarded a small number of PRIs to conservation-oriented businesses and intermediaries working in Latin America. The MacArthur Foundation no longer makes PRIs to conservation organizations in the United States.

16. I talked to one foundation that expected the abundance of state money for takeouts to drive its lending. It did not.

17. F. B. Heron Foundation, Heron Views, "New Frontiers in Mission-Related Investing": http://www.fbheron.org/message2.html (June 2006).

Chapter 16. Reducing Costs

1. D&R Greenway Land Trust Web site, Case Studies: http://www.drgreenway.org/case_studies.html.

2. Thank you to Stephen Small for articulating this important point.

3. Many, but not all, opinions on the conditions under which a land trust signs Form 8283 require the land trust to be comfortable with the valuation of the gift part of a bargain sale. See chapter 4 on legal and ethical considerations, the subsection on Form 8283.

4. A very interesting book on partnerships is edited by Eve Endicott, *Land Conservation through Public / Private Partnerships* (Washington, D.C.: Island Press, 1993). The book describes the range of these collaborations.

5. The stated IRS position in conservation-buyer transactions is outlined in Internal Revenue Bulletin: 2004–28, July 12, 2004, notice 2004–41. IRS resolution of the issues raised in this notice is anticipated at some yet to be determined point.

6. Excerpted from Rebecca S. Toupal, "Conservation Partnerships: Indicators of Success," Social Sciences Institute, Technical Report 2, Release 7.1 (February 1998).

7. *Land Trust Standards and Practices:* 8I: Evaluating Partnerships.

Chapter 17. Putting It All Together

1. LTA Accreditation Commission Web site: http://www.lta.org/accreditation/.

2. Land Trust Alliance, *Assessing Your Organization* (Washington, D.C.: Land Trust Alliance, 2005).

3. Hopper, Kim and Ernest Cook. *Conservation Finance Handbook.* (San Francisco: Trust for Public Land, 2004).

Conclusion: How It *Could* Come Together in the Future

1. Rob Aldrich, personal e-mail dated September 12, 2006. Numbers based on Land Trust Alliance research, USDA/ERS Natural Resource Inventory and Sprawl Costs: Economic Impact of Unchecked Development [Robert W. Burchell, Anthony Downs, Barbara McCann, and Sahan Mukherji (Washington, DC: Island Press, 2005)], and "Our Built and Natural Environments," http://www.epa.gov/piedpage/pdf/built.pdf#search=%22Our%20Built%20and%20Natural%20Environments%22 (numbers not available after 2003).

   An estimate for annual land developed is approximately 2.2 million acres per year. Land conserved averages approximately 2.3 million acres for national conservation organizations, between five hundred thousand and eight hundred thousand acres for land trusts, and an undetermined additional amount for additional public agency expenditures above what is allocated to projects lead by private conservation organizations (and accounted for in their numbers). Public funding accounts for nearly 88 percent of permanent conservation funding based on Frank Casey, "Contours of Conservation Finance," *From Walden to Wall Street,* James N. Levitt, ed. (Washington, DC: Island Press, 2005), 37–50.

2. Casey, "Contours of Conservation Finance."

3. Casey, "Contours of Conservation Finance."

4. Estimates of this rate vary. American Farmland Trust gives reports that urbanized land is increasing at 3.4 times the population (Farming on the Edge Report: http://www.farmland.org/resources/fote/default.asp) and Keith Schneider's article reports sprawl growing at seven times the population. ("420 Million: America's New Population Boom: Smart Growth Can Cut Congestion, Pollution in Emerging Supercities," Elm Street Writers Group, 2004, http://www.mlui.org/fullarticle.asp?fileid=16761).

5. Schneider, "420 Million."

6. American Farmland Trust, Farming on the Edge Report.

7. Casey, "Contours of Conservation Finance."

8. Lucy Bernholz, *Creating Philanthropic Capital Markets: The Deliberate Evolution* (New York: John Wiley & Sons, 2004).

9. Patrick Coady, "Conservation Finance Viewed As A System," *From Walden to Wall Street,* James N. Levitt, ed. (Washington, DC: Island Press, 2005).

Glossary

1. *Dictionary of Banking Terms,* 2000.

2. *Dictionary of Banking Terms.*

3. LTA, *The Standards and Practices Guidebook,* 9–12 appendix 9.1.

4. *The Standards and Practices Guidebook.*

5. *The Standards and Practices Guidebook.*

6. *Dictionary of Banking Terms,* 2000.

7. *Dictionary of Banking Terms.*

8. LTA, *The Standards and Practices Guidebook,* 9–12 appendix 9.1.

9. *Dictionary of Banking Terms*, 2000.

10. *Dictionary of Banking Terms*.

11. *Dictionary of Banking Terms*.

12. *Dictionary of Banking Terms*.

13. *Dictionary of Banking Terms*.

14. *Dictionary of Banking Terms*.

15. *Dictionary of Banking Terms*.

16. *Dictionary of Banking Terms*.

17. *Dictionary of Banking Terms*.

18. *Dictionary of Banking Terms*.

19. *Dictionary of Banking Terms*.

20. LTA, *The Standards and Practices Guidebook*, 9–12 appendix 9.1.

21. *Dictionary of Banking Terms*, 2000.

22. *Dictionary of Banking Terms*.

23. LTA, *The Standards and Practices Guidebook*, 9–12 appendix 9.1.

24. *The Standards and Practices Guidebook*.

25. *Dictionary of Banking Terms*, 2000.

26. *Dictionary of Banking Terms*.

27. *Dictionary of Banking Terms*.

Bibliography

Baxter, Christine I. *Program-related Investments: A Technical Manual for Foundations.* New York: Wiley, 1999.

Bernholz, Lucy. *Creating Philanthropic Capital Markets: The Deliberate Evolution.* Hoboken, NJ: Wiley, 2004.

Birchard, Bill. *Nature's Keepers.* San Francisco: Jossey-Bass, 2005.

Block, Stanley B., and Geoffrey A. Hirt. *Foundations of Financial Management.* 7th ed. Boston: Irwin, 1994.

Brewer, Richard. *Conservancy: The Land Trust Movement in America.* Hanover, NH: University Press of New England, 2003.

Brick, Philip, Donald Snow, and Sarah Van de Wetering, eds. *Across the Great Divide: Explorations in Collaborative Conservation and the American West.* Washington, DC: Island Press, 2001.

Byers, Elizabeth, and Karin Marchetti Ponte. *The Conservation Easement Handbook.* 2nd ed. Washington, DC: Land Trust Alliance; San Francisco: Trust for Public Land, 2005.

Ciconte, Barbara L., and Jeanne G. Jacob. *Fundraising Basics: A Complete Guide.* 2nd ed. Gaithersburg, MD: Aspen, 2001.

Cummings, Jack. *Real Estate Finance and Investment Manual.* Paramus, NJ: Prentice Hall, 1997.

Dove, Kent E., Alan M. Spears, and Thomas W. Herbert. *Conducting a Successful Major Gifts & Planned Giving Program: A Comprehensive Guide and Resource.* San Francisco: Jossey-Bass, 2002.

Downes, John, and Jordan W. Goodman. *Dictionary of Finance and Investment Terms.* 6th ed. Hauppauge, NY: Barron's Educational Series, 2003.

Endicott, Eve, ed. *Land Conservation through Public/Private Partnerships.* Washington, DC: Island Press, 1993.

Fairfax, Sally K., Lauren Gwinn, Mary Ann King, Leigh Raymond, and Laura A. Watt. *Buying Nature: The Limits of Land Acquisition as a Conservation Strategy, 1780–2004.* Cambridge, MA: MIT Press, 2005.

Fairfax, Sally K., and Darla Guenzler. *Conservation Trusts.* Lawrence: University Press of Kansas, 2001.

Feyerabend, Borrini, et al. *Co-management of Natural Resources: Organising, Negotiating, and Learning-by-doing.* Switzerland: International Union for Conservation of Nature and Natural Resources, 2000.

Fisher, Roger, and William Ury. *Getting to Yes.* 2nd ed. New York: Penguin Books, 1991.

Fitch, Thomas P. *Dictionary of Banking Terms.* 4th ed. Hauppauge, NY: Barron's Educational Series, 2000.

Flanagan, Joan. *The Grass Roots Fundraising Book: How to Raise Money in Your Community.* Lincolnwood, IL: NTC/Contemporary Books, 1995.

The Foundation Center. *The PRI Directory: Charitable Loans and Other Program-related Investments by Foundation.* 2nd ed. New York: The Foundation Center, 2003.

Freyfogle, Eric T. *The Land We Share.* Washington, DC: Island Press, 2003.

Friedman, Jack P. *Dictionary of Business Terms.* 3rd ed. Hauppauge, NY: Barron's Educational Series, 2000.

Garner, Bryan A., ed. *Black's Law Dictionary.* 8th ed. St. Paul, MN: West Publishing, 2004.

Ginn, William. *Investing in Nature: Case Studies of Land Conservation in Collaboration with Business.* Washington, DC: Island Press, 2005.

Giving USA. "Giving USA 2005. The Annual Report on Philanthropy for the Year 2004. 50th Annual Issue." Indianapolis, IN: Giving USA Foundation, AAFRC Trust for Philanthropy, 2005.

Groves, Craig R. *Drafting a Conservation Blueprint.* Washington, DC: Island Press, 2003.

Heffernan, Shelagh. *Modern Banking.* London: Wiley, 2005.

Herman, Robert D., and Associates. *The Jossey-Bass Handbook of Nonprofit Leadership and Management.* 2nd ed. Hoboken, NJ: Jossey-Bass, 2004.

Hopkins, Alix W. *Groundswell: Stories of Saving Places, Finding Community.* San Francisco: Trust for Public Land, 2005.

Hopkins, Bruce. *Law of Tax-exempt Organizations.* 7th ed. New York: Wiley, 1998.

Hopper, Kim, and Ernest Cook. *Conservation Finance Handbook.* San Francisco: Trust for Public Land, 2004.

Klebaner, Benjamin J. *American Commercial Banking: A History.* Boston: G. K. Hall, 1990.

Klein, Kim, *Fundraising for the Long Haul.* Chardon Press Series. San Francisco: Jossey-Bass, 2000.

Klein, Kim and Stephanie Roth, eds. *Raise More Money: The Best of the Grassroots Fundraising Journal.* Chardon Press Series. San Francisco: Jossey-Bass, 2001.

Land Trust Alliance. *Appraising Easements: Guidelines for Valuation of Land Conservation and Historic Preservation Easements.* 3rd ed. Washington, DC: Land Trust Alliance and the National Trust for Historical Preservation, 1999.

———. *Assessing Your Organization: Using Land Trust Standards and Practices.* Washington, DC: Land Trust Alliance, 2004.

———. *Doing Deals: A Guide to Buying Land for Conservation.* Washington, DC: Land Trust Alliance; San Francisco: Trust for Public Land, 1995.

———. *Land Trust Standards and Practices.* Washington, DC: Land Trust Alliance, 2004.

———. *Starting a Land Trust: A Guide to Forming a Land Conservation Organization.* Washington, DC: Land Trust Alliance, 2000.

Levitt, James N., ed. *From Walden to Wall Street: Frontiers of Conservation Finance.* Washington, DC: Island Press, 2005.

McKee, Michael. "The Care and Feeding of Volunteers." In *Grassroots Fundraising Journal* (September/October 2005): 4–8.

National Research Council. *Setting Priorities for Land Conservation.* Washington, DC: National Academy Press, 1993.

Piedmont Environmental Council. *Sources of Funds for Conservation: A Handbook for Landowners and Non-Profit Organizations.* Warrenton, VA: Piedmont Environmental Council, 2003.

Robinson, Ellis M. M., and Kim Klein, eds. *The Nonprofit Membership Toolkit.* San Francisco: Jossey-Bass, 2003.

Rose, Peter S. *Commercial Bank Management.* 5th ed. New York: McGraw-Hill, 2002.

Schaff, Terry, and Doug Schaff. *The Fundraising Planner: A Working Model for Raising the Dollars You Need.* San Francisco: Jossey-Bass, 1999.

Small, Stephen J. *The Federal Tax Law of Conservation Easements.* 4th ed. Washington, DC: Land Trust Alliance, 1997.

———. *Preserving Family Lands.* 3rd ed. Vols. 1–3. Boston: Landowner Planning Center, 1997 (vol. 1), 1998 (vol. 2), 2002 (vol. 3).

Stein, Bruce A., Lynn S. Kutner, and Jonathan S. Adams. *Precious Heritage: The Status of Biodiversity in the United States.* New York: Oxford University Press, 2000.

Susskind, Lawrence, Sarah McKearnan, and Jennifer Thomas-Larmer, eds. *The Consensus Building Handbook: A Comprehensive Guide to Reaching Agreement.* Thousand Oaks, CA: Sage, 1999.

Wondolleck, Julia M., and Steven L. Yaffee. *Making Collaboration Work: Lessons from Innovation in Natural Resource Management.* Washington, DC: Island Press, 2000.

About the Author

Story Clark is a consultant specializing in land conservation organizational development and conservation finance. She has advised numerous conservation organizations, land trusts and foundations in the Rocky Mountain Region and nationally. She has been involved in land conservation and land use planning for thirty years and serves on the boards of several conservation organizations including Conservation International and the Tuckernuck Land Trust. She is a former board member of the Land Trust Alliance and is a frequent lecturer at Land Trust Alliance conferences.

Before establishing her consulting business in 2000, she was senior director at the Jackson Hole Land Trust and founding executive director of the Jackson Hole Conservation Alliance. Previously she worked for the National Park Service, the Alaska Coalition, and as a land use planner for Teton County, Wyoming. In 1996, Ms. Clark received the National Park Foundation?s Citizen Leadership Medal for continued leadership in the preservation and protection of the United States? scenic and historic heritage. She has a B.A. in creative writing and biology from Hampshire College. Ms. Clark lives with her husband and two daughters on their family's ranch in Wilson, Wyoming.

Index